THE BRITISH ACADEMY
CLASSICAL AND MEDIEVAL LOGIC TEXTS
General Editors: P. T. Geach and W. Kneale

PAUL OF VENICE
LOGICA MAGNA
PART II
FASCICULE 6

PAULI VENETI
LOGICA MAGNA

SECUNDA PARS

TRACTATUS DE VERITATE ET FALSITATE PROPOSITIONIS

ET

TRACTATUS DE SIGNIFICATO PROPOSITIONIS

Edited with notes on the sources by
FRANCESCO DEL PUNTA

Translated into English
with explanatory notes by
MARILYN McCORD ADAMS

Published for
THE BRITISH ACADEMY
by the
OXFORD UNIVERSITY PRESS
1978

Oxford University Press, Walton Street, Oxford OX2 6DP

OXFORD LONDON GLASGOW NEW YORK
TORONTO MELBOURNE WELLINGTON CAPE TOWN
IBADAN NAIROBI DAR ES SALAAM LUSAKA ADDIS ABABA
KUALA LUMPUR SINGAPORE JAKARTA HONG KONG TOKYO
DELHI BOMBAY CALCUTTA MADRAS KARACHI

ISBN 0 19 725962 6

*Printed in Great Britain
at the University Press, Oxford
by Vivian Ridler
Printer to the University*

CONTENTS

INTRODUCTION

Life

PAUL OF VENICE was born in Udine, Italy, around 1369. After entering
the Augustinian convent of S. Stefano in Venice, he studied first at Padua.
In 1390 he was assigned to Oxford where he spent at least three years.
By May 1408, he had achieved the status of Doctor of Arts and Theology
and lector in philosophy at the University of Padua.

Although the full details of his biography have yet to be established, it
is clear that Paul had an active career in the political and religious as well
as the academic sphere. More than once he served as ambassador of
Venice to foreign rulers and proved himself an effective diplomat. At
various times he held positions of leadership in his order, including that
of Rector and Vicar General (1409–10), Prior Provincial of Siena (1420),
Prior Provincial of Marche Tarvisine (1420–1), and Regent of the Siena
convent (1421). During his lifetime, he enjoyed international recognition
as a philosopher, and because of this the friars of his convent at S. Stefano
were allowed to wear the black biretta of the patricians (1417). He taught
intermittently at Padua until the end of his life, but also lectured at
Siena (1420), was deputed to lecture at Bologna (1424), and was later
professor at Siena (1427) and rector of the University (1428). He died on
15 June 1429.[1]

Works

Many works in philosophy and theology have been attributed to Paul
of Venice, although a definitive study of their dating, authenticity, and
interrelations has yet to be undertaken. For present purposes, it will be
enough to list the logical writings among them:

(A) Commentaries on Aristotle's *Organon*:

1. *Expositio super Universalia Porphyrii et in Artem Veterem Aristotelis*
   (*Exposition of Porphyry's 'Universals' and the 'Old Logic' of Aristotle*)
2. *In Aristotelis Praedicamenta de Ordine Praedicabilium* (*On Aristotle's
   Categories Concerning the Order of the Predicables*)
3. *Commentarius in Libros Posteriorum Aristotelis* (*Commentary on
   Aristotle's Posterior Analytics*)
4. *Commentarius in Peri Hermeneias Aristotelis* (*Commentary on Aristotle's
   Peri Hermeneias*)

[1] The above biographical data are taken from A. B. Emden, *A Biographical Register of
the University of Oxford to A.D. 1500* (Oxford, Clarendon Press, 1959), vol. 3, 'Paolo
Veneto', pp. 1944–5. Further bibliography on Paul's life is available in this article.

(B) Other Logical Works:

1. *Logica Parva sive Summulae* (*The Small Logic or Short Summary*)
2. *Logica Magna* (*The Great Logic*)
3. *Sophismata Aurea* (*Golden Sophismata*)
4. *Quadratura sive De Quattuor Dubiis* (*The Square or On Four Doubts*)
5. *De Universalibus* (*On Universals*)[1]

Some of these—e.g. the *Commentarius in Libros Posteriorum Aristotelis* and the *Logica Parva*—circulated widely and survive in numerous manuscripts and editions. In fact, the *Logica Parva* was a popular textbook and was even commented on by several fifteenth-century philosophers.[2] No doubt in part because of its voluminous size—200 folios on both sides with double columns, the rough equivalent of 2,500 modern octavo pages[3]—the *Logica Magna* was not reproduced so often. Wilhelm Risse[4] knows of only two printings—Venice, 1499 (H. 12505), and Venice, 1559—and of these the second does not represent an independent edition but only a reissuing of the first. In addition, there is one surviving complete manuscript: Codex Vaticanus Latinus 2132.[5] A heading on the manuscript added in a later hand attributes the work to Paul of Venice, as does the Venice 1499 edition. We do not know exactly when the *Logica Magna* was written. But assuming that Paul of Venice is the author, there is some reason to fix a date after Paul's sojourn in England (see pp. x–xii below).

As impressive in scope as in length, the *Logica Magna* contains chapters on most major topics in medieval logic. The 1499 edition tabulates its contents as follows:

TRACTATUS PRIMAE PARTIS	TREATISES OF PART I
Primus tractatus de terminis	*Treatise 1:* On Terms
Secundus de suppositionibus termino-rum	*Treatise 2:* On the *Suppositio* of Terms

[1] All of these works except for (B5) are listed by Emden, op. cit., p. 1945.
[2] For example, by Menghus Blanchellus Faventinus (Domenico Bianchelli), Jacobus Ritius Aretinus, and Manfredus de Medicis. See *Menghi Faventini Subtilissime Expositiones Questionesque super Summulis Magistri Pauli Veneti, una cum Argutissimis Additionibus Jacobi Ritii Aretini et Manfredi de Medicis* (Venetiis, 1542).
[3] This calculation is made by Allan Perreiah in his introduction to *Logica Magna, Tractatus de Suppositionibus*, edited and translated by Allan Perreiah (The Franciscan Institute, St. Bonaventure, 1971), p. xiii.
[4] Wilhelm Risse, *Bibliographia Logica: Verzeichnis der Druckschriften zur Logik mit Angabe ihrer Fundorte*, Band I (Hildesheim, Georg Olms Verlagbuchhandlung, 1965), pp. 23, 70.
[5] For a description of the manuscript, see A. Maier, *Codices Vaticani Latini, Codices 2118-2192* (Romae, 1961), pp. 27–8. C. H. Lohr, in his 'A Note on the Manuscripts of Paulus Venetus Logica', *Manuscripta*, 1973, pp. 35–6, lists 19 other manuscripts of the *Logica Magna*. Of these, one does contain material from Part I, Treatise 23–viz. Venezia, Biblioteca Marciana, Lat. cl. VI. 30 (2547), ff. 44ra–61rb—but all of the other 18 contain the *Logica Parva* instead.

We have edited and translated two treatises from Part II: Treatise 10
(hereafter *OTF*), which is mainly concerned with a general formulation
of the conditions under which propositions are true or false; and Treatise
11 (hereafter *OSP*), which deals primarily with the ontological status of
that which is signified by the whole proposition, and not just by one of
its parts. Other treatises will appear in other fascicles.

Structure and Sources of OTF *and* OSP

Paul of Venice's method in *OTF* and *OSP* represents an extension
of the standard medieval practice, implicit in the structure of the *quaestio*,
of discussing and refuting the opinions of others. Collecting an array of
opinions about the matter under discussion, he encapsulates each in one
or more theses (*conclusiones*) and systematically gives arguments for and
against them. Each treatise culminates in an opinion that is presented as
Paul's own and that is specifically designed to avoid the difficulties uncovered in the earlier positions. Clearly, his aim is not merely to develop
the problems of truth and signification—indeed in neither case is the final
view worked out in as much detail as one would like—but to provide the
reader with a digest of opinions and their refutations on which he could
call in the sophistical debates which were a standard part of philosophical
training at that time.

Further, it is clear that our treatises are skilful compilations from other
sources. Research by the editor of this fascicle has uncovered Paul of
Venice's extensive dependence on the two English philosophers, Richard
Feribrigge and John 'Venator'[1] in composing *OTF* and *OSP*. The *Logic*
of Venator is itself a compilation which organizes competing views into
theses and counter-arguments and quotes among others the opinion of
Feribrigge as stated in his *Treatise on the Truth of Propositions*. From the
works of these philosophers, Paul takes not only his statements of their
own opinions, but also those of the Second, Third, and Fourth Ways of

---

[1] He may be the John Huntman listed by Emden, op. cit., vol. 2, pp. 987–8. The dates
are compatible with this hypothesis, and the manuscript does refer to 'Johannes Venator
Anglicus', so that the nationality is right, too. But there is no other positive evidence for
this identification.

OTF and the First and Second Opinions of *OSP*. In additon, he borrows from Feribrigge and Venator many more arguments which he directs against other positions, including his own, quoting them either verbatim or with small elaborations. These facts fit in well with the belief among some fifteenth-century philosophers that Paul of Venice brought back many books, including works of logic, from England.[1] Of course, he was also aware of the opinions of other logicians more accessible to him, such as Peter of Mantua, who preceded him as teacher of logic in the University of Padua, Albert of Saxony, Gregory of Rimini, and Peter of Ailly.

Following the medieval custom of not mentioning other writers by name except as a sign of special respect, Paul only once explicitly identifies the author of the opinion under discussion—viz. when he cites Gregory of Rimini, a distinguished doctor and former Rector and Vicar General of his Order, as the proponent of the Third Opinion of *OSP*. Other authors were suggested by Prantl[2] and/or were easily recognizable as sources from the early printed editions of their works. The editor's further investigations combine with these to yield the following table of identifications:

OTF	*OSP*
1st Way: Albert of Saxony	1st Opinion: ?
2nd Way: ?	2nd Opinion: ?
3rd Way: ?	3rd Opinion: Gregory of Rimini
4th Way: ?	4th Opinion: Peter of Ailly
5th Way: Richard Feribrigge	5th Opinion: Paul of Venice
6th Way: Peter of Ailly	
7th Way: John Venator	
8th Way: Peter of Mantua	
9th Way: Paul of Venice	

[1] Bruno Nardi notes that Antonio Cittadini wrote the following in a polemical commentary on the *Logica Minor* around 1476: 'Ferunt autem quidam non auctoritate indigni, hunc libellum in Britannia, ubi olim et dialecticae et philosophiae studia floruerunt, in antiquissimis litteris compertum esse, ut ex illis constaret, prius opusculum hoc extructum fuisse quam Paulus Venetus natus esset. Quod eo magis a non nullis creditur, quod certum est Paulum apud Britanos visendorum gymnasiorum gratia aliquando commoratum esse, ac postea in Italiam revertentem multos libros secum detulisse, quorum auctores Italis penitus erant incogniti.' (Cod. Urb. lat. 1381, f. 2r, *Saggi sull'aristotelismo Padovano dal secolo XIV al XVI* (G. C. Sansoni Editore, Firenze 1958) c. 3, pp. 75–6.)

[2] In connection with the First Way of *OTF*, Prantl cites John Buridan and Albert of Saxony; for the Fourth, Buridan and Peter of Ailly; and for the Sixth, Peter of Ailly (*Geschichte der Logik im Abendlande*, v. IV (Photostatically reproduced by Akademische Druck und Verlagsanstalt, Graz, 1955), c. 20, p. 134, Anm. 558). Buridan is not Paul of Venice's immediate source for either the First or the Fourth Ways, however; nor is Ailly an adherent of the Fourth. Prantl correctly identifies Gregory of Rimini and Peter of Ailly as the authors of the Third and Fourth Opinions of *OSP*, however (ibid., Anm. 559). Dr. Del Punta's hypothesis regarding Paul's sources for the positions he discusses, has already been accepted by Norman Kretzmann in his article 'Medieval Logicians on the Meaning of the *Propositio*', *Journal of Philosophy*, vol. 65 (1970), pp. 767–87. As he acknowledges, his references are dependent on Dr. Del Punta's research.

Although the Second, Third, and Fourth Ways of *OTF* and the First and Second Opinions of *OSP* echo numerous medieval logicians more or less remote in time from Paul of Venice, the editor has not discovered any near contemporaries or recent predecessors who held precisely these positions. Nevertheless, whoever may have been their adherents, Paul of Venice's immediate sources for them are demonstrably Richard Feribrigge, John Venator, and William Heytesbury. It is the purpose of the Fontes printed at the end of the text to inform the reader of Paul's immediate sources for the opinions and arguments that he gives, and to document these identifications. Since, with the exception of Gregory of Rimini's commentary on the *Sentences*,[1] the works of the above authors are not readily available, we have quoted the relevant passages from Albert of Saxony, Peter of Ailly, Peter of Mantua, and William Heytesbury in the Fontes. Since Paul of Venice depends so heavily on Richard Feribrigge and John Venator, however, it seemed better to collect all of the passages cited from their works into two appendixes. This enables the reader to capture the flow of their discussions and to assess the connections between them as well as the dependence of *OTF* and *OSP* on them, for himself. Feribrigge's *Treatise on the Truth of Propositions* and Venator's *Logic* exist only in manuscripts, and the texts in the appendices represent provisional editions of them. The editor is currently preparing a critical edition of the former, and so has corrected the text of the cited manuscript against that of other codices. For the latter he used the only complete manuscript,[2] and only the obvious mistakes are corrected. The editor intends to produce a critical edition of it as well.

Method

In establishing the text of *OTF* and *OSP*, we have used the Bodleian library's copy of the Venice 1499 edition (shelfmark: Auct. 2 Q 3.5), together with the manuscript. At least where *OTF* and *OSP* are concerned, there are seldom substantial differences between these two witnesses. Nevertheless, in the few cases in which they do arise and where we have been able to check the readings against those of Paul's sources, the manuscript has agreed more often with the sources. Accordingly, we have followed the general policy of preferring the manuscript to the edition, unless there are compelling reasons to do otherwise. The critical apparatus lists all the variants except evident omissions, transpositions and simple inversions that do not change the sense, scribal mistakes, repetitions of the same word and repetitive additions, and in a few cases obvious synonymy. Because of

---

[1] See Fontes, *Tractatus de Significato Propositionis*, c. 3, note 1, p. 211 below.
[2] The manuscript is described by A. Maier, *Codices Vaticani Latini, Codices 2118–2192* (Romae, 1961), pp. 21–2.

the nature of this work, however, we have been conservative in our judge-ments. And when a reading, however apparently mistaken, is witnessed by both the manuscript and the edition, we have always noted it in the apparatus. Within reason, we have standardized the spelling to the received classical forms as an aid to the reader—e.g. where appropriate supplying the 'ae' diphthong for 'e'. But we have retained certain very characteristic spellings of words such as 'Sortes' (for 'Socrates'), 'correlarium' (for 'corollarium'), and 'Parisius' (for 'Parisiis'). Finally it should be noted that the manuscript has characteristic Italian spellings (e.g. -x- for -ss- as in 'poxit', 'poxet' for 'possit', 'posset') which are not recorded in the apparatus. Modern logical terminology has sometimes been employed in the trans-lation in preference to cognate translations: e.g. 'molecular', not 'hypo-thetical', for '*hypothetica*'.

The text of *OTF* and *OSP* contains a number of references to other parts of the *Logica Magna*, but none explicitly to other works attributed to Paul of Venice. We have found that other relevant parts of the *Logica Magna* are not only consistent with our treatises, but also often sufficient to illuminate otherwise puzzling passages. This is especially true of the discussion of primary and secondary signification in Part I, Treatise 1 'On Terms', and of Treatises 4 and 5 of Part I concerning exclusive terms. This self-contained character of the *Logica Magna* is one of the reasons why we have made it a general policy not to refer to other works attributed to Paul of Venice. Another is that while the common authorship of the *Logica Magna*, the *Logica Parva*, the *Sophismata*, and the *Quadratura* is highly probable, it has not been proved with certainty. And invoking the text of one to explain a passage in another would seem to presuppose that this had been established. We have found that the teachings of the *Logica Parva* are in any event often inconsistent with those of the *Logica Magna*. For example, the author of the *Logica Magna* argues against the view that propositions must be expressions in the indicative mood (Part II, Treatise 1 'On Propositions', f. 101rb lin. 2–21),[1] but the *Logica Parva* states that

A proposition is an indicative expression that signifies the true or the false. For example, 'A man runs.' First, 'expression' is posited as the genus, because every proposition is an expression and not vice versa. I say 'indicative', since only an indicative expression is a proposition and not an imperative, or optative. . .'[2]

Again, in *OTF* the Seventh Way is rejected on the ground that it fails to take account of the case of insoluble propositions (such as 'This proposi-tion—where "this" indicates the proposition of which it is a part—is false') whose primary significatum is true, according to Paul, although the

---

[1] See English note a on ch. 8, pp. 262–3 below.
[2] *Logica Parva*, Venetiis, 1544, f. 3 v C.

proposition is false (see *OTF*, c. 7, Counter-Thesis 5, pp. 55–7 below). But the *Logica Parva* explains that

> . . . A true categorical proposition is one whose primary and adequate significatum is true. For example, 'You are a man.' . . . A false categorical proposition is one whose primary and adequate significatum is false. For example, 'You are a donkey.'[1]

And it makes no exception for insolubles. It is noteworthy that such discrepancies between the two works were already recorded by at least one fifteenth-century commentator on the *Logica Parva*, and he seems nevertheless to have taken it for granted that Paul of Venice was the author of both works.[2]

Many arguments in *OTF* and *OSP* are initially puzzling, turning as they do on special rules about the scope and function of terms such as 'precisely' and 'wholly', or on the doctrine of primary and secondary signification, or on ambiguities that are difficult to decipher in Latin and almost impossible to reflect in English. To make the treatises more readily understandable, the translator has supplied a set of notes which inform the reader of relevant doctrine from other parts of the *Logica Magna* and which attempt to unravel the more difficult arguments. Frequent reference is made to Part I, Treatise 1 'On Terms', which has been edited and translated and will appear in a forthcoming fascicle by Norman Kretzmann. In the interests of uniformity, the translator has followed Kretzmann's translations when quoting from this treatise.

Acknowledgements

The preparation of this fascicle has been facilitated by assistance from several sources. Thanks are due to Alina Del Punta for help in transcribing and collating the manuscript and edition; to Peter Geach for suggestions which have resulted in substantial improvements in the translation; to Dr. Richard Hunt for helpful advice regarding the edition and construction of the *Apparatus Fontium*; to Bernard Dod of the Clarendon Press for careful copy editing; to Robert M. Adams for useful advice and suggestions on many points; and to Odette Mousalam and Lynn Hill for typing the translation. We are also grateful to the American Philosophical Society for a grant from the Penrose Fund which enabled us to purchase necessary xeroxes and microfilms, as well as airplane tickets which made transatlantic

---

[1] *Logica Parva*, Venetiis, 1544, f. 4rC–vA.

[2] See Menghus Blanchellus Faventinus (Domenico Bianchelli), *Commentarius super Logicam Pauli Veneti* (Tarvisii, 1476) sign. a²ra, a³ra, a⁶va, b⁵ra. Fifteenth-century opinion seems not to have been unanimous on this point, however. See the remarks of Antonio Cittadini quoted by Nardi and reproduced in p. xi note 1 above. It is difficult to know how much to infer from what Cittadini says, however, since the passage occurs in a polemical work.

collaboration possible. Part of the translator's work was financed by a fellowship from the U.S. National Endowment for the Humanities. The editor's research connected with this fascicle was carried out while he was attached to Linacre College, Oxford, on a scholarship from the Italian Ministry of Education and subsequently from the British Council. He wishes to dedicate his labour to the late A. N. Prior of Balliol College, who first gave impulse to his research. Finally, we wish to thank the General Editors of this series and the British Academy for undertaking the publication of this work.

As for the division of labour between us Francesco Del Punta is primarily responsible for the edition; Marilyn Adams, for the translation. The identification of external sources was entirely a product of Dr. Del Punta's research. The location of internal references and references to Aristotle was a work of collaboration.

ADDENDA ET CORRIGENDA

p. 209 (Fontes Cap. 1, p. 80 n. 1) Et ultra, G. Nuchelmans, *Theories of the Proposition, Ancient and Medieval Conceptions of the Bearers of Truth and Falsity*, Amsterdam–London, 1973, pp. 281–8.

p. 228** *Continuetur sic.* Et alia significat quod aliquam chimaeram esse est intelligibile per hanc propositionem 'Aliqua chimaera est', si sit-quod sic intellectum non potest esse verum.

p. 230* Cf. *Categoriae*, editio composita: 'dum enim res est' etc. (Aristoteles latinus I. 1–5, p. 76 lin. 19–20); transl. autem Guillelmi de Moerbeka: 'eo enim quod res est' etc. (ibidem, p. 115 lin. 1–2).

p. 269 (Notes Ch. 4) p. 109 n. c. Literally, we have 'a verb taken as significant cannot render a *suppositum* to a verb'. But the principal verb of a proposition does not have *suppositio*. *Suppositum* here must be taken in its grammatical sense as equivalent to 'subject'. Cf. L. M. De Rijk, *Logica Modernorum* II (Assen, 1967), pp. 529–33.

LOGICAE MAGNAE

SECUNDA PARS

TRACTATUS DE VERITATE ET FALSITATE PROPOSITIONIS

B

SIGLA ET ABBREVIATIONES

$M =$ Codex manuscriptus Vaticanus Latinus 2132
    (saec. xv, ante an. 1443).
$E =$ Editio typographica Venetiis 1499.
[. . .] Includunt verba superflua.
⟨. . .⟩ Includunt verba ab editore addita.
Numeri arabici superscripti indicant notas de fontibus.

SIGNS AND ABBREVIATIONS USED IN THE TRANSLATION

⟨. . .⟩ Enclose words added by the translator.
Superscript lower-case letters indicate English explanatory notes.

DE VERITATE ET FALSITATE
PROPOSITIONIS

(158rb E)

Ad probandum sophismata et alias quascumque enuntiationes diversi
5 diversimode viis variis antecedenter procedunt, terminum quaerentes
eundem.

⟨*Prima Via*   *Capitulum Primum*⟩

Prima (201vb M) igitur via[1] veritatem propositionis concludit ex quibusdam
conclusionibus, quarum prima est ista:

10   Ad veritatem propositionis affirmativae requiritur subiectum et
       praedicatum supponere pro eodem.

Probatur: Nam in propositione affirmativa copula verbalis manet affirmata.
Igitur significat subiectum et praedicatum supponere pro eodem.

       2a conclusio: Ad veritatem propositionis negativae sufficit quod
15   subiectum et praedicatum non supponant pro eodem.[2]

Probatur, quia ad veritatem affirmativae requiritur quod supponant pro
eodem. Igitur ad veritatem negativae sibi oppositae sufficit quod non
supponant pro eodem.

       3a conclusio: Non ad cuiuslibet propositionis veritatem sufficit et
20   requiritur quod sic sit sicut per illam significatur.[3]

Probatur: Nam illa

       Homo est animal

non significat sicut est; igitur nec aliqua alia. Consequentia tenet. Et
antecedens probatur, quia si significat sicut est, igitur significat qualiter-
25 cumque est. Consequentiam arguit per hoc quod ly .sicut. confundit
confuse et distributive.[4] Et falsitas consequentis patet, quia non significat
taliter qualiter est Deum esse, nec taliter qualiter est hominem currere,
et sic de aliis.

---

1 Incipit tractatus de veritate et falsitate propositionis *E, titulum om. M*   14 sufficit]
et requiritur *add. E.*   16–17 probatur . . . eodem *om.* (*hom.*) *E*   17 negativae]
affirmativae *M, correxi*   23 significat non *transp. E*   25 quod ly] quia *M*
26 et$^{1-2}$ *om. E*

ON THE TRUTH AND FALSITY
OF PROPOSITIONS

In proving sophismata and any other sort of theses, different ⟨authors⟩, seeking the same end, proceed towards it in different manners and in various ways.

⟨*The First Way*   *Chapter One*⟩

The first way infers the truth of propositions from the following theses.

> *Thesis 1*: It is a necessary condition of the truth of an affirmative proposition that the subject and the predicate supposit for the same thing.

Proof: In an affirmative proposition the copulative verb occurs ⟨as⟩ affirmed. Therefore, an affirmative proposition signifies that the subject and the predicate supposit for the same thing.

> *Thesis 2*: It is a necessary and sufficient condition of the truth of a negative proposition that the subject and the predicate do not supposit for the same thing.

Proof: It is a necessary condition of the truth of an affirmative proposition that they supposit for the same thing. Therefore, it is a sufficient condition of the truth of the negative proposition opposite to it that they do not supposit for the same thing.[a]

> *Thesis 3*: It is not a necessary and sufficient condition of the truth of any proposition whatever, that things are so as the proposition signifies.

Proof: The proposition

A man is an animal

does not signify as things are. Therefore, neither does any other proposition. The inference holds. Proof of the premiss: If it signifies as things are then it signifies in every way as things are. ⟨The author of this way⟩ argues for the inference on the basis that 'as' renders the *suppositio* confused and distributive.[b] The falsity of the conclusion is clear. For 'A man is an animal' does not signify in the way in which it is the case that God is, or that a man runs, and so on.

4a conclusio: Ad veritatem propositionis requiritur quod ipsa significet taliter qualiter est, et non significet aliqualiter aliter quam est.

Probatur: Nam si aliqua propositio significat taliter qualiter est, et cum hoc significat aliter quam est, ipsa est falsa; quia non ita est qualitercumque

5 per ipsam significatur, quod requiritur ad hoc quod propositio sit vera.⁵

Ex praedictis haec via elicit quaedam correlaria.

Primum: Omnis propositio affirmativa significat se esse veram.

Probatur, quia omnis propositio affirmativa, ratione copulae verbalis, significat illud pro quo supponit subiectum esse illud pro quo supponit

10 praedicatum.⁶

2um correlarium: In omni propositione negativa, quando subiectum et praedicatum non supponunt pro eodem, propositio est vera; et quando supponunt pro eodem, propositio est falsa.⁷

3um correlarium: Universaliter, quaelibet affirmativa de praesenti,

15 cuius subiectum pro nullo supponit, est falsa.

Patet, quia ad veritatem affirmativae requiritur quod subiectum et praedicatum supponant pro eodem.⁸

Haec sunt dicta huius primae opinionis.

⟨*Conclusiones contra primam viam*⟩

20 Contra hanc viam,⁹ quae discrete, iudicio meo, ducit ad terminum principaliter intentum, pono aliquas conclusiones.

Prima est ista: Aliqua est propositio affirmativa vera cuius non subiectum et praedicatum supponunt pro eodem.

Huius conclusionis veritas elicitur ex qualibet propositione non habente

25 extrema, sicut patet de consequente huius condicionalis

Si Sortes currit, movetur,

et de secunda parte huius copulativae

Animal est homo et e converso.

Sed forte dicitur quod illud dictum debet intelligi de propositione

30 habente extrema. Adhuc iste intellectus est falsus. Nam ista propositio est vera et affirmativa

Populus est populus,

et tamen subiectum et praedicatum non supponunt pro eodem. Et haec similiter

35 Sortes et Plato sunt homines,

et tamen extrema non supponunt pro eodem, eo quod non supponunt pro aliquo, sed bene pro aliquibus.

5 quod²] aliqua *add. E*   20 discrete] discordantiam *E*   22 vera *om. E*   37 sed] et *add. M*

Thesis 4: It is a necessary condition of the truth of a proposition that it signifies as things are and does not signify in any way otherwise than things are.

Proof: If a proposition signifies as things are and together with this signifies otherwise than things are, it is false. For it is not the case that things are so in whatever way the proposition signifies—which is a necessary condition of the truth of a proposition.

The first way infers certain corollaries from the preceding theses.

⟨*Corollary*⟩ *1*: Every affirmative proposition signifies that it itself is true.

Proof: Every affirmative proposition, because of the copulative verb, signifies that what the subject supposits for is what the predicate supposits for.

Corollary 2: Every negative proposition is true when the subject and the predicate do not supposit for the same thing and false when they do supposit for the same thing.

Corollary 3: Universally, any present-tense affirmative proposition whose subject supposits for nothing is false.

This is clear, since it is a necessary condition of the truth of an affirmative proposition that its subject and predicate supposit for the same thing.

These are the claims made by the first opinion.

⟨*Theses against the First Way*⟩

The first way leads to the principally intended end discretely,[c] in my judgement. I assume some theses against it.

⟨*Counter-*⟩*Thesis 1*: There is a true affirmative proposition that is not such that its subject and predicate supposit for the same thing.[d]

The truth of this thesis is obtained from ⟨considering⟩ any ⟨true⟩ proposition that lacks extremes. This is clear with respect to the consequent of the conditional

Socrates is running, only if moving,

and with respect to the second part of the conjunctive proposition

An animal is a man and conversely.

But perhaps someone will say that the claim ought to be understood ⟨as made only⟩ with respect to propositions that have extremes. Still, so understood, Thesis 1 is false. The proposition

People are people

is true and affirmative. Nevertheless, its subject and predicate do not supposit for the same thing. Similarly the proposition

Socrates and Plato are men

⟨is true and affirmative⟩. Nevertheless, its extremes do not supposit for the same thing, because they do not supposit for some thing but for some *things*.

Ex his sequitur correlarie contra 2am conclusionem huius viae, quod

Aliqua est negativa falsa, et tamen subiectum et praedicatum non
supponunt pro eodem.

Patet de contradictoriis propositionum propositarum.

5   Item non sequitur:

In propositione (158va E) affirmativa copula principalis manet affirmata.

Igitur significat subiectum et praedicatum supponere pro eodem.

2a conclusio: Licet aliqua propositio vera significet sicut est, non
10   tamen significat qualitercumque est.

Probatur: Nam illa

Homo est animal

non significat qualitercumque est, ut patet, et tamen significat sicut est.
Probatur: Nam ita est sicut per ipsam significatur. Igitur ipsa significat
15   sicut est. Consequentia patet, quia non magis videtur distribuere ly .sicut.
quam ly .ita. Antecedens vero concedit praedicta opinio saepissime et in
pluribus locis, ut patet suam *Logicam* intuenti.[10] Nec est verum quod
semper ly .sicut. distribuat, sicut fuit ostensum in Prima Parte, capitulo
De Gradu Positivo.[11]

20   *3a conclusio*: Aliqua est propositio vera et necessaria, quae tamen
significat aliter quam est.

Patet de illa

Homo est animal,

quae significat hominem esse asinum, sicut in principio Primae Partis est
25   clare deductum.[12]

Item, haec est vera

Deus est vel homo est asinus,

quae etiam significat aliter quam est, (202ra M) eo quod significat hominem
esse asinum. Probatur: Nam ipsa significat Deum esse; igitur et hominem
30   esse asinum. Patet consequentia, quia non plus concurrit illa

Deus est

ad constitutionem illius disiunctivae quam illa

Homo est asinus.

Confirmatur: Nam si illa

35   Homo est asinus

1 secundam] primam *E*   11–13 probatur . . . est¹ *om. (hom.?) E*   16 praedicta]
prima *M*   32 disiunctivae] disiuncti *E*

From these remarks, a corollary follows against Thesis 2 of this way.

⟨*Corollary*:⟩ There is some false negative proposition whose subject and predicate nevertheless do not supposit for the same thing.

This is clear with respect to the contradictories of the proposed propositions.[e]

Again,[f] this does not follow—

The principal copula of an affirmative proposition occurs ⟨as⟩ affirmed.

Therefore, it signifies that the subject and the predicate supposit for the same thing.

⟨*Counter-*⟩*Thesis 2*: Even though a true proposition may signify as things are, nevertheless it does not signify in whatever way things are.[g]

Proof: The proposition

A man is an animal

does not signify in whatever way things are, as is clear. Nevertheless, it signifies as things are. Proof: Things are so as it signifies. Therefore, it signifies as things are. The inference is clear, since 'as' apparently does not distribute more than 'so' does. But the above opinion grants the premiss very often and in many places, as is clear to one who considers his *Logic*. Nor is it true that 'as' always distributes, as was shown in Part I, chapter 'On the Positive Degree'.

⟨*Counter-*⟩*Thesis 3*: There is some true and necessary proposition that nevertheless signifies otherwise than things are.[h]

This is clear with respect to the proposition

A man is an animal,

which signifies that a man is a donkey, as was clearly deduced in the beginning of Part I.[i]

Again, the proposition

God is or a man is a donkey

is true and it also signifies otherwise than things are, because it signifies a man being a donkey.[j] Proof: It signifies God existing. Therefore, it also signifies a man being a donkey. The inference is clear. For the proposition

God is

does not pertain to the constitution of that disjunctive proposition more than the proposition

A man is a donkey

does. Confirming argument: If the proposition

A man is a donkey

esset necessaria—dato quod cetera essent sicut nunc—illa disiunctiva significaret hominem esse asinum. Sed idem esset adhuc significatum primarium tunc quod est nunc. Igitur et nunc idem significat.

Et si diceretur quod nec significat Deum esse nec hominem esse asinum;
5 hoc non videtur mihi verum, ex quo significat Deum esse vel hominem esse asinum.

Item, illa disiunctiva redditur vera ratione partis verae. Quomodo igitur non significabit significatum partis verae?

Item, intellectus non potest ferri super illam disiunctivam nisi prius
10 feratur super primam partem. Igitur non potest significare suum adaequatum significatum nisi prius significet significatum primae partis. Quare etc.

> *4a conclusio*: Non omnis propositio affirmativa significat se esse veram.

Probatur: Nam ista est vera

15   Homo est animal

et non significat se esse veram. Igitur etc. Consequentia patet cum maiori. Et minorem probo: Illa propositio non significat aliquod significatum nisi ex compositione suarum partium. Sed nulla pars illius propositionis significat illam propositionem. Igitur illa tota propositio non significat se
20 ipsam propositionem esse veram.

Ex quo sequitur contra eandem opinionem quod

> Non omnis propositio affirmativa significat quod subiectum et praedicatum pro eodem aut pro eisdem supponunt; nec omnis propositio negativa significat quod non pro eodem aut pro eisdem
25   supponunt.

Patet ex conclusione.

> *5a conclusio*: Aliqua est propositio negativa vera, et tamen subiectum et praedicatum supponunt pro eodem.

Patet de ista

30   Antichristus non est Antichristus.

Ipsa enim est vera, ut patet, et tamen subiectum et praedicatum supponunt pro eodem, quia pro Antichristo.

Item, conceditur quod

> Aliqua est negativa falsa, et tamen subiectum et praedicatum non
35   supponunt pro eodem.

Patet de secunda parte huius copulativae

> Omnis homo non est animal et e converso,

2 adhuc] ad hoc *E*   5 mihi verum] possibile *E*   10 super] in *E*   11 quare *om. (etiam infra, sed ultra non notavi) E*   14 probatur *om. E*   24 aut] vel *E*
32 quia pro Antichristo] ut patet *M*   36 huius] illius *E*   37 non *om. M*

were necessary, granted that everything else is just as it is now, the disjunctive would signify a man being a donkey. But still the primary significatum would be the same in that case as it is now. Therefore, it signifies the same thing now, too.

Suppose someone said that it signifies neither God existing nor a man being a donkey. This does not seem true to me, because it does signify God existing or a man being a donkey.*k*

Again, the disjunctive proposition is rendered true because of its true part. How, then, will it fail to signify the significatum of its true part?

Again, the intellect cannot grasp the disjunctive proposition, if it does not first grasp the first part. Therefore, the proposition cannot signify its adequate significatum, if it does not first signify the significatum of the first part. Thus, etc.

⟨Counter-⟩*Thesis 4*: Not every affirmative proposition signifies that it itself is true.*l*

Proof: The proposition

A man is an animal

is true and does not signify that it itself is true. Therefore, etc. The inference is clear, as is the major. Proof of the minor: The proposition signifies some significatum only by the composition of its parts. But no part of the proposition signifies that proposition. Therefore, the proposition as a whole does not signify that that proposition itself is true.*m*

It follows from this against the same opinion that

Not every affirmative proposition signifies that its subject and predicate supposit for the same thing or things,*n*

and

Not every negative proposition signifies that its subject and predicate do not supposit for the same thing or things.*o*

This is clear from ⟨Counter-⟩Thesis 4.

⟨Counter-⟩*Thesis 5*: There is a true negative proposition whose subject and predicate nevertheless do supposit for the same thing.

This is clear with respect to the proposition

The Antichrist is not the Antichrist.

The proposition is true, as is clear. Nevertheless, its subject and predicate supposit for the same thing, since they supposit for the Antichrist.

Again, this is granted:

There is a false negative proposition whose subject and predicate do not supposit for the same thing.*p*

This is clear with respect to the second part of the conjunctive proposition

Every man is not an animal, and conversely,

et de ista

Populus non est populus,

ut primitus dicebatur.

5 *6a conclusio*: Admisso quod ille terminus 'chimaera' pro nullo nec pro aliquibus possit supponere, aliqua est propositio de praesenti affirmativa vera, cuius subiectum pro nullo nec pro aliquibus supponit.

Patet de talibus:

Chimaera intelligitur,

10 Chimaera est opinabilis.

Ultima conclusio contra eandem positionem est ista: Privatio significati alicuius termini ex natura rei non tollit pro eodem suppositionem eiusdem.

Volo dicere quod, licet significatum illius termini 'chimaera' non sit in 15 rerum natura, nec possit esse, adhuc ille terminus 'chimaera' in ista propositione

Chimaera est chimaera,

vel in ista

Chimaera intelligitur,

20 pro aliquo supponit, quia pro chimaera.[13] Probatur: Nam si significatum illius termini esset a parte rei, in tali propositione iste terminus 'chimaera' pro aliquo supponeret. Sed tunc iste terminus 'chimaera' non aliter se haberet quam nunc. Igitur et nunc pro eodem supponit.

Secundo, iste terminus 'chimaera' in praedicta propositione supponit 25 determinate, secundum regulas huius viae.[14] Igitur pro aliquo aut pro aliquibus determinate supponit. Consequentia patet, quia non videtur imaginabile oppositum contradictorium consequentis cum antecedente.

Tertio, in ista propositione

Antichristus est Antichristus,

30 subiectum supponit (158vb E) pro aliquo [et pro aliquo supponit]. Igitur similiter in illa

Chimaera est chimaera.

Consequentia patet, quia sicut significatum unius non est ex parte rei, ita nec alterius.

35 Antecedens probatur: Et sumo hanc copulativam

Antichristus est Antichristus et ille non erit,

et quaero utrum ly .Antichristus. supponat pro Antichristo vel non. Si sic,

6 affirmativa *om.* E   11–12 significati *om.* E   25 secundum] duas *add.* E

and with respect to the proposition

People are not people,

as was said in the beginning.

⟨*Counter-*⟩*Thesis* 6: If one admits that the term 'chimera' can supposit for no thing or things, there is a true affirmative present-tense proposition, whose subject supposits for no thing or things.[q]

This is clear with respect to propositions such as

A chimera is thought of,

and

A chimera is believed in.

The last thesis against this same position is this:

⟨*Counter-Thesis* 7⟩: The fact that the significatum of some term does not exist in reality does not prevent that term from suppositing for that significatum.

What I mean is that although the significatum of the term 'chimera' does not and could not exist in reality, still the term 'chimera' supposits for something in the proposition

A chimera is a chimera,

or in the proposition

A chimera is thought of,

since it supposits for a chimera. Proof: If the significatum of that term did exist in reality, the term 'chimera' in such a proposition would supposit for something. But the term 'chimera' would not be any different in the case supposed from the way it is now. Therefore, it supposits for the same thing even now.[r]

Second, the term 'chimera' supposits determinately in the above-mentioned proposition, according to the ⟨two⟩ rules of this way. Therefore, it supposits determinately for some thing or things. The inference is clear. For the contradictory opposite of the conclusion together with the premiss does not seem imaginable.

Third, in the proposition

The Antichrist is the Antichrist,

the subject supposits for something. Therefore, similarly in the proposition

A chimera is a chimera.

The inference is clear. For just as the significatum of one does not exist in reality, so neither does the significatum of the other.

Proof of the premiss: Take the conjunctive proposition

The Antichrist is the Antichrist and he will not be.

I ask whether 'Antichrist' supposits for the Antichrist or not. If so, I have

habetur intentum. Si non, sequitur quod secunda pars illius copulativae est vera. Patet consequentia, quia quaelibet negativa cuius subiectum pro nullo supponit est vera, secundum istam viam.[15] Sed sic est in proposito, quia si antecedens pro nullo, nec relativum, ut dicit eadem opinio.[16]

5 Igitur etc.

Quarto arguitur sic: In ista propositione

Chimaera est futura

subiectum pro aliquo supponit; igitur positio illa falsa.

Consequentia tenet, et antecedens probatur: Nam in tali propositione
10 subiectum ampliatur pro eo quod erit. Igitur supponit pro eo quod erit. Consequentia tenet, ab inferiori ad suum superius cum omnibus requisitis. Et antecedens patet, per auctores huius viae ponentes regulariter quod

Copula existente de praesenti, praedicato vero existente de futuro, subiectum ampliatur pro eo quod erit.[17]

15 Quinto arguitur sic: In ista propositione

Chimaera erit alba

subiectum pro aliquo supponit; igitur positio falsa.

Consequentia patet, et antecedens probatur: Nam illius propositionis praedicatum appellat suam formam.[18] Igitur subiectum pro aliquo sup-
20 ponit. Antecedens patet, per ipsos regulariter concedentes (202ʳᵇ M) quod

In omni propositione de futuro, praedicatum sequens verbum appellat suam formam.

Et consequentia patet, per eosdem eandem regulam declarantes. 'Id est,' inquiunt ipsi, 'in eadem forma erit aliquando verificabile in propositione
25 de praesenti, de pronomine demonstrante illud pro quo supponit subiectum illius propositionis de futuro.'[19] Quare etc.

Sicut ergo haec positio habet concedere quod ly .chimaera. aliquid significat, ita et quod pro aliquo supponit. Non enim magis est amplia-tivum illud verbum 'significat' quam illud verbum 'supponit', sicut
30 ostensum fuit in Prima Parte, circa principium, ubi haec materia diffusius declaratur, obiectiones contra me factas clare solvendo.[20] Quare etc.

⟨*Secunda Via*   *Capitulum Secundum*⟩

Secunda via[1] ponit unicam conclusionem quae est ista in forma:

Si haec propositio vel ista—quacumque demonstrata—significat
35   praecise sicut est, haec propositio est vera,

---

10 igitur . . . erit *om.* (*hom.?*) M   11 tenet] patet (*etiam infra, sed ultra non no-tavi*) M   12 auctores] auctoritatem M   ponentes] ponentem M   regulariter realiter (*etiam infra, lin.* 21) E

my intended conclusion. If not, it follows that the second part of the copulative proposition is true. The inference is clear, since any negative proposition whose subject supposits for nothing is true, according to this way.
This is the way it is in the proposed proposition. For if the antecedent ⟨of
a relative pronoun⟩ does not supposit for anything, then neither does the
relative pronoun, as the same opinion says. Therefore, etc.*

Fourth, I argue this way: In the proposition

A chimera is future,

the subject supposits for something. Therefore, this position is false.

The inference holds. Proof of the premiss: In such a proposition the
subject is ampliated* so as to stand for a thing that will be. Therefore, it
supposits for a thing that will be. The inference holds from the inferior
to its superior, when all of the required conditions are met. The premiss is
clear, according to the authors of this way. For they posit as a rule that

When the copula is present-tense but the predicate is future-tense,
the subject is ampliated for a thing that will be.

Fifth, I argue this way: In the proposition

A chimera will be white,

the subject supposits for something. Therefore, this position is false.

The inference is clear. Proof of the premiss: The predicate of that proposition appellates its own form. Therefore, the subject supposits for
something. The premiss is clear, according to them, since they grant as
a rule that

In every future-tense proposition, the predicate following the verb
appellates its own form.

The inference is clear, according to the same authors who posit this same
rule. 'That is,' they themselves say, '⟨the predicate⟩ in the same form will
at some time be truly predicated in a present-tense proposition of a pronoun indicating that for which the subject of the future-tense proposition
supposits.'* Thus, etc.

Therefore, just as this position has to concede that 'chimera' signifies
something, so also it has to concede that it supposits for something. For
the verb 'signifies' is not more ampliative than the verb 'supposits'. This
was shown towards the beginning of Part I, where I give a rather extended
explanation of this subject-matter by clearly solving objections made
against me. Thus, etc.

⟨*The Second Way*   *Chapter Two*⟩

The second way posits a single thesis which, stated as an inference, is as
follows.

Thesis: If this or that proposition (where any proposition is indicated)
signifies precisely as things are, the proposition is true.

quam probat sic: Si haec propositio significat praecise sicut est, haec
propositio significat sicut est et haec propositio non significat sicut non est.
Patet consequentia, ab exposita ad exponentes ipsius. Et ultra, si haec
propositio significat sicut est et haec propositio non significat sicut non
5 est, haec propositio est et haec propositio non est falsa. Et sequitur ultra

Igitur haec propositio est vera.

Igitur, a primo ad ultimum,

Si haec propositio significat praecise sicut est, haec propositio est
vera.

10 Quare etc.

⟨*Conclusiones contra secundam viam*⟩

Contra istam viam pono duas conclusiones.

⟨1⟩ *Prima*: Non si *A* propositio significat praecise sicut est, *A* propositio est vera.[2]

15 Haec conclusio demonstrata est in Prima Parte, capitulo De exclusivis,
ubi assignatur modus exponendi propositionem exclusivam quarti ordinis.[3]

⟨1.1⟩ Sed quia forte illa expositio non esset grata huic viae, ideo secundum propriam expositionem, meam conclusionem probo, alteram consequenter destruendo.

20 Et pono quod *A* sit illa propositio

Homo est asinus,

quae soli Sorti obiciatur, et non apprehendatur per ipsam nisi hominem
esse animal vel aliud verum, sic quod nullum falsum. Isto posito, patet
quod *A* est propositio falsa, et tamen significat praecise sicut est; quia
25 significat sicut est, ut patet, et non significat sicut non est—quod probo
sic: Sortes non apprehendit per ipsam sicut non est. Et ipsa nulli alteri
significat. Igitur non significat sicut non est. Consequentia patet, quia
significare est repraesentare virtuti cognitivae. Antecedens vero ponit
casus.

30 ⟨1.2⟩ Secundo arguitur sic: Haec propositio

Homo est asinus

significat praecise sicut est, et tamen est falsa, ut patet. Igitur etc. Consequentia patet, cum minori. Et maiorem probo ex eo quod quaelibet
propositio cuiuslibet suae partis significatum significat. Non enim est

3 exposita ad exponentes] exposito ad exponens *E*   8 est] igitur *add. (etiam
infra, sed ultra non notavi) E*   13 non] nam *E*   praecise *om. M*   16 quarti]
tertii *ME, correxi (cf. Fontes p. 204)*   17 ideo] iam *E*   18 conclusionem probo]
consequentiam probabo *E*   19 destruendo] destruam *E*   22 apprehendatur]
apprehendenti *M*   24 falsa *om. E*   25 significat[1]] praecise *add. M*   31 homo
est asinus] hominem esse asinum est praecise sicut est *M*

Proof: If the proposition signifies precisely as things are, the proposition signifies as things are and the proposition does not signify as things are not. The inference from the expounded proposition to the propositions expounding it is clear. Further, if the proposition signifies as things are and the proposition does not signify as things are not, the proposition exists, and the proposition is not false. It follows further,

Therefore, the proposition is true.

Therefore, inferring from the first ⟨antecedent⟩ to the last ⟨consequent⟩,

If the proposition signifies precisely as things are, then the proposition is true.

Thus, etc.

⟨*Theses Against the Second Way*⟩

I assume two theses against this way.

⟨*Counter-*⟩*Thesis 1*: It is not the case that if proposition *A* signifies precisely as things are, then proposition *A* is true.

This ⟨counter-⟩thesis has been demonstrated in Part I, chapter 'On Exclusives', where the way to expound exclusive propositions of the fourth order is assigned.[a]

⟨1.1⟩ But perhaps that exposition would not be acceptable to ⟨adherents of⟩ this way. Therefore, I shall prove my thesis according to their exposition,[b] thereby destroying their thesis.

I assume that *A* is the proposition

A man is a donkey

which is presented to Socrates alone; and that only that a man is an animal or some other truth and no falsehood is apprehended through it. When this has been assumed, it is clear that proposition *A* is false. Nevertheless, it signifies precisely as things are. It is clear that it signifies as things are. I prove that it does not signify as things are not, this way: Through it, Socrates does not apprehend as things are not. The proposition signifies to no one else. Therefore, it does not signify as things are not. The inference is clear. For to signify is to represent to a cognitive power.[c] And the premiss is laid down in the case assumed.

⟨1.2⟩ Second, I argue this way: The proposition

A man is a donkey

signifies precisely as things are. Nevertheless, it is false, as is clear. Therefore, etc. The inference is clear, as is the minor. I prove the major from the fact that any proposition signifies the significatum of any of its parts.

imaginabile quod significaret significatum totius et non significata partium. Nullus enim sanae mentis diceret quod ista

    Homo est animal

significat hominem esse animal, et non significaret hominem et animal.
5 Est enim primo signum sui, secundario vero cuiuscumque suae partis significati.

    Ex praedictis rationibus patet quod neutra illarum consequentiarum (159ra E) valet, qua arguit praedicta via suam conclusionem. Stat enim quod ly .praecise. non teneatur exclusive, et sic non arguitur ab exposita
10 ad exponentes ipsius. Dato etiam quod teneatur exclusive, secunda consequentia non valet, quia stat propositionem illam non significare suum adaequatum significatum, sed aliquod secundarium, secundum quod ratio prima ostendit.

    ⟨2⟩ *2a conclusio* est ista: Non si *A* propositio est vera, *A* propositio
15   significat praecise sicut est.[4]

    ⟨2.1⟩ Patet quia stat quod *A* sit propositio Sacrae Scripturae convertibilis cum una revelata a Spiritu Sancto et clausa in libro, nulli significans aut suum significatum alicui repraesentans. Igitur etc.

    Nec est dicendum, sicut alias audivi,[5] quod si *A* propositio est vera,
20 ipsa significat suum significatum intellectui divino; quia nulla res creata repraesentat se aut suum significatum intellectui divino, sed sola essentia divina, quae est species intelligibilis repraesentativa sui et cuiuslibet alterius citra se, significat intellectui divino propositionem illam et suum significatum.

25   ⟨2.2⟩ Secundo arguitur sic: Aliqua est negativa de praesenti vera, et aliqua de praeterito, et de futuro vera, quarum nulla significat primo sicut est. Igitur etc.

    Antecedens probatur.

    ⟨2.2.1⟩ Et primo de negativa. Nam si aliqua esset, maxime videtur ista
30   Nulla chimaera est,

quae (202va M) est vera, ut patet. Quod autem non significet sicut est primo, probatur: quia si

    Nulla chimaera est

significat primo sicut est, et ipsa primo significat quod nulla chimaera est;
35 igitur ita est quod nulla chimaera est. Consequens est falsum; igitur et antecedens.

4 significaret] significet *M*   9 exposita] exposito *M*   13 ostendit] ostendidit *ME* (*etiam infra M, sed ultra non notavi*)   14 *A* propositio² *om.*(*etiam infra, sed ultra non notavi*) *E*   20–21 intellectui¹⁻²] in intellectu *M*   26–7 primo sicut est significat *transp. E*   29 nam] quia (*etiam infra, sed ultra non notavi*) *E*   videtur] esse *add. E*   35 ita *om. M* (ita *Venator*, sic *Feribrigge*)

For it is not imaginable that it should signify the significatum of the proposition as a whole and not the significata of its parts. No one in his right mind would say that the proposition

A man is an animal

signified that a man is an animal, and did not signify a man and an animal. For a proposition is primarily a sign of its own significatum, but secondarily of the significata of each of its parts.

From these arguments, it is clear that neither of the inferences by which this way argues for its thesis holds good. For no contradiction is involved in not taking the 'precisely' as an exclusive. In that case there is no argument from the proposition expounded to the proposition expounding it. Even granted that it is taken as an exclusive, the second inference does not hold good. For it is consistent that the proposition does not signify its own adequate significatum, but signifies some secondary significatum, as my first argument has shown.

⟨*Counter-*⟩*Thesis* 2 : It is not the case that if proposition A is true, it signifies precisely as things are.

⟨2.1⟩ This is clear. For it is consistent that A should be a proposition of the Sacred Scriptures, interchangeable with a proposition revealed by the Holy Spirit, and that A should be in a closed book and not signify or represent its significatum to anyone. Therefore, etc.

Nor should one say, as I have heard elsewhere, that if proposition A is true, it signifies its significatum to the Divine Intellect. For no created thing represents itself or its significatum to the Divine Intellect. But the Divine Essence alone, which is an intelligible species representative of Itself and of everything else other than Itself, signifies that proposition and its significatum to the Divine Intellect.

⟨2.2⟩ Second, I argue this way: There is a true negative present-tense proposition, a ⟨true⟩ past-tense proposition, and a true future-tense proposition, none of which signifies primarily as things are. Therefore, etc.

Proof of the premiss:

⟨2.2.1⟩ First, with respect to a negative proposition. If there were some such negative proposition, the most obvious example would be the proposition

No chimera is,

which is true, as is clear. But that it does not signify primarily as things are, is proved this way: If

No chimera is

signifies primarily as things are, and it signifies primarily that no chimera is, then it is so that no chimera is. The consequent is false. Therefore, so is the antecedent.

Falsitas consequentis probatur. Nam quod nulla chimaera est, non est aliquid nec aliqualiter nec aliqua.

⟨2.2.1A⟩ Quod probatur sic, quia si nullam chimaeram esse, esset aliquid, aliqua, vel aliqualiter, et nullam chimaeram esse non est primum
5 simpliciter; igitur nullam chimaeram esse habet causam. Sed nulla est causa propter quam est quod nulla chimaera est. Igitur non est ita quod nulla chimaera est.

Consequentia patet cum maiori. Et minorem probo: Nam nullam chimaeram esse non est causa quare est quia nulla chimaera est. Nec est aliqua
10 alia causa positiva. Igitur, nulla est causa quare est nullam chimaeram esse.

Antecedens probatur pro utraque parte.

⟨2.2.1Aa⟩ Et primo pro prima, quia non sequitur:

Nulla chimaera est.

Igitur ita est quod nulla chimaera est.

15 Primo, quia ex negativa non praegnante non sequitur affirmativa sine termino modali.[6] Secundo, quia oppositum consequentis est imaginabile cum antecedente. Probatur: Nam si nihil nec aliqualiter esset, nulla chimaera esset. Et si nihil nec aliqualiter esset, non esset nullam chimaeram esse—quod est oppositum consequentis. Igitur etc.

20 ⟨2.2.1Ab⟩ Secunda pars illius antecedentis probatur—videlicet quod nulla est causa positiva quare est quod nulla chimaera est—quia non est aliqualiter in re, quin taliter non existente, sicut omnino nulla chimaera esset, qualiter nunc nulla chimaera est. Igitur nihil est causa positiva quare est quod nulla chimaera est.

25 Confirmatur: Nam non est ratio quare aliquid est causa quare nulla chimaera est, quin quodlibet et qualitercumque sit causa quare est quod nulla chimaera est. Consequens est falsum, quia nec homo nec hominem esse est causa quare est quod nulla chimaera est, cum causa et causatum ad invicem proportionentur. Modo hominem esse et nullam chimaeram
30 esse non possunt ad invicem proportionari.

⟨2.2.1B⟩ Secundo principaliter, si aliquid vel aliqualiter est nullam chimaeram esse, et non est maior ratio de uno quam de alio, igitur quodlibet vel qualitercumque est nullam chimaeram esse. Sed contingens est aliquid vel aliqualiter esse. Igitur, contingens est nullam chimaeram esse—
35 quod tamen non conceditur, quia necessarium est nullam chimaeram esse.

⟨2.2.1C⟩ Tertio, si est nullam chimaeram esse, vel est esse inhaerentiae vel esse per se. Non primo modo, quia nullo existente omnino, nulla chimaera esset, qualiter nunc nulla chimaera est. Igitur in nullo est subie-

---

4 primum] p^m M (principium *Feribrigge*)   6 ita *om.* M   14 ita *om.* M
22 existente] existat E   23 est¹] esset E   25 confirmatur] consimiliter M   quare]
quod E   31 secundo] tertio ME, *correxi*   34 esse¹ *om.* M   36 tertio]
quarto ME, *correxi*   37 nullo] uno E   38 qualiter nunc] nec E

Proof of the falsity of the consequent: There being no chimera is not anything, not anyhow, and not any things.

⟨2.2.1A⟩ Proof: If there being no chimera were something, some things, or somehow; and that no chimera is, is not the absolutely First ⟨Being⟩; then there being no chimera has a cause. But there is no cause by which it is that no chimera is. Therefore, it is not so that no chimera is.

The inference is clear, as is the major. Proof of the minor: There being no chimera, is not the cause by which it is that no chimera is. Nor is there any other positive cause. Therefore, there is no cause by which it is that no chimera is.

Proof of each of the premisses: ⟨2.2.1Aa⟩ First, of the first premiss:[d] This does not follow:

> No chimera is.
> Therefore, it is so that no chimera is.

First, because an affirmative proposition without any modal term does not follow from a non-pregnant[e] negative proposition. Second, because the opposite of the conclusion is imaginable together with the premiss. Proof: If there were not anything and not anyhow, no chimera would be. If there were not anything and not anyhow, that no chimera is, would not be— which is the opposite of the conclusion. Therefore, etc.

⟨2.2.1Ab⟩ Proof of the second premiss—viz. that there is no positive cause by which it is that no chimera is. For there is no way in which things are in reality, which is such that if things were not in that way, it would not be that no chimera is, in the way in which it is now that no chimera is. Therefore, nothing is the positive cause by which it is that no chimera is.

Confirming argument: If there were a reason why something would be the cause by which no chimera is, then anything whatever, and in any way whatever, would be the cause by which it is that no chimera is. The consequent is false, since neither a man nor that a man is, is the cause by which it is that no chimera is. For the cause and the caused are mutually proportioned. But that a man is, and that no chimera is, cannot be mutually proportioned.

⟨2.2.1B⟩ Second principal argument: If there being no chimera is something or somehow, and there is no more reason why it is one thing or one way rather than another, then there being no chimera is anything or anyhow. But a contingency is something or is somehow. Therefore, it is a contingency that no chimera is—which nevertheless ought not to be granted, since it is necessary that no chimera is.

⟨2.2.1C⟩ Third, if there being no chimera is, its being is either inherent or per se. Not the first way, since if nothing at all existed, no chimera would be, just as no chimera is now. Therefore, it is not inherent in anything

ctive; quia si in aliquo est subiective, igitur et in quolibet est subiective quod nulla chimaera est. Consequens est falsum, quia tunc unum accidens migraret de subiecto in subiectum—quod est contra Philosophum in primo *De Generatione*.[7] Et permanentius esset subiective in impermanen-
5 tiori, quia necessarium in contingenti—quod est simpliciter impossibile. Si autem nullam chimaeram esse, est esse per se, ita quod non in aliquo, sed quocumque alio non existente, adhuc nulla chimaera esset; igitur nullam chimaeram esse est primum simpliciter, (159rb E) cum non praesupponit alterius esse.

10 ⟨2.2.1D⟩ Quarto, si nullam chimaeram esse est, sequitur quod tu differs a nullam chimaeram esse. Consequens falsum, quia differentia non cadit nisi inter extrema positiva. Modo nullam chimaeram esse non est ens positivum, cum non sit substantia vel accidens, ut probatum est.

Sed consequentia probatur, quia tu es, et nullam chimaeram esse est,
15 et tu non es nullam chimaeram esse. Igitur, tu differs a nullam chimaeram esse. Consequentia patet, ab exponentibus ad expositum. Sed tertia pars probatur, quia si tu es nullam chimaeram esse, igitur nullam chimaeram esse est tu—per conversionem simplicem. Igitur nullam chimaeram esse est substantia—quod est contra omnes suppositam materiam sustinentes.

20 ⟨2.2.2 & 2.2.3⟩ Consimilibus formis hucusque factis probandum est quod non est sicut propositio de praeterito vel de futuro vera significat primo, cuius propositionis subiecto non correspondet significatum quod sit aliquid vel aliqualiter a parte rei. Cuiusmodi sunt istae:

Adam fuit,

25   Antichristus erit.

⟨2.2.2A⟩ Sicut enim non stat Deum esse sine Deo, nec te esse sine te, ita non stat Adam fuisse sine Adam. Sed Adam non est. Igitur Adam (202vb M) fuisse non est.

⟨2.2.2B⟩ Secundo, subductis omnibus absolutis a Deo, et hac proposi-
30 tione

Adam fuit

cum suis partibus sic significantibus, adhuc haec propositio esset vera, significando primo Adam fuisse. Sed tunc Adam fuisse non esset. Igitur, per idem, nec nunc, ex quo Adam non est.

3–4 in primo *om. E*   4–5 impermanentiori] impermanenti *M*   5 simpliciter] similiter *E*   7 non *om. E*   13 vel] nec *E*   29 absolutis] absolute *E* (absolutis *Venator*) a Deo] adeo *ME* (a deo *Venator*)   32 significantibus] significando *ME, quod correxi ex Venatore*

as in a subject. For if it is inherent in something as in a subject, then that no chimera is, is also inherent in anything whatever as in a subject. The consequent is false, since then one accident would pass from subject to subject—which is contrary to what the Philosopher says in *On Generation and Corruption*, Book I ⟨327^{b}22⟩. And the more permanent would inhere in the less permanent as in a subject, since the necessary would be in the contingent—which is absolutely impossible. Suppose, on the other hand, there being no chimera is a being *per se*, so that it is not inherent in something, but if there were nothing else, still there would be no chimera; then there being no chimera is the absolutely First ⟨Being⟩, since it does not presuppose the existence of anything else.

⟨2.2.1D⟩ Fourth, if there being no chimera *is*, it follows that you differ from there being no chimera. The consequent is false, since difference obtains only between positive extremes. But there being no chimera is not a positive being, since it is neither substance nor accident, as has been proved.

Proof of the inference: You are; and there being no chimera *is*. You are not there being no chimera. Therefore, you are different from there being no chimera. The inference is clear from the expounding propositions to what is expounded. The third premiss is proved this way: If you are there being no chimera, then there being no chimera is you—by simple conversion. Therefore, there being no chimera is a substance—which is contrary to all those who take sides in the matter under discussion.

⟨2.2.2 & 2.2.3⟩ Arguments similar to those already given should be used to prove that it is not ⟨so⟩ as is primarily signified by a true past-tense or future-tense proposition, whose subject has corresponding to it no significatum that is something or somehow in reality. The propositions

Adam was

and

The Antichrist will be

are propositions of this sort.

⟨2.2.2A⟩ For just as that God is, cannot stand without God, or that you are without you, so that Adam was, cannot stand without Adam. But Adam is not. Therefore, that Adam was, is not.

⟨2.2.2B⟩ Second, suppose that all absolute things have been annihilated by God, and that the proposition

Adam was,

together with its parts, signifies thus. Still that proposition signifying primarily that Adam was, would be true. But then that Adam was, would not be. Therefore, by the same reasoning, it is not now, because Adam is not.

⟨2.2.2C⟩ Tertio, Deum esse est Deus, et Sortem esse est Sortes. Igitur si Adam fuisse est, Adam fuisse est Adam praeteritus. Consequens est falsum, quia nihil nec aliqualiter est Adam praeteritus.

⟨2.2.3⟩ Et ita potest argui de illa

5　　Antichristus erit,

et de qualibet negativa vera, reducendo omnia priora argumenta, quibus probatur non esse quod nulla chimaera est.

Pro solutione quasi omnium istorum argumentorum, dicunt communiter doctores ordinis mei quod nullam chimaeram esse non est aliquid, nec
10 aliqua, sed aliqualiter; nec primum simpliciter, nec aliquid fluens ab ipso; non causa, nec causatum; non dependens, nec independens; non ens per se, nec ens in alio. Et sic multa quae non solum veritati et dictis doctorum approbatorum repugnant, verum et imaginationi, sicut inferius ostendam ubi de significato propositionis agetur.[8]

15 ⟨*Tertia Via*　　　　　　　　　　*Capitulum Tertium*⟩

Tertia via[1] e converso ponit illam conclusionem:

Si praecise sicut est significat haec propositio vel illa—quacumque demonstrata—illa propositio est vera.

Probatur: Nam si praecise sicut est significat *A* propositio, sicut est
20 significat *A* propositio, et non aliter quam est significat *A* propositio. Igitur *A* propositio est vera.

Consequentia prima patet, ab exposito ad suas exponentes. Secunda consequentia probatur quia ex opposito consequentis sequitur oppositum antecedentis. Sequitur enim

25　　*A* propositio est falsa.

Igitur aliter quam est ista significat.

Quare etc.

⟨*Argumenta cuiusdam magistri contra conclusionem*⟩

Contra istam conclusionem, arguit unus magister multipliciter.[2]
30 ⟨1⟩ Et primo sic: Praecise sicut est significat *A* propositio falsa. Igitur non si praecise sicut est significat haec propositio, haec propositio est vera.

Patet consequentia, et antecedens probatur: Et sit *A* ista propositio

Deus est asinus.

---

6 et] de illa negativa vel *add.* E　　　13 ostendam] ostendetur E　　　19 si *om.* M

⟨2.2.2C⟩ Third, that God is, is God, and that Socrates is, is Socrates. Therefore, if *that Adam was*ᶠ is, *that Adam was* is the past Adam. The consequent is false, since there is not anything or any way that the past Adam is.

⟨2.2.3⟩ And one can argue this way about the proposition

The Antichrist will be,

and about any true negative, by redirecting all the previous arguments used to prove that there being no chimera is not.ᵍ

By way of a solution to almost all of these arguments, the doctors of my order commonly say that there being no chimera is not something or some things, but somehow. It is neither the absolutely First ⟨Being⟩, nor something flowing from it; neither a cause, nor caused; neither dependent nor independent; neither a being *per se* nor a being inherent in another. Thus ⟨they say⟩ many things which are inconsistent, not only with the truth and the claims of approved doctors, but also with the imagination, as I will show below, where I deal with the significatum of a proposition.

⟨The Third Way   Chapter Three⟩

Conversely, the third way posits the following thesis.

> *Thesis*: If precisely the way it is, is signified by this or that proposition (where any proposition whatever is indicated), then the proposition is true.ᵃ

Proof: If precisely the way it is, is signified by proposition A, then the way it is, is signified by proposition A, and no other way than the way it is, is signified by proposition A. Therefore, proposition A is true.

The first inference, from the proposition expounded to the propositions expounding it, is clear. The second inference is proved from the fact that the opposite of the premiss follows from the opposite of the conclusion. For this follows:

Proposition A is false.

Therefore, another way than it is, is signified by this proposition.

Thus, etc.

⟨A Certain Master's Arguments against this Thesis⟩

One Master advances many arguments against this thesis.

⟨1⟩ First argument: Precisely the way it is, is signified by A, a false proposition. Therefore, it is not the case that if precisely the way it is, is signified by this proposition, then this proposition is true.

The inference is clear. Proof of the premiss: Let A be the ⟨false⟩ proposition

God is a donkey.

Tunc sic: Praecise sicut est significans est *A* propositio falsa. Igitur praecise sicut est significat *A* propositio falsa.

Probatur consequentia: Praecise sicut est significans est *A* propositio falsa. Igitur sicut est significans est *A* propositio falsa, et non sicut non 5 est significans est *A* propositio falsa. Patet consequentia, ab exposito ad eius exponentes.

Et sequitur ultra:

> Igitur, sicut est significat *A* propositio falsa, et non sicut non est significat *A* propositio falsa.

10 —quod sic probatur, quia ex opposito consequentis sequitur oppositum antecedentis. Nam sequitur:

> Sicut non est significat *A* propositio falsa.
> Igitur, sicut non est significans est *A* propositio falsa.

De alia parte patet. Patet igitur consequentia.

15 Antecedens probatur sic: *A* propositio falsa est praecise sicut est significans. Igitur, praecise sicut est significans est *A* propositio falsa. Consequentia patet, per conversionem simplicem.

⟨1.1⟩ Confirmatur idem sic: In quacumque indefinita affirmativa denotatur praedicatum particulariter dici de subiecto, sic quod subiecti et 20 praedicati sit eadem suppositio et aequalis, seu convertibilis praecise. Igitur, si ponitur unus terminus pro subiecto sive alius, non (159ᵛᵃ E) est differentia quoad veritatem vel falsitatem enuntiandam. Patet per a simili:

> Homo est animal,
25 Animal est homo.

Cum igitur in ista propositione

> *A* propositio falsa est praecise sicut est significans

sit huiusmodi, sequitur quod non erit differentia dicere

> *A* propositio falsa est praecise sicut est significans,
30 et
> Praecise sicut est significans est ⟨*A*⟩ propositio falsa.

⟨1.2⟩ Confirmatur iterum idem antecedens sic: Aliquod praecise sicut est significans est *A* propositio falsa. Igitur praecise sicut est significans est *A* propositio falsa. Consequentia patet, a particulari ad indefinitam. 35 Unde propositio singularis, sola demptione signi, fit indefinita. Et ita est in proposito.

---

2 falsa *om. E*   3 significans] est significans *A* propositio *M*   22 per *om. E*
23 simili] simile *M*   29 falsa *om. E*   32 aliquod] aliquid *M* (aliquod *Feribrigge*)

Then ⟨he argues⟩ this way: Precisely the way it is a sign is A a false proposition. Therefore, precisely the way it is, is signified by A, a false proposition.[b]

Proof of the inference: Precisely the way it is a sign is A a false proposition. Therefore, the way it is a sign is A a false proposition, and not the way it is not a sign is A a false proposition. The inference, from what is expounded to the propositions expounding it, is clear.

This follows further:

Therefore, the way it is, is signified by A, a false proposition, and it is not so that the way it is not, is signified by A, a false proposition.[c]

This is proved from the fact that the opposite of the premiss follows from the opposite of the conclusion. For this follows:

The way it is not, is signified by A, a false proposition.

Therefore, the way it is not a sign is A a false proposition.

⟨The inference⟩ with respect to the other part, is clear.[d] Therefore, the inference is clear.

Proof of the premiss: A is a false proposition precisely the way it is a sign. Therefore, precisely the way it is a sign is A a false proposition. The inference is clear by simple conversion.[e]

⟨1.1⟩ The same thing is confirmed this way: In any indefinite affirmative proposition, it is denoted that the predicate is said particularly of the subject, in such a way that the subject and the predicate have the same and equal, or precisely convertible, *suppositio*. Therefore, whether one term or the other is in the subject position, it makes no difference to the truth or falsity of the proposition. This is clear by analogy with

A man is an animal,

and

An animal is a man.

Therefore, since the proposition

A is a false proposition precisely the way it is a sign

is a proposition of the same kind, it follows that it will make no difference whether you say

A is a false proposition precisely the way it is a sign,

or

Precisely the way it is a sign is ⟨A⟩ a false proposition.

⟨1.2⟩ Again, the same premiss is confirmed this way: Something ⟨that is⟩ precisely ⟨of⟩ the way it is a sign is A a false proposition. Therefore, precisely the way it is a sign is A a false proposition. The inference, from the particular to the indefinite, is clear. Thus, a singular proposition becomes indefinite when only its applicative is removed.[f] This is the way it is in the proposed ⟨inference⟩.

⟨2⟩ Secundo principaliter contra conclusionem arguitur sic: Et pono quod omnis propositio falsa significet sicut est. Tunc sic:

Omnis propositio falsa significat sicut est.
Igitur praecise sicut est significat propositio falsa.

5 Consequentia patet, ab universali ad exclusivam, de terminis transpositis. Igitur non si praecise sicut est significat aliqua propositio, illa propositio est vera.

(203ʳᵃ M) ⟨3⟩ Tertio principaliter: Praecise sicut est significat haec propositio

10   Antichristus est,

et ipsa est falsa. Igitur, non si praecise sicut est significat haec propositio, haec propositio est vera.

Tenet consequentia, et antecedens probatur: Praecise quod Antichristus est haec propositio significat, et sic est. Igitur, praecise sicut est 15 haec propositio significat.

Minor sic arguitur:

Tali modo est.
Igitur sic est.

Consequentia patet, quia ly .sic. denotat similitudinem duorum similium 20 sicut hoc nomen 'talis'. Et antecedens probatur: Aliquo tali modo est. Igitur tali modo est. Patet consequentia, a particulari ad indefinitam. Antecedens probatur: Quod tu es homo, est. Et quod tu es homo, est aliquis talis modus qualis est quod Antichristus est. Igitur aliquo tali modo est. Confirmatur: Uterque illorum modorum est possibilis. Igitur talis est 25 unus illorum qualis est alter. Quare etc.

⟨*Responsio ad argumenta*⟩

Sed quia haec argumenta possent contra omnem viam reduci, et contra quamplurima dicta mea, ideo ad ipsa respondendo, taliter dissolvuntur:

⟨R1⟩ Cum enim arguitur

30   Praecise sicut est significans est propositio falsa.

Igitur, praecise sicut est significat propositio falsa,

quaeratur an ly .significans. in antecedente sit pars subiecti vel praedicati. ⟨a⟩ Si primum, negatur consequentia. Et ad probationem, concedo primam consequentiam et nego secundam, videlicet

35   Non sicut non est significans est *A* propositio ⟨falsa⟩.

Igitur, non sicut non est significat *A* propositio falsa.

---

7 vera] falsa *M*   8 principaliter *om. M*   18 est *om. E*   19 sic] sicut *M*
denotat] significat *E*   duorum similium *om. E*   28 quamplurima] suam plurima *E*
respondendo] respondeo *M*   32 quaeratur] quaeritur *E*

⟨2⟩ His second principal argument against the thesis is this. I posit that every false proposition signifies the way it is.*g* Then I argue this way:

Every false proposition signifies the way it is.
Therefore, precisely the way it is, a false proposition signifies.

The inference from the universal to the exclusive with the terms transposed, is clear.*h* Therefore, it is not ⟨the case⟩ that if precisely the way it is, some proposition signifies, then the proposition is true.

⟨3⟩ His third principal argument is this: Precisely the way it is, is signified by the proposition

The Antichrist is.

It is false. Therefore, it is not ⟨the case⟩ that if precisely the way it is, is signified by this proposition, the proposition is true.

The inference holds. Proof of the premiss: Precisely that the Antichrist is, is signified by this proposition, and so it is. Therefore, precisely the way it is, is signified by this proposition.

⟨He⟩ proves the minor this way:

It is in such a mode.
Therefore, it is so.

The inference is clear. For 'so' denotes a similarity between two similar things, just as the word 'such' does. Proof of the premiss: It is in some such mode. Therefore, it is in such a mode. The inference from the particular to the indefinite, is clear. Proof of the premiss: That you are a man, is. That you are a man, is some such mode as that the Antichrist is, is. Therefore, it is in some such mode. Confirming argument: Each of these modes is possible. Therefore, one of them is the same kind as the other. Thus, etc.

⟨*Reply to these Arguments*⟩

But these arguments could be directed against all the ways, as well as against very many of my own claims. Therefore, replying to them, I will resolve them in the following way.

⟨R1⟩ When ⟨he⟩ argues

Precisely the way it is a sign is ⟨*A*⟩ a false proposition.
Therefore, precisely the way it is, is signified by ⟨*A*⟩ a false proposition,

let us ask whether 'sign' in the premiss is part of the subject or part of the predicate. ⟨a⟩ If the first, I deny the inference. In reply to the proof, I grant the first inference*i* and deny the second—viz.

Not: the way it is not a sign is *A* a ⟨false⟩ proposition.
Therefore, not: the way it is not signifies *A*, a false proposition.

Nec ex opposito sequitur oppositum, quia non sequitur:

Sicut non est significat *A* propositio falsa.

Igitur, sicut non est significans est *A* propositio falsa.

Antecedens enim est verum, ut patet. Et consequens falsum, quia sua
5 convertens simpliciter est falsa, videlicet

A propositio falsa est sicut non est significans,

eo quod negatio transit super ly .significans. Quare per propositionem
asseritur quod *A* propositio falsa est sicut nullum significans est—quod
manifeste est falsum.

10   ⟨b⟩ Si autem concedatur quod ly .significans. in antecedente sit pars
praedicati, concedatur consequentia, et negetur antecedens. Et tunc ad
probationem negatur consequentia, quia non est conversio simplex.
Primo, quia illa

Praecise sicut est significans est *A* propositio falsa

15 non est alicuius quantitatis. Secundo, quia in antecedente ly .praecise. fuit
pars praedicati, in consequente vero est pars subiecti. Ideo debuit sic argui:
A propositio falsa est praecise sicut est significans. Igitur aliquid praecise
sicut est significans est ⟨*A*⟩ propositio falsa—quod conceditur, sicut et
antecedens.

20   ⟨R1.1⟩ Ad primam confirmationem dico tres propositiones.

Prima est quod non in quacumque affirmativa indefinita praedicatum
sic dicitur de subiecto quod sit aequalis suppositio.

Sicut patet in ista

Homo est iste homo.

25   *2a propositio*, quod in ista propositione
Praecise sicut est significans est *A* propositio falsa,
ly .praecise sicut est. non est subiectum.

Patet, quia ly .praecise. non est pars subiecti, ex demonstratione facta in
Prima Parte.[3]

30   *3a propositio*: In ista propositione
A propositio falsa est praecise sicut est significans,
ly .praecise sicut est significans. est praedicatum.

Patet ex communi schola.

Ex quibus patet quod in praedicta consequentia non ponitur subiectum
35 pro praedicato, nec e contra. Quare non mirum si aliqua differentia oritur
ex eisdem quoad veritatem vel falsitatem enuntiandam.

⟨R1.2⟩ Ad aliam confirmationem, nego similiter consequentiam. Nec
arguitur a particulari ad indefinitam, quia consequens non est alicuius

---

3 falsa *om. M*   10–11 concedatur[1-2]] conceditur *E*   11 negetur] negatur *E*
17–18 sicut est praecise[2] *transp. E*   20 tres *om. M*   36 enuntiandam *emendavi*
(*cf. supra p.* 26 *lin.* 22), explanandam *M*, explicandam *E*

Nor does the opposite ⟨of the premiss⟩ follow from the opposite ⟨of the conclusion⟩, since this does not follow:

The way it is not is signified by *A* a false proposition.
Therefore, the way it is not a sign is *A* a false proposition.*j*

The premiss is true, as is clear. The conclusion is false, since its direct converse—viz.

A is a false proposition the way it is not a sign

—is false. For the negation governs 'a sign'. Thus the proposition affirms that *A* is a false proposition in that it is no sign—which is clearly false.

⟨b⟩ But if it is granted that 'a sign' in the premiss is part of the predicate, I grant the inference and deny the premiss. Then, in reply to the proof ⟨of the premiss⟩, I deny the inference, since it is not a simple conversion. First, because the proposition

Precisely the way it is a sign is *A* a false proposition

has no quantity.*k* Second, because 'precisely' in the premiss was part of the predicate, but in the conclusion it is part of the subject. Therefore, ⟨he⟩ should argue this way: *A* is a false proposition precisely the way it is a sign. Therefore, something precisely the way it is a sign is ⟨*A*⟩ a false proposition—which I grant, along with the premiss.*l*

⟨R1.1⟩ In reply to the confirming argument, I maintain three theses.

⟨*Thesis*⟩ *1*: It is not the case that in any affirmative indefinite proposition, the predicate is said of the subject in such a way that they have equal supposition.

This is clear in the proposition

A man is this man.
Thesis 2: In the proposition
   Precisely the way it is a sign is *A* a false proposition
   the 'precisely the way it is' is not the subject.

It is clear from a demonstration made in Part I that 'precisely' is not part of the subject.

Thesis 3: In the proposition
   A is a false proposition precisely the way it is a sign
   the 'precisely the way it is a sign' is the predicate.

This is clear from the common school.

It is clear from these theses, that in the previously stated inference the subject is not put in the predicate position, nor vice versa. Thus, it is not surprising if these propositions differ with respect to truth and falsity.

⟨R1.2⟩ Similarly, ⟨in reply⟩ to the other confirming argument, I deny the inference. Nor is there any argument from the particular to the indefinite,

quantitatis, ut dictum est. Si enim ista ratio valeret, probarem quod tantum Deus est, quia

Aliquid tantum Deus est.

Igitur tantum Deus est.

5 Et ad probationem, cum dicitur

Propositio (159vb E) singularis, sola demptione signi, fit indefinita, certum est quod haec locutio est impossibilis, de virtute sermonis. Si tamen intelligitur quod dempto signo remanet propositio indefinita, dico quod hoc non est universaliter verum, ubi dempto signo aliud signum remanet.

10 Sicut hic

Iste omnis homo currit,

certum est quod si dematur signum, remanet universalis propositio et non indefinita. Et ita in proposito. Sicut ergo huius

Iste omnis homo currit

15 indefinita est ista

Ens omnis homo currit,

vel ista

Homo omnis homo currit,

ita et istius

20   Aliquid praecise sicut est significans est propositio falsa

indefinita est illa

Ens praecise sicut est significans est propositio falsa.

Quare etc.

⟨R2⟩ Ad secundam rationem principalem, admisso casu, nego con-

25 sequentiam. Nec arguitur per regulam, ut patet. Sed ex illa universali debet concludi quod

Praecise significans sicut est, est propositio falsa,

quae est propositio vera, sicut antecedens.

⟨R3⟩ Ad tertiam rationem, nego quod praecise sicut est significat haec

30 propositio

Antichristus est.

Et nego quod sic est—demonstrando Antichristum esse. Et illam similiter,

Aliquo tali modo est.

1 ut . . . est] quare etc. Et M   12 dematur] demonstratur M, demonstretur E,
correxi   15 ista] ita E   18 homo¹] hic E   21 est] sicut *add.* E   24 ratio-
nem] responsionem (*etiam lin. 29*) E   25 patet] intuenti *add.* E

since the conclusion is not of any quantity, as has been said.[m] If this argument held good, I would prove that only God is, since

> Something ⟨that is⟩ only God is.
> Therefore, only God is.[n]

To the proof, when it is said:

> The singular proposition becomes indefinite when only its applicative is removed,

it is certain that this saying is impossible taken literally. Nevertheless, if one understands that when the applicative is removed what remains is an indefinite proposition, I say that this is not universally true where, when an applicative is removed, another applicative remains. For example, with the proposition

> This ⟨which is⟩ every man runs,

it is certain that if an applicative is removed, a universal, not an indefinite, proposition remains. So also in the proposed case. Therefore, just as the indefinite of the proposition

> This ⟨which is⟩ every man runs

is the proposition

> What is every man runs

or the proposition

> A man ⟨that is⟩ every man runs;

so also the indefinite of the proposition

> Something ⟨that is⟩ precisely ⟨of⟩ the way it is a sign is A, a false proposition

is

> What is precisely ⟨of⟩ the way it is a sign is A, a false proposition.

Thus, etc.

⟨R2⟩ In reply to the second principal argument, I admit the case and deny the inference. Nor is the argument according to the ⟨cited⟩ rule, as is clear. But from that universal he ought to conclude

> Precisely a sign ⟨of⟩ the way it is, is a false proposition,

which is a true proposition, as is its premiss.[o]

⟨R3⟩ In reply to the third argument, I deny that precisely the way it is, is signified by the proposition

> The Antichrist is.

I deny that things are so (where ⟨'so'⟩ indicates that the Antichrist is). Similarly, I deny the proposition

> In some such mode it is.

Et admisso quod te esse hominem sit aliquis modus (203rb M)—quod tamen est falsum—nego illam
    ⟨Quod⟩ tu es homo est aliquis talis modus qualis est quod Antichristus est,

5 quia quod Antichristus est, non est modus, quia non est. Et cum dicitur
    Uterque illorum modorum est possibilis,
concedo.
    Igitur, talis est unus qualis est reliquus,
nego consequentiam. Sicut non sequitur:

10   Uterque illorum est possibilis—demonstratis te et Antichristo.
    Igitur, talis tu es qualis est Antichristus.

⟨*Conclusiones contra tertiam viam*⟩

Contra igitur illam suppositam viam, arguo ponendo duas conclusiones, sicut contra praecedentem.

15   *Prima* est: Non si praecise sicut est significat *A* propositio, *A* propositio est vera.

Haec conclusio potest persuaderi ex rationibus factis contra secundam opinionem superius recitatam.

Verumtamen arguo sic: Si oppositum huius conclusionis sit verum,
20 a pari haec condicionalis est bona:
    Si praecise sicut est significant *A* et *B* propositiones, *A* et *B* propositiones sunt verae.

Patet consequentia, quia si valet in singulari, oportet quod etiam valeat in plurali. Sed consequens est falsum, quod probo sic, ponendo quod *A* sit
25 ista propositio
    Tu es Sortes,
et *B* illa
    Tu es Plato,
quarum quaelibet sit falsa. Quo posito, patet quod *A* et *B* sunt proposi-
30 tiones falsae. Et tamen praecise sicut est significant, quia sicut est significant, eo quod te esse significant et non aliter quam sicut est significant. Probatur: Nam nullum falsum significant. Igitur non aliter quam sicut est significant.

Consequentia patet, quia contradictorium consequentis repugnat ante-
35 cedenti. Antecedens vero probatur: Nam nec te esse Sortem *A* et *B* significant, nec te esse Platonem *A* et *B* significant, ut patet. Et non videtur aliud falsum assignandum quod *A* et *B* significant. Igitur etc.

---

3 quod *supplevi ex p.* 28, *lin.* 22-3   10 demonstratis] demonstrato *E*   29 posito *om. M*   31 sicut *om. E*   37 quod] quam *E*

And granted that you are a man, is some mode (which nevertheless is false), I deny that

> That you are a man, is a mode of the same kind as that the Antichrist is, is.

For that the Antichrist is, is not a mode, since it is not. When ⟨he⟩ says

> Each of these modes is possible,

I grant it. ⟨And when he concludes⟩

> Therefore, one is of the same kind as the other,

I deny the inference. In the same way, this does not follow:

> Each of these is possible (where you and the Antichrist are indicated). Therefore, you are of the same kind as the Antichrist is.

⟨*Theses against the Third Way*⟩

Therefore, I argue against the supposed way by assuming two theses, just as I did in arguing against the preceding way.

> ⟨*Counter-*⟩*Thesis 1*: It is not the case that if precisely the way it is, is signified by proposition A, proposition A is true.

One can be persuaded of this thesis by the arguments made against the second opinion recited above.

Nevertheless, I offer this argument. If the opposite of this thesis were true, then by parity of reasoning, the conditional

> If precisely the way it is, is signified by propositions A and B, then propositions A and B are true

would hold good. The inference is clear. For if it holds good in the singular, it must also hold good in the plural. But the consequent is false—which I prove this way. I assume that A is the proposition

> You are Socrates,

and B the proposition

> You are Plato,

—each of which is false. When this has been assumed, it is clear that A and B are false propositions. Nevertheless, precisely the way it is, is signified by A and B. For the way it is, is signified by A and B because they signify that you are. And no other way than the way it is, is signified by A and B. Proof: Nothing false is signified by A and B. Therefore, no other way than the way it is, is signified by A and B.

The inference is clear, since the contradictory of the conclusion is inconsistent with the premiss. Proof of the premiss: For A and B signify neither that you are Socrates nor that you are Plato, as is clear.[p] It seems that no other falsehood can be assigned which A and B signify. Therefore, etc.

Ad rationem ergo opinionis patet quod non procedit. Conceditur enim illa stare simul:

A propositio est falsa,

et tamen

5   Non aliter quam sicut est A propositio significat,

sicut ostensum est in priori capitulo.

> 2a conclusio est ista: Non si A propositio est vera, praecise sicut est significat A propositio.

Haec conclusio deducitur sicut deducebatur secunda conclusio in altero
10 capitulo.⁴

Tamen arguitur sic: Haec propositio est vera

Homo est animal,

et tamen non praecise sicut est illa significat. Igitur etc. Consequentia patet cum maiori, et minorem probo: Nam aliter quam est illa significat,
15 seu sicut non est illa significat. Igitur, non praecise sicut est illa significat. Antecedens patet, quia hominem esse asinum illa significat, ut saepissime dictum est. Igitur[etc.], aliter quam est illa significat.

Et sic patet quod haec opinio non sufficienter probat intentum.

⟨Quarta Via   *Capitulum Quartum⟩*

20 Quarta viaⁱ ponit talem conclusionem:

> Si ita est totaliter sicut haec propositio vel illa significat, haec propositio vel illa est vera.

Probatur: Nam si ita est totaliter sicut haec propositio significat, totale significatum illius est verum. Et si sic, illa propositio est vera.

25 *⟨Conclusiones contra quartam viam⟩*

Contra istam viam pono duas conclusiones.

> ⟨1⟩ *Prima* est ista:² Non si ita est totaliter sicut A propositio significat,
>
> A propositio est vera.
>
> ⟨1.1⟩ Probatur: Et capio istam propositionem

30   Tu es asinus.

Tunc patet quod ipsa est falsa.

> ⟨1.1.1⟩ Et quod ita est totaliter sicut ipsa significat probatur: Te esse est totaliter sicut A propositio significat, et te esse est ita. Igitur, ita est (160ʳ a E) totaliter sicut A propositio significat.

35   Vel sic: Verum est totaliter sicut A propositio significat. Igitur, ita est

---

7 non] nam (*etiam infra, sed ultra non notavi*) E

Therefore, in reply to the argument for the opinion, it is clear that it does not follow. For I grant that these two things are consistent:

Proposition *A* is false,

and nevertheless

No other way than the way it is, is signified by proposition *A*,

as has been shown in an earlier chapter.

⟨*Counter-*⟩*Thesis 2*: It is not the case that if proposition *A* is true, precisely the way it is, is signified by proposition *A*.

This ⟨counter-⟩thesis can be deduced in the same way as the second ⟨counter-⟩thesis of another chapter.

Nevertheless, I argue this way. The proposition

A man is an animal

is true. Nevertheless, it is not the case that precisely the way it is, is signified by this proposition. Therefore, etc. The inference is clear, as is the major. Proof of the minor: Another way than it is, or the way it is not, is signified by the proposition ⟨'A man is an animal'⟩. Therefore, it is not the case that precisely the way it is, is signified by this proposition. The premiss is clear. For it signifies that a man is a donkey, as has very often been said. Therefore, another way than it is, is signified by it.

Thus, it is clear that this opinion does not sufficiently prove the intended conclusion.

⟨*The Fourth Way*   *Chapter Four*⟩

The fourth way posits the following thesis:

⟨*Thesis:*⟩ If things are so wholly as this or that proposition signifies, the proposition is true.

Proof: If things are so wholly as the proposition signifies, the whole significatum of the proposition is true. If so, the proposition is true.

⟨*Theses against the Fourth Way*⟩

I assume two theses against this way.

⟨*Counter-*⟩*Thesis 1*: It is not the case that if things are so wholly as proposition *A* signifies, proposition *A* is true.[a]

⟨1.1⟩ Proof: Take the proposition

You are a donkey.

Then it is clear that it is false.

⟨1.1.1⟩ Proof that things are so wholly as the ⟨proposition *A*⟩ signifies:[b] That you are, is wholly as proposition *A* signifies. That you are, is so. Therefore, things are so wholly as proposition *A* signifies.

Or this way: It is true wholly as proposition *A* signifies. Therefore,

totaliter sicut *A* propositio significat. Consequentia patet, quia 'verum' et 'ita' convertuntur.

Antecedens probatur, ut prius: Te esse est totaliter sicut *A* propositio significat, et te esse est verum. Igitur verum est totaliter sicut *A* propositio
5 significat. Consequentia patet, et antecedens pro prima parte probatur: Te esse est aliqualiter totaliter sicut *A* significat. Igitur te esse est totaliter sicut *A* significat. Consequentia patet, ex eo quod ex opposito consequentis sequitur oppositum antecedentis. Unde bene sequitur in aliis:

Tu es aliqualis totus homo.
10   Igitur, tu es totus homo.

⟨1.1.2⟩ Secundo, arguitur (203ᵛᵃ M) idem sic: Te esse est totaliter qualiter *A* significat. Igitur te esse est totaliter sicut *A* significat. Consequentia patet, eo quod ly .sicut. tenetur relative, sicut ly .qualiter.

Antecedens probatur: Te esse est totaliter, et taliter *A* significat. Igitur
15 te esse est totaliter qualiter *A* significat. Patet consequentia, eo quod ly .qualiter. convertitur cum ly .[et] et taliter. quando non praecedit impedimentum, sicut contingit in proposito, sicut ly .qualis. in ly.[et] et talis. Sequitur enim:

Tu es aliqualis qualis est Plato.
20   Igitur, tu es aliqualis et talis est Plato.

Antecedens vero pro qualibet parte patet intuenti.

⟨1.1.3⟩ Tertio: Te esse est totale significatum *A* propositionis. Igitur, te esse est totaliter sicut *A* propositio significat. Consequentia est nota, et similiter antecedens, quia te esse est aliquod totale significatum *A* proposi-
25 tionis.

⟨1.1.4⟩ Quarto: Te esse est aliqualiter sicut *A* propositio significat. Igitur, te esse est totaliter sicut *A* propositio significat. Patet consequentia, quia qualitercumque est totaliter, est aliqualiter, et e contra; sicut qualecumque est aliquale, est totum et totale, et e contra.

30   Licet, ergo, ista argumenta concludant quod ita est totaliter sicut *A* propositio significat, non tamen concludunt quod totaliter ita est sicut *A* propositio significat, quia ex ipsa sequitur quod qualitercumque ita est sicut *A* propositio significat. Sicut non sequitur:

Currens est totus Sortes.
35   Igitur, totus Sortes est currens.

---

5 patet] bona (*vel* est bona *etiam infra, sed ultra non notavi*) M   13 patet] ex *add.* (*etiam infra, sed ultra non notavi*) E   sicut¹] sic E   24 aliquod totale] aliquod tale M, aliquid totale E   28–9 qualecumque] qualitercumque E

things are so wholly as proposition A signifies. The inference is clear, since 'true' and 'so' convert.

I prove the premiss as before: That you are, is wholly as proposition A signifies. That you are, is true. Therefore, it is true wholly as proposition A signifies. The inference is clear. Proof of the first premiss: That you are, is somehow wholly as A signifies. Therefore, that you are, is wholly as A signifies. The inference is clear, because the opposite of the premiss follows from the opposite of the conclusion. Thus, by analogy, it follows that

> You are some kind of whole man.
> Therefore, you are a whole man.

⟨1.1.2⟩ Second, I argue for the same conclusion this way. That you are, is wholly how A signifies. Therefore, that you are, is wholly as A signifies. The inference is clear because 'as' is taken relatively, just as 'how' is.

Proof of the premiss: That you are, is wholly. A signifies in that way. Therefore, that you are is wholly how A signifies. The inference is clear because 'how' is interchangeable with 'in that way', when no preceding logical operator prevents this, as none does in the proposed ⟨case⟩. In the same way, 'of which kind' is interchangeable with 'of that kind'. For this follows:

> You are of some kind of which kind Plato is.
> Therefore, you are of some kind and Plato is of that kind.

Either part of the premiss is intuitively clear.

⟨1.1.3⟩ Third: That you are, is a whole significatum of proposition A. Therefore, that you are is wholly as proposition A signifies. The inference is clear. So is the premiss, since that you are, is a whole significatum of proposition A.

⟨1.1.4⟩ Fourth: That you are, is somehow as proposition A signifies. Therefore, that you are, is wholly as proposition A signifies. The inference is clear. For however it is wholly, it is somehow, and vice versa. In the same way, what is of any kind whatever is of some kind, it is as a whole and a whole, and vice versa.[c]

Therefore, although these arguments conclude that things are *so wholly* as proposition A signifies, nevertheless they do not conclude that *wholly* things are so as proposition A signifies. For it follows from this that in any way whatever, things are so as proposition A signifies. In the same way, this does not follow:

> A runner is Socrates, as a whole.
> Therefore, Socrates as a whole, is a runner.[d]

Et non sequitur:

> Aliqualiter totaliter ita est sicut *A* propositio significat.
> Igitur, totaliter ita est sicut *A* propositio significat,

sicut non sequitur:

5   Aliquis totus Sortes currit.
Igitur totus Sortes currit.

⟨1.2⟩ Item ad conclusionem arguitur sic: Chimaeram esse est totaliter sicut haec propositio

> Chimaera est

10 significat—quae sit *B*. Igitur, ita est totaliter sicut haec propositio significat—demonstrando per ly .ita. chimaeram esse.

Consequentia patet, et antecedens probatur: Chimaeram esse est totale significatum *B* propositionis, et illud totale significatum *B* propositionis est totaliter sicut *B* propositio significat. Igitur etc.

15   Consequentia tenet, et prima pars antecedentis probatur: Nam chimaeram esse est significatum ab illa propositione. Et non aliud quam chimaeram esse est significatum ab illa propositione—semper demonstrando *B*—iuxta loquentes praedictos. Igitur, chimaeram esse est totale significatum ab illa propositione. Quare sequitur quod

20   Chimaeram esse est totale significatum *B* propositionis.

Secunda pars antecedentis probatur: Nam aliqualiter totaliter sicut haec propositio significat est illud totale significatum *B* propositionis. Igitur illud totale significatum *B* propositionis est totaliter sicut *B* significat. Consequentia patet, per conversionem simplicem. Antecedens vero
25 probatur demonstrative, modis prioribus. Ista enim convertuntur

> Haec propositio significat totale significatum *B* propositionis

et

> Haec propositio significat totaliter sicut *B* propositio significat.

Igitur etc.

30   Ad rationem ergo opinionis, nego illam consequentiam:

> Ita est totaliter sicut haec propositio significat.
> Igitur, totale significatum illius est verum.

Stat enim oppositum consequentis cum antecedente, sicut ostendit ratio haec propinqua.

35   *2a conclusio*:[3] Non si *A* propositio est vera, ita est totaliter sicut *A* propositio significat.

---

7 item] iterum *E*   13 totale] totum *E*   19 quare] quae *M*, quia *E*, *correxi*
35 *A*¹] aliqua *E*

And this does not follow:

> Somehow wholly things are so as proposition A signifies.
> Therefore, things are so as proposition A signifies.

In the same way, this does not follow:

> Some Socrates as a whole, runs.
> Therefore, Socrates as a whole runs.[e]

⟨1.2⟩ Again, I argue for ⟨Counter-⟩Thesis 1 this way: That a chimera is, is wholly as the proposition

> A chimera is

(let it be B) signifies. Therefore, things are so wholly as this proposition signifies (where that a chimera is, is indicated by 'so').[f]

The inference is clear. Proof of the premiss: That a chimera is, is a whole significatum of proposition B. That whole significatum of proposition B is wholly as proposition B signifies. Therefore, etc.

The inference holds. Proof of the first premiss: That a chimera is, is what is signified by that proposition. Nothing other than that a chimera is, is what is signified by that proposition (where 'that' indicates B throughout the argument), according to the above-mentioned theorists. Therefore, that a chimera is, is a whole significatum of that proposition. Thus, it follows that

> That a chimera is, is a whole significatum of proposition B.

Proof of the second premiss: Somehow wholly as this proposition signifies is that whole significatum of proposition B. Therefore, that whole significatum of proposition B is wholly as B signifies. The inference is clear by simple conversion. But the premiss is proved by a demonstration of the sort used before. For the propositions

> This proposition signifies a whole significatum of proposition B

and

> This proposition signifies wholly as proposition B signifies

are interchangeable. Therefore, etc.

Therefore, in reply to the argument of this opinion, I deny the inference:

> Things are so wholly as this proposition signifies.
> Therefore, the whole significatum of the proposition is true.

For the opposite of the conclusion is consistent with the premiss, as the argument immediately above shows.

⟨Counter-⟩Thesis 2: It is not the case that if a proposition A is true, things are so wholly as proposition A signifies.

Patet ista conclusio ex superius dictis contra alias opiniones.⁴ Stat enim
A propositionem esse veram et non significare, vel si significat, non
significare suum adaequatum significatum.

Item, dato quod illa propositio

5   Homo est animal

cras significet solem esse primo, et non hominem esse animal, patet quod
cras ipsa erit vera. Et tamen falsum erit quod ita est totaliter sicut ipsa
significat—semper demonstrando per ly (160ʳᵇ E) .ita. hominem esse
animal.

10 ⟨*Quinta Via*   *Capitulum Quintum*⟩

Quinta via,¹ volens ostendere antecedens concludens aliquam propositionem esse veram, ponit tres conclusiones.²

      ⟨1⟩ *Prima* est ista: Ex eo quod propositio aliqua praecise quod est,
          significat esse, vel quod non est, significat non esse, est propositio
15   affirmativa vel negativa de praesenti vera.

      2a conclusio: Ex eo quod propositio aliqua quod erit, significat fore,
          vel quod non erit, significat non (203ᵛᵇ M) fore, est propositio
          affirmativa vel negativa de futuro vera.

      3a conclusio: Ex eo quod propositio aliqua significat rem fuisse quae
20   fuit, vel non fuisse quae non fuit, est propositio affirmativa vel
          negativa de praeterito vera.

Et sumit hic haec positio 'rem' generalius quam 'aliquid', pro omni tali
de quo potest esse ratio, cum hoc nomen 'res' dicatur de 'reor–reris'.

Prima conclusio exemplariter³ sic declaratur: Sit *A* ista

25   Tu curris

et *B* ista

      Tu non curris.

Tunc ex eo quod *A* praecise quod tu curris significat, et tu curris, haec
est vera

30   Tu curris.

Et ex eo quod *B* praecise significat quod tu non curris, et tu non curris,
haec est vera

      Tu non curris.

Et ita aliae conclusiones, a simili, suis modis, exemplariter⁴ declarantur.

2 *A om. E*   vel] et *E*   7 ita *om. M*   8 ita] sicut *E*   9 animal] etc. *add. E*
13–17 quod est . . . quod non est . . . quod erit . . . quod non erit *ME et Venator*, rem quae
est . . . rem quae non est . . . rem quae erit . . . rem quae non erit *Feribrigge*   16 et 19
aliqua] praecise *add. Feribrigge (non autem Venator)*   22 hic *om. E*

This thesis is clear from the claims made above against the other opinions. For it is consistent that proposition A is true and does not signify, or if it does signify, does not signify its own adequate significatum.

Again, granted that tomorrow the proposition

A man is an animal

signifies primarily that the sun is and not that a man is an animal, it is clear that tomorrow it will be true. Nevertheless, it will be false that things are so wholly as the proposition signifies (where that a man is an animal is always indicated by 'so').

⟨*The Fifth Way*   *Chapter Five*⟩

⟨The author of⟩ the fifth way, wishing to set out a basis that implies when a proposition is true, assumes three theses.

Thesis 1: What makes a proposition a true affirmative or negative present-tense proposition, is the fact that it precisely signifies that what is, is or precisely signifies that what is not, is not.

Thesis 2: What makes a proposition a true affirmative or negative future-tense proposition, is the fact that it ⟨precisely⟩ signifies that what will be, will be, or that what will not be, will not be.

Thesis 3: What makes a proposition a true affirmative or negative past-tense proposition, is the fact that it ⟨precisely⟩ signifies that a thing that was, was, or that a thing that was not, was not.

Here this position takes 'thing' more generally than 'something',[a] taking 'thing' for whatever is thinkable. For the noun 'thing' is derived from 'to think'.[b]

Thesis 1 is explained this way, by means of an example. Let A be the proposition

You are running,

and B, the proposition

You are not running.

Then, because A precisely signifies that you are running, and you are running, the proposition

You are running

is true. Because B precisely signifies that you are not running, and you are not running, the proposition

You are not running

is true. And so, the other theses are similarly explained by means of examples, in ways appropriate to them.

Ex his infert haec opinio duas regulas universales.⁵

⟨1R⟩ *Prima* est quod omnis propositio finite vel determinate praecise
verum significans, est propositio vera.

⟨2R⟩ *Secunda* est quod omnis propositio finite vel determinate praecise
5   falsum significans, est falsa.

Et intelligit hic 'verum' vel 'falsum' pro significato vero vel falso.

⟨*Conclusiones contra quintam viam*⟩

Contra istam viam procedunt multa argumenta contra alias vias deducta,
ut potest patere subtiliter intuenti. Verumtamen in speciali pono aliquas
10 conclusiones:

Prima est ista: Aliqua est propositio affirmativa de praesenti falsa,
et tamen ipsa praecise quod est significat esse.

Patet de illa propositione

Hoc quod est, est

15 —demonstrato Antichristo. Et ita probatur quod aliqua affirmativa de
praeterito falsa praecise quod fuit significat fuisse, sicut patet de illa

Hoc quod fuit, fuit

—demonstrato Antichristo. De futuro similiter conceditur quod aliqua
est propositio de futuro falsa quae praecise quod erit, significat fore, sicut
20 patet de illa

Hoc quod erit, erit

—demonstrato Caesare vel Adam—sumendo semper ly .praecise. modo
quo haec positio sumit.

2a conclusio est ista: *A* propositio praecise hominem currere significat,
25   et homo currit, et tamen *A* propositio est falsa.

Probatur: Et sit *A* ista

Iste homo currit

—demonstrato Antichristo—supponendo quod homo currat. Quo posito,
A propositio est falsa, et homo currit. Sed quod *A* praecise hominem
30 currere significet, probatur: Nam *A* praecise istum hominem currere
significat, secundum istam viam. Igitur *A* praecise hominem currere
significat. Patet consequentia, ab inferiori ad suum superius stans confuse
tantum, per notam exclusionis, quocumque alio impedimento deducto.⁶
Sequitur enim universaliter:

35   Tantum iste homo currit.

Igitur, tantum homo currit.

---

15 affirmativa] propositio *E*   17 fuit *alterum om. E*   22 demonstrato] Antichristo
add. E   33 notam] rationem *E*

From these theses, this opinion infers two universal rules:

⟨*Rule*⟩ *1*: Every proposition that finitely or determinately precisely signifies the truth, is a true proposition.

⟨*Rule*⟩ *2*: Every proposition that finitely or determinately precisely signifies a falsehood, is false.

Here ⟨this opinion⟩ understands 'truth' or 'falsehood' for a true or false significatum.

⟨*Theses against the Fifth Way*⟩

Many of the arguments that I brought against the other ways, tell against this way, as can be obvious upon careful inspection. Nevertheless, I assume some theses ⟨against the fifth way⟩ specifically.

⟨*Counter-*⟩*Thesis 1*: There is some false affirmative present-tense proposition, and nevertheless it precisely signifies that what is, is.

This is clear from the proposition

This which is, is

(where 'this' indicates the Antichrist).[c] In the same way, it is proved that some false affirmative past-tense proposition precisely signifies that what was, was, as is clear with respect to the proposition

This which was, was

(where 'this' indicates the Antichrist). Similarly, for the future tense, I grant that there is some false future-tense proposition that precisely signifies that what will be, will be. This is clear with respect to the proposition

This which will be, will be

(where 'this' indicates Caesar or Adam[d] and where 'precisely' is always taken in the way in which this position takes it[e]).

⟨*Counter-*⟩*Thesis 2*: Proposition A precisely signifies that a man runs, and a man runs. Nevertheless, proposition A is false.[f]

Proof: Let A be the proposition

This man runs

(where 'this man' indicates the Antichrist). Suppose that a man runs. When this has been posited, proposition A is false and a man runs. Proof that A precisely signifies that a man runs: A precisely signifies that that man runs, according to this way. Therefore, A precisely signifies that a man runs. The inference is clear from the inferior to its superior, where the superior term has merely confused *suppositio* because of the exclusion-sign, and where every other logical operator blocking the inference has been removed.[g] For this follows universally:

Only this man runs.

Therefore, only a man runs.

Etiam sequitur:

    Tu praecise Sortem vides.

    Igitur, tu praecise hominem vides.

    3a conclusio: Aliqua est propositio falsa quae tamen finite et deter-
5   minate est praecise verum significans.

Patet de ista

    Homo est asinus,

quae est falsa. Et quia ipsa est verum significans, ideo ipsa est praecise
verum significans, cum quaelibet affirmativa non denominata ab obliquo
10 implicite vel explicite, convertatur cum se ipsa, dictione exclusiva addita
praedicato.[7] Et ita potest concludi quod aliqua est propositio vera quae est
praecise falsum significans. Ista enim est vera

    Homo est animal,

et tamen est praecise falsum significans; quia est falsum significans, cum
15 significet hominem esse asinum, capram et bovem et huiusmodi.

⟨*Sexta Via*   *Capitulum Sextum*⟩

Sexta via,[1] inter multas conclusiones quas determinat, ponit illam:

    Quaelibet propositio ad placitum significans, ideo praecise vera est
    vel falsa quia sibi correspondet mentalis vera aut falsa.

20 Probatur, quia talis propositio ad placitum significans ideo praecise est
propositio quia sibi correspondet propositio mentalis proprie dicta.
Igitur etc. Antecedens est clarum—ait—et ab omnibus concessum. Et
consequentia patet, quia ab eodem denominatur talis propositio vera vel
falsa a quo ipsa denominatur propositio.

25 (160va E) ⟨*Conclusiones contra sextam viam*⟩

    Haec positio incomplete procedit quia non ponit antecedens universale
concludens propositionem mentalem esse veram. Posset enim dicere quod
A est propositio vera, quia *B* cum qua convertitur est propositio vera. Sed
certum est quod hoc non est antecedens concludens, quia iterum quaero
30 quid est antecedens concludens *B* esse verum? Et si dicitur quod *A* esse
verum, erit circulatio insufficiens et inutilis. Si autem dicatur quod *C* esse
verum, deducam processum in infinitum ad probandum unam propositionem esse veram—quod nullus sani capitis concederet.[2]

---

4 et] vel *E*   8 est³ *om. E*   9 obliquo] aliquo *M*   13 homo est animal *om.*
E   15 bovem] leonem *E*   20 ideo] iam *E* (ideo *Petrus de Aliaco*)   22 ait *om.*
E   concessum] conclusum *M* (concessum *Petrus de Aliaco*)   26 universale] uni-
versaliter *E*   27 posset] possem *M*   29 quaero] quaeram *M*   31 erit] est
E   quod *om. E*

This follows, too:

> You precisely see Socrates.
> Therefore, you precisely see a man.[h]
> ⟨Counter-⟩Thesis 3: There is some false proposition that nevertheless finitely and determinately, precisely signifies the truth.

This is clear with respect to the proposition

> A man is a donkey,

which is false. Since it is a sign of the truth, then it is precisely a sign of the truth.[i] For any affirmative proposition that is not implicitly or explicitly so called from an oblique ⟨term⟩, converts with the proposition formed by adding an exclusive to its predicate. In this way, too, one can conclude that there is some true proposition that is precisely the sign of a falsehood. The proposition

> A man is an animal

is true. Nevertheless, it is precisely a sign of a falsehood. For it is a sign of a falsehood, when it signifies that a man is a donkey, a goat, a cow, etc.

⟨The Sixth Way   Chapter Six⟩

The sixth way assumes, among the many theses it settles on, the following.

> ⟨Thesis:⟩ Any proposition that signifies by convention is true or false precisely because a true or false mental proposition corresponds to it.

Proof: Such a proposition that signifies by convention is a proposition precisely because a mental proposition properly so called corresponds to it. Therefore, etc. The premiss is clear, he says, and granted by all. The inference is clear. For such a proposition is called true or false from the same thing from which it is called a proposition.

⟨Theses against the Sixth Way⟩

This position starts out from an incomplete basis. For it does not lay down a universal premiss that implies when a mental proposition is true. He could say that *A* is a true proposition, because *B* with which it is interchangeable is a true proposition. But it is certain that this ⟨thesis⟩ is not a ⟨universal⟩ premiss ⟨that⟩ implies ⟨when a mental proposition is true⟩. For, again, I will ask what is the premiss that implies that *B* is true? If it is said 'that *A* is true', there will be an inadequate and useless circle. But if it is said 'that *C* is true', I will deduce that an infinite process is necessary to prove that one proposition is true—which no one in his right mind would grant.

Tamen pro maiori improbatione istius conclusionis (204ra M), et unius dicti[3] improbatione, pono aliquas conclusiones.

Prima est ista: Nulla propositio vocalis vel scripta essentialiter et intrinsece denominatur talis, sed solum extrinsece ex sui significati
5   apparentia aliquali.

Ista conclusio patet, per istam viam ponentem propositionem ad placitum significantem esse propositionem per solam habitudinem ad propositionem mentalem. Quare etc.

Probatur tamen conclusio ratione: Non implicat contradictionem hoc
10 esse et non esse propositionem—demonstrando propositionem vocalem vel scriptam. Igitur, nulla talis est intrinsece et essentialiter propositio.

Consequentia patet, a simili, quia bene sequitur:

Hoc esse, et non esse album vel nigrum, aut patrem vel filium, non implicat contradictionem.

15   Igitur, hoc non est intrinsece et essentialiter tale.

Antecedens vero patet, quia sicut stat aliquas res materiales esse et non esse signa verorum vel falsorum complexe significabilium; ita et hoc— demonstrando propositionem quamcumque. Confirmatur: Aliqua fuit prima propositio imposita ad significandum. Igitur illa potuit esse absque
20 aliqua impositione sui aut cuiuscumque ei consimilis. Et per consequens, illa numquam fuit intrinsece et essentialiter propositio. Quare sequitur, a pari, quod nec aliqua alia.

2a conclusio: Nulla propositio animae quae dicitur mentalis essentialiter et intrinsece denominatur talis.

25 ⟨2.1⟩ Ista conclusio probatur sicut praecedens, quia hoc esse—demonstrando talem mentalem—et non esse propositionem, non implicat contradictionem.

⟨2.2⟩ Item, si Deus talem propositionem mentalem poneret in uno lapide, ipsa non esset propositio. Igitur, dum fuit in mente non fuit
30 intrinsece et essentialiter propositio. Consequentia patet. Et antecedens probatur, quia si esset propositio, vel igitur mentalis, vocalis, vel scripta. Sed nullo istorum modorum, ut patet. Igitur, etc.

⟨2.3⟩ Item, si illa tunc esset propositio et non denominaretur talis ab aliqua mentali, igitur—per idem—nec propositio aliqua vocalis vel scripta,
35 aut ad placitum instituta, debet vocari talis ex habitudine ad propositionem mentalem—quod est fundamentaliter contra hanc viam.

4–5 ex . . . aliquali] est . . . aliqualis *M*   6 propositionem] et *add. E*   13 aut *om. E*   vel²] aut *E* (*etiam infra, nunc M nunc E, sed ultra non notavi*)   16 aliquas res materiales] alias res naturales *M*   17 signa] vel *add. E*   vel] sed *E* 20 aliqua] alia *M*   25 quia] illa *add. M*   29 non¹ *om. M*   31 scripta] vel sculpta *add. E*

Nevertheless, to give a fuller disproof of this thesis and of one claim ⟨on which it is based⟩, I assume some theses.

⟨*Counter-*⟩*Thesis 1*: No spoken or written proposition is so called essentially and intrinsically, but only extrinsically, because its significatum somehow appears through it.

This thesis is clear, according to this way, since it posits that a proposition that signifies by convention is a proposition only through its relation to a mental proposition. Thus, etc.

Nevertheless, the thesis is proved by this argument: That this is and is not a proposition (where 'this' indicates a spoken or written proposition) does not imply a contradiction. Therefore, no such proposition is a proposition intrinsically and essentially.

The inference is clear, by analogy. For this does follow:

That this is and is not white or black, father or son, does not imply a contradiction.

Therefore, this is not intrinsically and essentially such.

The premiss is clear. Just as it is consistent that certain material things are and are not signs of truths or falsehoods that can be signified by a complex, so also with this (where any ⟨spoken or written⟩ proposition is indicated). Confirming argument: Some proposition was the first one imposed for signifying. Therefore, that could be without any imposition of itself or of any equiform with it. Consequently, it never was intrinsically and essentially a proposition. Thus, it follows by parity of reasoning, neither was any other.

⟨*Counter-Thesis*⟩ *2*: No proposition of the mind, which is called 'mental', is called ⟨a proposition⟩ essentially and intrinsically.

⟨2.1⟩ This thesis is proved in the same way as the preceding one. For that this is and is not a proposition (where 'this' indicates such a mental proposition) does not imply a contradiction.[a]

⟨2.2⟩ Again, if God were to place such a mental proposition in a stone, it would not be a proposition. Therefore, it was not intrinsically and essentially a proposition when it was in the mind. The inference is clear. Proof of the premiss: If it were a proposition, then it would be mental, spoken, or written. But it would be a proposition in none of these ways, as is clear. Therefore, etc.

⟨2.3⟩ Again, ⟨suppose⟩ it were then a proposition and not so called from some mental proposition. Then, by the same reasoning, no spoken or written proposition, or proposition instituted by convention, ought to be so called from a relation to such a mental proposition—which is fundamentally contrary to this way.

3a conclusio: Nulla propositio vocalis vel scripta, ad placitum instituta, ex habitudine ad propositionem mentalem denominatur talis.

Patet. Nam tam ad placitum instituta quam naturaliter significans extrinsece denominatur propositio. Igitur neutra illarum denominatur talis per
5 habitudinem ad aliam—quod est contra istam viam.

4a conclusio: Nulla propositio extrinsece denominatur talis ex habitudine ad potentiam vitalem actualiter pertinentem.

Patet, quia etsi nullus intellectus intelligeret, adhuc multae essent propositiones in libro clauso secundum quod alias clarissime est ostensum.[4]

10 *5a conclusio*: Nulla propositio extrinsece denominatur talis ex habitudine ad suum significatum primarium vel adaequatum.

Patet, quia stat tale significatum esse et istam non esse propositionem.

6a conclusio: Quaelibet propositio extrinsece denominatur talis ex habitudine ad potentiam vere vel false quiescenter perceptivam.

15 Patet praedicta conclusio, discurrendo disiunctive et negative per omnes conclusiones praecedentes.

Et sic patet huius opinionis insufficientia.

⟨*Septima Via*   *Capitulum Septimum*⟩

Septima via[1] ponit quattuor conclusiones.

20 *Prima* est ista: Si Deus est et haec propositio—quacumque demonstrata—est propositio una significans primo quod Deus, haec propositio est vera.

Et dicitur 'una'—inquit—propter propositiones multiplices; quia dato quod esset una virtus infinitae potentiae activae, producens propositionem
25 simplicem per quam intelligeretur primo tam Deum esse quam chimaeram esse, haec propositio esset falsa, ut patet. Et de tali non sequitur:

Deus est.

Et haec propositio significat primo Deum esse.

Igitur, haec propositio est vera.

30 *2a conclusio* (160vb E) est ista: Si Sortes fuit, et haec propositio est una significans primo quod Sortes fuit, haec propositio est vera.

3a conclusio: Si Sortes erit, et haec propositio est una significans primo quod Sortes erit, haec propositio est vera.

4a conclusio: Si nulla chimaera est, et haec propositio est una signi
35 ficans primo quod nulla chimaera est, haec est vera.

5 aliam] aliquam *E*

⟨*Counter-*⟩*Thesis 3*: No spoken or written proposition instituted by convention is so called from a relation to a mental proposition.[b]

This is clear. For both those instituted by convention and those that signify naturally are called propositions extrinsically. Therefore, neither of these is so called through a relation to the other—which is contrary to this way.

⟨*Counter-*⟩*Thesis 4*: No proposition is so called extrinsically, from a relation to a vital power that is actually being applied or exercised.

This is clear. Even if no intellect were thinking ⟨of anything⟩, still there would be many propositions in a closed book—which I have very clearly shown elsewhere.

⟨*Counter-*⟩*Thesis 5*: No proposition is extrinsically so called from a relation to its own primary or adequate significatum.

This is clear. For it is consistent that such a significatum is, and that this is not a proposition.[c]

⟨*Counter-*⟩*Thesis 6*: Any proposition is extrinsically so called from a relation to a power, quiescently perceptive of the true or the false.

The thesis just stated is clear, running through all the above theses disjunctively and negatively.

Thus, the inadequacy of this opinion is clear.

⟨*The Seventh Way*   *Chapter Seven*⟩

The seventh way posits four theses.

Thesis 1: If God is and this proposition (where any proposition has been indicated) is one proposition that signifies primarily that God is, the proposition is true.

He says 'one' because of multiplex[a] propositions. If there were a power of infinite active potency that produced a simple proposition through which it was thought that God is no less primarily than that a chimera is, this proposition would be false, as is clear. With respect to such a proposition, this does not follow:

God is.

This proposition signifies primarily that God is.

Therefore, this proposition is true.

Thesis 2: If Socrates was, and this proposition is one that signifies primarily that Socrates was, this proposition is true.

Thesis 3: If Socrates will be, and this proposition is one that signifies primarily that Socrates will be, this proposition is true.

Thesis 4: If no chimera is, and this proposition is one that signifies primarily that no chimera is, then this proposition is true.

⟨*Conclusiones contra septimam viam*⟩

Haec positio insufficienter procedit.

Primo, quia non assignat universale antecedens universaliter concludens propositionem esse veram—quacumque demonstrata—sed cuilibet pro-
5 positioni proprium antecedens inferens talem propositionem esse veram, sicut patet in processu istarum conclusionum.

Secundo, similiter, quia superflue ponitur (204rb M) ly .una. Quaelibet enim propositio est una propositio. Sequitur enim:

Haec propositio est propositio significans primo Deum esse.

10 Igitur, haec propositio est propositio una significans primo Deum esse.

Et per consequens declaratio suae conclusionis destruit conclusionem primam.

Contra quam declarationem pono aliquas conclusiones.

15 *Prima* est ista: Aliqua est propositio falsa et impossibilis quae prius significat verum quam falsum aut impossibile.

Patet de ista

Homo est aliud ab homine,

quae per prius significat hominem esse quam hominem esse aliud ab
20 homine. Et ita sequitur correlarie quod

Aliqua est propositio vera et necessaria quae prius significat falsum et impossibile quam verum.

Patet de ista

Deus non est asinus,

25 quae prius significat Deum non esse quam Deum non esse asinum. Intellectus enim per prius fertur in partem quam in totum, ut alias dictum est.²

2a conclusio: Non si aliqua propositio significat aeque primo falsum sicut verum, est propositio falsa, et hoc tenendo ly .primo. exponi-
30 biliter gradualiter.³

Patet. Stat enim quod per illam propositionem

Homo est animal,

aeque primo a duobus concipiatur hominem esse animal et hominem esse asinum. Quo posito, adhuc illa esset vera, cum significatum non adaequa-
35 tum non sit in praeiudicium propositioni quoad veritatem vel falsitatem dicendam de ipsa.

3a conclusio: Non si esset una virtus infinitae potentiae activae producens propositionem simplicem per quam intelligeret primo tam

3 non *om. M*   12 conclusionem] consequentiam *E*

⟨*Theses against the Seventh Way*⟩

This position proceeds from an inadequate basis.

First, because it does not assign a universal premiss that universally implies when a proposition—where any one is indicated—is true. But it assigns a premiss proper to each proposition that implies when such a proposition is true, as is clear from the list of these theses.

Second, similarly, because 'one' is put in superfluously. For any proposition is one proposition. For this follows:

> This proposition is a proposition that signifies primarily that God is.
> Therefore, this proposition is one proposition that signifies primarily that God is.

Consequently, the explanation of his first thesis destroys it.*b*

Against this explanation, I assume some theses.

> ⟨*Counter-*⟩*Thesis 1*: There is some false and impossible proposition that signifies the truth prior to signifying the false or impossible.

This is clear with respect to the proposition

> A man is other than a man,

which signifies that a man is, prior to signifying that a man is other than a man.*c* Thus, this corollary follows:

> ⟨*Corollary*:⟩ There is some true and necessary proposition which signifies the false and impossible prior to signifying the truth.

This is clear with respect to the proposition

> God is not a donkey,

which signifies that God is not, prior to signifying that God is not a donkey. For the intellect apprehends the part prior to apprehending the whole, as I have said elsewhere.

> ⟨*Counter-*⟩*Thesis 2*: It is not ⟨the case⟩ that if some proposition signifies a falsehood no less primarily than the truth, the proposition is false (where 'primarily' is taken to be an exponible term of degree).

This is clear. For it is consistent that of two people, the one conceives through the proposition

> A man is an animal

that a man is an animal, no less primarily than the other conceives that a man is a donkey. Even on this hypothesis, that proposition would be true, since a significatum that is not adequate does not prejudice the truth or falsity of a proposition.

> ⟨*Counter-*⟩*Thesis 3*: It is not ⟨the case⟩ that if there were a power of infinite active potency that produced a simple proposition by means of which it had the thought that God is, no less primarily

Deum esse quam chimaeram esse, illa propositio esset falsa, tenendo ly .primo. ut prius.

Patet, quia stat cum toto antecedente quod Deum esse esset significatum adaequatum illius propositionis simplicis et non chimaeram esse.

5   *4a conclusio*: Si ly .primo. sumptum ut prius, excludit omnem prioritatem et posterioritatem simpliciter, videlicet durationis et naturae, nulla virtus finita aut infinita potest aeque primo intelligere Deum esse et chimaeram esse.

Patet. Nam Deus est virtus infinita, et tamen necessario prius intelligit
10 se esse quam chimaeram esse, immo et quascumque creaturas. Similiter, Deus prius intelligit quodcumque possibile positivum quam suam privationem aut negationem, cum quodlibet possibile positivum habeat propriam ideam in Deo in qua intellectus divinus tale possibile intelligit. Impossibilia, vero, privationes et negationes intelligit in ideis positivorum
15 et possibilium.

5a conclusio, militans contra totam positionem, est ista: Sumendo ly .primo. officiabiliter convertibiliter cum ly .adaequate.,[4] non si *A* est propositio una significans primo sic, et sic est, *A* est propositio vera.

20 Probatur: Et sit *A* illa propositio

Hoc est falsum—seipsa demonstrata.

Quo posito, patet quod *A* est propositio una significans primo hoc esse falsum, et hoc est falsum. Et tamen *A* est propositio falsa, cum asserat se esse falsam. Quod autem *A* sit propositio una, patet, cum non sit aequivoca.
25 Et quod significet primo hoc esse falsum, probatur: Nam hoc esse falsum est significatum adaequatum *A*. Igitur *A* significat primo hoc esse falsum.

Consequentia patet, et antecedens probatur, quia si hoc esse falsum non est adaequatum significatum *A*, quaero quid est illud, an categoricum vel hypotheticum? Non categoricum, quia quodcumque demonstratur, illius
30 oratio infinitiva non est oratio infinitiva huius

Hoc est falsum.

Nec etiam hypotheticum, per idem. Similiter:

Quodlibet significatum hypotheticum adaequat propositionem hypotheticam.

11 positivum] propositum M   11–12 suam privationem] suum privativum E
14 vero] non M   17 convertibiliter *om.* M   18 est³ *om.* E   20 propositio] vera
add. M   22 hoc esse] quod hoc est E   29 demonstratur] detur M

than the thought that a chimera is, the proposition would be false (where 'primarily' is taken as before).

This is clear, since it is consistent with the whole antecedent that that God is, should be the adequate significatum of that simple proposition, and not that a chimera is.

⟨Counter-⟩Thesis 4: If 'primarily', taken as before, excludes all priority and posteriority absolutely—viz. of duration and of nature—no power, finite or infinite, can have the thought that God is, no less primarily than the thought that a chimera is.

This is clear. For God is an infinite power. Nevertheless, He necessarily has the thought that He Himself is, prior to having the thought that a chimera is, and indeed even to having the thought that any creatures are. Similarly, God thinks of any possible positive thing prior to thinking of its privation or negation. For any possible positive thing has its own idea in God in which the Divine Intellect thinks of such a possible. But He thinks of impossibles, privations, and negations in the ideas of positive and possible things.*d*

Militating against the whole position is

⟨Counter-⟩Thesis 5: Taking 'primarily' as functionalizable*e* to and convertible with 'adequately', it is not the case that if *A* is one proposition that signifies primarily so and things are so, *A* is a true proposition.*f*

Proof: Let *A* be the proposition

This is false

(where 'this' indicates the proposition itself). When this has been assumed, it is clear that *A* is one proposition that signifies primarily that this is false, and this is false. Nevertheless, *A* is a false proposition, since it asserts that it itself is false. But that *A* is one proposition is clear, since *A* is not equivocal. Proof that it signifies primarily that this is false: That this is false, is the adequate significatum of *A*. Therefore, *A* signifies primarily that this is false.

The inference is clear. Proof of the premiss: If that this is false is not the adequate significatum of *A*, I ask what is: whether a categorical or a molecular? Not a categorical, since whatever categorical is indicated, its sentence-nominalization is not the sentence-nominalization*g* of the proposition

This is false.

It is not molecular either, by the same reasoning. Similarly,

Any molecular significatum is adequate to a molecular proposition.

Igitur, non categoricam.

Patet consequentia, eo quod impossibile est idem significatum esse significatum adaequatum categoricae et hypotheticae simul.

Ex quibus sequitur quod alicuius propositionis significatum primarium
5 aut adaequatum est verum, et tamen illa propositio est falsa. Patet de illa

Hoc est falsum—seipsa demonstrata.

Sed de hoc latius in materia insolubilium.[5]

⟨Octava Via   *Capitulum Octavum⟩*

(161[ra] E) Octava via[1] ponit duas regulas universales et breves.

10   ⟨1⟩ *Prima* est quod propositio vera est oratio indicativa, perfecta, univoca per quam adaequate intellectus redditur rectus.

(204[va] M) ⟨2⟩ Propositio autem falsa est oratio indicativa, perfecta, univoca per quam intellectus adaequate non redditur rectus.

Dicit autem propositionem reddere intellectum rectum, cum per eam
15 concipit intellectus ⟨affirmative⟩ rem esse quae est, vel negative rem non esse quae non est, vel rem non fuisse quae non fuit, vel rem non fore ⟨quae non erit⟩, et sic de aliis. Sicut enim res habet esse vel fuisse ⟨vel fore⟩, ita habet cognosci affirmative vel negative.

Redditur autem intellectus non rectus cum non correspondet composi-
20 tioni ex parte rei aliquid, vel non correspondebat aut ⟨non⟩ correspondebit, ad extra secundum tempus propositionis.

⟨Conclusiones contra octavam viam⟩

Contra istas regulas procedit conclusio quinta contra opinionem immediate praecedentem. Procedit etiam determinatio facta in primo capitulo
25 huius secundae partis ubi ostenditur quod non solum oratio indicativa est propositio, verum etiam imperativa, optativa et subiunctiva.[2] Igitur etc.

Contra autem regularum declarationem pono aliquas conclusiones.

Prima est ista: Aliqua est propositio per quam intellectus concipit rem esse quae est, et tamen ipsa est falsa.

30 Patet. Nam per istam

Antichristus est qui est,

3 et] vel *E*   10 oratio] propositio *ME, correxi (oratio Petrus Mantuanus). Usque ad lin. 21 Petri Mantuani textus citatur, cf. c. VIII, nota 1. Quem textum cito his siglis usus: C= Oxoniae, Bibl. Bodl., Can. misc. 219, f. 112v; Ma=Venetiis, Bibl. Nat. S. Marci, Lat. cl. vi. 128 (2559); Mn=Mantuae, Bibl. Commun., AIII 12, f. 46v; V=Vat. lat. 2135, f. 64r; Ω=omnium consensus*   12-13 propositio . . . rectus *om.* (hom.) *M*   12 perfecta] recta et *E* (perfecta *MaMnV, om. C*)   14 dicit] dicitur *E* (dico Ω)   15 affirmative *supplent* Ω   17 quae non erit *supplent MnV*   enim *om. M*   17-18 habet[1-2]] habent *E*   vel fore *supplent* Ω   19-20 compositioni] componi *M* (compositioni *CMaV*, componi *Mn*)   20 ex parte *om. E*   aliquid *post* correspondebit *transp.* Ω non *supplent MaMnV*   21 ad] aliquid *M* (ab *MaV*)   23 istas regulas] istam regulam *E*   24 praecedentem] sequentem *ME, correxi (cf. supra p. 54 lin. 16-p. 56 lin. 7)*   25 solum] sola *M*   26 etiam] et *M*   27 regularum declarationem] regulam *M*

Therefore, it is not adequate to a categorical.

The inference is clear, because it is impossible for the same significatum to be a significatum simultaneously adequate to a categorical and to a molecular proposition.

It follows from these theses that there is some proposition whose primary or adequate significatum is true and nevertheless the proposition is false. This is clear with respect to the proposition

This is false

(where 'this' indicates the proposition itself). But this will be discussed more fully when I come to the insolubles.

⟨*The Eighth Way*   *Chapter Eight*⟩

The eighth way assumes two brief and universal rules.

⟨*Rule*⟩ *1*: A true proposition is an indicative, perfect univocal expression through which the intellect is adequately rendered correct.

⟨*Rule*⟩ *2*: But a false proposition is an indicative, perfect univocal expression through which the intellect is not adequately rendered correct.

On the one hand, it is said that a proposition renders the intellect correct, because through it the intellect conceives ⟨affirmatively⟩ that a thing that is, is; or negatively, that a thing that is not, is not; or that a thing that was not, was not; or that a thing that will not be, will not be; etc. For as it pertains to a thing to be or to have been or to be going to be, so it pertains to it to be grasped affirmatively or negatively.

On the other hand, the intellect is rendered incorrect when nothing in reality corresponds to the composition ⟨of terms⟩ (or did correspond or will correspond, according to the tense of the proposition).

⟨*Theses against the Eighth Way*⟩

The fifth thesis ⟨advanced⟩ against the immediately preceding opinion goes against these rules. So does the view I settled on in Part II, chapter 1, where I show that not only expressions in the indicative mood are propositions, but also expressions in the imperative, optative, and subjunctive moods.[a] Therefore, etc.

I assume some theses against the explanation of these rules.

⟨*Counter-*⟩*Thesis 1*: There is some proposition through which the intellect conceives that a thing that is, is, and nevertheless the proposition is false.

This is clear. For through the proposition

The Antichrist, who is, is,

concipit intellectus rem esse quae est, cum concipiat significatum adaequatum illius.

> *2a conclusio*: Aliqua est propositio cui non correspondet aliquid a
> parte rei, nec correspondebat, nec correspondebit, et tamen intelle-
> ctus rectificatur per illam.

5

Patet. Nam per illam

Nulla chimaera est,

aut per illam

Nullus homo est asinus,

10 intellectus rectificatur. Et tamen illi non correspondet, nec correspondebat,
nec correspondebit aliquid a parte rei, supple adaequate; quia nullam
chimaeram esse, aut nullum hominem esse asinum, non potuit esse aliquid,
aliqua, vel aliqualiter, ut superius fuit ostensum.³

> *3a conclusio*: Licet rei quae est, fuit, vel erit, tanta sit praecise cogno-
> scibilitas ipsius quanta et ipsius existentia, tamen privationibus et
> negationibus correspondet intellectus, quibus nulla possibilis com-
> municatur essentia.

15

Prima pars patet per illud Philosophi secundo *Metaphysicae*:⁴

Sicut se habet res ad esse, ita ad cognosci.

20 Secunda pars similiter patet. Nam Deus et creaturae intelligunt privationes. Percipiunt enim peccata non fieri. Igitur intelligunt peccata.

Item, intelligunt tenebram opponi lumini, quietem motui, et peccatum
gratiae. Igitur intelligunt tenebram, quietem, et peccatum.

Hoc idem patet de negationibus. Intelligunt enim perfectionem creaturae
25 attendi penes distantiam a non esse simpliciter. Igitur intelligunt non esse
simpliciter.

Similiter, intelligunt chimaeram esse et nullam chimaeram esse opponi.
Igitur intelligunt tam chimaeram esse quam nullam chimaeram esse. Et
e contra.

30 Haec conclusio dirigitur contra hanc viam, asserentem quod nullus
potest intelligere non ens, nec aliquis potest intelligere non intellectum.
Arguit enim sic: Praecise ens potest intelligi. Igitur non potest intelligi
non ens. Antecedens patet, quia ens potest intelligi et nihil non ens potest
intelligi. Oppositum enim implicat contradictionem. Et similiter probat
35 quod tantum intellectum potest intelligi, ex quo concludit quod non potest
intelligi non intellectum.⁵

---

5 rectificatur] verificatur *M*   12 aut] vel *E*   14–15 cognoscibilitas ipsius] cognoscibilis *M*   16 possibilis] possibiliter *M*   21 percipiunt] praecipiunt *M*   23 tene-
bram] lumen *add. E*   32 ens] esse *E*   33 patet] arguitur *E*

the intellect conceives that a thing that is, is, since it conceives its adequate significatum.

⟨Counter-⟩Thesis 2: There is some proposition to which nothing in reality corresponds, corresponded, or will correspond, and nevertheless it renders the intellect correct.

This is clear. For the intellect is rendered correct through the proposition

No chimera is,

or through the proposition

No man is a donkey.

Nevertheless, nothing in reality corresponds, corresponded, or will correspond to them (where the correspondence is understood to be adequate correspondence). For that no chimera is, or that no man is a donkey, could not be anything, any things, or anyhow, as was shown above.[b]

⟨Counter-⟩Thesis 3: Although the knowability of a thing that is, was, or will be, is precisely proportional to its existence, nevertheless an act of intellect corresponds to privations and negations to which no possible essence is common.

The first part ⟨of the thesis⟩ is clear from what the Philosopher says in *Metaphysics*, Book II ⟨993^{b}30–1⟩, that

A thing is related to being known in the same way as it is related to existence.

Similarly, the second part is clear. God and creatures think of privations. For they perceive that sins are not committed. Therefore, they think of sins.

Again, they have the thought that darkness is opposed to light, rest to motion, and sin to grace. Therefore, they think of darkness, rest, and sin.

The same is clear with respect to negations. For they have the thought that the perfection of a creature is judged according to its remove from absolute non-existence. Therefore, they think of absolute non-existence.

Similarly, again, they have the thought that a chimera existing, and no chimera existing, are opposed. Therefore, they think no less of a chimera existing than of no chimera existing, and vice versa.

This thesis is directed against this way, which asserts that no one can think of non-being, nor can anyone think of what is not thought of. For he argues as follows: Precisely being can be thought of. Therefore, non-being cannot be thought of. The premiss is clear, since being can be thought of and nothing that is not a being can be thought of. The opposite implies a contradiction. Similarly, he proves that only what is thought of can be thought of, from which he concludes that what is not thought of cannot be thought of.

Dicitur quod si illa propositio

Praecise ens potest intelligi

exponitur modo dicto, non valet consequentia, sicut non sequeretur, secundum fautorem huius opinionis:

5   Praecise hoc album erit hoc album.

Igitur, non nigrum erit hoc album—semper eodem demonstrato.

Si autem exponitur illa secundum quod valentes theologi et metaphisici exponerent—videlicet, ens potest intelligi et non oppositum entis potest intelligi—negatur minor, quia bene oppositum entis potest intelligi.

10   Ulterius dicit haec opinio quod haec

Tu non es

non significat te non esse proprie, sed significat te esse privative et negative.[6] Sed hoc est falsum, quia haec

Antichristus non est

15 significat Antichristum non esse. Igitur et illa

Tu non es

significat te non esse.

Antecedens probatur: Ego intelligo Antichristum non esse. Igitur etc. Antecedens probatur: Ego credo Antichristum non esse. Igitur intelligo

20 Antichristum non esse. Patet consequentia, ab inferiori ad suum superius affirmative.

Item, Deus intelligit Antichristum non esse. Igitur et creatura potest idem intelligere. Consequentia patet, et antecedens probatur: Nam Deus vult Antichristum non esse. Igitur intelligit Antichristum non esse.

25 Consequentia patet, quia volitio praesupponit intellectionem, cum voluntas sit potentia superior ad intellectum. Antecedens vero concedit (161rb E) quilibet theologus.

Item, si illa propositio

Tu non es

30 significaret primo te esse, sequeretur quod illae convertuntur: (204vb M)

Tu es

et

Tu non es.

Patet consequentia, quia idem est adaequatum significatum utriusque.

---

6 non] hoc *add.* E   album] nigrum *ME, correxi*   8 videlicet *om.* E   18–19 Ego
. . . probatur *om. (hom.)* E   20 Patet consequentia *om.* E   25 volitio] velle *E*
intellectionem] intellectiones *E*   34 adaequatum *om.* E

I say that if the proposition

> Precisely being can be thought of

is expounded in the stated way, the inference does not hold good. In the same way, this inference would not hold good:

> Precisely this white thing will be this white thing.
> Therefore, no black thing will be this white thing

(where the same thing is always indicated by 'this')—as the author of this opinion admits.

But if the proposition in question is expounded as the theologians and metaphysicians would expound it—viz. being can be thought of and it is not the case that the opposite of being can be thought of—I deny the minor. For the opposite of being can indeed be thought of.

Further, this opinion states that the proposition

> You are not

does not properly signify that you are not, but signifies that you are, privatively and negatively. But this is false. For the proposition

> The Antichrist is not

signifies that the Antichrist is not. Therefore, the proposition

> You are not

signifies that you are not.

Proof of the premiss: I have the thought that the Antichrist is not. Therefore, etc. Proof of the premiss: I believe that the Antichrist is not. Therefore, I have the thought that the Antichrist is not. The inference from the inferior to its superior, affirmatively, is clear.

Again, God has the thought that the Antichrist is not. Therefore, creatures can also have the same thought. The inference is clear. Proof of the premiss: God wills that the Antichrist is not. Therefore, He has the thought that the Antichrist is not. The inference is clear. For volition presupposes an act of thought, since the will is a power superior to the intellect. Any theologian grants the premiss.

Again, if the proposition

> You are not

signified primarily that you are, it would follow that the proposition

> You are

and the proposition

> You are not

were interchangeable. The inference is clear, since the adequate significatum of both would be the same. Nor does it hold good to say that they

Nec valet dicere quod significant idem et non eodem modo, ita quod
syncategorema non mutat significatum, sed bene modum significandi.[7]
Nam hoc est falsum, quod non mutet significatum. Licet enim de se non
significet ex impositione, tamen cum alio significat; sicut illa vox 'mu',
licet de se non significet aliud a se et suis consimilibus, tamen cum alio
significat, dicendo 'murus'. Ubi patet quod non solum mutat modum
significandi, sed significatum. Et sic deberet haec opinio dicere quod
haec propositio

   Tu non es

significat propriissime te non esse. Et ly .non homo. significat proprie non
hominem. Non tamen nego quin significet hominem, sed hoc est de per
accidens.

⟨*Nona et ultima via quae est auctoris*   *Capitulum Nonum*⟩
Ultima via, quam inter ceteras reputo sustinendam, ponit aliquas conclusiones.

   Prima est si alicuius propositionis significatum adaequatum est verum,
   et non repugnat illam propositionem esse veram, sic significando
   adaequate, illa propositio est vera.

Haec conclusio patet. Nam aliquod est antecedens universale inferens propositionem esse veram, et non videtur aliquod nisi istud, sicut patet ex
reprobatione aliarum opinionum. Igitur istud est sufficiens.

   Notanter dicitur

   Non repugnat illam esse veram etc.

Nam, ut prius dicebatur, haec est falsa

   Hoc est falsum—seipso demonstrato,

et tamen adaequatum significatum est verum. Et hoc contingit, quia
repugnat ipsam esse veram sic significando adaequate, sicut patet intuenti.

   2a conclusio: Si aliqua propositio est vera, aliqualiter esse adaequate
   significans, suum adaequatum significatum est verum.

Patet discurrendo per singula.

   3a conclusio: Si alicuius propositionis significatum adaequatum est
   falsum, illa propositio est falsa.

Patet ut prius.

   4a conclusio: Si aliqua propositio est falsa, et non repugnat suum
   adaequatum significatum esse falsum, ipsum est falsum.

5 aliud] significatum *M*   6 murus] mutus *E*   30 discurrendo per] discurren-
ti *M*

signify the same thing and not in the same way, so that the syncategorematic terms do not change the significatum but rather the mode of signifying. For it is false that a syncategorematic term would not change the
significatum. Although it does not signify of itself by imposition, nevertheless it signifies together with another term. In the same way, the spoken
syllable 'mu' does not, of itself, signify something other than itself and
other syllables equiform with it. Nevertheless, it signifies together with
other letters, when one says 'mural'. Thus, it is clear that ⟨the syncategorematic term⟩ changes not only the mode of signifying, but also the significatum. Thus, this opinion ought to say that the proposition

> You are not

signifies most properly that you are not, and 'not man' signifies properly
not man. Nevertheless, I do not deny that 'not man' signifies man. But it
does so *per accidens*.

⟨*The Author's Way—The Ninth & Last*   *Chapter Nine*⟩

The last way, which of all the ways is the one I think ought to be supported,
assumes some theses.

⟨*Thesis*⟩ *1*: If the adequate significatum of a proposition is true and
it is not inconsistent that the proposition, thus adequately signifying,
should be true, then the proposition is true.

This thesis is clear. There is some universal premiss that implies when
a proposition is true. It seems not to be any other than this one, as is clear
from the refutation of the other opinions. Therefore, this premiss suffices.

Note that I say

> . . . it is not inconsistent that that proposition . . . should be true.

For, as I said earlier, the proposition

> This is false

(where 'this' indicates the proposition itself) is false. Nevertheless, its
adequate significatum is true. This happens because it is inconsistent that
the proposition, thus adequately signifying , should be true, as is intuitively
clear.

⟨*Thesis*⟩ *2*: If a proposition adequately signifying that things are in
some way, is true, its adequate significatum is true.

This is clear if one considers the instances one by one.

⟨*Thesis*⟩ *3*: If the adequate significatum of a proposition is false, the
proposition is false.

This is clear, as before.

⟨*Thesis*⟩ *4*: If a proposition is false, and it is not inconsistent that its
adequate significatum is false, its ⟨adequate significatum⟩ is false.

Patet ex dictis. Quare etc.

Ex praedictis sequitur quod

> Si aliqua propositio significat adaequate verum, et illa non est pro-
> positio insolubilis, illa est vera.

5 Unde propositio insolubilis communiter non dicitur falsa ratione sui
significati falsi, sed quia aut asserit se esse falsam, aut quia asserit se non
esse veram, aut quia sibi antecedit casualiter aliquod antecedens inferens
ipsam esse falsam. Sed de hoc latius in materia insolubilium, ubi huius
opinionis veritas clarius apparebit.[1] Quare etc.

10 ⟨*Argumenta contra ultimam viam*⟩

⟨1⟩ Contra secundam conclusionem, et consequenter contra totam
positionem, arguitur sic:[2] Haec propositio est vera

> Nulla chimaera est,

et tamen eius significatum adaequatum non est verum. Igitur etc.

15 ⟨1.1⟩ Consequentia patet cum maiori. Et minorem probo, quia si
adaequatum significatum illius

> Nulla chimaera est,

quae sit A, est verum, igitur adaequatum significatum illius est aliquod
verum.

20 Consequentia patet, quia ly .verum. non potest ibi stare modaliter, et
per consequens debet stare nominaliter. Sed consequens est falsum. Nam
si adaequatum significatum A est aliquod verum, sequitur quod illud
significatum est aliquid, aliqua, vel aliqualiter—quod est impossibile,
quia nullam chimaeram esse non est.

25 ⟨1.2⟩ Confirmatur: Nam si significatum adaequatum A est verum, verum
est significatum adaequatum A. Consequentia patet, per conversionem
simplicem, et ultra:

> Igitur, aliquod verum est significatum adaequatum A.

Patet consequentia, ab indefinita ad suam particularem. Sed consequens
30 est falsum, quia nihil, nec aliqua, nec aliqualiter est nullam chimaeram
esse.

⟨2⟩ Secundo arguitur sic:[3] Nulla propositio significat sicut non est. Et
quaelibet significat adaequate. Igitur, cuiuslibet propositionis adaequatum
significatum est verum. Et tamen aliqua propositio est falsa, ut patet.
35 Igitur etc.

Primum antecedens probatur sic, quia si aliqua, sit illa A. Contra:
A significat sicut non est. Igitur A significat aliqualiter qualiter non est.
Patet consequentia. Sed consequens est falsum, quod sic arguitur: A signi-

20 quia] ibi *add.* E   23 significatum *om.* E   25 confirmatur] consimiliter M

This is clear from what I have said. Thus, etc.

This follows from the above theses:

> If a proposition adequately signifies the truth, and the proposition is not an insoluble, the proposition is true.

Thus, an insoluble proposition commonly is not said to be false because of its false significatum, but because either it asserts that it itself is false, or because it asserts that it itself is not true, or because there is some premiss assumed in the case that implies that the proposition is false. But this is discussed more fully when I come to the insolubles, where the truth of this opinion will appear with greater clarity. Thus, etc.

⟨*Arguments against This Last Way*⟩

⟨1⟩ This argument is brought against Thesis 2, and consequently against the whole position: The proposition

> No chimera is

is true. Nevertheless, its adequate significatum is not true. Therefore, etc.

⟨1.1⟩ The inference is clear, as is the major. Proof of the minor: If the adequate significatum of the proposition

> No chimera is

(let it be *A*) is true, then its adequate significatum is something true.

The inference is clear, since 'true' there cannot be taken as a modal expression. Consequently, it ought to be taken as a nominal expression.[a] But the consequent is false. For if the adequate significatum of *A* is something true, it follows that the significatum is something, some things, or somehow—which is impossible, since that no chimera is, is not.

⟨1.2⟩ Confirming argument: If the adequate significatum of *A* is ⟨a⟩ truth, ⟨a⟩ truth is the adequate significatum of *A*.[b] The inference is clear by simple conversion. Further,

> Therefore, something true is the adequate significatum of *A*.

The inference from the indefinite to its particular, is clear. But the conclusion is false, since there is not anything, or any things, or any way that is that no chimera is.

⟨2⟩ Second, this argument is brought ⟨against Thesis 1⟩: No proposition signifies as things are not. Any proposition signifies adequately. Therefore, the adequate significatum of any proposition is true. Nevertheless, some proposition is false, as is clear. Therefore, etc.

The first premiss is proved this way: ⟨Suppose⟩ there were some proposition ⟨that signified as things are not⟩. Let it be *A*. On the contrary, *A* signifies as things are not. Therefore, *A* signifies in some way as things are not. The inference is clear. But the conclusion is false, as is proved

ficat aliqualiter qualiter non est. Igitur *A* significat aliqualiter et aliqualiter non est. Consequentia tenet ex hoc, quia arguitur a propositione affirmativa in qua ponitur terminus relativus, ad copulativam factam de eisdem terminis, sola mutatione facta termini relativi in antecedens eiusdem.

5   Et universaliter ubi sic arguitur, nulla negatione praeposita, (205ra M) vel signo distributivo, termino relativo, tenet consequentia, ut patet in similibus. Nam sequitur:

(161va E) Video hominem quem tu vides.
Igitur, video hominem, et hominem vides.

10 Et sequitur:

Aliqualiter Sortes currit, qualiter currit Plato.
Igitur, aliqualiter currit Sortes et aliqualiter currit Plato.

Similiter etiam sequitur quando negatio postponitur termino relativo, sic arguendo:

15 Aliqualiter currit Sortes, qualiter non currit Plato.
Igitur, aliqualiter currit Sortes, et aliqualiter non currit Plato.

⟨3⟩ Tertio arguitur sic:[4] Aliqua est propositio quae non est adaequate aliqualiter significativa. Et quaelibet propositio est vera vel falsa. Igitur, etc.
⟨3.1⟩ Antecedens pro prima parte probatur. Nam haec propositio:

20 Si Antichristus est albus, Antichristus est coloratus

est propositio cuius nullum potest assignari significatum. Nullus enim posset intelligere quid foret, ⟨quod⟩ si Antichristus est albus, Antichristus est coloratus, si foret.
⟨3.2⟩ Item, haec est propositio

25 Homo est non homo.

Et tamen non aliqualiter esse ista significat, nec est significativa. Probatur, quia si aliqualiter esse est significativa, vel igitur hominem esse, vel hominem esse non hominem.
⟨3.2.1⟩ Non primum, quia tunc, per idem, significaretur per illam

30 Homo est asinus

et per quamlibet propositionem trium terminorum, cuius subiectum esset ly .homo.—quod non est verum.
⟨3.2.2⟩ Nec etiam secundum, quia hominem esse non hominem, non potest intelligi. Sed quod non potest intelligi non potest significari. Igitur
35 ista propositio hominem esse non hominem non est significativa.
Consequentia patet cum minori. Et maiorem probo:

Nam hominem esse non hominem non potest intelligi esse ens.

---

1 aliqualiter³] taliter *E*   6 vel *om. M*

this way: *A* signifies in some way as things are not. Therefore, *A* signifies in some way and in some way things are not. The inference holds, since we argue from an affirmative proposition in which a relative term is posited, to a conjunctive proposition formed using these same terms with only a change of the relative term to its antecedent.

Universally, where the argument proceeds in this way—i.e. when no negation or distributive sign is placed before the relative term—the inference holds, as is clear in similar instances. For this follows:

I see a man whom you see.

Therefore, I see a man and a man you see.

And this follows:

Socrates runs some way as Plato runs.

Therefore, Socrates runs some way and some way Plato runs.

Similarly, it also follows when the negation is placed after a relative term, arguing this way:

Socrates runs some way as Plato does not run.

Therefore, Socrates runs some way and some way Plato does not run.

⟨3⟩ Third, the following argument is advanced ⟨against Theses 2 and 4⟩. There is some proposition that does not adequately signify in any way. Any proposition whatever is true or false. Therefore, etc.

⟨3.1⟩ The first premiss is proved this way. The proposition

If the Antichrist is white, the Antichrist is coloured

is a proposition to which no significatum can be assigned. For no one could understand what this would be if it were to be that if the Antichrist is white, the Antichrist is coloured.

⟨3.2⟩ Again, this

A man is a not-man

is a proposition. Nevertheless, it does not signify that things are in any way, nor is it significant. Proof: If it signifies that things are in some way, then it signifies either that a man is, or that a man is a not-man.

⟨3.2.1⟩ It does not signify the first, since then, by the same reasoning, that a man is, would be signified by the proposition

A man is a donkey

and by any proposition of three terms whose subject is 'a man'—which is not true.

⟨3.2.2⟩ It does not signify the second either, since that a man is a not-man, cannot be thought of. But what cannot be thought of, cannot be signified. Therefore, the proposition does not signify that a man is a not-man.

The inference is clear, as is the minor. Proof of the major:

That a man is a not-man, cannot be thought to be a being.

Igitur, non potest intelligi.

Patet consequentia, quia si potest intelligi, igitur intellectus potest esse obiectum. Sed nullum potest esse obiectum intellectus, nisi sub ratione entis. Igitur potest intelligi esse ens.[5]

5   ⟨3.3⟩ Item, haec copulativa

Tu es et tu non es

est propositio quae non aliqualiter esse significat vel est significativa. Igitur etc. Antecedens probatur, quia te esse et te non esse non potest intellectus simul apprehendere. Nec aliud significatum illa significat.

10 Igitur non aliqualiter esse illa significat.

Patet consequentia. Et probatur assumptum, quia si te esse et te non esse posset intellectus simul comprehendere posset, per idem, cuiuslibet consequentiae contradictorium consequentis intelligere cum antecedente— quod est falsum.

15 ⟨4⟩ Quarto principaliter arguitur sic:[6] Haec propositio

Antichristus est

non est insolubilis nec sibi pertinens. Et tamen eius adaequatum significatum est verum. Igitur etc.

Consequentia patet cum maiori. Et minorem probo: Nam praecise

20 sicut est illa propositio

Antichristus est

significat, et ipsa adaequate significat. Igitur eius adaequatum significatum est verum.

⟨4.1.1⟩ Consequentia patet cum minori. Et maiorem probo: Nam sicut

25 est illa significat, et non aliter quam sicut est illa significat. Igitur etc. Consequentia patet. Et maior illius antecedentis probatur, quia Antichristum esse illa significat. Et Antichristum esse potest intelligi. Igitur, sicut est illa significat. Patet consequentia, quia hoc verbum 'significat' extendit se a parte post usque in ea quae intelliguntur.

30 ⟨4.1.2⟩ Iam probatur quod non aliter quam sicut est illa significat, quia praecise possibiliter esse per illam intelligitur esse. Et praecise possibiliter esse est. Igitur, non aliter quam sicut est illa significat.

⟨4.2⟩ Confirmatur: Nam illa significat adaequate aliqualiter, et taliter est.

---

2 intellectus] sibi *ME, correxi* (*cf. p.* 72 *lin.* 28)   3 potest esse] est *E*   31 possibiliter] possibile *E*

Therefore, it cannot be thought of.

The inference is clear. For what can be thought of can be an object for the intellect. But something can be an object for the intellect only under the notion of being. Therefore, it can be thought to be a being.

⟨3.3⟩ Again, the conjunctive proposition

You are and you are not

is a proposition that does not signify that things are in some way, and is not significant. Therefore, etc. Proof of the premiss: The intellect cannot simultaneously apprehend that you are and that you are not. Nor does the proposition

⟨You are and you are not⟩

signify another significatum. Therefore, it does not signify that things are in some way.

The inference is clear. Proof of the assumption: If the intellect could simultaneously comprehend that you are and that you are not, it could by the same reasoning think the contradictory of the conclusion of any inference, together with its premiss—which is false.

⟨4⟩ The fourth principal argument is this: The proposition

The Antichrist is

is neither an insoluble proposition nor a proposition about itself. Nevertheless, its adequate significatum is true. Therefore, etc.

The inference is clear, as is the major. Proof of the minor: The proposition

The Antichrist is

signifies precisely as things are, and it signifies adequately. Therefore, its adequate significatum is true.

⟨4.1.1⟩ The inference is clear, as is the minor. Proof of the major: It signifies as things are and it does not signify otherwise than as things are. Therefore, etc. The inference is clear. Proof of the major premiss: It signifies that the Antichrist is. That the Antichrist is, can be thought of. Therefore, it signifies as things are. The inference is clear, since the verb 'signifies' ampliates the term following it ⟨to range⟩ over those things that are thought of.ᶜ

⟨4.1.2⟩ Again, that it does not signify otherwise than as things are, is proved ⟨as follows⟩:

Precisely the possibly-existing is thought of as existing, by means of this proposition.
Precisely the possibly-existing is.
Therefore, it does not signify otherwise than as things are.

⟨4.2⟩ Confirming argument: The proposition

⟨The Antichrist is,⟩

adequately signifies in some way, and things are that way.

Igitur significat adaequate sicut est. Igitur significat adaequate verum. Et est falsa non insolubilis nec pertinens eidem. Igitur etc.

⟨*Responsio auctoris ad argumenta contra ultimam viam*⟩

Ad haec respondetur.

5 ⟨R1.1⟩ Ad primum dico quod si proponitur ista

Significatum adaequatum *A* est verum,

quaeritur quomodo tenetur ly .verum.—an pure adiective vel in neutro genere substantivatum.

⟨a⟩ Primo modo, conceditur ista propositio, et sic continue tenetur in 10 meis conclusionibus. Et tunc non valet argumentum:

Igitur, significatum adaequatum *A* est aliquod verum.

Sed bene sequitur:

Igitur, significatum adaequatum *A* est significatum verum.

⟨R1.2⟩ Et per hoc patet responsio ad confirmationem, quod tenendo 15 ly .verum. in consequente sicut in antecedente, non sequitur:

Verum est significatum adaequatum *A*.

Igitur, aliquod verum est significatum adaequatum *A*.

Sed debet concludi pro sua particulari:

Igitur, aliquod verum significatum est significatum adaequatum *A*.

20 ⟨b⟩ Si autem in praeassumpta propositione tenetur ly .verum. in neutro genere substantivatum, negatur illa. Et sic non sumpsi in dictis meis.

⟨R2⟩ Ad secundum concedo[7] quod aliqua propositio (205rb M) significat sicut non est, sicut ista

Homo est asinus,

25 quae significat hominem esse asinum, et tale significatum non est. Immo et aliqua propositio vera significat sicut non est, sicut ista

Nulla chimaera est.

Significat enim nullam chimaeram esse, et nullam chimaeram esse (161vb E) non est. Et ita consequenter concedo quod aliqua propositio significat 30 aliqualiter qualiter non est, quia aliqua propositio falsa significat aliqualiter, et non qualitercumque significat propositio falsa, est. Et ulterius negatur consequentia:

Igitur, aliqua propositio significat aliqualiter, et aliqualiter non est.

---

8 substantivatum] substantivato *ME, correxi* (*etiam infra, lin.* 21. *Cf. Logica Magna, Pars I, tract.* 1 '*De terminis*', *ed. Venetiis 1499, f.* 2 *rb lin.* 38)   10–11 argumentum: igitur] consequentia *E*   12–13 sequitur: igitur *om. E*   18–19 sed . . . *A om.* (hom.?) *M*   25 quae *om. E*

Therefore, the proposition adequately signifies as things are. Therefore, it adequately signifies the truth. It is false and is neither an insoluble nor a proposition about itself. Therefore, etc.

⟨*Paul's Reply to the Arguments against the Last Way*⟩

I reply to these arguments.

⟨R1.1⟩ In reply to the first I say that if the proposition

The adequate significatum of *A* is true

is proposed, I ask how the 'true' is taken, whether purely adjectivally or in the neuter gender equivalent to a substantive.

⟨a⟩ If 'true' is taken in the first way, I grant the proposition. And in my theses I take 'true' continually in this way. And then the argument

Therefore, the adequate significatum of *A* is something true

does not hold good. But rather this follows:

Therefore, the adequate significatum of *A* is a true significatum.

⟨R1.2⟩ From this, my reply to their confirming argument is clear: viz. that taking 'true' in the conclusion in the same way as ⟨'a truth' is taken⟩ in the premiss, this does not follow:

⟨A⟩ truth is the adequate significatum of *A*.

Therefore, something true is the adequate significatum of *A*.

But the conclusion ought to be drawn to its own particular:

Therefore, some true significatum is the adequate significatum of *A*.

⟨b⟩ But if in the assumed proposition, 'true' is taken in the neuter gender equivalent to a substantive, I deny it. I have not taken it in this way in my claims.

⟨R2⟩ In reply to the second, I grant that some proposition signifies as things are not. For example, the proposition

A man is a donkey

signifies that a man is a donkey. Such a significatum is not. In fact, there is even a true proposition that signifies as things are not. For example, the proposition

No chimera is

signifies that no chimera is, and that no chimera is, is not. Thus, consequently, I grant that some proposition signifies in some way as things are not. For some false proposition signifies in some way. And it is not ⟨the case⟩ that things are whatever way a false proposition signifies. Further, I deny the inference:

Therefore, some proposition signifies in some way and in some way things are not.

Unde huiusmodi modus arguendi fallit cum istis verbis 'intelligo', 'signi-
fico', 'volo', 'nolo'. Immo non sequitur:

> Antichristus erit homo qui non est.

> Igitur, Antichristus erit homo, et homo non est.

5 Similiter:

> Ly .Antichristus. significat hominem qui non est.

> Igitur significat hominem, et homo non est.

Quod autem aliquando valeat, hoc est gratia materiae.

⟨R3⟩ Ad tertium argumentum dico quod nulla est propositio quae non
10 sit aliqualiter significativa.

⟨R3.1⟩ Et nego quod illa condicionalis non sit aliqualiter significativa.
Significat enim quod si Antichristus est albus, Antichristus est coloratus.
Et cum dicitur quod nullus posset intelligere quid foret quod si Antichristus est albus, Antichristus est coloratus, negatur. Unde quidam in-
15 telligunt quod si tale significatum esset, illud esset Deus, sicut dicit una
opinio[8] quod nullam chimaeram esse est Deus. Alii intelligunt quod si
illud esset, esset quodlibet. Alii intelligunt quod si illud esset, non esset
aliquid, nec aliqua, sed aliqualiter, sicut iam ponunt fautores complexe
significabilium.[9]

20 ⟨R3.2.2⟩ Ad confirmationem dico quod illa

> Homo est non homo

significat hominem esse non hominem. Et nego quod non posset intelligi
hominem esse non hominem. Et cum dicitur

> Non potest intelligi esse ens.

25 > Igitur, non potest intelligi,

nego consequentiam, quia adhuc potest intelligi esse falsum et impossibile.
Et ad probationem:

> Si potest intelligi, potest esse obiectum intellectus,

nego conditionalem illam, quia nullum falsum obicitur intellectui, sed
30 solum verum.

⟨R3.2.1⟩ Item, concedo quod illa

> Homo est non homo,

significat hominem esse. Et cum infertur:

> Igitur, per idem significatur per illam

35 >   Homo est asinus,

>   et per quamlibet propositionem trium terminorum, cuius subiectum
>   est ly .homo.,

---

8 aliquando] aliter *E*   12 significat] sicut *E*   quod *om. E*   15 esset Deus] esse
Deum *E*   29 intellectui] intelligi *E*

Thus this form of argument fails with the verbs 'think', 'signify', 'want', 'not want'. In fact, this does not follow:

The Antichrist will be a man who is not.

Therefore, the Antichrist will be a man, and a man is not.

Similarly, ⟨this does not follow⟩:

The term 'Antichrist' signifies a man who is not.

Therefore, it signifies a man and a man is not.

But that this form of inference holds good in other cases, depends upon the subject-matter.

⟨R3⟩ In reply to the third argument, I say that there is no proposition that is not in any way significant.

⟨R3.1⟩ I deny that that conditional is not in any way significant. For it signifies that if the Antichrist is white, the Antichrist is coloured. When ⟨they⟩ say that no one can understand what it would be—that if the Antichrist is white, the Antichrist is coloured—I deny it. Thus, some understand that if there were such a significatum, it would be God, just as one opinion says that that no chimera is, is God. Others understand that if there were that significatum, it would be anything whatever. Others understand that if there were that significatum, it would not be some thing, or some things, but somehow, as the partisans of what is complexly signifiable now suppose.[d]

⟨R3.2⟩ In reply to the confirming argument, I say that the proposition

A man is a not-man

signifies that a man is a not-man. I deny that it cannot be thought that a man is a not-man. When ⟨they⟩ say

It cannot be thought to be a being.

Therefore, it cannot be thought of,

I deny the inference, since even so ⟨that a man is a not-man,⟩ can be thought to be false and impossible. To the proof:

If it can be thought of, it can be an object for the intellect,

I deny that conditional. For nothing false is an object for the intellect, but only the truth.[e]

⟨R3.2.1⟩ Again, I grant that the proposition

A man is a not-man,

signifies that a man is. When ⟨they⟩ infer

Therefore, by the same reasoning, that a man is, is signified by the proposition

A man is a donkey,

and by any proposition of three terms whose subject is the term 'man',

concedo conclusionem.

Et nota quod non concedo illam significare hominem esse propter hoc quod ex ipsa sequitur materialiter aut formaliter suum signum, scilicet

Homo est.

5 Quia ad istam

Tu curris

sequitur illa

Deus est,

quae tamen non significat Deum esse. Ad istam etiam

10   Tu es aliud a te,

sequitur formaliter quod baculus stat in angulo. Et tamen illa non significat baculum stare in angulo. Sed concedo illam significare hominem esse, quia suum signum ex eadem formaliter sequitur, et formaliter sequeretur, dato quod illa esset propositio simpliciter et omniquaque contingens.

15 Dico igitur quod quaelibet propositio significat cuiuslibet propositionis significatum ad ipsam formaliter sequentis, dato adhuc quod sibi sola contingentia esset communicata. Et sic debet intelligi illud commune dictum

Quaelibet propositio significat quidquid sequitur ad eam,

20 quod quidem aliqui[10] parum naturales et metaphysici omnimode nituntur destruere.

⟨R3.3⟩ Ad aliam confirmationem, dico quod ista copulativa

Tu es et tu non es

significat adaequate te esse et te non esse. Secundario vero tam te non esse 25 quam te esse significat. Et cum dicitur:

Intellectus non potest simul intelligere te esse et te non esse,

dico quod hic potest esse locutio de simultate naturae aut durationis. Primo modo, concedo illam, et nego consequentiam, cum infertur:

Igitur, non aliqualiter ⟨esse⟩ illa significat.

3 signum] significatum (*etiam infra, lin.* 13) E   12 sed] si E   16 sibi *om.* M
20 aliqui] alii M

I grant the conclusion.

Notice I do not grant that the proposition

⟨A man is a not-man⟩

signifies that a man is, because its sign—viz.

A man is

follows materially or formally from the proposition

⟨A man is a not-man.⟩

For the proposition

God is

follows from the proposition

You are running,

which nevertheless does not signify that God is. Also, it follows formally from the proposition

You are other than yourself,

that a stick is standing in the corner. Nevertheless, the proposition

⟨You are other than yourself⟩

does not signify that a stick is standing in the corner. But I grant that the proposition

⟨A man is a not-man,⟩

signifies that a man is, because its sign follows formally from that proposition and would follow formally if it were granted that the proposition was absolutely and in every way contingent. Therefore, I say that any proposition signifies the significatum of any proposition that would follow from it formally, even if it were granted that contingency alone was predicated of it.ᶠ It is in this way that the common saying,

Any proposition signifies whatever follows from it,

ought to be understood. Certainly this is a claim which some superficial natural philosophers and metaphysicians try in every way to destroy.

⟨R3.3⟩ In reply to the other confirming argument, I say that the conjunctive proposition

You are and you are not

adequately signifies that you are and you are not. But secondarily it signifies that you are not, no less than that you are. When ⟨they⟩ say

The intellect cannot simultaneously have the thought that you are and that you are not,

I say that here they can be speaking of the simultaneity of nature or the simultaneity of duration. In the first way, I grant it.ᵍ I deny the inference when it is inferred:

Therefore, it is not the case that it signifies that things are in some way.

Secundo modo nego antecedens. Nam non solum intellectus divinus in instanti temporis intelligit te esse et te non esse, immo et intellectus beati, divinam essentiam intuentis, cum ibi non sit discursus durativus, sed praecise naturae. Et cum concluditur quod tunc intellectus simul posset
5 comprehendere cuiuslibet consequentiae contradictorium consequentis cum antecedente, concedo conclusionem, non solum de beatis, immo de viatoribus. Licet enim ista propositio

   Homo est asinus

per prius significet hominem quam (205va M) asinum, tamen pro aliquo
10 instanti significat ambo. Et sic intellectus intelligit ambo simul. Ita dico quod intellectus per prius intelligit antecedens quam consequens et oppositum consequentis, et tamen in fine illa omnia intelligit simul.

   ⟨R4.1⟩ Ad quartum argumentum, nego quod praecise sicut est illa

   Antichristus est

15 significat.

   ⟨R4.1.1⟩ Et cum dicitur:

   Nam sicut est illa significat,

concedo. Significat enim aliquid esse, et sic est.

   ⟨R4.1.2⟩ Sed nego quod non aliter quam sicut est illa significat. Immo,
20 aliter quam sicut est illa significat. Nam ipsa significat Antichristum esse, et Antichristum esse non est sicut est. Et ad probationem, cum dicitur

   Praecise (162ra E) possibiliter esse per illam intelligitur esse.

   Et praecise possibiliter ⟨esse⟩ est.

   Igitur, non aliter quam sicut est illa significat,

25 nego consequentiam, sicut non sequitur:

   Praecise possibile esse illa significat.

   Et praecise possibile est.

   Igitur, nullum significatum falsum illa significat.

   ⟨R4.2⟩ Ad confirmationem dico quod si ly .taliter. demonstrative tenetur
30 pro Antichristo, concedo consequentiam, et nego antecedens pro secunda parte. Si autem tenetur relative, nego consequentiam, et concedo antecedens. Nam taliter est qualiter significat illa

   Antichristus est

significando Antichristum esse. Quare etc.

---

6 conclusionem] consequentiam *E*   non . . . immo] immo non . . . sed etiam *E*
9 prius] primum *M*   10 intelligit ambo simul] simul intelligit illa *E*   19 sed]
et *M*

Understood in the second way, I deny the premiss. For not only does the Divine Intellect in an instant of time have the thought that you are and that you are not; but also the intellects of the blessed, intuiting the Divine Essence, where there is no discourse in time, but precisely a discourse of nature.[h] When ⟨they⟩ conclude that then the intellect could simultaneously comprehend the contradictory of the conclusion of any inference, together with its premiss, I grant the conclusion. In fact, ⟨this is true⟩ not only of the blessed, but also of those in this life. For, although the proposition

A man is a donkey

signifies a man prior to signifying a donkey, nevertheless at some instant it signifies both. So understood, the intellect simultaneously thinks both. Thus, I say that the intellect thinks of the premiss prior to thinking of the conclusion and the opposite of the conclusion. Nevertheless, in the end, it thinks of them all simultaneously.

⟨R4.1⟩ In reply to the fourth argument, I deny that the proposition

The Antichrist is

signifies precisely as things are.

⟨R4.1.1⟩ When they say:

It signifies as things are,

I grant it. For it signifies that something is, and things are so.

⟨R4.1.2⟩ But I deny that it does not signify otherwise than things are. In fact, it does signify otherwise than as things are. For it signifies that the Antichrist is, and that the Antichrist is, is not as things are. In reply to the proof when they say:

Precisely the possibly-existing is thought of as existing, by means of this proposition.
Precisely the possibly-existing is.
Therefore, it does not signify otherwise than as things are,

I deny the inference. In the same way, this does not follow:

It signifies that precisely the possible is.
Precisely the possible is.
Therefore, it signifies no false significatum.

⟨R4.2⟩ In reply to the confirming argument, I say that if the 'in that way' is taken as indicating the Antichrist, I grant the inference and deny the second premiss. But if it is taken relatively, I deny the inference and grant the premiss. For that is the way in which the proposition

The Antichrist is,

signifies, when it signifies that the Antichrist is. Thus, etc.

LOGICAE MAGNAE

SECUNDA PARS

TRACTATUS DE SIGNIFICATO PROPOSITIONIS

DE SIGNIFICATO PROPOSITIONIS

Quia in praecedentibus de significato adaequato propositionis[1] tangebatur, ideo de eodem restant videnda duo, ut consequentius valeat quis respondere. Primum erit de quidditate ipsius; secundum de sui signi
5 adaequatione.[2]

⟨De Quidditate Significati Propositionis⟩

Circa primum multae versantur opiniones.

⟨Prima Opinio   Capitulum Primum⟩

Prima ponit quod significatum propositionis verae est modus rei et non
10 res.[3] Et arguit sic:[4]

⟨1⟩ Primo, cuiuslibet propositionis verae significatum est ubique. Sed nihil praeter substantiam immaterialem est ubique. Igitur cuiuslibet propositionis verae significatum est modus rei et non res existens.

Assumptum probat sic, de hac propositione

15   Tu es.

Nam ubique est quod tu es. Et quod tu es haec propositio significat. Igitur etc. Maior probatur: Ubicumque scitur quod tu es, ibi verum est quod tu es. Sed nullum est ubi in mundo quin staret, sine mutatione tui, quod sciatur ibi quod tu es. Igitur, in omni loco, absque mutatione
20 tui, in quo tu non es, stat ibi verum esse quod tu es. Sed ubicumque est verum quod tu es, ibi est quod tu es. Igitur etc.

2° sic:

Nulla chimaera est

est propositio vera. Igitur suum significatum est verum. Igitur nullam
25 chimaeram esse est verum. Et ultra,

Igitur nullam chimaeram esse est.

Sed non res; igitur modus rei.

2–3 tangebatur] tunc agebatur *M*   12 immaterialem] materialem *M*   17 maior]
antecedens *E*   19 tui] a loco in quo es *add. Feribrigge*   sciatur] sciam *E*   21 ibi]
ita *add. E*

ON THE SIGNIFICATUM OF
A PROPOSITION

The adequate significatum of a proposition was touched on in the preceding chapters. Therefore, we must now examine two things in connection with it, so that ⟨in discussing such matters⟩ we will be able to make more consistent replies. The first concerns its quiddity; the second, the adequation of its sign.

⟨On the Quiddity of the Significatum of a Proposition⟩

About the first, there are many opinions under discussion.

⟨The First Opinion   Chapter One⟩

The first opinion assumes that the significatum of a true proposition is a mode of a thing and not a thing. ⟨Adherents of this opinion⟩ offer the following arguments.

⟨1⟩ First, the significatum of any true proposition is everywhere. But nothing except immaterial substance is everywhere. Therefore, the significatum of any true proposition is a mode of a thing and not an existent thing.

The assumption is proved this way, with respect to the proposition

You are.

That you are, is everywhere. This proposition signifies that you are. Therefore, etc. Proof of the major: Wherever it is known that you are, there it is true that you are. But, for any place in the world, it is consistent that without any change in you it is known there that you are. Therefore, it is consistent that in every place in which you are not, without any change in you, there it is true that you are. But wherever it is true that you are, that you are is there. Therefore, etc.

2. They argue this way:

No chimera is

is a true proposition. Therefore, its significatum is true. Therefore, that no chimera is, is true. And further,

Therefore that no chimera is, is.

But it is not a thing. Therefore, it is a mode of a thing.

⟨Argumenta contra primam opinionem⟩

Contra istam positionem arguitur sic:⁵

⟨1⟩ Ubicumque est significatum illius propositionis, ibi est significatum subiecti. Sed ubique, per opinionem, est significatum illius propositionis. Igitur ubique est significatum subiecti. Et per consequens, tu es ubique.

Consequentia patet, et prima pars antecedentis probatur: Ubicumque est significatum adaequatum per duo est utriusque illorum significatum. Sed ubique est significatum per illa duo, scilicet per subiectum et illud verbum 'est'. Igitur etc.

2° Te esse non distinguitur realiter a te, ut probabitur inferius.⁶ Sed te esse est ubique. Igitur tu es ubique.

3° Sequitur quod Sortem currere est ubique, supposito quod haec sit vera

Sortes currit,

et cum hoc quod Sortes incipiat currere. Tunc, ubique est Sortem currere postquam nullibi fuit Sortem currere. Igitur ubique efficitur Sortem currere. Et a nullo alio quam a Sorte. Igitur Sortes ubique efficit Sortem currere. Et si sic, igitur Sortes ubique efficit cursum suum—quod est falsum.

4° Sequitur quod si scio te esse, non scio aliud nisi hunc modum; et quod omnis scientia est scientia modorum; et quod Deus et intelligentiae non sciunt nisi modos rerum. Consequens est falsum, quia scientia quidditatum est prior scientia modorum, sicut quidditates modis sunt priores.

5° Si significatum propositionis verae sit modus rei, ita quod non res, aut igitur simplex aut compositus. Si simplex, igitur uno simplici nomine potest significari. Consequentia patet, quia conceptui simplici potest simplex pars orationis correspondere, cum iuxta variationem conceptuum variantur partes orationis. Et tunc sequitur quod non quodlibet incomplexorum significat substantiam vel qualitatem etc., cum illa vox non significet nisi modum rei. Si talis modus (205vb M) sit complexus, tunc non stat Deum esse, nullo complexo existente, nec stat intelligi Deum esse, pluribus non existentibus.

6° Si te esse est modus rei, vel igitur modus intrinsecus vel modus extrinsecus. Non modus extrinsecus, quia staret te esse et non esse te

---

4 ubique] ubicumque *M*   11 es] est *add. M*   16–18 igitur . . . currere *om.*
(hom.?) *M*   18 igitur *om. M*   31 nullo] uno *E*

⟨Paul's Arguments against the First Position⟩

I argue against this position this way:

⟨1⟩ Wherever the significatum of that proposition is, there is the significatum of its subject. But, according to this opinion, the significatum of the proposition

⟨You are⟩

is everywhere. Therefore, the significatum of the subject is everywhere. Consequently, you are everywhere.

The inference is clear. Proof of the first premiss: Wherever the adequate significatum of two ⟨terms⟩ is, ⟨there⟩ is the significatum of each of them. The significatum of these two ⟨terms⟩—viz. the subject and the verb 'are'— is everywhere. Therefore, etc.[a]

2. That you are, is not really distinct from you, as ⟨I⟩ will prove below. But that you are is everywhere. Therefore, you are everywhere.

3. Suppose that the proposition

Socrates runs,

is true, and together with this, that Socrates begins to run. It follows that *that Socrates runs* is everywhere. Then, that Socrates runs, is everywhere, after a time when that Socrates runs, was nowhere. Therefore, everywhere it is brought about that Socrates runs. This is brought about by no one other than Socrates. Therefore, everywhere Socrates brings it about that Socrates runs. If so, then everywhere Socrates brings about his own running—which is false.

4. It follows that if I know that you are, I know only this mode; and that all knowledge is knowledge of modes; and that God and the intelligences know only modes of things. The conclusion is false, because the knowledge of quiddities is prior to the knowledge of modes, just as quiddities are prior to modes.

5. If the significatum of a true proposition is the mode of a thing in such a way that it is not a thing, either it is a simple mode or a complex mode. If simple, then it can be signified by one simple name. The inference is clear. For a simple piece of discourse can correspond to a simple concept, since pieces of discourse are varied as concepts are varied. Then it follows that it is not the case that any non-complex whatever signifies substance or quality, etc., since that utterance would signify only the mode of a thing. If such a mode were complex, then it would not be consistent that God is when no complex is. Nor would it be consistently thought that God is and yet that it is not the case that there are many.[b]

6. If that you are, is a mode of a thing, then it is either an intrinsic mode or an extrinsic mode. It is not an extrinsic mode. For then it would be consistent that you are and that *that you are* is not—which is impossible.

esse—quod est impossibile. Si modus intrinsecus, sequitur quod realiter
et identice verificatur de illo cuius est modus. Patet consequentia, eo
quod modus intrinsecus est quadruplex: videlicet finitum vel infinitum,
actualis existentia realiter et haecceitas.[7] Sed quilibet istorum modorum
5 verificatur de illo vel de illis, a quo vel a quibus consurgit. Si enim haec
opinio melius considerasset quid est modus rei, non posuisset significatum
aliquod esse modum rei.

7° Si te esse est modus, vel igitur est modus in te vel extra te. Non
extra te, quia (162rb E) tunc ad corruptionem tui non desineret te esse,
10 eo quod nullum absolutum desineret esse ad mutationem factam in alio.
Nec te esse est modus in te, quia tu es naturaliter prior omni existente in
te. Et universaliter stat prius esse sine posteriori inter quae non est ordo
nec dependentia. Igitur stat te esse, quamvis te esse non sit—quod est
impossibile.

15   8° Te esse est modus. Igitur te esse est ens. Patet consequentia, eo quod
ly .ens. verificatur de quolibet termino ampliativo. Et sequitur:

    Te esse est ens.

    Igitur est substantia vel accidens.

Patet consequentia, quia ens sua primaria divisione sic dividitur. Et ultra,
20   Igitur te esse est res,
—quod est contra opinionem.

⟨*Responsio ad rationes opinionis*⟩
    ⟨R1⟩ Ad primam rationem huius opinionis,[8] nego quod cuiuslibet
propositionis verae et affirmativae de praesenti significatum est ubique.
25 Et nego quod te esse sit ubique. Et ad argumentum:
    Ubicumque scitur quod tu es, ibi verum est quod tu es,
concedo, tenendo ly .verum. modaliter. Et nego quod ubicumque verum
est quod tu es, ibi sit quod tu es.
    ⟨R2⟩ Ad secundam rationem, concedo quod nullam chimaeram esse est
30 verum, sumendo ly .verum. ut prius. Ex quo non sequitur quod nullam
chimaeram esse est, sicut inferius apparebit.[9]

⟨*Secunda Opinio et Duo Aliae Opiniones Derivatae*
                                    Capitulum Secundum⟩
Secunda opinio[1] ponit significatum propositionis verae esse compositionem
35 mentis vel intellectus componentis aut dividentis. Fundatur enim haec

---

3 quadruplex] quadrupliciter *E*   4 actualis] actualiter *E*   existentia realiter] ex nª
realit' (*forte pro*: existentia realitatis) *M*   5 consurgit] constat *M*   9 desineret]
destrueretur *E*   12 et] vel *E*   13 te1 *om. E*   19 primaria] prima *E*
23 rationem] responsionem *E*   25 sit] est *E*   29 secundam rationem] secundum
argumentum *E*   31 apparebit] etc. *add. E*

If it is an intrinsic mode, it follows that it is truly said to be really identical with the thing of which it is the mode. The inference is clear from the fact that the intrinsic mode is fourfold: viz. finite or infinite, actual existence in reality, and thisness.[c] But any of these modes is truly predicated of the thing or things to which it pertains. Thus, if this opinion had better considered what a mode of a thing is, it would not have assumed that any significatum is a mode of a thing.

7. If that you are, is a mode, then it is either a mode in you or a mode outside you. It is not a mode outside you, since then that you are would not cease to exist upon your ceasing to exist. For no absolute thing would cease to exist upon some change made in something else. That you are, is not a mode in you either, since you are naturally prior to everything existing in you. And, universally, where there is no order or dependence among things, it is consistent that the prior should be without the posterior.[d] Therefore, it is consistent that you are, although *that you are* is not—which is impossible.

8. That you are, is a mode. Therefore, that you are, is a being. The inference is clear, because 'being' is truly predicated of any non-ampliative term whatever. This follows:

That you are, is a being.
Therefore, it is a substance or accident.

The inference is clear, since this is the primary division of being. Further,

Therefore, that you are, is a thing

—which is contrary to this opinion.

⟨*Reply to Arguments for the First Opinion*⟩

⟨R1⟩ In reply to the first argument of this opinion, I deny that the significatum of any true affirmative present-tense proposition whatever is everywhere. I deny that that you are, is everywhere. In reply to the argument:

Wherever it is known that you are, there it is true that you are,

I grant it, taking the term 'true' as a modal expression.[e] I deny that wherever it is true that you are, that you are, is there.

⟨R2⟩ In reply to the second argument, I grant that *that no chimera is* is true, taking the term 'true' as before. From this, it does not follow that *that no chimera is* is, as will appear below.

⟨*The Second Opinion and Two Other Derivative Opinions*
                                        Chapter Two⟩

The second opinion assumes that the significatum of a true proposition is a composition of the mind or intellect, compounding or dividing. This

opinio super duo dicta Aristotelis et super ultima ratione primae opinionis.

⟨1⟩ Dicit Philosophus primo *Peri Hermeneias*[2] quod hoc verbum 'est'
significat quandam compositionem quam sine extremis non est intelligere.
5 Igitur significatum per totam illam propositionem

Sortes est homo

est aliquid, et non res extra mentem vel intellectum. Igitur est aliqua compositio mentis. Consequentia tenet per hoc quod huic verbo 'est' non
correspondet aliquid extra mentem, iuxta auctoritatem allegatam.

10 2° Fundatur haec opinio in secundo *Peri Hermeneias*,[3] ubi Philosophus
dicit quod 'necesse est esse' et 'impossibile est non esse' convertuntur.
Igitur

Necesse est nullam chimaeram esse

et

15 Impossibile non est nullam chimaeram esse

convertuntur. Ex quibus sequitur quod aliquid vel aliqualiter est nullam
chimaeram esse et non extra mentem. Igitur in mente.

3° Arguit sic haec opinio: Si significatum propositionis verae esset
extra mentem, tunc significatum propositionis verae negativae, et de
20 praeterito, et de futuro, cui vel quibus non correspondent aliquae res de
praesenti, esset extra mentem. Consequens falsum, quia nihil nec aliqualiter est nullam chimaeram esse vel Antichristum futurum.

⟨*Argumenta contra secundam opinionem*⟩

Contra istam opinionem arguitur sic:[4]
25 ⟨1⟩ Ista consequentia est bona:

Deus est.

Igitur, Deum esse est verum,

cum non stet oppositum consequentis cum antecedente. Et antecedens est
necessarium; igitur et consequens.

30 Tunc sic:

Necesse est Deum esse

est verum. Sed praecise contingenter est aliqua compositio mentalis.
Igitur, Deum esse non est aliqua compositio mentalis.

2° Arguitur sic: Nulla compositio mentalis est. Igitur Deum esse non
35 est possibile. Consequentia patet, quia haec propositio

Deum esse est possibile

7–8 compositio] propositio *E*   15 non *om. M* (*sed cf. infra, p.* 90, *lin.* 7–8)   non *et*
nullam *om. Feribrigge et Venator*   17 igitur in mente *om. M*

opinion is based on two claims of Aristotle as well as on the last argument of the first opinion.

⟨1⟩ The Philosopher says in *Peri Hermeneias*, Part I, ⟨c. 3 16ᵇ24–5⟩ that the verb 'is' signifies a certain composition that cannot be understood without extreme ⟨terms⟩. Therefore, what is signified by the whole proposition

Socrates is a man

is something. It is not a thing outside the mind or intellect. Therefore, it is some composition of the mind. The inference holds, since, according to the invoked authority, nothing outside the mind corresponds to the verb 'is'.

2. This opinion is based on *Peri Hermeneias*, Part II ⟨c. 13 22ᵃ14–ᵇ28⟩, where the Philosopher says that 'it is necessary to be' and 'it is impossible not to be' are interchangeable. Therefore,

It is necessary that no chimera is

and

It is not impossible that no chimera is

are interchangeable. From these propositions it follows that *that no chimera is* is something or somehow. It is not outside the mind. Therefore, it is in the mind.

3. This opinion argues this way: If the significatum of a true proposition were outside the mind, then the significatum of a true negative proposition, and of a past-tense proposition and of a future-tense proposition, to which no present things outside the mind correspond, would be outside the mind. The consequent is false. For that no chimera is, or that the Antichrist will be, is not anything or anyhow.

⟨Arguments against the Second Opinion⟩

I argue against this opinion in the following way.

⟨1⟩ This inference is good:

God is.

Therefore, that God is, is true.

For the opposite of the conclusion is not consistent with the premiss. The premiss is necessary. Therefore, so is the conclusion. Then I argue this way: The proposition

It is necessary that God is

is true. But a mental composition exists precisely contingently. Therefore, that God is, is not a mental composition.ᵃ

2. I argue this way: No mental composition is. Therefore, that God is, is not possible. The inference is clear. For the proposition

That God is, is possible

significat assertive quod haec compositio quae est Deum esse est possibilis. Tunc sic: Ista consequentia est bona. Antecedens fuit possibile, per eos, ante creationem mundi. Igitur et consequens.

Tunc sic: Deum esse non est possibile. Igitur Deum esse est impossibile.
5 Consequentia bona. (206ʳᵃ M) Antecedens est iterum possibile. Igitur et consequens—quod non est verum, cum non sit aliqua talis possibilis

Deum esse est impossibile.

3° Pono quod immediate post hoc nullus intellectus creatus intelliget, et quod iam aliquis intelligat Deum esse. Tunc immediate post hoc erit
10 ita quod nulla compositio est. Igitur, iam desinit esse ita quod Deus est. Patet consequentia ex opinione. Et consequens est falsum, quia necesse est Deum esse.

4° Illud quod significat propositio in mente, significat propositio sibi correspondens in voce vel in scripto. Sed propositio in mente significat
15 Deum esse extra mentem vel intellectum, quia aliter esset processus in infinitum. Igitur propositio vocalis vel scripta significat Deum esse extra mentem vel intellectum.

5° Haec propositio

Deus est

20 est una affirmativa solum habens duas partes ex quarum compositione significat. Sed subiectum significat aliquid extra mentem, et copula similiter. Igitur et tota propositio sic significat significatum resultans ex his. Consequentia patet cum maiori. Et minorem probo (162ᵛᵃ E), quia aliter haec mentalis esset falsa

25   Deus est,

quia significaret subiectum esse copulam.

6° Sequitur quod tu potes facere Deum esse, quia tu potes facere illam propositionem mentalem.

7° Deum esse fuit ante productionem mundi. Sed tunc non fuit aliqua
30 compositio mentalis. Igitur etc.

8° Essentia divina quae est quaedam propositio intellectui divino fuit propositio vera ante creationem mundi.[5] Sed tunc non fuit aliqua compositio mentalis. Et ipsa significabat intellectui divino Deum esse. Igitur etc.

35 ⟨*Responsio ad rationes pro secunda opinione*⟩

Ad rationes.

⟨R1⟩ Ad primam[6] dico quod illa auctoritas Aristotelis est falsa de virtute

---

2–3 fuit ... creationem] per eos fuit possibile quando creatio *M*   8 intelliget] intelli-geret *E*   16 vel scripta *transp. post* esse *E*   extra *om. M*   26 significaret] significat *E*   31 propositio] compositio *M* (propositio *Petrus de Aliaco*)

signifies assertorically that this composition, viz.

That God is,

is possible. Then, I argue this way: The inference is good. The premiss was possible, according to them, before the creation of the world. Therefore, so was the conclusion.

Then I argue this way: That God is, is not possible. Therefore, that God is, is impossible. The inference is good. Again, the premiss is possible. Therefore, so is the conclusion—which is not true, since there is no such possible proposition as

That God is, is impossible.

3. I assume that immediately after this instant, no created intellect will think of ⟨anything⟩, and that now someone has the thought that God is. Then, immediately after this, it will be so that there is no composition. Therefore, it now ceases to be so that God is. The inference is clear, according to this opinion. The conclusion is false, since it is necessary that God is.

4. That which a mental proposition signifies is signified by the corresponding spoken or written proposition. But the mental proposition signifies that God is outside the mind or intellect. Otherwise, there would be an infinite process. Therefore, the spoken or written proposition signifies that God is outside the mind or intellect.

5. The proposition

God is

is one affirmative proposition having only two parts by whose composition it signifies. But the subject signifies something outside the mind and so does the copula. Therefore, also, the proposition as a whole so signifies the significatum resulting from these significata. The inference is clear, as is the major. Proof of the minor: Otherwise, the mental proposition

God is

would be false, since it would signify that the subject is the copula.

6. It follows that you can make it to be that God is since you can make that mental proposition.

7. That God is, was before the production of the world. But there was no mental composition then. Therefore, etc.

8. The Divine Essence, which is a sort of proposition for the Divine Intellect, was a true proposition before the creation of the world. But there was no mental composition then, and the Divine Essence signified to the Divine Intellect that God is. Therefore, etc.

Replies to the arguments ⟨for the second opinion⟩:

⟨R1⟩ In reply to the first, I say that the authority of Aristotle is false,

sermonis. Verum debet intelligi ad istum sensum quod quaelibet propositio vocalis vel scripta de secundo adiacente subordinatur uni mentali
de tertio adiacente,[7] quia sola propositio de secundo adiacente non est
reperibilis in mente.

5   ⟨R2⟩ Ad secundam nego illam consequentiam:

> 'Necesse est esse' et 'impossibile est non esse' convertuntur.
>
> Igitur 'Necesse est nullam chimaeram esse' et 'Impossibile non est
> nullam chimaeram esse' convertuntur,

quia per idem sequeretur:

10   Igitur 'Necesse est te non esse' et 'Impossibile non est te non esse'
> convertuntur

—quod est falsum, quia prima est falsa et secunda vera. Sed bene sequitur:

> Igitur 'Necesse est te esse' et 'Impossibile est te non esse' convertun-
> tur.

15 Et ita sequitur in principali argumento:

> Igitur 'Necesse est chimaeram esse' et 'Impossibile est chimaeram
> non esse' convertuntur.

Et haec est intentio Philosophi. Verumtamen non sequitur:

> Necesse est nullam chimaeram esse.

20   Igitur aliquid vel aliqualiter est nullam chimaeram esse,

sicut inferius[8] ostendetur.

⟨R3⟩ Ad tertiam nego consequentiam, quia licet alicuius propositionis
significatum sit extra mentem, non tamen cuiuslibet. Nec tamen talium
significata sunt compositiones mentales. Nam si nihil nec aliqualiter esset,
25 non minus nullam chimaeram esse esset verum, sicut et Adam fuisse vel
Antichristum fore. Et tamen nullum istorum esset compositio mentalis.

Ex ista opinione pullularunt duae aliae opiniones falsae.

⟨*Opinio derivata*⟩

Prima[9] fuit quod significatum propositionis sit oratio infinitiva, sicut
30 Deum esse et hominem esse, et huiusmodi, quia Deum esse est significatum adaequatum illius

> Deus est.

Sed Deum esse est oratio infinitiva. Igitur, significatum adaequatum illius
est oratio infinitiva.

---

9 sequeretur] sequitur *E*   11 convertuntur *om. M*   22 propositionis] compositionis
M   27 opinione] falsa *add. M*   pullularunt] pullularent *M*

taken literally. But it ought to be understood in the following sense—that any spoken or written proposition of the second adjacent is subordinated to a mental proposition of the third adjacent. For a mere proposition of the second adjacent cannot be found in the mind.[b]

⟨R2⟩ In reply to the second, I deny the inference:

'It is necessary to be' and 'it is impossible not to be' are interchangeable.

Therefore, 'It is necessary that no chimera is' and 'It is not impossible that no chimera is' are interchangeable.

For by the same reasoning, it follows:

Therefore, 'It is necessary that you are not' and 'It is not impossible that you are not' are interchangeable,

which is false, since the first is false and the second is true. But rather it follows:

Therefore, 'It is necessary that you are' and 'It is impossible that you are not' are interchangeable.

Thus, it follows in the principal argument:

Therefore, 'It is necessary that a chimera is' and 'It is impossible that a chimera is not' are interchangeable.

This is the intention of the Philosopher. Nevertheless, this does not follow:

It is necessary that no chimera is.

Therefore, that no chimera is, is something or somehow,

as I will show below.

⟨R3⟩ In reply to the third, I deny the inference. Although the significatum of some proposition is outside the mind, nevertheless not the significatum of any proposition whatever. Nevertheless, the significata of those propositions ⟨whose significata are not outside the mind⟩ are not mental compositions. For if there were not anything and not anyhow, none the less that no chimera is, would be true, just as that Adam was, and that the Antichrist will be, would be true. Nevertheless, none of them would be a mental composition.

Two other false opinions arise from this one.

⟨*Derivative Opinion*⟩

The first was that the significatum of a proposition is a sentence-nominalization such as that God is, and that a man is, etc. For that God is, is the adequate significatum of the proposition

God is.

But that God is, is a sentence-nominalization. Therefore, the adequate significatum of that proposition is a sentence-nominalization.[c]

⟨*Argumenta contra opinionem derivatam*⟩

⟨1⟩ Contra istam opinionem arguitur sic: Nulla oratio infinitiva est **vera**
vel falsa. Igitur nullum significatum illius propositionis

Deus est

5 est verum vel falsum. Et per consequens, ipsa non est vera nec falsa—
quod negat haec opinio.

2° Ego scio Deum esse et me esse. Et non scio aliquam orationem in-
finitivam. Igitur etc.

3° Ante productionem mundi fuit Deum esse. Et tunc non fuit aliqua
10 oratio infinitiva. Igitur etc.

4° Sequitur quod ego possum facere Deum non esse et te esse asinum.
Immo quod ego possum facere duo contradictoria esse simul vera. Patet
consequentia ex quo huiusmodi non sunt nisi orationes infinitivae.

Ad rationem patet quod non procedit penes aliquam opinionem de
15 suppositione materiali vel simplici. Nam prima, ponens terminum posse
materialiter supponere absque limitatione praecedente,[10] negaret consequentiam propter mutationem suppositionis. Secunda[11] negaret (206rb M)
minorem—videlicet, quod Deum esse sit oratio infinitiva—sed bene ly
.Deum esse.

20 ⟨*Altera opinio derivata*⟩

Secunda opinio[12] surgens originaliter ex priori ponit quod significatum
propositionis est ipsamet propositio, ita quod idem est signum et significatum. Unde Deum esse, secundum istam viam, est illa propositio

Deus est,

25 quia omne verum est propositio. Sed Deum esse est verum. Igitur Deum
esse est propositio.

Et confirmatur, quia scire Deum esse non est nisi scire illam propositionem

Deus est,

30 et credere Deum esse est credere illam propositionem

Deus est.

⟨*Argumenta contra alteram opinionem derivatam*⟩

Contra istam opinionem procedunt duo argumenta ultima contra aliam
opinionem immediate praecedentem facta. Tamen arguitur sic:

35 ⟨1⟩ Ex illa opinione sequitur quod si nulla propositio foret, nihil foret,
quia si nulla propositio foret, non esset Deum esse, nec aliquid esse.

21 originaliter] quae originatur ex prima vel *E*   35 nihil] non *E*

⟨*Arguments against the Derivative Opinion*⟩

⟨1⟩ I argue against this opinion this way: No sentence-nominalization is true or false. Therefore, no significatum of the proposition

God is

is true or false. Consequently, that proposition is neither true nor false—which this opinion denies.

2. I know that God is and that I am. I do not know any sentence-nominalization. Therefore, etc.

3. That God is, was before the production of the world. There was no sentence-nominalization then. Therefore, etc.

4. It follows that I can make God not to be, and you to be a donkey. In fact, I can make two contradictories to be simultaneously true. The inference is clear, because things of this sort are only sentence-nominalizations.

In reply to the argument, it is clear that it does not proceed consistently with any opinion about material or simple *suppositio*. For the first, which posits that a term can supposit materially without any preceding limitation, would deny the inference because of a change of *suppositio*. The second would deny the minor—viz. that that God is, is a sentence-nominalization. But rather 'that God is' is a sentence-nominalization.[d]

⟨*Another Derivative Opinion*⟩

The second opinion that arises, taking its origin in the prior opinion, assumes that the significatum of a proposition is the proposition itself, so that the sign and the significatum are the same thing. Thus, according to this way, that God is, is the proposition

God is.

For everything true is a proposition. But that God is, is true. Therefore, that God is, is a proposition.

Confirming argument: To know that God is, is only to know the proposition

God is.

To believe that God is, is to believe the proposition

God is.

⟨*Arguments against this Derivative Opinion*⟩

The last two arguments made against the other, immediately preceding, opinion tell against this opinion. Nevertheless, I offer these arguments.

⟨1⟩ It follows from that opinion that if there were no proposition, there would be nothing. For if there were no propositions, it would not be that God is or that something is.

⟨2⟩ Item, isti non ponunt propositiones aliquas praeter propositiones creatas. Et tunc sequitur quod si nulla propositio foret, Deus non sciret aliquid esse, quia tunc Deus non sciret aliquam talem propositionem

Aliquid est.

5 Et satis possibile est quod nulla propositio creata sit, quia nec in voce, quia omnes homines possunt silere; nec in scripto, quia omnia scripta possunt comburi; nec in mente, quia possibile est omne animal dormire. Igitur etc.

Ad rationem nego quod omne verum est propositio (162ᵛᵇ E) quia
10 omne quod est ens est verum transcendenter. Et tamen non quodlibet quod est ens est propositio. Adhuc concessa illa maiori, negatur consequentia, si ly .verum. tenetur in maiori pro propositione vera, et in minori modaliter vel transcendenter.

Ad confirmationem nego quod scire Deum esse non est nisi scire talem
15 propositionem

Deus est.

Nam scire Deum esse est scire illam propositionem

Deus est,

et etiam aliud ab ea, quia suum significatum.

20   Et si proponitur:

Scire Deum esse est scire illam propositionem Deus est,

conceditur, quia aut significat assertive quod sciens Deum esse est sciens illam propositionem. Et hoc conceditur. Aut asserit quod scientia qua scitur Deum esse est scientia qua scitur ista propositio, et iterum concedo
25 eam; sicut concedo quod intelligere hominem est intelligere speciem hominis, quia intelligens hominem est intelligens speciem hominis, et intellectio qua intelligitur homo, est intellectio qua intelligitur species hominis. Utrum autem scientia qua scitur propositio et intellectio qua intelligitur species hominis distinguatur a quolibet tali quod scitur vel intelligitur, non
30 est praesentis negotii, sed magis ad metaphysicum vel librum *De Anima* pertinet. Quare etc.

⟨*Tertia Opinio*   *Capitulum Tertium*⟩

Tertia opinio, quae est communiter doctorum ordinis mei et praecipue Magistri Gregorii de Arimino,¹ ponit quod significatum propositionis est
35 aliqualiter esse et complexe significabile. Et cum quaeritur ab ipso utrum

---

1 praeter] propter *E*   25 sicut] ego *add. E*   34 Arimino] ordinis mei *add. M*

⟨2⟩ Again, ⟨adherents of this position⟩ do not suppose that there are any propositions besides created propositions. Then it follows that if there were no proposition, God would not know that something is, since then God would not know a proposition such as

Something is.

It is quite possible that no created proposition should exist: no spoken propositions, since all men can be silent; no written, since all writings can be burned; no mental, since it is possible that every animal should sleep. Therefore, etc.

In reply to the argument, I deny that everything true is a proposition. For everything that is a being is true, where 'true' is taken as a transcendental term. Nevertheless, it is not the case that any being whatever is a proposition. Even when the major has been granted, I deny the inference, if 'true' is taken for a true proposition in the major and as a modal or transcendental term in the minor.

In reply to the confirming argument, I deny that to know that God is, is only to know a proposition such as

God is.

To know that God is, is to know the proposition

God is

and also something else, since it is to know its significatum.

If someone proposes

To know that God is, is to know the proposition 'God is',

I grant it. For either it signifies assertorically that one who knows that God is, is one who knows the proposition—and I grant this. Or it asserts that the knowledge by which it is known that God is, is the knowledge by which the proposition is known—and again, I grant this. In the same way, I grant that to think of man is to think of the species of man. For one who thinks of man is one who thinks of the species of man; and the act of intellect by which man is thought of is the act of intellect by which the species of man is thought of. But whether the knowledge by which a proposition is known, and the act of intellect by which the species of man is thought of, are distinguished from any such that is known or thought of, does not pertain to the present business, but more to metaphysics or to ⟨Aristotle's⟩ book *On the Soul*. Thus, etc.[e]

⟨*The Third Opinion*   *Chapter Three*⟩

The third opinion, which is common among the doctors of my order and is chiefly the opinion of Master Gregory of Rimini, assumes that the significatum of a proposition is that things are in some way and is signifiable by a complex.[a] When it is asked whether what is thus signifiable is

tale significabile sit aliquid vel nihil, dicit ipse[2] quod hoc nomen 'aliquid'
et sibi synonyma 'res' et 'ens' possunt accipi tripliciter.

Uno modo communissime secundum quod omne significabile complexe
vel incomplexe, vere vel false, dicitur res et aliquid. Et isto modo dicit
5 quod Philosophus cepit illum terminum 'res' in *Praedicamentis*, capitulo
'De Priori',[3] cum ait, 'Dum res est vel non est, oratio vera aut falsa dicatur
necesse est.' Ibi enim capit illum terminum 'res' pro significato totali
propositionis, quod est complexe significabile secundum illam opinionem.

Secundo modo sumuntur pro omni significabili complexe vel etiam
10 incomplexe, sed vere, id est per veram enuntiationem. Quod autem false,
dicitur non ens. Et isto modo capit Philosophus, quinto *Metaphysicae*,
capitulo 'De Ente',[4] ubi dicit falsum esse non ens.

Tertio modo sumuntur dicta nomina ut significant aliquam essentiam
seu entitatem existentem. Et hoc modo quod non existit dicitur 'nihil',
15 iuxta illud Augustini, *Contra Epistulam Fundamenti*,[5] capitulo ultimo,
'Constat quod non est nihil esse.'

Dicit ergo haec opinio quod capiendo dictos terminos (206[va] M) primo
modo vel secundo modo, significatum propositionis est aliquid. Sed tertio
modo non est aliquid. Unde hominem esse animal non est aliquid, sed est
20 hominem esse substantiam animatam sensitivam rationalem. Nec hominem
esse risibilem est aliquid, sed est hominem posse ridere.

⟨*Argumenta contra tertiam opinionem*⟩

Contra istam opinionem arguitur.

⟨1.1⟩ Et primo contra distinctionem de ly .aliquid. arguitur. Et quaero
25 utrum ly .aliquid. primo vel secundo modo, sit terminus transcendens vel
non. Si sic, igitur immediate dividitur in substantiam et accidens vel saltim
in ens in actu et ens in potentia. Si ergo hominem esse est aliquid primo
vel secundo modo, igitur hominem esse est substantia vel accidens. Et
per consequens, hominem esse est aliquid tertio modo.

30 Si autem dicitur quod non est transcendens, et est terminus simplex,
vel igitur minus communis quam transcendens vel magis. Si minus, igitur
vel est in praedicamento, vel de ipso verificatur transcendens tertio modo.
Et sic adhuc sequitur quod si hominem esse est aliquid primo modo vel
secundo modo, quod est aliquid tertio modo. Si vero dicitur, sicut haberent

5 Praedicamentis] Praedicamento *M*, praesenti *E, correxi*   Praedicamentis . . .
Priori] Postpraedicamentis, capitulo De Oppositis *Gregorius de Arimino* (*iuxta ed. cit.*)
9 sumuntur] sumitur *M*   10 per veram enuntiationem] pro vera enuntiatione *M*
10–11 dicitur false *transp. E* (false tantum, dicitur *Gregorius de Arimino*, tantum false significatur, dicitur *Petrus de Aliaco*)   20 rationalem] rationabilem *M*   24 distinctionem]
illam *add. M*   arguitur] sic *add. E*   31 quam] terminus *add. E*   33–4 et . . .
modo[2] *om.* (*hom.?*) *E*

something or nothing, he says that this name 'something' and its synonyms 'thing' and 'being', can be taken in three ways.

In one way, it is taken most generally, in such a way that everything signifiable, whether by a complex or by a non-complex,[b] truly or falsely, is called a thing or something. He says that the Philosopher takes the term 'thing' in this way in the chapter 'On "Prior"' in the *Categories* ⟨14ᵇ21–2⟩, when he says 'It is necessary that an expression is called true or false when a thing is or is not.' For there ⟨the Philosopher⟩ takes the term 'thing' for the whole significatum of a proposition, which is signifiable by a complex, according to this opinion.

In the second way, these terms are taken for everything signifiable, by a complex or even by a non-complex, but truly—that is, by a true statement. But what is signifiable falsely is called non-being. And the Philosopher takes it in this way in *Metaphysics*, Book V, chapter 7 'On Being' ⟨1017ª31–2⟩, where he says that the false is non-being.

In the third way, the above-mentioned names are taken to signify an essence or an existing entity. In this way, what does not exist is called nothing. This accords with what Augustine says in the last chapter of *Against the Epistle of Manichaeus Called 'Fundamental'*, 'It is evident that it is not ⟨the case⟩ that nothing *is*.'

Therefore, this opinion says that when the above-mentioned terms are taken in the first or second way, the significatum of a proposition is something. But in the third way, it is not something. Thus, for a man to be an animal, is not something, but is for a man to be an animate, sensitive, rational substance. And for a man to be risible, is not something, but is for a man to be able to laugh.

Arguments aga inst the Third Opinion⟩

I argue against this opinion.

⟨1.1⟩ My first argument is against the distinction of the term 'something'. I ask whether or not 'something', taken in the first or second way, is a transcendental term. If so, then it is immediately divided into substance and accident, or at least into being in act and being in potency. Therefore, if that a man is, is something in the first or second way, then that a man is, is substance or accident. Consequently, that a man is, is something in the third way.

But if it is said that 'something' is not a transcendental, and that it is a simple term, then either it is less general than a transcendental term or more general. If less general, then either it is in a category, or the transcendental term taken in the third way is truly predicated of it. Thus, it still follows that if that a man is, is something in the first or second way, it is something in the third way. But if it is said, as they would have to say,

dicere, quod non est transcendens sed communior quam transcendens, sequitur quod est terminus ampliativus vel distrahens, ex quo est terminus simplex. Patet consequentia discurrendo in omnibus aliis, sicut 'possibile', 'imaginabile', 'intelligibile', et huiusmodi. Sed consequens est falsum, 5 quia tunc non valeret ista consequentia:

> Hominem esse est aliquid.
>
> Igitur hominem esse est,

cuius oppositum ipse teneret.

⟨1.2⟩ Secundo arguitur quod hominem esse animal non est hominem 10 esse substantiam animatam sensitivam rationalem. Sit enim primum A et secundum B. Et quaero utrum A et B sint idem vel diversa. Si idem, igitur sunt aliquid tertio modo. Si diversa, igitur A non (163ra E) est B. Si autem dicitur quod A et B nec sunt idem nec diversa, sequitur quod A est asinum esse animal et quodcumque aliud complexe significabile verum, 15 quia non videtur ratio quare A sit B et non asinum esse animal. Quare etc.

⟨2.1⟩ Iam contra opinionem arguitur sic: Hominem esse est substantia vel accidens. Igitur etc. Antecedens probatur: Omne quod est, est substantia vel accidens. Sed hominem esse est aliquid quod est. Igitur, hominem esse est substantia vel accidens. Consequentia est bona. Ante-20 cedens est Philosophi in *Praedicamentis*.[6] Et minor probatur: Nam hominem esse est aliquid, et illud est. Igitur hominem esse est aliquid quod est. Consequentia patet, quia relativum nominis convertitur in relativum pronominis sibi correspondens et notam copulationis ubi non fuerit impedimentum. Prima pars antecedentis conceditur ab eis. Et secunda similiter 25 debet concedi, quia aliter ly .aliquid. non posset esse antecedens alicuius relativi—quod non videtur verum.

Confirmatur: Omnia entia aut sunt in primis substantiis, aut de primis substantiis dicuntur. Sed huiusmodi complexe significabilia sunt aliqua. Igitur sunt in primis substantiis aut de primis substantiis dicuntur. Et per 30 consequens, sunt substantiae vel accidentia. Consequentia patet cum minori, sumendo ly .aliquid. tertio modo. Et maior est Aristotelis in *Praedicamentis*.[7]

⟨2.2⟩ Secundo arguitur sic: Istius propositionis

> Hominem esse est hominem esse

35 subiectum supponit determinate, cum sit indefinita. Igitur pro aliquo aut

---

10 animatam *om. M*   17–19 antecedens . . . accidens *om. (hom.)* E   23 notam] non E   25 antecedens] accidens M   27 entia] autem M   33 secundo] tertio E

that it is not a transcendental term, but is more general than a transcendental term, it follows that it is an ampliative or distracting[c] term, since it is a simple term. The inference is clear, if one reasons with respect to all the other terms such as 'possible', 'imaginable', 'intelligible', etc. But the conclusion is false, since ⟨if it were true⟩ this inference would not hold good:

That a man is, is something.
Therefore, that a man is, is

—which is the opposite of what he would hold.

⟨1.2⟩ Second, I argue that for a man to be an animal, is not for a man to be an animate, sensitive, rational substance. For let the first be A and the second B. I ask whether A and B are the same or different. If the same, then they are something in the third way. If different, then A is not B. But if it is said that A and B are neither the same nor different, it follows that A is that a donkey is an animal, and whatever else is true and signifiable by a complex. For there seems to be no reason why A should be B and not be that a donkey is an animal. Thus, etc.

⟨2.1⟩ Then, I argue this way against this opinion: That a man is, is substance or accident. Therefore, etc. Proof of the premiss: Everything that is, is substance or accident. But that a man is, is something that is. Therefore, that a man is, is substance or accident. The inference is good. The premiss is maintained by the Philosopher in the *Categories* ⟨c. 4 1^{b}25–7⟩. Proof of the minor: That a man is, is something, and the latter is. Therefore, that a man is, is something that is. The inference is clear, since, where there is no logical operator preventing it, a noun-relative is interchangeable with its corresponding pronoun-relative together with a sign of conjunction.[d] They grant the first part of the premiss. They ought similarly to grant the second, since otherwise 'something' could not be the antecedent of any relative pronoun—which seems untrue.

Confirming argument: All beings either are in first substances or are said of first substances. But ⟨significata⟩ of this sort, which are signifiable by a complex, are some things. Therefore, they are either in first substances or they are said of first substances. Consequently, they are either substances or accidents. The inference is clear, as is the minor, taking 'something' in the third way. The major is asserted by Aristotle in the *Categories* ⟨c. 1 2^{a}34–^{b}6⟩.

⟨2.2⟩ Second, I argue this way. The subject of the proposition

For a man to be, is for a man to be

has determinate *suppositio*, since the proposition is indefinite. Therefore,

pro aliquibus supponit, sumendo ly .aliquo. vel .aliquibus. tertio modo. Consequentia patet, quia si supponit determinate, contingit descendere ad omnia sua supposita. Sed quodlibet suppositum est aliquid tertio modo, et omnia supposita sunt aliqua tertio modo. Igitur, pro aliquo vel pro
5 aliquibus tertio modo supponit.

⟨2.3⟩ Tertio arguitur sic—et iam continue sumam terminum transcendentem tertio modo, propter brevitatem verborum: Si hominem esse non sit aliquid nec aliqua, sequitur quod Deus non potest facere hominem esse. Patet consequentia, quia si Deus faceret hominem esse, Deus esset causa
10 et hominem esse esset effectus divinus, et per consequens, esset aliquid. Consequens est (206vb M) falsum, quia

> Hominem esse incepit esse.
> Igitur Deus fecit hominem esse.

Consequentia bona. Et antecedens probatur, quia hominem esse nunc est.
15 Et hominem esse aliquando non fuit, quia non ante productionem mundi. Igitur hominem esse incipit vel incepit esse. Sed non incipit, ut patet. Igitur incepit.

Confirmatur: Sequitur quod Deus non potest facere Antichristum fore. Patet ut prius. Et consequens est falsum, quia si non potest facere Anti-
20 christum fore, igitur numquam determinavit Antichristum fore—quod est error.

⟨2.4⟩ Quarto,[8] sequitur ex ista opinione quod multa sunt aeterna quorum nullum est Deus. Consequens est error condemnatus Parisius,[9] ubi dicitur quod 'multa fuerint ab aeterno quae non sunt Deus. =Error'. Et con-
25 sequentia patet, quia secundum istam opinionem Deum esse et mundum fore fuerunt ab aeterno, quorum nullum est aliquid vel aliqua.

⟨2.5⟩ Quinto: ⟨a⟩ Essentia divina videt intuitive seipsam esse. Igitur visio illa unit potentiam cum obiecto. Sed non est unio sine terminis, nec terminus sine entitate. Igitur divinam essentiam esse est entitas aliqua.
30 ⟨b⟩ Item, visio illa intuitiva essentiae divinae vel terminatur intrinsece vel extrinsece. Non extrinsece, quia nullum extrinsecum causat visionem intuitivam in essentia divina. Sed intrinsece. Igitur ad se. Sed ista visio terminatur ad divinam essentiam esse. Igitur essentiam divinam esse est essentia divina, et per consequens, aliqua entitas existens.
35 ⟨c⟩ Item, sequeretur quod non semper intellectui divino primo obiceretur essentia divina. Consequens est contra theologicam veritatem. Et

---

3 omnia *om. M*   4 et . . . modo *om. M*   6 tertio] quarto *E*   14 nunc]
non *E*   22 quarto] quinto *E*   quod *om. E*   27 quinto] sexto *E*   esse *om. M*
31 non extrinsece *om. M*   visionem] unionem *M*   32 se] esse *M*   ista visio]
illa unio *M*   35 sequeretur] sequitur *E*   primo *om. E*

it supposits for something or some things, taking 'something' or 'some things' in the third way. The inference is clear. For if it has determinate *suppositio* it is possible to descend to all its supposita. But any suppositum whatever is something in the third way, and all supposita are some things in the third way. Therefore, it supposits for something or some things, taking 'something' or 'somethings' in the third way.

⟨2.3⟩ Third, I argue this way. (Now, in order to be brief, let me always take the transcendental term ⟨'something'⟩ in the third way.) If for a man to be, is not something or some things, it follows that God cannot make a man to be. The inference is clear. If God made a man to be, God would be the cause and *for a man to be* would be the divine effect. Consequently, it would be something. The conclusion is false, since

For a man to be, began to be.
Therefore, God made a man to be.

The inference holds good. Proof of the premiss: For a man to be, is now. But at some time, for a man to be, was not, since it was not before the production of the world. Therefore, for a man to be, begins to be or began to be. It is not beginning, as is clear. Therefore, it began.

Confirming argument: It follows that God cannot make the Antichrist to be in the future. This is clear, as before. The conclusion is false. For if He cannot make the Antichrist to be in the future, then He never decreed the Antichrist to be in the future—which is an error.

⟨2.4⟩ Fourth, it follows from this opinion that there are many eternal things none of which is God. This conclusion is an error condemned at Paris, where it is said to be an error to say that 'many things that are not God were from eternity'. The inference is clear. For according to this opinion, that God is, and that the world will be, were from eternity. But neither of them is something or things.

⟨2.5a⟩ Fifth, the Divine Essence intuitively sees that It is. Therefore, that vision unites the power with its object. But there is no union without termini ⟨of the union⟩, nor is there any terminus without an entity. Therefore, that the Divine Essence is, is some entity.

⟨b⟩ Again, this intuitive vision of the Divine Essence has either an intrinsic or an extrinsic terminus. Not an extrinsic terminus, since nothing extrinsic causes the intuitive vision in the Divine Essence. But an intrinsic terminus. Therefore, it is its own terminus. But that the Divine Essence is, is the terminus of this vision. Therefore, that the Divine Essence is, is the Divine Essence and consequently some existing entity.

⟨c⟩ Again, it would follow that the Divine Essence is not always the first object for the Divine Intellect. The conclusion is contrary to

consequentia patet, quia tali visioni, per opinionem, obicitur unum complexe significabile, quod non est essentia divina.

⟨2.6⟩ Sexto, sequitur quod si Deus est, infinita sunt quorum nullum est Deus. Patet, quia si Deus est, Deum esse est. Et si Deum esse est,
5 Deum esse esse est. Et sic in infinitum, multiplicando complexe significabilia. Consequens est dissonum veritati. Mirabile est enim quod non possit aliquid esse nisi infinita sint et infinities infinita.

⟨2.7⟩ Septimo, sequitur quod si tantum Deus est, non tantum Deus est. Immo, quod ante primum instans mundi tantum Deus fuit, quia tunc
10 Deus fuit, et tunc nihil aliud a Deo fuit, quia nullum horum complexe significabilium fuit aliquid. Tunc etiam fuit verum

Non tantum Deus est.
Nam sequitur:

Hoc est, et hoc non est Deus.
15   Igitur, non tantum Deus est,

⟨quia⟩ sic esse, sicut primo significatur per antecedens, ante primum instans mundi, fuit verum, quocumque complexe significabili aeterno demonstrato. Igitur, sic esse, sicut significatur per consequens, tunc fuit verum.

⟨2.8⟩ Octavo, si Deum esse non sit Deus, nec aliquid, nec aliqua, sequitur
20 quod inter illa non sit ordo nec dependentia. Et per consequens, utrumque illorum stat esse sine contradictione absque reliquo. Consequentia tenet discurrendo per omnia alia. Consequens est impossibile, quia non stat Deum esse et non esse Deum esse, nec e contra.

⟨2.9⟩ Nono, arguitur: Deum esse est. Igitur mensuratur aliqua mensura.
25 Consequentia patet, quia Deus (163rb E) mensuratur aliqua mensura, intelligentiae et aliae creaturae derivatae ab ipso Primo. Igitur, a pari, Deum esse. Sed non mensuratur mensura temporis, cum haec mensurat creaturas habentes inceptionem et desitionem. Nec mensura aevi, cum haec mensurat creaturas habentes initium et non desitionem. Igitur men-
30 sura aeternitatis. Et recte mensura aeternitatis, quia Deum esse est aeternum. Sed aeternitas non est mensura alicuius nisi essentiae divinae. Igitur Deum esse est essentia divina—quod est intentum.

⟨2.10⟩ Ultimo arguitur (207ra M) sic:[10] Haec positio concedit repugnantia imaginationi et rectae rationi. Igitur ipsa non est tolerabilis. Con-
35 sequentia patet. Et antecedens probatur: Nam haec positio habet concedere

3 sexto] septimo E   6 enim om. M   8 septimo] octavo E   17 significabili] significabit M   19 octavo] nono E   esse om. M   24 nono] decimo E   26 derivatae] determinatae E   27-9 haec ... haec] hoc ... hoc M   30 recte] recta M

theological truth. The inference is clear. For, according to this opinion, one ⟨significatum⟩ that is signifiable by a complex and that is not the Divine Essence, is an object for this vision.

⟨2.6⟩ Sixth, it follows that if God is, there is an infinite number of things, none of which is God. This is clear. For if God is, *that God is* is. And if *that God is* is, then that *that God is, is* is, and so on, multiplying ⟨significata⟩ that are signifiable by a complex to infinity. The consequent disagrees with the truth. For it is remarkable that something could be only if there were an infinity of things and infinity times infinity.

⟨2.7⟩ Seventh, it follows that if only God is, not only God is. In fact, it follows that before the first instant of the world, only God was. For God was then and nothing other than God was then, since then none of the ⟨significata⟩ that are signifiable by a complex was something. Even then,

Not only God is

was true. For this follows:

This is, and this is not God.
Therefore, not only God is.

Before the first instant of the world, it was true that things are so as the premiss primarily signifies (where anything eternal and signifiable by a complex is indicated). Therefore, it was true then that things are so as the conclusion signifies.

⟨2.8⟩ Eighth, if *that God is*, is not God, and not anything and not any things, it follows that there is no order or dependence between them. Consequently, it is consistent that each of them should exist without the other, without contradiction. The inference holds, ⟨as can be seen⟩ by applying the same reasoning to all the other examples. The conclusion is impossible, since it is not consistent that God is and *that God is* is not. Nor ⟨is it consistent that God is not and *that God is* is⟩.

⟨2.9⟩ Ninth, I argue this way: That God is, is. Therefore, that God is, is measured by some measure. The inference is clear, because God is measured by some measure. So are the intelligences and other creatures derived from the First Being Itself.*e* Therefore, by parity of reasoning, that God is, ⟨is measured⟩. But it is not measured by the measure of time, since this measures creatures that begin to be and cease to be. Nor by the measure of *aevum*, since this measures creatures that begin to be and do not cease to be. Therefore, it is measured by the measure of eternity, and rightly by the measure of eternity, since that God is, is eternal. But eternity is the measure of the Divine Essence alone. Therefore, that God is, is the Divine Essence—which is my intended conclusion.

⟨2.10⟩ Lastly, I argue this way. This position grants things inconsistent with the imagination and right reason. Therefore, it is unacceptable. The inference is clear. Proof of the premiss: This position has to grant that there

quod aliquid vel aliqualiter est, et illud vel taliter non est Deus nec
creatura; dependens nec independens; factivum nec factibile; corporeum
nec incorporeum; nec in mundo nec extra mundum; nec in praedicamento
nec extra praedicamentum; nec in anima nec extra animam; nec res nec
5　modus rei; nec positivum nec privativum; nec per se existens nec alteri
inhaerens; nec substantia nec accidens; nec actus nec potentia, nec compositum ex his; nec perfectum nec imperfectum; et tamen aeternum et
necesse esse. Quae imaginatio, iudicio meo, formata recta ratione non
potest admittere.

10　⟨3⟩ Ad illud igitur quod dicit haec opinio in principio, quod quodlibet
significabile complexe est res secundum Philosophum, nego. Et dico quod
propositio illa Philosophi est falsa de virtute sermonis. Tamen intellectus
Aristotelis fuit verus. Noluit enim dicere quod necessario, si aliquid est—
puta Sortes vel Plato—et aliqua propositio significat primo illud esse, illa
15　est vera. Et si idem non est, et illa propositio sic primo significat ut prius,
illa est falsa. Vocat igitur Aristoteles Sortem, Platonem et huiusmodi, res,
non tamen quodlibet significatum. Nihil enim nec aliqualiter apud Philosophum esset res, quod vel qualiter non esset ens positivum. Quare etc.

⟨*Quarta Opinio*　　　　　　　　　　　*Capitulum Quartum*⟩

20　Quarta opinio ponit aliquas conclusiones.[1]

　　⟨1⟩ *Prima* est ista, quod nihil est adaequatum significatum seu totale
　　alicuius propositionis mentalis proprie dictae.

Quia quaelibet talis ratione partium quibus aequivalet in significando,
significat plura ad invicem distincta, sicut patet cuilibet intuenti. Et per
25　consequens nihil est totale seu adaequatum significatum talis propositionis,
quia nihil est quodlibet significatum per eam.

　　2ᵃ conclusio: Quidquid significatur per aliquam propositionem men-
　　talem proprie dictam secundum eius totalem significationem,
　　etiam significatur per aliquam eius partem. Sed tamen bene ali-
30　　qualiter significatur per ipsam secundum eius totalem significa-
　　tionem, qualiter non significatur per aliquam eius partem.

Quia haec propositio

　　Homo est animal

aliqualiter—scilicet hominem esse animal—significat, qualiter non signi-
35　ficatur per aliquam eius partem.

---

2 nec²] vel *E*　　　13 verus] vocatus *add. M*　　　18 res *om. E*　　　34 significat
secundum eius totalem significationem *add. Petrus de Aliaco*

is something or things are in some way, and ⟨yet⟩ this, or this way, neither God nor creature is, neither what is dependent nor independent, neither what is capable of creating nor capable of being created, neither what is corporeal nor incorporeal, neither what is in the world nor outside the world, neither what is in a category nor outside a category, neither what is in the mind nor outside the mind, neither a thing nor a mode of a thing, neither something positive nor a privation, neither what exists *per se* nor what is inherent in another, neither substance nor accident, neither act nor potency, nor a composite of these, neither what is perfect nor imperfect, and nevertheless eternal and necessarily existent—which, in my judgement, no imagination formed by right reason can admit.

⟨3⟩ Therefore, when this opinion claims at the beginning, that, according to the Philosopher, whatever is signifiable by a complex is a thing, I deny it. I say that the Philosopher's postulate is false, when taken literally. Nevertheless, what Aristotle understood ⟨by it⟩ was true. For he did not wish to say that necessarily, if something is—say Socrates or Plato—and some proposition signifies primarily that it is, that proposition is true. ⟨Nor does he wish to say that⟩ if the same thing is not and, as before, the proposition then signifies primarily that it is, the proposition is false. Therefore, Aristotle calls Socrates and Plato, and so on, things, but he does not call any significatum whatever a thing. For, according to the Philosopher, there is not anything or any way a thing would be but that that thing, or that way ⟨of being⟩, would be a positive being. Thus, etc.

⟨*The Fourth Opinion*   *Chapter Four*⟩

The fourth opinion assumes some theses.

> *Thesis 1*: Nothing is the whole or adequate significatum of a mental
>   proposition properly so called.

Any such proposition, by virtue of the parts to which it is equivalent in signifying, signifies many things distinct from one another, as is intuitively clear. Consequently, nothing is the whole or adequate significatum of such a proposition, since nothing is whatever is signified by it.[a]

> *Thesis 2*: Whatever is signified by a mental proposition properly so
>   called, according to its whole signification, is also signified by one
>   of its parts. But, nevertheless, a proposition may signify according
>   to its whole signification, in some way in which none of its parts
>   signifies.

For the proposition

> A man is an animal

signifies in some way in which none of its parts does—viz. ⟨it signifies⟩ that a man is an animal.

3ª conclusio: Nullius propositionis mentalis proprie dictum sibi correspondens, sive oratio infinitivi modi sumpta significative, supponit pro aliqua re.

Verbi gratia, hoc dictum, seu haec oratio infinitivi modi,

5   Hominem esse animal,

quae correspondet huic propositioni

Homo est animal,

licet quando sumitur materialiter supponat pro aliqua re—scilicet pro illa propositione cui correspondet—tamen quando sumitur significative seu
10 personaliter, dicit quod non supponit pro aliqua re. Patet, quia cum talis oratio sic sumpta significet plura—scilicet omnia quae significat propositio sibi correspondens—non esset ratio quare magis supponeret pro uno suorum significatorum quam pro alio. Igitur vel pro quolibet vel pro nullo. Sed nullus diceret pro quolibet, quia sic illa oratio

15   Hominem esse animal

supponeret pro asino. Igitur, pro nullo. Et sicut dicit de ista, ita et de qualibet alia.

Ex his infert haec opinio quod Deum esse non est Deus, et hominem esse non est homo, quia pari ratione omnem hominem esse animal esset
20 homo—quod falsum est, quia de nullo homine verum est dicere quod est omnem hominem esse animal. Item etiam pari ratione hominem esse asinum esset homo—quod est falsum, quia non apparet ratio quare plus homo quam asinus. Etiam chimaeram non esse chimaeram esset aliquid— quod est falsum, quia non potest dici quid est nisi forte dicatur quod est
25 Deus. Et pari ratione quidquid est in mundo est chimaeram non esse chimaeram—quod est multum dissonum.

Si ergo quaeritur, quid est omnem hominem esse animal, aut hominem esse animal, apud istam opinionem quaestio est incongrua et ridiculosa, sicut si quaeratur (207ʳᵇ M) quid est omnem hominem. Et si arguatur sic:

30   Illa propositio
            Omnis homo est animal
        significat omnem hominem esse animal.

Igitur, omnem hominem esse animal significatur per eam,

dicit quod non est bona consequentia, (163ᵛᵃ E) quia antecedens est
35 congruum, consequens vero incongruum. Ad cuius declarationem ponit istam regulam quod

2 sive] puta *E*   11 scilicet] quia *E* (scilicet *Petrus de Aliaco*)   14 sic *om. E*
15 animal] significaret asinum vel *add. E*   24 quid] quod *E*   26 dissonum]
derisorium *Petrus de Aliaco*

Thesis 3: No dictum, or sentence-nominalization, taken as significant, corresponding to a mental proposition properly so called, supposits for some thing.

For example, ⟨take⟩ this dictum, or sentence-nominalization:

for a man to be an animal,

which corresponds to the proposition

A man is an animal.

Although when it is taken materially, it supposits for some thing—viz. for the proposition to which it corresponds—nevertheless, when it is taken as significant or personally, ⟨this opinion⟩ says, it does not supposit for any thing. This is clear, since such an expression, so taken, signifies many—viz. all the things that the proposition corresponding to it signifies. There would be no more reason why it should supposit for one of its significata than for another. Therefore, it supposits for any whatever or for none. But no one would say that it supposits for any whatever, since then the expression

for a man to be an animal

would supposit for a donkey. Therefore, it supposits for none.[b] What ⟨this opinion⟩ says about this proposition, it would say about any other.

From these theses, this opinion infers that for God to be, is not God; and for a man to be, is not a man. For, by parity of reasoning, for every man to be an animal, would be a man—which is false, since of no man is it true to say that he is *for every man to be an animal.* Again, also, by parity of reasoning, for a man to be a donkey, would be a man—which is false, since there appears to be no more reason why it would be a man than a donkey. Also, for a chimera not to be a chimera would be something—which is false, since one cannot say what it is, unless perhaps one says that it is God. By parity of reasoning, anything in the world is *for a chimera not to be a chimera*—which is quite unheard of.

Therefore, suppose one asks, what *for every man to be an animal* or *for a man to be an animal* is. According to this opinion, the question is ill-formed and ridiculous, as would be the question, what for every man is? ⟨Suppose⟩ one argues this way:

The proposition

Every man is an animal

signifies every man to be an animal.

Therefore, for every man to be an animal, is signified by it.

⟨This opinion⟩ says that the inference does not hold good, because the premiss is well-formed, while the conclusion is ill-formed. To explain this, he lays down the following rule.

Quaelibet oratio in qua ponitur a parte subiecti, sicut totale subiectum, verbum infinitivi modi [cum accusativo], supponens significative seu personaliter, et acceptum verbaliter, est incongrua.
Sicut ista

5   Sedere est.

Patet, quia verbum significative sumptum non potest reddere suppositum
verbo. Ideo haec est incongrua

Sedeo est,

et pari ratione

10   Sedere est.

Dicit autem notanter 'verbum . . . acceptum personaliter et verbaliter',
quia quandoque verbum infinitivi modi accipitur significative nominaliter,
seu loco unius nominis verbalis, et tunc est nomen. Sicut in ista

Sedere est quiescere,

15 quae tantum valet sicut ista

Sedens est quiescens.

Ulterius dicit haec opinio quod istae sunt congruae:

Volo Sortem currere,

Scio hominem esse animal,

20   Haec oratio significat Deum esse,

Volo currere,

Scio arguere,

et sic de aliis.

⟨*Conclusiones contra quartam opinionem*⟩

25   Contra istam opinionem pono aliquas conclusiones.

⟨1⟩ *Prima* est ista: Aliqua est propositio vera mentalis proprie dicta,
quae ratione suarum partium non significat plura realiter condi-
stincta.

Patet de hac propositione et qualibet simili

30   Hoc est hoc—eodem demonstrato.

Subiectum enim et praedicatum significant idem simpliciter.

2ᵃ *conclusio*: Licet propositio aliqua distincta significet ratione suarum
partium, non tamen ipsius significatum absolvitur ab alicuius veri-
ficatione.

---

1 oratio] propositio *E*   sicut *om. M*   2 cum accusativo *om. hic et habet in sequenti*
secunda regula quam ponit, Petrus de Aliaco   7 verbo] verbum *M*   11 verbum]
autem add. M   12 quandoque] quando *E*   15 quae] mihi *add. E*   21 volo
currere] nolo, curo *E*   22 arguere] arguo *E*   32 licet] enim *add. E*

⟨*Rule*:⟩ Any proposition in which there is, placed in the subject position as the whole subject, a verb that (i) is in the infinitive mood, and (ii) supposits significantly or personally, and (iii) is taken as a verb, is ill-formed.

For example, the proposition

To sit, is.

This is clear, since a verb taken as significant cannot function as the subject of a verb.ᶜ Therefore, the proposition

I sit, is

is ill-formed, and by parity of reasoning, so is

To sit, is.

Note that he says, 'a verb . . . that is taken personally and as a verb'. For sometimes a verb in the infinitive mood is taken as significant and nominally or in place of a verbal noun, and then it is a noun—for example, in the proposition

To sit, is to rest,

which has the same force as the proposition

One who sits, is one who rests.

Further, this opinion says that the following expressions are well-formed:

I want Socrates to run,
I know a man to be an animal,
This expression signifies God to exist,
I want to run,
I know how to argue,

and so on.

⟨*Theses against the Fourth Opinion*⟩

I assume some theses against this opinion.

⟨*Counter-*⟩*Thesis 1*: There is a true mental proposition properly so called, that does not, by reason of its parts, signify many things really distinct from one another.

This is clear from the proposition

This is this

(where the same thing is indicated ⟨by each 'this'⟩) and other similar propositions. For the subject and the predicate signify absolutely the same thing.

⟨*Counter-*⟩*Thesis 2*: Even if a proposition were to signify distinct things by reason of its parts, nevertheless its significatum depends on what some part is true of.

Patet de ista

Sortes est videns asinum,

quae significat Sortem et asinum, et tamen Sortem videre asinum est Sortes, sicut superius[2] probabatur.

5   *3ᵃ conclusio*: Alicuius propositionis mentalis significatum est aliquid.

Probatur: Nam secundum istam opinionem, essentia divina est sibi propositio significans seipsam esse. Aut igitur significatum illius est aliquid vel nihil. Si aliquid, habeo intentum. Si nihil, contra, divinam essentiam esse est aliquid. Patet, quia illa propositio quae est essentia divina est 10 aliquid. Igitur divinam essentiam esse est aliquid. Consequentia patet, secundum opinionem, quia oratio infinitiva non incongrue ponitur quando materialiter pro propositione supponit.

2° Ista propositio in mente

Hoc est falsum—seipsa demonstrata—

15 significat quod est aliquid. Igitur etc. Antecedens probatur: Nam ipsa significat hoc esse falsum. Et hoc esse falsum est aliquid, quia haec propositio

Hoc est falsum

est aliquid, secundum istam opinionem. Igitur, hoc esse falsum est aliquid. 20 Patet consequentia sustinendo eandem positionem.

3° Significatum huius adaequatum

Tu es tu

est, quia cuiuslibet partis significatum est. Igitur et totius significatum est. Sed non est aliqua, ut patet. Igitur est aliquid. Patet consequentia secun- 25 dum istam opinionem, quia negat huiusmodi complexe significabilia. Et antecedens similiter, eo quod tu non es aliqua, saltim totalia, sicut debet intelligi illud antecedens.

4ᵃ conclusio: Alicuius propositionis mentalis proprie dictum sibi correspondens, sive oratio infinitivi modi sumpta significative, 30   supponit pro aliqua re.

Probatur: Et capio istam mentalem in creatura

Deus est,

et quaero si habet significatum adaequatum sibi. Non est dicendum quod non habet significatum adaequatum, quia ipsa est signum. Igitur alicuius

---

4 superius probabatur] *pro* inferius probabitur? (*cf. infra p. 212 n. 2*)   8 contra *om. M*   11 infinitiva] infinitive *M*   19 esse] est *ME, correxi*   20 positio- nem] suppositionem *M*   32 est] Deus *add. M*   34 signum] significatum *E*

This is clear from the proposition

Socrates is a beholder of a donkey,

which signifies Socrates and a donkey. Nevertheless, for Socrates to behold a donkey is Socrates, as was proved above.[d]

⟨Counter-⟩Thesis 3: The significatum of some mental proposition is something.

Proof: According to this opinion, the Divine Essence is a proposition which signifies Itself to be, to Itself. Therefore, either the significatum of this proposition is something or it is nothing. If it is something, I have my intended conclusion. But suppose it is nothing: on the contrary, for the Divine Essence to be, is something. This is clear ⟨as follows⟩: The proposition that is the Divine Essence is something; therefore, for the Divine Essence to be, is something. The inference is clear, according to this opinion. For ⟨an expression⟩ is not ill-formed when the infinitive expression in it supposits materially for a proposition.

2. The mental proposition

This is false

(where 'this' indicates the proposition itself) signifies what is something. Therefore, etc. Proof of the premiss: The proposition signifies this to be false. For this to be false, is something. For, according to this opinion, the proposition

This is false

is something. Therefore, for this ⟨to be⟩ false, is something. The inference is clear, according to the same position.

3. The adequate significatum of the proposition

You are you

is, since the significatum of any of its parts is. Therefore, the significatum of the whole is, too. But it is not some things, as is clear. Therefore, it is something. The inference is clear, according to this opinion, since it denies ⟨significata⟩ of the sort that are signifiable by a complex.[e] Similarly, the premiss, too, since you are not some things—at least not some whole things—which is the way the premiss ought to be understood.

⟨Counter-⟩Thesis 4: There is some mental proposition properly so-called, whose corresponding dictum or sentence-nominalization, taken as significant, supposits for something.

Proof: I take the proposition

God is

in the mind of a creature and ask if it has a significatum adequate to it. One ought not to say that it does not have an adequate significatum, since it is

significati adaequati signum. Igitur ipsa habet adaequatum significatum.

Similiter, quaelibet pars eius habet significatum adaequatum. Et ipsa non significat nisi ex compositione suarum partium. Igitur ipsa similiter 5 habet significatum adaequatum.

Si ergo habet significatum adaequatum, quaero quid est significatum adaequatum illius. Et sequitur quod Deum esse est significatum adaequatum illius. Quaero tunc utrum illa oratio infinitiva sumatur significative vel materialiter. Non (207ᵛᵃ M) materialiter, quia tunc significaret quod 10 haec propositio

Deus est

esset significatum adaequatum sui ipsius—quod est falsum. Si autem significative, habetur intentum.

5ᵃ conclusio: Oratio infinitiva verbaliter et significative subiciens
15   propositioni cuius est pars incongruitatem non tribuit seu ridiculum.

Probatur: Nam oratio aliqua indicativa verbaliter et significative subiciens propositioni cuius est pars incongruitatem non reddit. Igitur nec oratio infinitiva sic sumpta. Consequentia patet, quia non potest assignari ratio diversitatis. Et antecedens est manifestum de qualibet tali

20   Quod currit movetur,

ubi subiectum est ly .quod currit. Et est oratio indicativa, cum ibi sit verbum indicativi modi. Et supponit personaliter verbaliter, quia ly .currit. non potest in praedicta propositione sumi nominaliter. Igitur etc.

2° Ista oratio

25   Hominem esse

est oratio infinitiva, quae verbaliter sumpta significat non quiescenter significatum distinctum a se et quocumque suo consimili. Igitur sic sumpta pro eodem potest in propositione supponere. Consequentia patet discurrendo in omnibus aliis, etc.

30   3° Arguitur sic: Et praesuppono quod ex omni propositione sequitur una propositio in qua (163ᵛᵇ E) ly .verum. praedicatur de suo dicto. Hoc communiter conceditur. Deinde suppono quod ex suppositione personali

a sign. Therefore, it is the sign of some adequate significatum. Therefore, it has an adequate significatum.

Similarly, each of its parts has an adequate significatum. It signifies only by the composition of its parts. Therefore, similarly, it has an adequate significatum.

Therefore, if it has an adequate significatum, I ask what its adequate significatum is. It follows that for God to be, is its adequate significatum. Then I ask whether the infinitive expression is taken as significant or materially. Not materially, since then it would signify that the proposition

God is

was the adequate significatum of itself—which is false. But if it is taken as significant, I have my intended conclusion.

⟨*Counter*-⟩*Thesis* 5: If an infinitive expression is made the subject of the proposition of which it is a part—where its verb is taken as a verb and the expression is taken as significant—this does not render that proposition ill-formed and ridiculous.

Proof: If an expression in the indicative mood is made the subject of the proposition of which it is a part—where its verb is taken as a verb and the expression is taken as significant—this does not render the expression ill-formed. Therefore, neither ⟨does making⟩ an infinitive expression so taken, ⟨the subject of the proposition of which it is a part⟩. The inference is clear, since there seems to be no reason to distinguish ⟨between infinitive and indicative expressions in this respect⟩. The premiss is obvious with respect to any proposition such as

What runs, moves,

where the subject is 'what runs'. It is an indicative expression, since it contains a verb in the indicative mood. It has personal *suppositio* taken as a verb, since 'runs' cannot be taken as a noun in the above proposition.ᶠ Therefore, etc.

2. The expression

for a man to be

is an infinitive expression that—when its verb is taken as a verb—signifies non-quiescentlyᵍ a significatum distinct from itself and from others equiformʰ with it. Therefore, so taken, it can supposit for the same thing in a proposition. The inference is clear, when one applies the same reasoning to all other examples.

3. I argue this way. I presuppose that from every proposition there follows a proposition in which 'true' is predicated of its dictum. This is commonly granted. Then I suppose that ⟨a proposition in which a term⟩ has material *suppositio* does not follow from ⟨a similar proposition in which⟩

non sequitur suppositio materialis respectu eiusdem. Hoc etiam communiter conceditur respectu eiusdem, et leviter probaretur. Tunc facio istam consequentiam:

Deus est.

5   Igitur Deum esse est verum.

Consequentia patet per primam suppositionem. Et in antecedente ly .Deus. non supponit materialiter. Igitur nec in consequente. Nec per idem ly .esse. Igitur, nec tota oratio infinitiva. Patet consequentia, cum non significet nisi ex compositione suarum partium. Si enim supponeret

10   materialiter et partes significative, non significaret ex compositione partium.

4° Arguitur, probando istam consequentiam:

A significat hominem esse.

Igitur hominem esse significatur ab *A*.

15   Nam sequitur:

A significat hominem esse.

Igitur hominem esse *A* significat.

Igitur hominem esse significatur ab *A*.

Ultima consequentia tenet, ab activa ad suam passivam. Et prima probatur:

20   Nam bene sequitur:

A significat hominem.

Igitur hominem *A* significat.

Igitur per idem et alia est bona. Consequentia est bona, quia sicut illud verbum 'significat' potest incomplexum ante se determinare, quod requiri-

25   tur a parte post, ita et complexum.

Dico igitur quod oratio infinitiva verbaliter sumpta et significative non reddit incongruam orationem, immo congruam, sicut oratio composita ex adiectivo et substantivo. Unde dicendo

Deum esse est verum,

30   ly .Deum esse. est oratio infinitiva, quia ly .esse. est verbum infinitivi modi verbaliter tentum. Aliter non videtur quare non congrue diceretur

Deus esse est verum,

sicut

Deum esse est verum.

35   Est ergo ly .Deum. accusativi casus et ly .esse. verbum ex quibus fit

---

1 respectu eiusdem *om. E*   2 leviter probaretur] sequitur probabiliter et *E*
12 arguitur probando] arguo *E*   14 ab *A* significatur *transp. E*   15–17 Nam . . .
significat *om. E*

the same term has personal *suppositio*. This is commonly granted, too, and is easily proved. Then I infer

God is.
Therefore, for God to be, is true.

The inference is clear by the first assumption. In the premiss, 'God' does not have material *suppositio*. Therefore, it does not have material *suppositio* in the conclusion. By the same reasoning, the term 'to be' does not have material *suppositio* either. Therefore, neither does the whole infinitive expression. The inference is clear, since ⟨the infinitive expression⟩ signifies only by the composition of its parts. If it did supposit materially and its parts significantly, it would not signify by the composition of its parts.

4. I argue by proving this inference:

A signifies a man to be.
Therefore, a man to be, is signified by *A*.

For this follows:

A signifies a man to be.
Therefore, a man to be, *A* signifies.
Therefore, a man to be is signified by *A*.

The last inference, from an active to its passive, holds. Proof of the first inference: This follows:

A signifies a man.
Therefore, a man *A* signifies.

Therefore, by the same reasoning, the other inference is good, too. The inference is good. For just as the verb 'signifies' can determine a non-complex that normally occurs after it ⟨in the proposition⟩, when it occurs before it; so also it can govern a complex that occurs before it.

Therefore, I say that an infinitive expression—where its verb is taken as a verb and the expression is taken as significant—does not render an expression ill-formed, but well-formed; just as an expression composed of an adjective and a substantive is well-formed. Thus when one says

For Him[i] to be, is true,

'for Him to be' is the infinitive expression, since 'to be' is a verb in the infinitive mood taken as a verb. Otherwise, there seems to be no reason why

For He to be, is true

would not be a well-formed statement, just as

For Him to be, is true

is. Therefore, it is 'Him' in the accusative case and the verb 'to be', from

oratio infinitiva. Et quia illud verbum 'est' debet habere suppositum per nominativum, ideo illa oratio tota est nominativi casus.

Et cum dicitur ab opinione ista quod pari ratione posset supponere ly .sedeo. in ista

5   Sedeo est

personaliter, sicut ly .sedere. in ista

Sedere est,

sumendo verbaliter utrumque; dico quod non est similitudo, quia ly .sedeo. potest esse propositio, sed non ly .sedere. Sicut enim ly .homo est
10 albus. non potest subici personaliter et tamen bene potest subici ly .homo albus., ita in proposito ly .sedere. et non ly. sedeo.

Si ergo quaeratur, quid est chimaeram non esse chimaeram, non debet ridiculum causari loco responsionis, nec quaerentem repellere, sed debet dici quod chimaeram non esse chimaeram non est aliquid, nec aliqua, nec
15 aliqualiter. Similiter, hominem esse asinum non est aliquid, nec aliqua, nec aliqualiter, cum sit impossibile. Sed cum quaeritur, quid est omnem hominem esse animal, dicatur quod nihil est, sed est aliqua. Est enim omnes homines actu existentes. Et talis oratio pro multis supponit, quia pro Sorte, pro Platone et huiusmodi.

20 ⟨*Aliae conclusiones et dicta magistri quartae opinionis*⟩

Adhuc pro maiori declaratione huius opinionis notandae sunt tres conclusiones quas ipse ponit.

⟨1⟩ *Prima* est quod praeter omnem propositionem creatam est aliquod verum seu aliqua veritas extra animam.

25 Patet, quia (207vb M) Deus est veritas et notitia vera.

2ª conclusio est quod praeter omnem propositionem creatam vel increatam, nullum est verum seu nulla est veritas extra animam.

Quia sicut veritas creata est ipsa propositio creata quam formamus, sic veritas increata, quae est Deus, est propositio increata.

30   *3ª conclusio*, quod Deus sive notitia divina est ipsi intellectui divino propositio vera.

Patet, quia significat intellectui divino quiescenter quod Antichristus erit, aut quod ipse est.

⟨*Primum Dictum*⟩ Item, dicit haec opinio quod antequam aliquid esset
35 praeter Deum, verum erat mundum fore, si haec oratio 'mundum fore'

1–2 per nominativum] nominativi casus *E*   3 quod *om. M*   posset] possit *M*
16 omnem *om. M*   30 divino *om. E*   35 verum *om. M*   si]sed *ME, correxi*
(si *in ms.,* sed *in edd. Petrus de Aliaco*)

which the infinitive expression is made. And since the verb 'is' ought to have a suppositum through the nominative case, then the expression as a whole is of the nominative case.

When this opinion says that by parity of reasoning, 'I sit' could have personal *suppositio* in

I sit, is,

just as 'to sit' does in the proposition

To sit, is

—where each is taken as a verb—I say that the examples are not similar. For 'I sit' can be a proposition ⟨on its own⟩, but 'to sit' cannot. For just as 'A man is white' cannot be a subject that has personal *suppositio* but 'white man' can be a subject that has personal *suppositio*; so in the proposed case 'to sit' can be, but 'I sit' cannot be.

Therefore, if someone should ask what is for a chimera not to be a chimera, ⟨the question⟩ ought not to evoke ridicule instead of a reply. Nor should one try to put the questioner off. But one should say that for a chimera not to be a chimera, is not anything or any things, or anyhow. Similarly, for a man to be a donkey, is not anything, any things, or anyhow, since it is impossible. But when one asks what is for every man to be an animal, one should say that it is nothing, but is some things. For it is all actually existing men. Such an expression supposits for many, since it supposits for Socrates and for Plato, etc.

⟨Other Theses and Claims of the Master of the Fourth Opinion⟩

Still, for more explanation of this opinion, one ought to take note of the following three theses which ⟨the Master who holds this opinion⟩ assumes.

> *Thesis 1*: In addition to every created proposition, there is something true or some truth outside the mind.

This is clear, since God is truth and true cognition.

> *Thesis 2*: In addition to every created or uncreated proposition, there is nothing true or no truth outside the mind.

For just as created truth is the created proposition itself, which we form; so uncreated truth, which is God, is the uncreated proposition.

> *Thesis 3*: God or the Divine Cognition is a true proposition for the Divine Intellect itself.

This is clear, since it quiescently signifies that the Antichrist will be, or that It Itself is, to the Divine Intellect.

⟨*First Claim*:⟩ Again, this opinion says that before there was anything besides God, that the world will be, was true, if the expression 'that the

capiatur materialiter, non pro se ipsa, sed pro propositione cuius est dictum, et illud verum seu illa propositio vera erat Deus. Et si arguitur:

Illud verum erat contingens, et Deus erat necessarium . . .

dicit quod illud verum erat ens necessarium sicut Deus, sed tamen illud
5 verum erat contingenter verum. Sicut scientia Dei quod Antichristus erit est ens necessarium, et tamen est contingenter scientia quod Antichristus erit.

⟨2*um* Dictum⟩ ⟨a⟩ Item, concedit illam condicionalem

Si nulla propositio esset, adhuc verum esset nullam propositionem
10   esse,

quia antecedens est impossibile. Sicut enim, inquit, impossibile est Deum non esse notitiam, ita impossibile est Deum non esse propositionem veram.

⟨b⟩ Si tamen nulla propositio creata esset, verum esset nullam talem esse, et illud verum esset Deus.

15 ⟨3*um* Dictum⟩ Item concedit illa opinio quod ab aeterno fuit propositio vera, cui non correspondebat propositio falsa. Quia ab aeterno fuit Deus propositio vera et sibi ab aeterno non correspondebat aliquod falsum, quia nec falsum quod fuit deitas, nec aliquod aliud positiva entitas.

⟨*Responsio ad conclusiones et dicta*⟩

20   Quia horum dictorum aliqua sunt vera, sicut prima et tertia conclusio et tertium dictum cum prima parte secundi, ⟨1⟩ ideo contra conclusionem secundam arguo sic:

Aliqua est entitas quae non est Deus nec aliqua propositio creata.
Igitur aliqua est veritas quae non est aliquod istorum.

25 Consequentia patet, ex eo quod 'entitas' et 'veritas' convertuntur sicut 'ens' et 'verum'.

2° sic: Obiectum huius propositionis mentalis in creatura

Homo est animal

est aliquod verum vel aliqua veritas. Et non veritas increata, (164ra E)
30 quia tunc a pari illa esset obiectum cuiuscumque propositionis verae, necessariae vel contingentis—quod est falsum. Similiter stat quod per illam quis assentiat vel dissentiat non habendo aliquem conceptum divinum. Igitur etc. Nec etiam veritas creata, quae est ipsamet propositio, est quodlibet obiectum illius, quia tunc non staret te intelligere hominem
35 esse animal et percipere te intelligere quando ⟨non⟩ perciperes te intelligere

---

1-2 cuius est dictum *om. Petrus de Aliaco*   15-18 item . . . entitas *om. E*   22
arguo] arguitur *E*   23 creata] increata *ME, correxi* (*cf. supra p. 116, lin. 26*)
25 convertuntur] distinguuntur *M*   31 quod² *om. M*   33 veritas *om. E*   ipsa-
met] ipsa videlicet *E*   34 est] ita *E*

world will be' is taken materially, not for itself, but for the proposition whose dictum it is; and that that truth or that true proposition was God. And if one argues,

That truth was contingent, and God was necessary . . .

this opinion says that that truth was a necessary being, just as God is. Nevertheless, that truth was contingently a truth. In the same way, God's knowledge that the Antichrist will be, is a necessary being, and nevertheless it is contingently knowledge that the Antichrist will be.

⟨Second Claim:⟩ ⟨a⟩ Again, this opinion grants the conditional

If there were no proposition, still that no proposition is, would be true,

since the antecedent is impossible. For this opinion says, just as it is impossible for God not to be a cognition, so it is impossible for God not to be a true proposition.

⟨b⟩ Nevertheless, if there were no created proposition, it would be true that no such proposition is, and that truth would be God.

⟨Third Claim:⟩ Again, this opinion grants that from eternity there was a true proposition to which no false proposition corresponded. For from eternity, God was a true proposition. And nothing false corresponded to Him from eternity, since there was nothing false which was the Deity, and there was no other positive entity.

⟨Replies to the Theses and Claims⟩

Some of these claims are true—e.g. Theses 1 and 3, and the third claim together with the first part of the second. ⟨1⟩ Therefore, I argue against Thesis 2 this way:

There is some entity which is not God and not a created proposition.
Therefore, there is some truth which is not one of these.

The inference is clear, because 'entity' and 'truth' are interchangeable, just as 'being' and 'true' are.

2. I argue this way: The object of the created mental proposition

A man is an animal

is something true or some truth. It is not the uncreated truth. For if it were, by parity of reasoning, the uncreated truth would be the object of any true proposition whatever, whether necessary or contingent—which is false. Similarly, it would be consistent that through the uncreated truth someone would assent or dissent without having any divine concept. Therefore, etc. Nor is the created truth, which is the proposition itself, the object of that proposition. For then it would not be consistent that you think that a man is an animal, and perceive yourself to think of it, when you do not perceive yourself to think of such a sign—which is false and

tale signum—quod est falsum et contra experientiam. Igitur oportet dicere quod aliquod obiectum illius est veritas distincta tam a Deo quam a propositione creata.

3° sic: Ego scio aliqualiter esse scientia proprie dicta a priori et demon-
5 strative. Igitur illa scientia est propositionis increatae aut propositionis creatae solum aut alterius sciti quod non est aliqua propositio. Non potest dici primum, eo quod propositio increata, quae Deus est, non scitur a viatore aliquo istorum modorum. Nec potest dici secundum, quia scientia proprie dicta est de incorruptibilibus et impossibilibus aliter se habere,
10 primo *Posteriorum*.³ Sed quaelibet talis propositio est corruptibilis et possibilis aliter se habere. Igitur etc. Oportet igitur dari tertium, et habetur intentum.

⟨*Contra secundam partem secundi dicti*⟩

Similiter aliud dictum est falsum—videlicet quod si nulla propositio
15 creata esset, nullam propositionem creatam esse esset Deus—quia a pari Deus esset nullam chimaeram esse. Consequens est falsum, quia nulla negatio sicut nec aliqua privatio est verificabilis identice de Deo. Patet. Nam nihil est identice Deus nisi illud proprio conceptu concipiatur ab intellectu divino. Sed intellectus divinus non intelligit istas negationes nec
20 privationes in propriis rationibus idealibus, sicut nec falsitates et impossi- bilitates. Igitur etc.

2° Nulla negatio est communicabilis alicui nisi sua positiva oppositio sit etiam communicabilis, quia magis videtur de affirmatione quam de negatione. Sed chimaeram esse non est communicabile alicui. Igitur nec
25 nullam chimaeram esse.

(208ᵃ M) 3° Si mundum fore fuit Deus ante creationem mundi, per idem, iam est Deus, quia sicut tunc fuit talis propositio increata, ita et nunc. Cum igitur iam aliqua propositio creata enuntiat mundum fore, sequitur quod mundum fore, per idem, est propositio creata. Arguo tunc
30 sic: Hoc fore est propositio increata—demonstrando mundum fore. Et hoc fore est propositio creata. Igitur propositio creata est propositio increata.

4° Sequitur ex illo dicto quod aliqua est propositio simpliciter contingens et tamen eius adaequatum significatum est simpliciter necessarium. Patet
35 de illa

---

3 creata] causata *E*   8 nec . . . secundum *om. M*   9 incorruptibilibus et] conceptibus *M*   12 habetur] habebitur *E*   14 aliud] illud *M*   15 crea- tam] increatam *E*   30 fore² *om. M*   34 tamen *om. E*

contrary to experience. Therefore, it is necessary to say that something is the object of that proposition, and that it is a truth distinct both from God and from a created proposition.

3. I argue this way: I know that things are in some way, with knowledge properly speaking, *a priori* and demonstrative. Therefore, that knowledge is of an uncreated proposition, or only of a created proposition, or of another known which is not a proposition. The first cannot be said, because the uncreated proposition, which is God, is not known by those in this life in any of these ways. Nor can the second be said, since knowledge properly speaking is of incorruptibles and of things that cannot be otherwise than they are (*Posterior Analytics*, Book I ⟨c. 2, 71^{b}15–16; c. 8, 75^{b}24–5⟩). But any such proposition is corruptible and can be otherwise than it is. Therefore, etc. Therefore, it is necessary to grant the third, and I have my intended conclusion.

⟨*Against the Second Part of the Second Claim*⟩

Similarly, the other claim is false—viz. that if there were no created proposition, for no created proposition to be,would be God. For by parity of reasoning, God would be that no chimera is. The conclusion is false, since just as no privation, so also no negation, is truly predicable of God with the 'is' of identity. This is clear. For nothing is identical with God unless the Divine Intellect conceives of it in a proper concept. But the Divine Intellect does not think of those negations or privations in proper ideal concepts. Nor does it think of falsehoods and impossibilities ⟨in proper ideal concepts⟩. Therefore, etc.^{j}

2. A negation is predicable of something only if its own positive opposite is also predicable ⟨of something⟩, since to be predicable seems to pertain more to the affirmation than to the negation. But that a chimera is, is predicable of nothing. Therefore, that no chimera is, is predicable of nothing.

3. If that the world will be, was God before the creation of the world, by the same reasoning, it is God now. For just as there was such an uncreated proposition then, so also there is one now. Therefore, when some created proposition now states that the world will be, it follows by the same reasoning, that *that the world will be* is the created proposition. Then I argue this way: That this will be, is the uncreated proposition (where 'this' indicates that the world will be). That this will be, is a created proposition. Therefore, a created proposition is the uncreated proposition.

4. It follows from that claim that there is some absolutely contingent proposition whose adequate significatum is absolutely necessary. This is clear from the proposition

Antichristus erit,

cuius significatum est Antichristum fore, quod est Deus.

5° Sequitur quod aliqua propositio vera erit falsa, et tamen eius adaequatum significatum numquam erit falsum. Patet de illa propositione 5 creata

Antichristus erit,

cuius significatum adaequatum est primum simpliciter quod numquam erit falsum.

⟨*Ultima Opinio: Prima conclusio*　　*Capitulum Quintum*⟩

10 Multae aliae opiniones tractandae et in quibusdam reprobandae forent. Sed quia aliqualiter discrepando, in maiori parte conveniunt, asserentes plura quae meo iudicio vera sunt, defendenda atque pro viribus sustinenda, ideo de his fundetur opinio ultima, pluribus munita conclusionibus, quarum prima sit ista:

15　　⟨1⟩ Nullius propositionis negativae adaequatum significatum est
　　　　aliquid, aliqua, vel aliqualiter, quovis modo †latum†.

Patet. Nam nullam chimaeram esse non est aliquid, aliqua, nec aliqualiter. Igitur nec aliquod aliud significatum tale. Consequentia patet, et antecedens fuit probatum in improbatione secundae opinionis huius tractatus.[1]

20 ⟨*Conclusio cuiusdam magistri*⟩

Ista conclusio est repugnans conclusioni octavae, quam determinat una de opinionibus dimissis.[2] Et est ista in forma:

Deum non esse solem est Deus.

⟨1.1⟩ Probatur: Deus est, et Deus non est sol. Igitur Deus est Deum 25 non esse solem. Patet consequentia. Nam sequitur generaliter: Ego sum, et ego sum albus; igitur ego sum me esse album. Ego sum, et ego ero; igitur ego sum me fore. Igitur per idem in proposito.

⟨1.2⟩ Item, tota ratio movens aliquos ad oppositum, ait iste magister, est ista:

30　　Si nihil nec aliqualiter esset, Deum non esse solem non esset.
　　Sed iam aeque bene Deus non est sol, sicut tunc non esset sol.
　　Igitur, per idem, iam Deum non esse solem, non est.

Sed quod ista ratio non debeat movere arguit sic: Nam data ista responsione, sequitur ista conclusio

---

7 est] et *E*　　　quod *om. E*　　　10 reprobandae] repellendae *E*　　　12 meo] nostro *E*　　pro *om. M*　　　13 his] omnibus *add. E*　　ultima fundetur opinio transp. E*　　　14 prima] conclusio *add. E*　　　16 latum *M* (*pro* late?), argumentum *E* (*cf. supra p. 96, lin. 2 sqq.*)　　　18 aliquod] aliquid *M*　　　19 in *om. E* tum *E* (*cf. supra p. 96, lin. 2 sqq.*)　　　18 aliquod] aliquid *M*　　　19 in *om. E* 26 et ego sum *om. M*

The Antichrist will be,

whose significatum is that the Antichrist will be—which is God.

5. It follows that some true proposition will be false and nevertheless its adequate significatum never will be false. This is clear from the created proposition

The Antichrist will be,

whose adequate significatum is the absolutely First Being, which never will be false.

⟨*The Last Opinion: Thesis 1*   *Chapter Five*⟩

There are many other opinions that ought to be discussed and refuted on certain ⟨points⟩. But although there are some differences among them, they agree for the most part. And they assert many things that are true, in my judgement, and that ought to be defended and maintained to the best of one's ability. Therefore, the last opinion, armed with many theses, draws on all of these opinions.

> *Thesis 1*: The adequate significatum of a negative proposition is not anything, any things, or anyhow, however broadly construed.

This is clear. For that no chimera is, is not anything, any things, or anyhow. Therefore, neither is any other such significatum. The inference is clear. The premiss was proved in disproving the second opinion of this treatise.

⟨*A Certain Master's Thesis*⟩

This thesis is inconsistent with Thesis 8 of one of the opinions that I have not discussed. It is of this form:

> That God is not the sun, is God.

⟨1.1⟩ Proof: God is, and God is not the sun. Therefore, God is that God is not the sun. The inference is clear. For in general, this follows: I am, and I am white; therefore I am that I am white. I am, and I will be; therefore, I am that I will be. Therefore, the same reasoning holds in the proposed example.

⟨1.2⟩ Again, this master says, the whole argument that moves others to assert the opposite*a* is this:

> If there were not anything or anyhow, then that God is not the sun, would not be.
>
> But, God is not the sun the way things are now, just as much as He would not be the sun in the case supposed.
>
> Therefore, by the same reasoning, that God is not the sun, is not now.

But he argues in the following way, that this argument ought not to be persuasive: Given this reply, the conclusion

Deus non est.

Probatur sic: Deum esse non est. Igitur Deus non est. Consequentia patet, et antecedens probatur: Deum esse vel Deum non esse non est. Sed quidquid et qualitercumque est Deum esse vel Deum non esse, est
5 Deum esse. Igitur Deum esse non est. Tenet consequentia, et antecedens probatur: Si nihil nec aliqualiter esset, Deum esse vel Deum non esse, non esset. Sed iam aeque bene Deus est vel Deus non est, sicut (164rb E) tunc Deus esset vel Deus non esset. Igitur iam Deum esse vel Deum non esse non est.
10   ⟨2⟩ Item arguit sic:

Deum esse non solem est Deus.

Igitur Deum esse et Deum non esse solem est Deus.

Patet consequentia, quia arguitur a convertibili ad convertibile. Et ultra, igitur Deum non esse solem est Deus. Et quod sic arguitur probatur:
15 Istae propositiones convertuntur—scilicet ista copulativa

Deus non est sol et Deus est

et ista

Deus est non sol.

Et dicta istarum propositionum sunt. Igitur dicta istarum convertuntur.

20 ⟨*Argumenta contra conclusionem eiusdem magistri*⟩

Ad haec respondetur[3] negando consequentiam, quia ex ipsa sequitur quod Deus est sol—cuius oppositum ponit illa opinio.

⟨1⟩ Et probatur consequentia: Nam Deum non esse solem est Deus. Et Deum non esse solem est sol. Igitur sol est Deus, et e contra. Con-
25 sequentia tenet cum minori; quia non videtur quare alicuius propositionis significatum adaequatum communicetur identice significato subiecti et non significato praedicati, cum propositio aeque bene constituatur a praedicato sicut a subiecto.

⟨2⟩ Item arguitur sic, ex modo arguendi secundae deductionis: Deum
30 non esse solem est solem non esse Deum. Sed Deum non esse solem est Deus, et solem non esse Deum est sol. Igitur Deus est sol. Consequentia tenet cum minori ex opinione, et maiorem probo: Nam istae propositiones convertuntur

Deus non est sol

---

12 et] vel *E*   14 arguitur] arguatur *E*   21 consequentiam] illam *add. E*
26 communicetur] communiter *E*   27 constituatur] constituitur *E*   31 sol est
Deus *transp. M*

God is not,

follows. Proof: That God is, is not. Therefore, God is not. The inference is clear. Proof of the premiss: That God is or that God is not, is not. But whatever, and whatever way, that God is or that God is not, is: that, or in that way, that God is, is. Therefore, that God is, is not. The inference holds. Proof of the premiss: If there were not anything or anyhow, that God is or that God is not, would not be. But God is, or God is not, the way things are now, just as much as God would be, or would not be, in the case supposed. Therefore, that God is or that God is not, is not now.

⟨2⟩ Again, he argues this way:

That God is a not-sun, is God.

Therefore, that God is and God is not the sun, is God.

The inference is clear, since the argument is from one proposition to a proposition interchangeable with it. Further,

Therefore, that God is not the sun, is God.

Proof that the argument is ⟨an inference from one interchangeable proposition to another⟩: These propositions—viz. the conjunctive proposition

God is not the sun and God is   ●

and the proposition

God is a not-sun

are interchangeable. The nominalizations of these propositions exist. Therefore, their nominalizations are interchangeable.

⟨*Arguments against that Master's Thesis*⟩

I reply to these arguments by denying the inference ⟨in 1.1⟩. For by this inference, it follows that God is the sun—which is the opposite of what that opinion assumes.

⟨1⟩ Proof of the inference: For that God is not the sun, is God. That God is not the sun, is the sun. Therefore, the sun is God, and vice versa. The inference holds, as does the minor. There seems to be no reason why the adequate significatum of a proposition should be predicated in the manner of identity of the significatum of the subject and not of the significatum of the predicate. For the proposition is constituted just as much by the predicate as by the subject.

⟨2⟩ Again, I argue this way, using the mode of argument ⟨that this master uses⟩ in the second deduction ⟨i.e. in 2⟩: That God is not the sun, is that the sun is not God. But that God is not the sun, is God; and that the sun is not God, is the sun. Therefore, God is the sun. The inference holds, according to his opinion, as does the minor. Proof of the major: The propositions

God is not the sun

et

    Sol non est Deus.

Et sua dicta sunt. Igitur convertuntur. Igitur quodlibet istorum est de altero verificabile significative. Consequentia patet, ex quo possunt
5 personaliter supponere.

    3° Arguo quod Deum non esse solem est sol, ex modo primae deductionis. Nam sequitur:

    Sol est. (208rb M)

    Et sol non est Deus.

10   Igitur Deum non esse solem est Deus.

Patet consequentia. Nam sequitur generaliter: Album est, et album est Sortes; igitur Sortes est Sortem esse album. Etiam sequitur: Aliquid fore est, et idem fore est Sortes; igitur Sortes est Sortem fore.

⟨*Responsio ad rationes pro conclusione eiusdem magistri*⟩

15   ⟨R1.1⟩ Ad rationem ergo primam, nego consequentiam. Et ad probationem dico quod licet sequatur universaliter affirmative, non tamen sic sequitur negative. Quare similitudo non est ad propositum.

    ⟨R1.2⟩ Et ulterius dico quod illa ratio illorum concludit. Et ad improbationem nego illam

20   Deus non est,

et illam similiter

    Deum esse non est.

Et tunc ad rationem:

    Deum esse vel Deum non esse non est.

25   Sed quidquid et qualitercumque est Deum esse vel Deum non esse, est Deum esse.

    Igitur Deum esse non est.

non valet argumentum, quia nota disiunctionis in prima propositione tenetur divisive convertibiliter cum disiunctiva. In secunda autem pro-
30 positione tenetur collective ratione signi distributivi determinantis ipsam.[4] Sed haec deberet esse prima propositio

    Aliqualiter qualiter est Deum esse vel Deum non esse, non est

---

15–16 probationem] ergo *add.* M   18–19 improbationem nego] probationem dico
negando *E*   19 illam] quod *add. E*   22 non esse *transp.* M   29 convertibiliter]
et convertitur *E*

and

> The sun is not God

are interchangeable. Their dicta exist. Therefore, their nominalizations are interchangeable. Therefore, the nominalization of each, taken significantly, is truly predicated of the nominalization of the other. The inference holds because they can have personal *suppositio*.

3. I argue that that God is not the sun, is the sun, using the mode of argument in his first deduction ⟨i.e. in 1.1⟩. For this follows:

> The sun is.
> The sun is not God.
> Therefore, that God is not the sun, is God.

The inference is clear. For in general, this follows: A white thing is, and a white thing is Socrates; therefore Socrates is that Socrates is a white thing. This follows, too: That something will be, is. That the same thing will be, is Socrates. Therefore, Socrates is that Socrates will be.

⟨*Reply to Arguments for the Same Master's Thesis*⟩

⟨R1.1⟩ Therefore, in reply to the first argument, I deny the inference. In reply to the proof, I say that although the affirmative would follow universally, nevertheless, the negative does not thus follow. Thus, the analogy does not hold good with the proposed case.

⟨R1.2⟩ Further, I say that that argument of his opponents holds good. In reply to his disproof, I deny the conclusion

> God is not

and similarly the premiss

> That God is, is not.

Then in reply to the argument

> That God is, or that God is not, is not.
> But whatever, and whatever way, that God is or that God is not, is:
>   that, or in that way, that God is, is.
> Therefore, that God is, is not,

the argument does not hold good. For the sign of disjunction is taken with divisive force in the first proposition, so that it is interchangeable with a disjunctive proposition. But in the second proposition, it is taken collectively, because of the distributive sign that governs it.[b] But, ⟨for the argument to hold good⟩, the first proposition ought to be

> Some way in which that God is or that God is not, is, is such that things are not that way,

—quae negatur. Unde suum contradictorium est verum—videlicet

    Qualitercumque est Deum esse vel Deum non esse, est.

Nam quidquid et qualitercumque est Deum esse vel Deum non esse, est
Deum esse. Sed Deum esse est. Igitur etc.

5   ⟨R2⟩ Ad secundam rationem concedo quod Deum esse non solem est
Deus. Sed nego illam consequentiam:

    Deum esse non solem est Deus.

    Igitur Deum esse et Deum non esse solem est Deus.

Nec arguitur ab uno convertibili ad reliquum. Et cum dicitur:

10   Illa copulativa convertitur cum illa categorica,

concedatur.

    Et dicta ipsarum sunt,

verum est.

    Igitur illa dicta convertuntur,

15 non valet consequentia, quia huiusmodi dicta supponere possunt personaliter et non illae propositiones. Unde in simili non sequitur:

    'Tu differs a me' et 'Ego differo a te' convertuntur.

    Et ipsarum dicta sunt.

    Igitur illa convertuntur.

20 Patet quod non valet consequentia, quia antecedens est verum et consequens falsum. Si enim illa dicta converterentur, et possunt subici vel
praedicari, personaliter supponendo, tunc illa esset possibilis

    Te differre a me est me differre a te,

quod est falsum, ut patebit inferius.[5]

25 ⟨Dubia⟩

    ⟨1⟩ Circa praedicta posset dubitari primo de hoc quod dicitur:

    Deum esse vel Deum non esse, est Deum esse.

    ⟨1.1⟩ Nam arguo sic: Deum non esse non est Deum esse. Igitur Deum
esse vel Deum non esse, non est Deum esse. Patet consequentia a parte
30 disiuncti ad totum sine impedimento praecedente.

4 etc. om. M   21 et om. M   29 consequentia] prima E

which I deny. Thus its contradictory is true, viz.

Whatever way that God is or that God is not, is, is such that things are that way.

For whatever, and whatever way, that God is or that God is not, is: that, or in that way, that God is, is. But that God is, is. Therefore, etc.

⟨R2⟩ In reply to the second argument, I grant that that God is a not-sun, is God. But I deny the inference:

That God is a not-sun, is God.
Therefore, that God is and God is not the sun, is God.

Nor is there any argument from one of ⟨two⟩ interchangeable propositions to the other. When he says:

That conjunctive proposition is interchangeable with that categorical,

I grant it. ⟨And when he asserts:⟩

And their nominalizations exist,

it is true. ⟨And when he concludes:⟩

Therefore, their nominalizations are interchangeable,

the inference does not hold good. For such nominalizations can have personal *suppositio* and the propositions cannot. Thus, analogously, this does not follow:

'You are different from me' and 'I am different from you' are interchangeable.
Their nominalizations exist.
Therefore, these nominalizations are interchangeable.

It is clear that the inference does not hold good, since the premiss is true and the conclusion false. For if those nominalizations were interchangeable, then since they can be a subject or predicate with personal *suppositio*, then the proposition

For you to be different from me, is for me to be different from you

would be possible—which is false, as will become clear below.

⟨*Doubts*⟩

⟨1⟩ Doubts can be raised about the preceding remarks. First, about the claim that

That God is or that God is not, is that God is.

⟨1.1⟩ For I argue this way: That God is not, is not that God is. Therefore, that God is or that God is not, is not that God is. The inference from a part of a disjunctive proposition to the whole, where there is no preceding logical operator to prevent this, is clear.

⟨1.2⟩ Secundo arguo sic: Huius disiunctivae

Deus est vel Deus non est

significatum est disiunctum ex significatis ambarum partium. Sed secundae partis significatum adaequatum non est. Igitur nec ipsius totius disiun-
5 ctivae.

⟨1.2.1⟩ Patet consequentia dupliciter. Primo, quia bene sequitur: A est, et B non est; igitur aggregatum ex A et B non est.

⟨1.2.2⟩ Secundo, quia bene sequitur:

A et B

10 copulativae significatum est copulatum ex significatis adaequatis partium illius. Sed unius istarum significatum adaequatum non est. Igitur, nec totius copulativae.

2° Dubitatur similiter de concessione huius

Deum esse non solem est Deus,

15 quia videtur quod Deum esse non solem non sit. (164va E) Nam huius propositionis

Deus est non sol

significatum non est. Igitur etc.

Antecedens probatur, quia praedicati significatum non est. Igitur illius
20 propositionis significatum non est. Antecedens patet, cum significatum illius sit pura negatio. Et consequentia probatur: Nam huius propositionis

Antichristus est futurus

significatum adaequatum non est, quia significatum subiecti non est. Sed aeque bene concurrit ad compositionem existentia praedicati sicut subiecti.
25 Igitur si alicuius propositionis praedicati significatum adaequatum non est, ipsius totius significatum adaequatum non est.

⟨*Responsio ad dubia*⟩

⟨R1⟩ Ad haec dubia respondeo, concedendo ut prius quod Deum esse vel Deum non esse, est Deum esse.
30 ⟨R1.1⟩ Et illam similiter

Deum esse vel Deum non esse, non est Deum esse.

Nec ista sunt opposita, sicut nec ista:

Sortes vel Brunellus est homo,
Sortes vel Brunellus non est homo.

---

1 arguo] arguitur *E*   3 significatis] significatione *E*   9 et] vel *ME, correxi*
11 adaequatum *om. E*   19 quia *om. E*   24 existentia] essentia *M*   25 pro-
positionis] verae *add. M*   28 respondeo concedendo] respondendo concedo *E*

⟨1.2⟩ Second, this argument is made: The significatum of the disjunctive proposition

God is or God is not

is a disjunction formed from the significata of both of the parts. But the adequate significatum of the second part is not. Therefore, the adequate significatum of the whole disjunctive proposition is not.

⟨1.2.1⟩ The inference is doubly clear. First, because this follows: *A* is and *B* is not; therefore, the aggregate formed from *A* and *B* is not.

⟨1.2.2⟩ Second, because this follows: the significatum of the conjunctive proposition

A and *B*

is the conjunction formed from the adequate significata of those parts. The adequate significatum of one of them is not. Therefore, the adequate significatum of the whole conjunctive proposition is not.

⟨2⟩ Similarly, a doubt is raised about my granting the proposition

That God is a not-sun, is God,

because it seems that *that God is a not-sun*, is not. For the significatum of the proposition

God is a not-sun

is not. Therefore, etc.

Proof of the premiss: The significatum of the predicate is not. Therefore, the significatum of the proposition is not. The premiss is clear, since the predicate's significatum is a pure negation. Proof of the inference: The adequate significatum of the proposition

The Antichrist is future

is not, since the significatum of the subject is not. But the existence of the predicate contributes as much to the composition as the existence of the subject does. Therefore, if the adequate significatum of the predicate of a proposition is not, the adequate significatum of the whole is not.

⟨*Reply to the Doubts*⟩

⟨R1⟩ Replying to these doubts, I grant, as before, that *that God is* or *that God is not*, is that God is.

⟨R1.1⟩ Similarly, I grant the proposition

That God is or that God is not, is not that God is.

Nor are these propositions opposed, just as

Socrates or Brownie is a man

and

Socrates or Brownie is not a man

are not opposed.

⟨R1.2⟩ Ad secundam rationem contra idem, nego consequentiam. Unde sicut ad veritatem disiunctivae sufficit veritas unius partis, ita ad existentiam sui adaequati significati sufficit (208va M) existentia significati unius partis principalis.

5 ⟨R1.2.1⟩ Et ad primam probationem consequentiae dico quod illa nihil probat; quia bene concedo quod aggregatum ex illis significatis non est, ex quo enim significatum adaequatum secundae partis non est, ex ipso nihil nec aliqualiter aggregatur. Licet enim disiunctiva illa significet ex compositione suarum partium, tamen significatum illius non componitur

10 ex compositione suarum partium, sumendo 'componi' ad intentionem argumenti.

⟨R1.2.2⟩ Similiter alia probatio non procedit, propter dissimilitudinem. Sicut enim ad veritatem copulativae significantis ex compositione suarum partium, requiritur utriusque partis veritas; ita ad existentiam sui signi-

15 cati, requiritur utriusque partis significati existentia. Sed quia primum non requiritur in disiunctiva, ut dictum est, propterea nec secundum, debet concludi. Hoc potest declarari in propositionibus de copulato et disiuncto extremis. Nullus enim diceret quod significatum illius non esset

Tu es homo vel chimaera.

20 Et tamen alterius partis significatum non est. Sed illius

Tu es homo et chimaera

significatum adaequatum non est, quia illius termini 'chimaera' significatum non est, non obstante quod totius residui significatum sit.

⟨R2⟩ Ad secundam dubitationem, concedo quod Deum esse non solem

25 est Deus.

Et ad improbationem eius posset responderi per ea quae dicta sunt nunc ultimo, negando illam consequentiam:

Significatum praedicati non est.

Igitur nec totius propositionis,

30 sicut non sequitur:

Significatum secundae partis huius complexi significantis Antichristum, non est.

Igitur, et illius complexi significatum adaequatum non est.

---

1 contra] conceditur M   3 significati² om. E   5 primam] partem principalem add. M   quod] per add. E   6 probat] probatur E   14 veritas] et existentia add. E   16 requiritur] reperitur E   21–2 chimaera¹⁻²] chimaerae E   31 significantis] significans ME, correxi

⟨R1.2⟩ In reply to the second argument against the same concession, I deny the inference. Thus, just as for the truth of a disjunctive proposition, the truth of one of its parts suffices; so for the existence of its adequate significatum, the existence of the significatum of one of the principal parts suffices.

⟨R1.2.1⟩ In reply to the first proof of the inference, I say that it proves nothing. I gladly grant that the aggregate of these significata is not. For because the adequate significatum of the second part is not, there is not anything or anyhow, formed from aggregating together the significata of the first and the second part. For although the disjunctive proposition signifies by the composition of its parts, nevertheless its significatum is not composed from the composition of its parts (where 'to be composed' is taken in the way intended in the argument).

⟨R1.2.2⟩ Similarly, the other proof ⟨of the inference in the second argument⟩ is not telling, because of a disanalogy. For just as for the truth of a conjunctive proposition that signifies by the composition of its parts, the truth of each of the parts is required; so for the existence of its significatum, the existence of the significatum of each of its parts is required. But, since the first is not required in a disjunctive proposition, as has been said, one ought to conclude that, for that reason, the second is not required either. This can be explained ⟨by reference⟩ to propositions with conjunctive or disjunctive extremes. For no one would say that the significatum of the proposition

You are a man or a chimera

is not. Nevertheless, the significatum of its second part is not. But the adequate significatum of

You are a man and a chimera

is not, because the significatum of the term 'chimera' is not, notwithstanding that the significatum of the whole of the remainder is.

⟨R2⟩ In reply to the second doubt, I grant that *that God is a not-sun*, is God.

I could reply to its disproof by means of those things I have said just now, by denying this inference:

The significatum of the predicate is not.
Therefore, the significatum of the whole proposition is not.

In the same way, this does not follow:

The significatum of the second part of this complex that signifies the Antichrist, is not.
Therefore, the adequate significatum of the complex is not.

Verumtamen magis realiter et ad propositum respondendo, dico quod illius propositionis

Deus est non sol

praedicatum infinitum potest dupliciter teneri aut simpliciter negative
5 aut aliqualiter positive. Primo modo nego illam propositionem. Nec ad illum sensum ipsam concessi. Asserit enim isto modo quod Deus est negatio solis—quod est falsum. Et si arguitur sic:

Deus non est sol.
Et Deus est.
10 Igitur Deus est non sol,

sic sumendo, non valet argumentum. Nec arguitur cum debito medio quando sic sumitur, sed oportet addere in antecedente

Negatio solis est,

quod est falsum.
15 Secundo modo concedo propositionem illam, quia ipsa asserit cum suo adaequato significato quod Deus est aliquid quod non est sol. Et ad illum sensum concessi eam. Et sic sumendo, bene sequitur:

Deus non est sol.
Et Deus est.
20 Igitur Deus est non sol.

Et sic semper sumebam quotiens tales consequentias dixi esse bonas. Ex praedictis patet quod significatum illius, sumptae secundo modo, est. Quare argumentum non procedit.

Item sicut dico de infinito termino incomplexo, dico similiter de infinito
25 complexo. Si ergo proponitur

Tu es nullam chimaeram esse,

quaeratur an illud infinitum complexum supponat simpliciter negative aut aliqualiter positive. Primo modo negatur illa, quia significat assertive quod tu es talis negatio nullam chimaeram esse. Et si arguitur ut prius:

30 Tu non es chimaeram esse.
Et tu es.
Igitur tu es nullam chimaeram esse,

patet consequentiam non valere. Debet enim sumi medium ut dictum est.
35 Secundo modo concedatur quod tu es nullam chimaeram esse, quia quidquid et qualitercumque est in mundo, est nullam chimaeram esse et nullum hominem esse asinum. Quia tu es aliquid quod non est chimaeram

1 respondendo] respondeo *M* 37 aliquid] aliquod *E*

Nevertheless, replying more to the point, and to the proposed example, I say that the infinite predicate of the proposition

God is a not-sun

can be taken in two ways—either absolutely negatively, or somehow positively. Taken in the first way, I deny the proposition, nor have I granted it in this sense. For, taken in this way, it asserts that God is the negation of the sun—which is false. If one argues this way:

God is not the sun.
God is.
Therefore, God is a not-sun,

taking the infinite predicate in this way, the argument does not hold good. Nor is the argument made with the required means ⟨of proof⟩, when the infinite predicate is so taken. But it is necessary to add in the premiss:

The negation of the sun is,

which is false.

Taken in the second way, I grant the proposition, since it asserts with its adequate significatum, that God is something that is not the sun. It is in that sense that I have granted it. So taken, this does follow:

God is not the sun.
God is.
Therefore, God is a not-sun.

I have always taken it thus, as many times as I have said that such inferences are good. From the preceding remarks it is clear that the significatum of that proposition taken in the second way, is. Thus, the argument does not proceed.

Again, I say the same things about an infinite complex as I say about an infinite non-complex term. Therefore, if someone proposes

You are no chimera existing,[c]

one should ask whether the infinite complex supposits absolutely negatively or somehow positively. Taken in the first way, I deny it, since it signifies affirmatively that you are such a negation as not-any-chimera-existing. And if one should argue as before:

You are not a chimera existing.
You are.
Therefore, you are no chimera existing,

it is clear that the inference does not hold good. For an additional premiss ought to be taken, as has been said.[d]

In the second way, I grant that you are no chimera existing. For whatever, and whatever way, is in the world, is no chimera existing and no man being a donkey. For you are something that is not a chimera existing (and

esse, et quidquid est in mundo similiter, quia bene sequitur isto secundo modo:

> Tu non es chimaeram esse.
> Et tu es.

5   Igitur tu es nullam chimaeram esse.

Et ita conceditur quod nullam chimaeram esse est, et nullum hominem esse asinum est aliquid, aliqua vel aliqualiter. Et si dicitur, 'Prius negasti tales propositiones', dico (164vb E) quod ipsas negavi ad primum sensum et non ad secundum sensum.

10   Iterum si quis vellet introducere oppositum conclusionis dicendo:

> Aliquid est nullam chimaeram esse.
> Sed significatum adaequatum illius negativae 'Nulla chimaera est' est
>   nullam chimaeram esse.
> Igitur significatum adaequatum propositionis negativae est aliquid.

15 Patet quod si ly .nullam chimaeram esse. in antecedente difformiter sumatur, non valet argumentum. Si autem uniformiter, vel igitur primo modo vel secundo modo. Si primo modo, negatur prima pars antecedentis. Si secundo modo, negatur secunda, quia nullum est significatum propositionis negativae nisi quatenus (208vb M) est pura negatio.

20   Item si proponeretur

> Tu es te non esse asinum,

debet simpliciter negari, quia nulla infinitatio ibi est.
Et si arguitur:

> Tu es non te esse asinum.

25   Igitur tu es te non esse asinum,

quaeratur, ut prius, de infinitatione antecedentis, quomodo sumitur, primo vel secundo modo. Primo modo, concedatur consequentia et negatur antecedens. Secundo modo, concedatur antecedens et negatur consequentia. Quare etc.

30 ⟨*Ultima Opinio: Secunda Conclusio*   *Capitulum Sextum*⟩

> *Secunda conclusio* in ordine est ista: Nullius propositionis categoricae
> affirmativae cuius subiecto vel praedicato implicito vel explicito
> nihil praeter signum correspondet in rerum natura, significatum
> adaequatum est aliquid vel aliqualiter, quale aut quantum, creator
35   vel creatura.

---

4 et] nullam chimaeram esse est et *add. E*   6 et²] ita *add. E*   14 adaequatum
om. E   22 simpliciter] similiter *E*   33 correspondet] correspondendo *M*

so for anything in the world). For in the second way ⟨of taking the negated extremes⟩, this follows:

You are not ⟨a⟩ chimera existing.
You are.
Therefore, you are no chimera existing.

In this way I grant that no chimera existing, is; and that no man being a donkey is something, some things, or somehow. If someone says, 'You have denied such propositions before', I say that I have denied them taken in the first sense and not taken in the second sense.[e]

Again, suppose someone wished to introduce the opposite of Thesis 1, saying:

Something is no chimera existing.
The adequate significatum of the negative proposition 'Not any chimera exists' is no chimera existing.
Therefore, the adequate significatum of a negative proposition is something.

It is clear that if 'no chimera existing' is taken differently in the two premisses, the argument does not hold good. But if it is taken in the same way, then either in the first way or in the second way. If in the first way, I deny the first premiss.[f] If in the second way, I deny the second ⟨premiss⟩,[g] since no significatum of a negative proposition is, except in so far as it is a pure negation.

Again, if someone proposes:

You are you not being a donkey,

it ought to be absolutely denied, since there is no term negation there. And if someone argues:

You are not you being a donkey.
Therefore, you are you not being a donkey,

one should ask, as before, whether the infinite ⟨predicate⟩ in the premiss is taken in the first way or in the second way. Taken in the first way, I grant the inference and deny the premiss. Taken in the second way, I grant the premiss and deny the inference.[h] Thus, etc.

⟨*The Last Opinion: Thesis 2*   *Chapter Six*⟩

The second thesis in order is the following:

Thesis 2: No affirmative categorical proposition whose subject or predicate, implicit or explicit, has nothing over and above a sign corresponding to it in the nature of things, has an adequate significatum that is something or somehow, some kind or so much, creator or creature.

Haec conclusio patet de istis:

Antichristus erit,

Adam fuit,

Hoc potest esse—demonstrato uno possibili quod non est nec erit.

5 Unde quia Antichristus non est, Antichristum fore non est. Et per idem,
Adam fuisse vel hoc posse esse, non est. Sed concedo quod Adam fuisse
fuit; et quod Antichristum fore erit.

Non tamen concedo, sicut alii concedunt, quod Adam fuisse est Adam
praeteritus, et Antichristum fore est Antichristus futurus, negantes
10 Antichristum fore esse, et similiter Adam fuisse esse. Nam ex primo sequitur secundum. Sequitur enim bene:

Antichristum fore est Antichristus futurus,

Igitur, Antichristum fore est.

Patet consequentia, a tertio adiacente ad secundum adiacens affirmative,
15 sine verbo vel praedicato distrahente termino.

Verumtamen conceditur quod Antichristum fore est Antichristus futurus,
et Adam fuisse est praeteritus Adam, sumendo ly .praeteritum. et .futu-
rum. participialiter, quia Antichristum fore erit Antichristus, et Adam
fuisse fuit Adam.

20 ⟨*Argumenta contra conclusiones primam et secundam ultimae opinionis*⟩

⟨1.1⟩ Contra istas duas conclusiones arguitur communiter[1] sic: Antichristum fore est verum. Igitur Antichristum fore est aliquid. Patet consequentia, quia 'verum' et 'aliquid' convertuntur. Et antecedens probatur:
Nam haec propositio

25   Antichristus erit

est vera, quae significat adaequate Antichristum fore. Igitur Antichristum
fore est verum.

⟨1.2⟩ Secundo sic: Antichristum fore est verum. Igitur verum est Antichristum fore. Consequentia patet, quia conversio simplex. Et antecedens
30 est verum, ut argutum est. Igitur et consequens. Tunc sic: Verum est
Antichristum fore. Igitur aliquod verum est Antichristum fore. Patet
consequentia, ab indefinita ad suam particularem. Et ex consequenti
sequitur quod aliquid, aliqua, vel aliqualiter est Antichristum fore.

⟨1.3⟩ Tertio: Antichristum fore est verum. Sed non est aliquod verum

This thesis is clear with respect to the following propositions:

The Antichrist will be,
Adam was,
This can be,

(where 'this' indicates a possible that neither is nor will be). Thus, since the Antichrist is not, that the Antichrist will be, is not. By the same reasoning, that Adam was or that this can be, is not. But I grant that *that Adam was* was; and that *that the Antichrist will be* will be.

Nevertheless, I do not grant, as others do, that *that Adam was* is the past Adam, and *that the Antichrist will be* is the Antichrist to be,[a] while denying that *that the Antichrist will be* is, and similarly that *that Adam was* is. For the second follows from the first. For this does follow:

That the Antichrist will be, is the Antichrist to be.
Therefore, that the Antichrist will be, is.

The inference is clear, from the third adjacent to the second adjacent,[b] where the propositions are affirmative and in the absence of any distracting[c] verb or predicate term.

Nevertheless, I grant that *that the Antichrist will be* is the Antichrist to be, and that *that Adam was* is the past Adam, taking the terms 'past' and 'to be' to be part of a periphrastic tense formation.[d] For that the Antichrist will be, will be the Antichrist; and that Adam was, was Adam.

⟨*Arguments against Theses 1 and 2 of the Last Opinion*⟩

⟨1.1⟩ The following argument is commonly made against the ⟨above⟩ two theses: That the Antichrist will be, is ⟨a⟩ truth.[e] Therefore, that the Antichrist will be, is something. The inference is clear, since '⟨a⟩ truth' and 'something' are interchangeable. Proof of the premiss: The proposition

The Antichrist will be   ˙

is ⟨a⟩ truth. It signifies adequately that the Antichrist will be. Therefore, that the Antichrist will be, is ⟨a⟩ truth.

⟨1.2⟩ Second, this argument is advanced: That the Antichrist will be, is ⟨a⟩ truth. Therefore, ⟨a⟩ truth is that the Antichrist will be. The inference is clear, since it is a simple conversion. The premiss is true, as has been argued. Therefore, so is the conclusion. Then, this argument: ⟨A⟩ truth is that the Antichrist will be. Therefore, something true is that the Antichrist will be. The inference is clear, from the indefinite to its particular. From the conclusion it follows that something is, or some things are, or somehow it is that the Antichrist will be.

⟨1.3⟩ Third: That the Antichrist will be, is ⟨a⟩ truth. But it is not

praeter Antichristum fore. Igitur Antichristum fore est Antichristum fore. Et ex consequenti sequitur quod

Antichristum fore est.

⟨1.4⟩ Quarto: Antichristum fore est scitum. Igitur Antichristum fore
5 est. Consequentia tenet, a tertio adiacente ad secundum adiacens. Et antecedens patet, quia Antichristum fore creditur sine haesitatione.

Omnia ista argumenta possunt fieri contra primam conclusionem.

⟨*Responsio cuiusdam magistri ad argumenta contra conclusionem*⟩

Ad haec argumenta de significato propositionis negativae respondet unus
10 magister,[2] negans simpliciter tales consequentias:

Nullum hominem esse asinum est verum.

Igitur verum est nullum hominem esse asinum.

Te non esse est possibile.

Igitur possibile est te non esse.

15 Concedit ergo quod nullum hominem esse asinum est verum, et tamen non est verum nullum hominem esse asinum. Nullam chimaeram esse est possibile et necessarium, et tamen non est possibile nec necessarium nullam chimaeram esse. Te non esse est contingens, et tamen non est contingens te non esse.

20 ⟨2.1⟩ Ait enim: Si verum est nullum hominem esse asinum, igitur aliqua veritate verum est nullum hominem esse asinum. Igitur veritate rei vel compositionis aut intellectus. Non primo modo, ut patet. Nec secundo modo, quia veritas intellectus vel compositionis est adaequatio intellectus ad rem. Modo nullum hominem esse asinum non est res. Igitur etc.

25 ⟨2.2⟩ Item, si possibile est nullum hominem esse asinum, et solum illud quod possibile est esse potest esse, igitur nullum hominem esse asinum potest esse.

⟨2.3⟩ Item, si possibile est nullum hominem esse asinum, et possibili posito in esse non sequitur inconveniens, igitur sequitur quod posito in
30 esse quod nullus homo est asinus nullum sequitur inconveniens. Consequens falsum, quia eadem inconvenientia sequuntur quae modo, dato quod esset nullum hominem esse asinum.

⟨2.4⟩ Item, si contingens est te non (165ᵃ E) esse, et cum contingentia sit potentia ad utramque partem contradictionis, igitur te non esse est
35 aliqua potentia potens terminare actum. Consequens falsum, quia quod non est nec potest esse non potest terminare nec terminari.

---

9 argumenta] facta *add. E*   10 negans] negando *E*   30 nullum *om. E*   31
sequuntur] sequeretur *M*   32 quod] quae *M*   36 terminari] terminat *M*

something true other than that the Antichrist will be. Therefore, that the Antichrist will be, is that the Antichrist will be. From the conclusion it follows that

That the Antichrist will be, is.

⟨1.4⟩ Fourth: That the Antichrist will be, is known. Therefore, that the Antichrist will be, is. The inference from the third adjacent to the second adjacent, holds. The premiss is clear, since that the Antichrist will be, is believed without hesitation.

All these arguments can be made against Thesis 1.

⟨*A Certain Master's Reply to Arguments against the Thesis*⟩

One Master replies to these arguments concerning the significatum of a negative proposition by absolutely denying such inferences as:

That no man is a donkey, is ⟨a⟩ truth.

Therefore, ⟨a⟩ truth is that no man is a donkey.*f*
and

That you are not, is ⟨a⟩ possibility.

Therefore, ⟨a⟩ possibility is that you are not.

Therefore, he grants that that no man is a donkey, is ⟨a⟩ truth, and nevertheless that it is not ⟨a⟩ truth that no man is a donkey. ⟨He grants that⟩ that no chimera is, is ⟨a⟩ possibility and ⟨a⟩ necessity, and nevertheless neither ⟨a⟩ possibility nor ⟨a⟩ necessity is that no chimera is; that you are not, is ⟨a⟩ contingency and nevertheless that it is not ⟨a⟩ contingency that you are not.

⟨2.1⟩ For he says, if ⟨a⟩ truth is that no man is a donkey, then according to some kind of truth, ⟨a⟩ truth is that no man is a donkey. Therefore, according to the truth of things, or according to the truth of a composition or of the intellect. Not in the first way, as is clear. Nor in the second way, since the truth of the intellect or of a composition is the adequation of the intellect to things. But that no man is a donkey, is not a thing. Therefore, etc.

⟨2.2⟩ Again, if ⟨a⟩ possibility is that no man is a donkey, and only the possible can be; then that no man is a donkey, can be.

⟨2.3⟩ Again, if ⟨a⟩ possibility is that no man is a donkey, and no difficulty follows from assuming ⟨a⟩ possibility actualized; then it follows that no difficulty follows from assuming ⟨the possibility⟩ that no man is a donkey, actualized. The consequent is false, since the same difficulties would follow, as they do when it is granted that that no man is a donkey, is.

⟨2.4⟩ Again, if ⟨a⟩ contingency is that you are not, since contingency is a potency for either side of a contradiction, then that you are not, is some potency able to be the terminus of an act. The consequent is false, since what neither is nor can be, can neither be a terminus nor have a terminus.

⟨*Contra responsionem eiusdem magistri reductio ad conclusiones absurdas*⟩

Contra istam responsionem arguo deducendo plures (209ʳᵃ M) conclusiones absurdas.

⟨1⟩ *Prima* est ista: Aliqua sunt duo contradictoria inter se contra-
5　　dicentia, et tamen non est ita sicut aliquod illorum significat.

Patet de istis contradictoriis

Homo est asinus

et

Non homo est asinus.

10 Quod autem non sit ita sicut primum significat patet, cum suum significatum adaequatum sit falsum et impossibile. Et quod non sit ita sicut
secundum adaequate significat, similiter patet, quia non est verum nullum
hominem esse asinum, secundum istam responsionem.

2ᵃ *conclusio*: Aliqua est consequentia bona et formalis, et ita est sicut
15　　significatur adaequate per antecedens, et tamen non est ita sicut
adaequate significatur per consequens.

Patet sic arguendo: Tu es homo. Igitur tu non es asinus. Nam, secundum
istam responsionem, verum est te esse hominem, et non est verum te non
esse asinum.

20　　3ᵃ *conclusio*: Aliqua est condicionalis vera, et possibile est ita esse sicut
significatur per antecedens adaequate; et tamen nec possibile, nec
impossibile, nec necessarium, nec contingens est ita esse sicut
significatur adaequate per consequens.

Patet de ista

25　Si tu es homo, tu non es lapis.

Et sic multae aliae sequuntur volenti advertere.

Haec enim responsio videtur mihi irrationalis, quia sicut ly .verum.
vel aliquis terminus modalis potest participialiter modaliter teneri a parte
praedicati, ita a parte subiecti. Immo a fortiori, quia magis videtur terminus
30 officiabilis emittere vim suam quando praecedit quam quando subsequitur.³

Nec aliqua rationum illarum procedit contra me quin aequaliter pro-
cedat contra ipsum. Arguam enim sic contra ipsam: Nullum hominem
esse asinum est verum. Igitur, nullum hominem esse asinum est verum
aliqua veritate. Vel igitur veritate rei vel veritate compositionis . . . Et sic

28 participialiter] vel *add.* M　　30 officiabilis] officialis M

⟨*The Author Infers Absurd Conclusions against that Master's Reply*⟩

I argue against this reply by deducing many absurd conclusions from it.

First ⟨*Absurd*⟩ *Conclusion*: There exist two contradictories that are mutually contradictory and nevertheless things are not so as one of them signifies.[g]

This is clear from the contradictories

A man is a donkey

and

It is not the case that a man is a donkey.

But that things are not so as the first signifies, is clear, since its adequate significatum is false and impossible. That things are not so as the second adequately signifies, is similarly clear, since it is not ⟨a⟩ truth that no man is a donkey, according to this reply.

Second ⟨*Absurd*⟩ *Conclusion*: There is some good and formal inference, such that things are so as the premiss adequately signifies, and nevertheless not so as the conclusion adequately signifies.[h]

The inference is clear, when one argues this way: You are a man. Therefore, you are not a donkey. For according to this reply, ⟨a⟩ truth is that you are a man and it is not ⟨a⟩ truth that you are not a donkey.

Third ⟨*Absurd*⟩ *Conclusion*: There is some true conditional, such that ⟨a⟩ possibility is that things are so as the antecedent adequately signifies, and nevertheless neither ⟨a⟩ possibility nor ⟨an⟩ impossibility, neither ⟨a⟩ necessity nor ⟨a⟩ contingency, is that things are so as the consequent adequately signifies.

This is clear from the proposition

If you are a man, you are not a stone.

One who considers the matter will see that many other absurd conclusions follow in the same way.

This ⟨master's⟩ reply seems irrational to me. For, just as '⟨a⟩ truth' or a modal term can be taken as a participle and modal term when it occurs in the predicate position; so it can be taken as a participle and modal term when it occurs in the subject position. In fact, *a fortiori*, since a functionalizable term seems more to have force when it precedes the expression it governs than when it follows it.

Nor does any of these arguments proceed against me that does not proceed equally well against him. For I should argue against his opinion this way: That no man is a donkey, is ⟨a⟩ truth. Therefore, that no man is a donkey, is ⟨a⟩ truth according to some truth. Therefore, either according to the truth of things or according to the truth of a composition . . .

ultra continue deducendo a parte praedicati sicut ipse deducit a parte subiecti.

Dico igitur[4] aliter quod ly .verum., .possibile., .impossibile., .necessarium. et .contingens., et alii termini modales, possunt dupliciter teneri:

5 nominaliter resolutorie aut modaliter officiabiliter. Primo modo nego istas propositiones:

    Nullam chimaeram esse est verum,

    Verum est nullam chimaeram esse,

    Antichristum fore est possibile,

10   Possibile est Antichristum fore,

    Nullum hominem esse asinum est necessarium,

    Necessarium est nullum hominem esse asinum,

    Te non esse est contingens,

    Contingens est te non esse.

15 Ex qualibet enim illarum sequitur significatum tale esse aliquid, aliqua, vel aliqualiter—quod est falsum. Sed tenendo secundo modo concedo easdem propositiones, sive modus ponatur a parte subiecti sive a parte praedicati.

Eodem modo est dicendum si proponeretur

20   Ita est sicut haec propositio adaequate significat

        Nullus homo est asinus,

vel isto modo

    Sic est sicut haec propositio adaequate significat

        Antichristus erit,

25 quaerendum est de modo sumendi istos terminos 'ita' et 'sic', an nominaliter demonstrative, vel resolutorie, aut officiabiliter modaliter. Primo modo negetur quaelibet istarum. Secundo modo concedatur, quia apud me idem est

    Ita est quod nullus homo est asinus

30 et

    Verum est quod nullus homo est asinus;

    Sic est quod Antichristus erit,

    Verum est quod Antichristus erit.

⟨*Responsio auctoris ad argumenta contra conclusiones*⟩

35 Ad rationes igitur principales:

⟨R1.1⟩ Ad primam distinguendo de ly .verum. in antecedente an tran-

---

17 modus ponatur] modi praeponantur *E*   25 ita] est *add. M*   sic] sicut *E*   26
demonstrative] denominative *E*   27 concedatur] conceditur *E*

And so on continually deducing ⟨with respect to 'a truth'⟩ in the predicate position, what he deduced ⟨with respect to 'a truth'⟩ in the subject position.

Therefore, I maintain otherwise, that '⟨a⟩ truth', '⟨a⟩ possibility', '⟨an⟩ impossibility', '⟨a⟩ necessity', and '⟨a⟩ contingency', and other modal terms can be taken in two ways: as nominal and resoluble terms,[i] or as modal and functionalizable terms. Taking ⟨such terms⟩ in the first way, I deny the following propositions:

That no chimera is, is ⟨a⟩ truth,
⟨A⟩ truth is that no chimera is,
That the Antichrist will be, is ⟨a⟩ possibility,
⟨A⟩ possibility is that the Antichrist will be,
That no man is a donkey, is ⟨a⟩ necessity,
⟨A⟩ necessity is that no man is a donkey,
That you are not, is ⟨a⟩ contingency,
⟨A⟩ contingency is that you are not.

For it follows from any of them that such a significatum is something, some things, or somehow—which is false. But taking them in the second way, I grant the same propositions, whether the modal term is placed in the subject position or in the predicate position.

One ought to say the same thing if someone proposed

So it is as the proposition
No man is a donkey
adequately signifies,

or similarly

Thus[j] it is as the proposition
The Antichrist will be
adequately signifies.

One ought to ask how the terms 'so' and 'thus' are taken—whether as nominal and demonstrative or resoluble terms, or as modal and functionalizable terms. Taken in the first way, I would deny each of the propositions. Taken in the second way, I would grant them. For, on my view,

So it is that no man is a donkey,

and

⟨A⟩ truth is that no man is a donkey;
Thus it is that the Antichrist will be,

and

⟨A⟩ truth is that the Antichrist will be,

are the same.

⟨*The Author's Reply to Arguments against his Theses*⟩

Therefore, ⟨replying⟩ to the principal arguments:

⟨R1.1⟩ I reply to the first by distinguishing with respect to '⟨a⟩ truth' in

scendenter sumatur vel modaliter. Primo modo concedo consequentiam et nego antecedens. Secundo modo nego consequentiam, nec sic convertitur cum ente.

⟨R1.2⟩ Ad secundam rationem, quaero utrum ly .verum. difformiter 5 vel uniformiter sumatur in antecedente et in consequente. Si difformiter, patet consequentiam non valere. Si uniformiter, igitur nominaliter resolutorie vel officiabiliter modaliter. Primo modo nego antecedens. Secundo modo concedo consequentiam et consequens. Et tunc ad argumentum:

Verum est Antichristum fore.

10   Igitur aliquod verum est Antichristum fore,

non valet argumentum. Et ad probationem, dico quod antecedens non est alicuius quantitatis. Et si quaeritur quae est indefinita consequentis, dico quod antecedens, si ly .verum. tenetur transcendenter, vel sicut in sua particulari.

15   ⟨R1.3⟩ Ad tertiam rationem, nego consequentiam, quia deberet sumi in maiori

Antichristum fore est aliquod verum

—quod est falsum.

Aliter potest ad haec omnia brevius responderi dicendo quod huiusmodi 20 termini 'verum', 'falsum', (165ʳᵇ E) et huiusmodi possunt dupliciter teneri: primo modo, nominaliter resolutorie; secundo modo nominaliter officiabiliter seu modaliter. Primo modo sumitur quando dicto propositionis non coniungitur vel si coniungitur per aliud adiectivum determinatur, ut

Deus, seu aurum, est verum

25 vel

Nullam chimaeram esse est aliquod verum.

Sed secundo modo sumitur quando huiusmodi dicto coniungitur sive ante sive post, (209ʳᵇ M) limitatione deducta quacumque, ut

Verum est nullam chimaeram esse,

30   Nullum hominem esse asinum est necessarium,

Quod homo est asinus est impossibile,

Possibile est quod Antichristus sit.

---

1 vel] an *E*   5 sumatur] sumitur *E*   12 consequentis] consequenter *E*   13 tenetur] teneretur *M*   15 deberet] debet *E*

the premiss whether it is taken as a transcendental or as a modal term. ⟨Taken⟩ in the first way, I grant the inference and deny the premiss. ⟨Taken⟩ in the second way, I deny the inference. Nor, so taken, does '⟨a⟩ truth' convert with 'being'.

⟨R1.2⟩ In reply to the second argument, I ask whether '⟨a⟩ truth' is taken differently or in the same way in the premiss and conclusion. If differently, it is clear that the inference does not hold good. If in the same way, then either as a nominal and resoluble term or as a modal and functionalizable term. Taken in the first way, I deny the premiss. Taken in the second way, I grant the inference and the conclusion. Then, in reply to the argument:

⟨A⟩ truth is that the Antichrist will be.
Therefore, something true is that the Antichrist will be,

the argument does not hold good. In reply to the proof, I say that the premiss is not of any quantity. And if someone asks what is the indefinite proposition that corresponds to the conclusion, then I say that the premiss is, if '⟨a⟩ truth' is taken as a transcendental term or as it is taken in the ⟨corresponding⟩ particular.[k]

⟨R1.3⟩ In reply to the argument, I deny the inference, since one ought to assume in the major

That the Antichrist will be, is something true,

which is false.

⟨One⟩ can reply to all three of these arguments in a different way and more briefly, by saying that terms such as 'true' ⟨or 'a truth'⟩ and 'false' ⟨or 'a falsehood'⟩, etc. can be taken in two ways.[l] In the first way, as nominal and resoluble terms. In the second way, as functionalizable or modal terms. They are taken in the first way, when they are not joined to the nominalization of a proposition, or, if they are joined, they are governed by another adjective. For example,

God, or gold, is true,

or

That no chimera is, is something true.

But they are taken in the second way, when they are joined to such a nominalization, whether before ⟨it⟩ or after ⟨it⟩ (where any limitation has been removed). For example,

⟨A⟩ truth is that no chimera is,
That no man is a donkey, is ⟨a⟩ necessity,
That a man is a donkey, is ⟨an⟩ impossibility,
⟨A⟩ possibility is that the Antichrist is.

Quotienscumque ergo proponitur

    Verum est nullam chimaeram esse

aut

    Nullam chimaeram esse est verum;

5   Possibile est Antichristum fore,

aut e converso, concedo quamlibet istarum sine distinctione. Sed nego
illas:

    Nullam chimaeram esse est aliquod verum,

    Aliquod necessarium, vel aliquod possibile est nullum hominem esse

10   asinum, vel Antichristum fore.

Secundum ergo istum modum continue sumam in sequentibus, quia
taediosum foret continue distinctionibus laborare. Quare etc.

    ⟨R1.4⟩ Ad quartam nego consequentiam, quia arguitur cum termino
distrahente. Unde ly .scitum., .verum., .falsum. et huiusmodi termini

15 modales sunt termini ampliativi et distrahentes copulam principalem.

    ⟨*Responsio auctoris ad rationes eiusdem magistri*⟩

    Ad rationes vero illius magistri respondeo, ita pro eo sicut pro me.

    ⟨R2.1⟩ Cum dicitur:

    Verum est nullam chimaeram esse.

20   Igitur aliqua veritate verum est nullam chimaeram esse,

nego consequentiam. Unde si nihil nec aliqualiter esset, verum esset
nullam chimaeram esse. Et tamen nulla veritate, quia nec veritate prima
nec veritate secunda, nec veritate rei nec veritate compositionis, cum non
esset aliqua harum veritatum. Et si concluditur:

25   Igitur, per idem, verum est Antichristum fore et tamen nulla veritate

      verum est Antichristum fore,

nego consequentiam, quia si nihil nec aliqualiter esset, nihil nec aliqualiter
foret nec fuisset nec posset esse. Et per consequens, non verum esset
Antichristum fore, vel posse esse, vel Adam fuisse.

30 Huiusmodi ergo veritates:

    Antichristum fore,

6 distinctione] determinatione *E*   21 nihil] esset *add. M*   aliqualiter] aliter *M*

Therefore, whenever ⟨someone⟩ proposes

⟨A⟩ truth is that no chimera is,

or

That no chimera is, is ⟨a⟩ truth;
⟨A⟩ possibility is that the Antichrist will be,

or

That the Antichrist will be, is ⟨a⟩ possibility;

I grant each of them without distinction. But I deny these propositions:

That no chimera is, is something true,
Something necessary or something possible is that no man is a donkey
or that the Antichrist will be.

Therefore, in what follows, I will continually take such terms in this second way, since it would be tedious continually to belabour these distinctions. Thus, etc.

⟨R1.4⟩ In reply to the fourth, I deny the inference, since the argument is made with a distracting term. Thus 'known', '⟨a⟩ truth', '⟨a⟩ falsity', and modal terms of this kind are ampliative terms and they distract the principal copula.[m]

⟨*The Author's Reply to that Master's Arguments*⟩

I reply to the arguments of that master, as much on his behalf[n] as on my own.

⟨R2.1⟩ When it is said:

⟨A⟩ truth is that no chimera is.
Therefore, according to some kind of truth, ⟨a⟩ truth is that no chimera is,

I deny the inference. Thus, if there were not anything or anyhow, ⟨a⟩ truth would be that no chimera is. Nevertheless, it would be ⟨a⟩ truth according to no truth, since it would be ⟨a⟩ truth neither according to the first truth, nor according to a second;[o] neither according to the truth of things, nor according to the truth of a composition; since none of these truths would be. If he concludes:

Therefore, by the same reasoning, ⟨a⟩ truth is that the Antichrist will be, and nevertheless according to no truth ⟨a⟩ truth is that the Antichrist will be,

I deny the inference. For if there were not anything or anyhow, then there would neither be nor have been nor could possibly be anything or in any way. Consequently, it would not be ⟨a⟩ truth that the Antichrist will be or can be, or that Adam was. Therefore, such truths as

that the Antichrist will be,

Adam fuisse,

Hoc posse esse,

originantur a prima veritate, quae est immensa divinitas. Et sic originari
non est esse, saltem in proprio genere, sed solummodo in intellectu divino
5 vel voluntate ipsius. Unde si Deus non esset, nihil nec aliqualiter esset.
Et si nihil nec aliqualiter esset, non verum esset Antichristum fore vel
aliquid huiusmodi. Et per consequens, huiusmodi sunt vera prima veritate.

Sed non sic est de negationibus, privationibus, falsitatibus et impossi-
bilitatibus, quae non possunt originari a prima veritate, cum in ea nulla sit
10 falsitas, negatio aut privatio. Nec ab aliqua prima falsitate, cum nulla sit
talis opposita primae veritati a qua originentur falsitates vel huiusmodi,
cum originari dicat principium positivum. Modo negationes, privationes,
falsitates et impossibilitates, quae non sunt signa, non sunt entia positiva,
ut pluries dictum est.

15   ⟨R2.2⟩ Ad aliud, nego consequentiam:

Possibile est nullum hominem esse asinum.

Et solum possibile potest esse.

Igitur, nullum hominem esse asinum potest esse,

quia debuit sumi pro maiori:

20   Aliquod possibile est nullum hominem esse asinum,

vel ista:

Possibile est nullum hominem esse asinum esse,

quarum quaelibet est falsa.

⟨R2.3⟩ Ad aliud:

25   Possibile est nullum hominem esse asinum.

Et possibili posito in esse nullum sequitur inconveniens,

concedo.

Igitur, posito in esse quod nulla chimaera est, nullum sequitur inconveniens.

30 Dico quod si istud consequens sic intelligatur quod posita alicui ista de
inesse

Nulla chimaera est,

nullum sequitur inconveniens, concedo. Si autem intelligatur quod posito
quod sit nullam chimaeram esse, non sequitur inconveniens, nego con-
35 sequentiam. Nec sic intelligitur illud dictum

Possibili posito in esse nullum sequitur inconveniens,

sed primo modo.

⟨R2.4⟩ Ad ultimum nego consequentiam. Ratio autem quare patet
intuenti.

11 originentur falsitates] originetur falsitas E   13 entia om. E

that Adam was,

that this can be,

arise from the first truth, which is the immeasurable Divinity. And to arise thus is not to be, at least in a proper genus, but only to be in the Divine Intellect or Will. Thus, if God were not, there would not be anything or anyhow. If there were not anything or anyhow, it would not be ⟨a⟩ truth that the Antichrist will be, or some such thing. Consequently, ⟨significata⟩ of this kind are truths according to the first truth.

But this does not apply to negations, privations, falsehoods, and impossibilities, which cannot arise from the first truth. For in the first truth there is no falsehood, negation, or privation. Nor do they arise from some first falsehood, since there is no such falsehood opposite to the first truth, from which falsehoods or the like could arise. For to arise bespeaks a positive principle. But negations, privations, falsehoods, and impossibilities that are not signs, are not positive beings, as has been said many times.

⟨R2.2⟩ In reply to another argument, I deny the inference:

⟨A⟩ possibility is that no man is a donkey.

Only the possible can be.

Therefore, that no man is a donkey, can be.

For one ought to take as the major

Something possible is that no man is a donkey,

or the proposition

⟨A⟩ possibility is that *that no man is a donkey* is,

each of which is false.

⟨R2.3⟩ In reply to another:

⟨A⟩ possibility is that no man is a donkey.

No difficulty follows from assuming ⟨a⟩ possibility actualized,

I grant them.

Therefore, no difficulty follows from assuming ⟨the possibility⟩ that no chimera is, actualized.

I say that if the conclusion is understood to mean that no difficulty follows from proposing the non-modal proposition

No chimera is

to someone, I grant it. But if it is understood to mean that no difficulty follows from assuming that *that no chimera is* is, I deny the inference. Nor is the claim

No difficulty follows from assuming ⟨a⟩ possibility actualized

so understood. Rather it is understood in the first way.

⟨R2.4⟩ In reply to the last, I deny the inference. My reason for doing so, however, is intuitively clear.

⟨*Sententia auctoris de quibusdam auctoritatibus Philosophi*⟩

Ex quo igitur ut constat argumenta non procedunt, ostendendo hanc opinionem fuisse de intentione Philosophi, ita quod secundum Philosophum non sequitur:

5   Possibile est sic esse, vel necessarium est nullam chimaeram esse aut nullum hominem esse asinum.

    Igitur, aliquid vel aliqualiter est nullum hominem esse asinum, aut sic esse.

Oppositum tamen ponit opinio contraria, asserens quamlibet talem ponere
10 in esse per aliquid, aliqua vel aliqualiter.

    Philosophus namque in secundo *Peri Hermeneias*,[5] ponit illa esse contradictoria

    Possibile est esse

et

15   Impossibile est esse,

et

    Contingens est non esse

et

    Necessarium est esse

20 vel

    Necesse est esse.

Ex quo sequitur quod illa sunt contradictoria

    Possibile est chimaeram esse

et

25   Impossibile est chimaeram esse,

et ista similiter

    Contingens est nullam chimaeram esse

et

    Necesse est chimaeram esse.

30 Si ergo quaelibet istarum poneret in esse, ut dicit ista opinio, contradictoria invicem contradicentia (209va M) extra materiam insolubilium forent simul falsa—quod tamen omnibus est absurdum.

    2° Arguitur sic: Ista convertuntur (165va E)

    Non possibile est Antichristum fore

35 et

    Impossibile est Antichristum fore,

---

2 ostendendo] ostendo *E*   14–16 et . . . et *om. M*   17 est] etiam *E*   19
necessarium . . . vel *om. M*   33 ista] illae *M*

⟨*The Author's Opinion about Certain Authoritative Passages from the Philosopher*⟩

For this reason, therefore, as is clear, these arguments cannot be seen to hold good by showing that this opinion accords with the intention of the Philosopher. Thus, according to the Philosopher, this does not follow:

⟨A⟩ possibility is that it is so, or ⟨a⟩ necessity is that no chimera is or that no man is a donkey.

Therefore, something or somehow is that no man is a donkey, or that it is so.

Nevertheless, the contrary opinion assumes the opposite, asserting that any such proposition assumes ⟨a possibility⟩ actualized by something, some things, or somehow.

For the Philosopher, in *Peri Hermeneias*, Part II ⟨c. 13, 22ᵃ32–8⟩, posits that

⟨A⟩ possibility is ⟨for such and such⟩ to be

and

⟨An⟩ impossibility is ⟨for such and such⟩ to be;
⟨A⟩ contingency is not ⟨for such and such⟩ to be

and

⟨A⟩ necessity is ⟨for such and such⟩ to be

are pairs of contradictories. It follows from this that the propositions

⟨A⟩ possibility is that a chimera is

and

⟨An⟩ impossibility is that a chimera is;

and similarly

⟨A⟩ contingency is that no chimera is

and

⟨A⟩ necessity is that a chimera is

are pairs of contradictories. Therefore, if one assumed the non-modal propositions corresponding to any of the above whatever, as this opinion says, contradictories that are mutually contradictory outside the matter of insolubles would be simultaneously false—which nevertheless everyone finds absurd.

2. I argue this way. According to Aristotle in the previously cited book, the propositions

Not ⟨a⟩ possibility is that the Antichrist will be

and

⟨An⟩ impossibility is that the Antichrist will be

per Aristotelem in libro praeallegato. Sed ex prima non sequitur quod aliquid, aliqua vel aliqualiter sit Antichristum fore. Igitur, nec ex secunda. Similiter et illae convertuntur

Contingens est te non esse

5 et

Non necesse est te esse,

per Aristotelem ibidem. Sed secunda non ponit in esse, ut patet secundum istam opinionem quae reprobatur, et omnes alias. Igitur nec prima.

3° Hoc idem patet per eundem Philosophum in eodem libro,[6] parum
10 infra textum allegatum, ponentem quod

Possibile aequivoce sumitur. Nam uno modo pro possibili coniuncto actui, ut possibile est ambulare quoniam ambulat. Alio modo pro possibili in potentia quod non est actui coniunctum, ut possibile est ambulare quoniam ambulabit.

15 Ecce ex textu Philosophi expresse habetur quod non sequitur:

Possibile est aliquem ambulare.

Igitur, aliquid vel aliqualiter est aliquem ambulare.

Et in primo *Peri Hermeneias* circa finem,[7] dicit quod 'hanc vestem possibile est incidi et non inciditur, sed prius exteritur', id est vetustate consumitur,
20 'similiter autem et non incidi possibile est. Non enim esset prius exteri nisi esset possibile non incidi.' Ex quo textu satis patet quod non sequitur:

Hanc vestem possibile est non incidi.

Igitur, aliquid vel aliqualiter est illam non incidi.

Nec sequitur:

25 Illam possibile est incidi.

Igitur, aliquid vel aliqualiter est illam incidi.

4° Idem ostenditur ex sententia Philosophi in fine eiusdem primi *Peri Hermeneias*,[8] ponentis quod de futuris contingentibus non est determinata veritas, ita quod demonstrata utraque parte contradictionis, non necesse
30 est hoc fore, nec necesse est hoc non fore, sed necesse est hoc fore vel hoc non fore. Ait enim in littera:

'Dico autem necesse est futurum esse bellum navale cras vel futurum

15 habetur] sequitur *E*   19 exteritur id est] exterius a *E*   20 exteri] exterius *E*
28 quod *om. E*

convert. But it does not follow from the first that something, some things, or somehow is that the Antichrist will be. Therefore, it does not follow from the second either. Similarly, according to Aristotle in the same place, the propositions

⟨A⟩ contingency is that you are not

and

Not ⟨a⟩ necessity is that you are

also convert. But the second does not assume a possibility actualized, as is clear according to the opinion which I am disproving, as well as all others. Therefore, neither does the first.

3. This same point is made clear by the same Philosopher, in the same book, a little below the cited text ⟨23ᵃ7–11⟩, where he posits that

'Possible' is taken equivocally. In one way, for the possible conjoined to the actual. For example, ⟨a⟩ possibility is that he walks, because he walks. In another way, for the possible in potency which is not conjoined to actuality. For example, ⟨a⟩ possibility is that he walks because he will walk.

Here we have explicitly from the text of the Philosopher that this does not follow:

⟨A⟩ possibility is that someone walks.
Therefore, something or somehow is that someone walks.

And in *Peri Hermeneias*, Part I ⟨c. 9, 19ᵃ12–16⟩, towards the end, he says that 'This coat is possibly cut up and it is not cut up, but is worn out first'—i.e. it is destroyed with age. 'But, similarly, it is also possible for it not to be cut up. For it would not be that it wears out first, if it were not possible for it not to be cut up.' This text makes it clear enough that this does not follow:

This coat is possibly not cut up.
Therefore, something or somehow is that it is not cut up.

Nor does it follow:

This is possibly cut up.
Therefore, something or somehow is that this is cut up.

4. The same thing is shown by the opinion that the Philosopher lays down at the end of *Peri Hermeneias*, Part I ⟨c. 9, 19ᵃ27–32⟩, that where future contingents are concerned, there is no determinate truth, so that it is not ⟨a⟩ necessity that *this*—pointing to either side of the contradiction—will be, nor ⟨a⟩ necessity that this will not be. But ⟨a⟩ necessity is that this will be or that this will not be. For he says literally:

'. . . But I mean: ⟨a⟩ necessity is that either there will be a sea fight

non esse. Sed non futurum esse bellum navale cras necesse est vel non futurum, futurum autem esse vel non esse necesse est.'

Ex quo textu patet quod non sequitur:

Necesse est sic fore vel non fore sic.

5   Igitur, aliquid vel aliqualiter est sic fore vel sic non fore.

Et aliquantulum supra,[9] probando idem ait:

'Amplius, si est album nunc, verum erat dicere primo quoniam erit album. Quare semper verum fuit dicere quodlibet eorum quae facta sunt quoniam erit.'

10   Ex quo textu patet quod secundum Philosophum non sequitur:

Verum erat dicere quod hoc erit album.

Igitur, aliquid vel aliqualiter erat quod hoc erit album.

Aliter sua condicionalis foret falsa.

⟨5⟩ Ultimo arguitur ex hoc: Nam ista opinio destruit totum processum
15 Philosophi primo *Priorum*.[10] Probatur, quia data ista, numquam praemissae officiabiles forent verae ubi aliquis talis modus praecederet dictum negatum, quod tamen ibidem communiter fit. Etc.

⟨*Ultima Opinio: Tertia Conclusio*   *Capitulum Septimum*⟩

Tertia conclusio in ordine est ista: Cuiuslibet propositionis adaequate
20   complexe significabile quod in natura ponitur a suo incomplexe significabili per subiectum vel praedicatum enuntiabile aliqualiter distinguitur.

Volo dicere quod Deum esse et Deus distinguuntur; hominem esse distinguitur ab homine; te esse distinguitur a te.

25   ⟨1⟩ Probatur conclusio: Nam Deum esse et Deus significative distinguuntur. Igitur, aliqualiter distinguuntur. Consequentia tenet, ab inferiori ad suum superius sine impedimento. Antecedens probatur: Nam Deum esse est adaequate complexe significabile et non incomplexe significabile. Sed Deus est adaequate incomplexe significabile et non complexe signi-
30 ficabile. Igitur significative distinguuntur.

---

7 nunc] non *M*   9 erit] erunt *E*   11 erit] erat *E*   16 officiabiles] affirmativae *M*   17 etc. *om. E*   23 distinguuntur] distinguitur *M* (*etiam infra, ubicumque, usque ad p. 158 lin. 6–7*)

tomorrow or that there will not be a sea fight tomorrow. But I do not say that there will be a sea fight tomorrow, is ⟨a⟩ necessity or that there will not be one tomorrow, is ⟨a⟩ necessity. But that there will be or will not be is ⟨a⟩ necessity.'

From this text ⟨in *Peri Hermeneias* 19ᵃ30–3⟩, it is clear that this does not follow:

⟨A⟩ necessity is that things will be so or that things will not be so. Therefore, something or somehow is that things will be so or that things will not be so.

And a little above, proving the same thing, he says,

'Further, if it is white now, ⟨a⟩ truth it was to say first that it will be white. Thus, always ⟨a⟩ truth it was to say that any of those things that have happened will be.'

It is clear from the text ⟨*Peri Hermeneias*, c. 9, 18ᵇ9–11⟩ that this does not follow according to the Philosopher:

⟨A⟩ truth it was to say that this will be white. Therefore, something or somehow was that this will be white.

Otherwise, his own conditional would be false.

⟨5⟩ Finally, I argue from the fact that this opinion destroys the Philosopher's whole procedure in the *Prior Analytics*, Book I ⟨c. 3, 25ᵃ27–ᵇ26; c. 13, 32ᵃ18–ᵇ3⟩. Proof: If this opinion is granted, functionalizable premisses would never be true where some such mode preceded a negated nominalization. But ⟨the Philosopher⟩ commonly ⟨advances such premisses⟩ in that same work, etc.ᵇ

⟨*Last Opinion: Thesis 3*   *Chapter Seven*⟩

The third thesis in order is this.

Thesis 3: What is adequately and complexly signifiable by any proposition and has a place in reality,ᵃ is somehow distinct from what is non-complexly signifiable through its statable subject or predicate.

I mean that that God is and God are distinct; that a man is, is distinct from a man; that you are, is distinct from you.

⟨1⟩ Proof of the thesis: For that God is, and God are distinct with respect to signification. Therefore, they are somehow distinct. The inference holds from the inferior to its superior without any interfering logical operator. Proof of the premiss: That God is, can be adequately signified by a complex and not by a non-complex. But God can be adequately signified by a non-complex and not by a complex. Therefore, they are distinct with respect to signification.

2° Arguitur sic: Deus et Deum esse originaliter distinguuntur. Igitur aliqualiter distinguuntur. Consequentia tenet ut prius. Et antecedens probatur: Nam ratio divinitatis originatur ex omnibus rationibus essentialibus divinis. Sed ratio Deum esse oritur ex ratione entitatis et ratione
5 divinitatis. Igitur etc.

3° Deum esse et Deus formaliter distinguuntur. Igitur aliqualiter distinguuntur. Consequentia tenet ut prius. Et antecedens probatur: Nam ratio divina ut sic est ratio incomplexi. Sed ratio Deum esse ut sic, est ratio complexi. Cum igitur ratio complexi et ratio incomplexi (209vb M)
10 formaliter distinguantur, sequitur quod Deus et Deum esse formaliter distinguuntur.

Confirmatur sic: Entitas divina formaliter distinguitur a ratione vitae in Deo. Igitur et Deus a Deum esse. Consequentia patet, quia sicut ratio vitae in Deo est posterior ratione entitatis in ipso, ita ratio complexa
15 divina est posterior ratione incomplexa ipsius. Antecedens probatur: Nam alia ratione (165vb E) est Deus productivus entis quod non est vita et alia entis quod est vita; quia si non alia, non posset aliquid producere quod non esset vita. Igitur illae rationes distinguuntur. Sed non realiter. Igitur formaliter.

20 Consimilibus rationibus potest probari quod hominem esse distinguitur ab homine, et te esse a te. Quia unius est ratio complexi et alterius incomplexi, quia ratio hominis, quae est humanitas, oritur ex tanto gradu latitudinis perfectionis simpliciter. Sed ratio huius complexi hominem esse consurgit ex humanitate et ratione essendi in gradu illo. Similiter, ratio
25 tui individualis oritur ex tanto gradu latitudinis specificae. Sed ratio illius complexi te esse oritur ex eadem ratione ⟨tui, et ratione essendi in gradu illo⟩. Et ita dicatur in aliis complexe significabilibus, ut hominem vivere oritur ex ratione hominis, ratione entitatis et ratione vitae; te currere ex ratione individuali tui, ratione entitatis et ratione cursus specifica vel
30 individuali.

Ex quibus sequitur quod etiam est distinctio formalis inter complexe significabilia sicut inter incomplexe significabilia et inter complexe et incomplexe significabilia simul; ita quod Deum esse et Deum vivere formaliter distinguuntur; hominem esse hominem et hominem esse
35 animal formaliter distinguuntur. Sicut enim prius est esse in Deo quam vita, et in homine prius animalitas quam humanitas; ita Deum esse prius est quam Deum vivere, et hominem esse animal prius est quam hominem

4 Deum] divini M (etiam lin. 8)   entitatis] entis M (etiam infra, lin. 14, 27, 28 et p. 160 lin. 13. Cf. autem hic infra, lin. 16–17)   5 divinitatis] veritatis E   13 et om. E 16–17 entis$^{1-2}$] entitatis E   22 humanitas] humanitatis E   24 ratione] ratio M 24–7 in . . . illo om. (hom.?) E   27 significabilibus] significantibus E   29 ratione^3] ipse ME, correxi   36 animalitas . . . humanitas] animalitatis . . . humanitatis M

2. I argue this way: God and God existing[b] are distinct in their origin. Therefore, they are somehow distinct. The inference holds as before. Proof of the premiss: The notion[c] *Divinity* takes its origin from all the essential notions of the Divine. But the notion *God existing*, takes its origin from the notions of existence and Divinity. Therefore, etc.

3. God existing, and God are formally distinct.[d] Therefore, they are somehow distinct. The inference holds as before. Proof of the premiss: The notion of the Divine is, as such, the notion of a non-complex. But the notion *God existing* is, as such, the notion of a complex. Since, therefore, the notion of a complex and the notion of a non-complex are formally distinct, it follows that God and *God existing* are formally distinct.

Confirming argument: The Divine Existence is formally distinct from the notion *life* in God. Therefore, God is formally distinct from *God existing*. The inference is clear. For just as the notion *life* in God is posterior to the notion of His existence, so a complex notion of the Divine is posterior to the non-complex notion of Him. Proof of the premiss: The notion of God *qua* productive of being that is not life is one notion, and the notion of God *qua* productive of being that is life is another. For if it were not another, then He could not produce something that was not life. Therefore, these notions are distinct. But not really distinct. Therefore, formally distinct.

By similar arguments, it can be proved that a man existing is distinct from a man, and you existing is distinct from you. For the notion of one is the notion of a complex; and the notion of the other, of a non-complex. For the notion of man, which is humanity, arises from a certain degree of breadth of absolute perfection. But the notion of the complex *a man existing* arises from humanity and the notion of being in that degree. Similarly, the notion of the individual you arises from a certain specific degree. But the notion of the complex *you existing* arises from the same notion of you together with the notion of being in that degree. The same sort of thing may be said about others that are signifiable by a complex. For example, *a man living* arises from the notion *man*, the notion *existence*, and the notion *life*; *you running*, from the notion of the individual you, from the notion *existence*, and from the notion, specific or individual, of running.

From these remarks, it follows that there is also a formal distinction among those that are signifiable by a complex, just as there is among those signifiable by a non-complex; at the same time, there is also a formal distinction between those signifiable by a complex and those signifiable by a non-complex. Thus, that God is, and that God lives, are formally distinct; that a man is a man, and that a man is an animal, are formally distinct. For just as existence is prior to life in God, and animality prior to humanity in man; so God existing is prior to God living, and a man being an animal

esse hominem. Sed ubicumque est prioritas et posterioritas, ibi est aliqua distinctio, saltem formaliter. Igitur inter illa complexe significabilia est aliqua distinctio quae non potest esse nisi formalis.

Ex praedictis sequitur quod magis distinguuntur Deus et Deum esse, 5 quam homo et hominem esse. Nam Deus et Deum esse immense et infinite distinguuntur, sed homo et hominem esse praecise finite distinguuntur. Igitur etc. Consequentia tenet. Et maiorem probo: Nam quaecumque duae rationes tante distinguuntur, quantae sunt. Sed quaelibet illarum rationum est immensa et infinita formaliter. Igitur etc. Secunda 10 pars similiter probatur: Nam ratio hominis est formaliter finita, et ratio similiter huiusmodi complexe significabilis. Igitur, homo et hominem esse praecise finite distinguuntur. Tamen plus distinguitur quam asinus et asinum esse, quia etiam maioris et perfectioris entitatis sunt rationes a quibus fundamentaliter originantur. Quare etc.

15 ⟨*Argumenta contra tertiam conclusionem*⟩

⟨1⟩ Contra istam conclusionem arguitur sic: Si Deus et Deum esse formaliter distinguuntur, sic quod prius est Deus quam Deum esse, et cum omne prius stet absque contradictione esse absque suo posteriori, igitur stat Deum esse et non esse Deum esse absque contradictione—quod 20 est impossibile.

2° Arguitur sic: Ratio illius incomplexi est ratio sui complexi. Igitur non formaliter distinguuntur. Consequentia tenet. Et antecedens probatur: Nam ratio incomplexi est Deus. Et ratio complexi est Deus. Igitur ratio incomplexi est ratio complexi. Consequentia tenet. Et antecedens similiter, 25 quia in divinis non cadit distinctio realis nisi in personis divinis.

3° Sumo Deum praecise secundum se, absque aliquo alio quoquo modo ab eo distincto. Aut igitur ipse est Deum esse aut non. Non secundum, quia tunc distinguerentur realiter. Si primum, igitur vel Deum esse non distinguitur a Deo—quod est propositum—vel in Deo sunt plura Deum 30 esse—quod est error. Sicut enim non est nisi unus Deus, ita nec nisi unum Deum esse.

4° Sequitur quod Deus non est Deus quo est Deum esse, sed alia et alia ratione. Consequens falsum, quia tunc in Deo non esset summa simplicitas.

---

1 ibi *om. M*   5 immense et *om. E*   8 quaelibet] qualibet *M*   10 similiter] igitur *E*   25 in² *om. M*   26 quoquo modo] quo quomodo *M (cf. infra p. 164, lin. 10)*   28 vel *om. E*

is prior to a man being a man. But wherever there is priority and posteriority there is some distinction there, at least formally. Therefore, among those that are signifiable by a complex, there is some distinction which can be only a formal distinction.

From the preceding remarks, it follows that God, and that God is, are more distinct than a man, and that a man is. For God, and that God is, are immeasurably and infinitely distinct. But a man, and that a man is, are precisely finitely distinct. Therefore, etc. The inference holds. Proof of the major: How much any two notions are distinct, varies with how much they are. Either of these two notions is immeasurable and formally infinite. Therefore, etc. Similarly, the second premiss is proved this way: The notion of man is formally finite. So is the notion of ⟨a man existing⟩ which is signifiable by a complex. Therefore, man, and that a man is, are precisely finitely distinct. Nevertheless, they are more distinct than a donkey, and that a donkey is, since the formal principles from which ⟨a man, and that a man is⟩ fundamentally originate are formal principles of greater and more perfect entity than those from which ⟨a donkey, and that a donkey is,⟩ originate. Therefore, etc.

⟨Arguments against Thesis 3⟩

⟨1⟩ Thesis 3 is argued against, this way. Suppose God and God existing[e] are formally distinct in such a way that God is prior to God existing. Since it is consistent that anything prior exists without what is posterior to it, then it is consistent that God is, and that *God existing* is not, without any contradiction—which is impossible.

2. This argument is made. The notion of that non-complex is the notion of its complex. Therefore, they are not formally distinct. The inference holds. Proof of the premiss: The notion of the non-complex is God. The notion of the complex is God. Therefore, the notion of the non-complex is the notion of the complex. The inference holds. So does the premiss, since in the realm of Divinity real distinction occurs only among the Divine Persons.

3. I[f] take God precisely in Himself, apart from anything else in any way distinct from Him. Either He is God existing, or not. Not the second, since they they would be really distinct. If the first, then either God existing is not distinct from God—which is what was to be proved—or in God there are many Gods existing—which is an error. For just as there is only one God, so there is only one God existing.[g]

4. It follows that God is not God by that by which He is God existing, but is one under one notion and the other under another notion. The conclusion is false, since then God would not be simple in the highest degree.

5° Sequitur quod duo sunt Dei. Probatur: Nam Deus est unus Deus et Deum esse est alius Deus. Igitur etc. Consequentia tenet cum prima parte antecedentis. Et secundam probo: Nam Deus non est Deum esse. Et quilibet illorum est Deus. Igitur etc. Consequentia tenet cum minori.
5   Et maiorem probo: Nam Deus distinguitur a Deum esse, per conclusionem. Igitur Deus non est Deum esse. Consequentia tenet, ab exposito ad unam suarum exponentium.

⟨*Responsio ad argumenta contra tertiam conclusionem*⟩

Ad rationes:

10 ⟨R1⟩ Ad primam, concedo quod Deus est prius quam Deum esse, et nego quod universaliter stet prius esse sine posteriori, licet stet (210ra M) intelligi sine posteriori. Possum enim intelligere Deum et non intelligere ipsum esse. Unde aliquando posterius est ita intrinsecum priori quod non stat sine contradictione esse primum sine secundo. Sicut per prius est in
15 divina essentia ratio vitae vel intellectivae quam ratio immensitatis, necessitatis vel independentiae, cum isti sint modi intrinseci consurgentes ex rationibus essentialibus divinis. (166ra E) Et tamen non stat primum esse sine secundo. Similiter, in creatura per prius est esse, vivere, vel te esse intellectivum, quam esse finitum vel infinitum, cum isti sint modi illarum
20 rationum essentialium. Et tamen non stat primum esse sine secundo, quia quod aliqua creatura sit quae non sit finita nec infinita implicat contradictionem.

⟨R2⟩ Ad secundam, nego quod ratio complexi sit ratio incomplexi vel e contra. Et ad probationem nego illam consequentiam:

25   Ratio complexi est Deus.
        Et ratio incomplexi est idem Deus.
        Igitur, ratio complexi est ratio incomplexi.

Nam in qualibet parte antecedentis est suppositio realis vel identica, et in consequente suppositio formalis. Sicut in simili non sequitur:

30   Pater est essentia divina.
        Et Filius est essentia divina.
        Igitur Pater est Filius,

quia in antecedente est suppositio essentialis, in consequente vero suppositio personalis. Sed deberet concludi:

35   Igitur, Pater est illud quod est Filius.

6 exposito] exposita *M*   15 intellectivae] intelligere *M*   16 independentiae] dependentiae *E*   sint] sunt (*etiam lin. 19*) *E*   17 essentialibus *om. M*   18 vel] etiam *add. M*   19 quam . . . infinitum *om. M*   29 sicut] similiter *E*   31 est . . . divina] similiter *M*   33 suppositio²] sola *M*

5. It follows that there are two Gods. Proof: God is one God and God existing is another God. Therefore, etc. The inference holds as does the first part of the premiss. Proof of the second part of the premiss: For God is not God existing. Each of them is God. Therefore, etc. The inference holds, as does the minor. Proof of the major: God is distinct from God existing, according to Thesis 3. Therefore, God is not God existing. The inference holds from the expounded proposition to one of the propositions expounding it.

⟨*Reply to the Arguments against Thesis 3*⟩

In reply to the arguments:

⟨R1⟩ In reply to the first, I grant that God is prior to God existing. I deny that universally it is consistent that the prior exists without the posterior, although it is consistent that the prior is thought of without the posterior. For I can think of God and not think of Him existing. Thus, sometimes the posterior is so intrinsic to the prior, that it is not consistent and without contradiction that the first is without the second. For example, the notion *life* or *intellectual power* exists in the Divine Essence prior to the notions *immensity*, *necessity*, or *independence*; for the last are intrinsic modes that arise from the essential notions of the Divine. Nevertheless, it is not consistent that the first is without the second. Similarly, being, living, or you being intellectual, is in a creature prior to being finite or infinite, since the last are modes of the earlier-mentioned essential formal principles. Nevertheless, it is not consistent that the first is without the second. For that some creature is neither finite nor infinite implies a contradiction.

⟨R2⟩ In reply to the second, I deny that the notion of the complex is the notion of the non-complex, or vice versa. In reply to the proof, I deny the inference:

The notion of the complex is God.

The notion of the non-complex is the same God.

Therefore, the notion of the complex is the notion of the non-complex.

For in each part of the premiss, the *suppositio* is real and identical, and in the conclusion the *suppositio* is formal.[h] Similarly, analogously, this does not follow:

The Father is the Divine Essence.

The Son is the Divine Essence.

Therefore, the Father is the Son.

For in the premiss the *suppositio* is essential, but in the conclusion personal.[i] But one ought to conclude:

Therefore, the Father is that which is the Son.

Ita in priori consequentia debuit concludi ex illis praemissis:

Igitur, ratio incomplexi est illud quod est ratio complexi, vel e contra.

Et isto modo concedo consequentiam et consequens. Unde ad concludendum tale consequens debuit sumi continue suppositio formalis—videlicet:

5   Ratio incomplexi est formaliter Deus.

Et ratio complexi est formaliter Deus.

Igitur etc.

Isto modo concederem consequentiam et negarem minorem.

⟨R3⟩ Ad tertiam, cum dicitur:

10   Sumo Deum praecise secundum se absque aliquo alio quoquo modo
ab eo distincto,

casus est impossibilis, quia non potest sumi posterius sine priori. Modo Deus sive ratio divinitatis praesupponit infinitas rationes essentiales sine quibus non potest sumi, sicut rationem entitatis, vitae, intellectivae. Et hoc

15 certum est, quod si quis vellet sumere humanitatem absque animalitate, vellet impossibile. Et tamen humanitas et animalitas invicem distinguuntur. Tamen quia stat sumi per intellectum prius sine posteriori, ideo admitto quod sumatur Deus sine Deum esse. Et tunc cum quaeritur, utrum sit Deum esse vel non, dico quod est Deum esse. Et ad improba-

20 tionem, nego consequentiam pro qualibet parte disiunctivae consequentis.

⟨R4⟩ Ad quartam concedo quod Deus non est Deus quo est Deum esse, sed alia ratione Deus et alia ratione Deum esse. Prima est incomplexa et secunda complexa. Et cum concluditur:

Igitur in Deo non est summa simplicitas,

25 nego consequentiam, quia cum infinita simplicitate reali vel essentiali stant infinitae distinctiones rationum formalium.

⟨R5⟩ Ad quintam nego quod sunt duo Dei. Et concedo quod Deum esse est Deus. Sed non alius Deus a Deo. Et cum dicitur:

Deus distinguitur a Deum esse.

30   Igitur non est Deum esse,

non valet consequentia. Nec arguitur ab exposito ad alteram suarum exponentium, quia ly .distinguitur. debet primo probari aliqualiter resolutorie sic:

Aliqua distinctione distinguitur,

6 Et . . . Deus *om.* (*hom.*) M   10 quoquo modo] quo quomodo M   11 distincto] demonstrato E   13 divinitatis] deitatis M   14 intellectivae] intelligentiae M   15 animalitate] sumere *add.* M   17 tamen] tum E
27 sunt] sint M

Thus, in the prior inference one ought to have concluded from these premisses:

Therefore, the notion of the non-complex is that which is the notion of the complex and vice versa.

In this way, I grant the inference and the conclusion. Thus, for inferring such a conclusion, one ought continually to have taken the *suppositio* to be formal throughout the argument, viz.:

The notion of the non-complex is formally God.
The notion of the complex is formally God.
Therefore, etc.

Taken in this way, I would grant the inference and deny the minor.

⟨R3⟩ In reply to the third, when it is said:

I take God precisely in Himself apart from anything else distinct from Him in any way,

the case is impossible. For the posterior cannot be taken without the prior. But God or the notion of Divinity presupposes an infinite number of essential notions without which it cannot be, such as the notion of existence and of life and intellectual power. And this is certain: that if someone wished to take humanity without animality, he would wish the impossible. Nevertheless, humanity and animality are distinct from one another. Nevertheless, since it is consistent that the prior is taken without the posterior by the intellect, then I admit that God is taken without God existing. Then, when it is asked whether or not He is God existing, I say that He is God existing. In reply to the disproof, I deny the inference for each part of the disjunctive conclusion.

⟨R4⟩ In reply to the fourth, I grant that God is not God by that by which He is God existing, but is God under one notion and is God existing under another notion. The first is non-complex and the second is complex. When it is concluded:

Therefore, God would not be simple in the highest degree,

I deny the inference, since an infinite number of distinctions of formal principles is consistent with infinite, real or essential simplicity.

⟨R5⟩ In reply to the fifth, I deny that there are two Gods. I grant that *God existing* is God, but no other God than God. When it is said:

God is distinct from God existing.
Therefore, He is not God existing,

the inference does not hold good. Nor is there an argument from the expounded proposition to one of the propositions expounding it. For one ought first to prove 'is distinct' somehow resolubly, this way:

It is distinct by some distinction,

ex quo stat determinate pro multis distinctionibus disiunctive. Ex quo debet concludi quod Deus aliqua distinctione non est Deum esse—quod est verum. Et si dicitur quod bene sequitur:

Deus differt a Deum esse.

5   Igitur Deus non est Deum esse,

concedo quod bene sequitur, sed antecedens est falsum. Et si dicitur:

Deus aliqua differentia differt a Deum esse.

Igitur differt a Deum esse,

concedo consequentiam et nego antecedens. Et si arguitur sic:

10   Deus aliqua distinctione distinguitur a Deum esse.

Igitur aliqua differentia distinguitur a Deum esse.

Et si sic,

igitur aliqua differentia differt a Deum esse,

nego primam consequentiam.

15 Unde dico quod licet inter rationes formales divinas sit aliqualis distinctio, non tamen differentia, quia distinctio potest esse inter ea quae non distinguuntur realiter, sed differentia non reperitur nisi inter ea quae distinguuntur realiter. Propterea universaliter sequitur:

A differt a *B*.

20   Igitur *A* non est *B*.

Unde conceditur in divinis quod Pater differt a Filio et distinguitur ab eodem. Non tamen conceditur quod Pater differat ab essentia divina, licet distinguatur ab ipsa.

⟨*Ultima Opinio: Quarta Conclusio*   *Capitulum Octavum*⟩

25   *Quarta conclusio* et ultima in ordine est ista: Cuiuslibet propositionis verae et affirmativae de praesenti sine verbo (210rb M) ampliativo aut termino distrahente aliqualiter, adaequatum significatum subiecti aut praedicati principali significato est communicabile identice realiter.

30 Volo dicere quod huius propositionis

Deus est

adaequatum significatum est idem realiter cum significato adaequato subiecti, ita quod idem est realiter Deus et Deum esse, homo et hominem esse, Sortes et Sortem esse.

35   Notanter dico 'subiecti vel praedicati', quia significatum adaequatum

17–18 sed . . . realiter *bis habet* (hom.) M, *om.* (hom.?) E   26 sine] termino vel *add.* E
33 Deus] est *add.* M

because 'distinct' has determinate *suppositio* for many distinctions dis-junctively. One ought to conclude from this that God by some distinction is not God existing—which is true. And if it is said that this does follow:

God differs from God existing.

Therefore, God is not God existing,

I grant that it does follow. But the premiss is false. And if it is said:

God, by some difference, differs from God existing.

Therefore, He differs from God existing,

I grant the inference and deny the premiss. And if this argument is advanced:

God, by some distinction, is distinct from God existing.

Therefore, He is distinct from God existing, by some difference.

And if so,

Therefore, by some difference He differs from God existing,

I deny the inference.

Thus, I say that although there is some sort of distinction among divine formal principles, nevertheless there is not a difference. For distinction can be among those things that are not really distinct. But difference obtains only among those things that are really distinct. For this reason, this follows universally:

A differs from B.

Therefore, A is not B.

Thus, it is granted in the realm of the Divine that the Father differs from the Son and is distinct from Him. Nevertheless, it is not granted that the Father differs from the Divine Essence, although He is distinct from it.ʲ

⟨*Last Opinion: Thesis 4*   *Chapter Eight*⟩

The fourth and last thesis in order is this:

Thesis 4: For any true and affirmative present-tense proposition, that has no ampliative verb or a term that is somehow distracting, the adequate significatum of the subject or the adequate significatum of the predicate is really identical with its principal significatum.

I mean that the adequate significatum of the proposition

God is

is really identical with the adequate significatum of the subject, so that God and that God is, a man and that a man is, Socrates and that Socrates is, are really the same.

Notice I say '⟨the adequate significatum⟩ of the subject or ⟨the adequate sig-nificatum⟩ of the predicate'. For the adequate significatum of a proposition

propositionis est aliquando idem significato (166ʳᵇ E) subiecti et non significato praedicati, supple adaequato. Aliquando e converso. Sicut

     Hic asinus est hominis.

Nam asinum esse hominis est asinus et non homo, nec in recto nec in
5 obliquo. Similiter

     Sortem est videns Plato,

significatum adaequatum non est Sortes, sed Plato.

     Item notandum quod licet propositio plura significet totalia et distincta,
non tamen adaequatum significatum est illa totalia, nisi pro ipsis fiat
10 extremaliter substantive, implicite vel explicite, verificatio propositionis.
Sicut haec

     Homo est animal.

Haec propositio significat hominem, asinum, leonem et huiusmodi. Et
tamen significatum illius non est asinus vel leo, quia ratione nullius
15 istorum propositio vera est. Sed quia ratione hominis propositio ista
dicitur vera, ideo significatum adaequatum est identice homo.

     Item significatum illius adaequatum

     Sortes differt a Platone

est Sortes, et non Sortes et Plato, sicut aliqui dicunt.[1] Quia licet pro ipsis
20 propositio verificetur, non tamen extremaliter substantive implicite nec
explicite, ut patet cum non sit praedicatum ly .Platone. Sed istius propositionis

     Homines sunt homines

aut illius

25   Populus est

significatum adaequatum est identice plura, quia pro illis extremaliter
substantive implicite vel explicite propositio vera est.

     Ex quibus sequitur quod huiusmodi propositionis

     Sol calefacit domum

30 adaequatum significatum est sol, et non sol et domus, sicut dicunt illi.
Nam solem calefacere domum est sol praecise, ut ipsi dicunt, et tale est
adaequatum significatum illius. Igitur etc. Minor patet, quia solem calefacere domum et domum calefieri a sole est significatum copulativum.

is sometimes identical with the significatum of the subject and not with the significatum of the predicate (where by 'significatum' 'adequate significatum' is understood); sometimes, the other way around. For example, in

This donkey is a man's,

that the donkey is a man's, is a donkey and not a man ⟨no matter whether a man is supposited for⟩ by a term in the nominative case or by a term in an oblique case. Similarly, the adequate significatum of

Socrates' beholder is Plato

is not Socrates, but Plato.

Again, notice that although a proposition signifies many whole and distinct significata, nevertheless its adequate significatum is not those wholes, unless the proposition comes out true when its substantival extremes, whether they be implicit or explicit, ⟨are taken to supposit⟩ for those wholes. For example, the proposition

A man is an animal

signifies a man, a donkey, a lion, and the like. Nevertheless, its significatum is not a donkey or a lion. For it is not by reason of anything of these kinds that the proposition is true. But since the proposition is said to be true by reason of a man, then the adequate significatum is identical with a man.

Again, the adequate significatum of the proposition

Socrates is different from Plato

is Socrates, and not Socrates and Plato, as some say. For although the proposition comes out true with respect to them, nevertheless not with respect to its implicit or explicit substantival extremes, as is clear since 'Plato' is not the predicate. But the adequate significatum of the proposition

Men are men

or of the proposition

There are people

is identical with many, since the proposition is true for many, implicitly or explicitly, with respect to its substantival extremes.

It follows from these remarks that the adequate significatum of a proposition such as

The sun heats the house

is the sun, and not the sun and the house, as they say. For that the sun heats the house, is precisely the sun, as they themselves say. ⟨That the sun heats the house,⟩ is its adequate significatum. Therefore, etc. The minor is clear, since *that the sun heats the house and the house is heated by the sun* is a conjunctive significatum. Therefore, it does not adequately

Igitur adaequate non correspondet propositioni categoricae. Consequentia patet et declarabitur inferius.² Dicendum ergo quod illae duae propositiones convertuntur

Sol calefacit domum

5 et

Domus calefit a sole,

et tamen significata non sunt idem realiter, quia nec domus nec sol.

Item sequitur ex praedictis quod hominem esse album non est homo et albedo, sicut dicit unus magister ordinis mei.³ Sed est praecise homo vel
10 album, quia pro quolibet illorum fit verificatio propositionis et non pro albedine. Quare etc.

⟨*Contra quartam conclusionem, reductio ad conclusiones absurdas*⟩

Contra istam conclusionem arguo multipliciter, multas deducendo conclusiones absurdas, quas communiter⁴ concludunt viam suppositam negan-
15 tes.

⟨1⟩ *Prima* est quod falsum scitur.

Probatur: Nam falsum esse scitur. Sed quodlibet falsum esse est falsum. Igitur falsum scitur. Patet consequentia, quia in tertio vel in quarto tertiae figurae.

20 *2ª conclusio*: Possibile est impossibile.

Probatur: Hoc esse est impossibile, demonstrando propositionem impossibilem. Et hoc esse est possibile. Igitur possibile est impossibile. Patet consequentia, quia syllogismus demonstrativus in tertia figura. Secunda pars antecedentis probatur: Nam hoc esse est verum. Igitur hoc esse est
25 possibile. Prima pars antecedentis probatur: Nam hoc est impossibile, demonstrando illam

Tu es asinus.

Et hoc est hoc esse. Igitur hoc esse est impossibile. Consequentia patet, ut prius, et antecedens est conclusionis. Igitur etc.

30 *3ª conclusio*: Eandem propositionem scis et dubitas.

Probatur: Istam propositionem dubitas

Rex sedet

ut suppono, et istam eandem scis. Probatur, quia istam esse scis, et istam esse est ista. Igitur istam scis.

35 *4ª conclusio*: Aliqua est propositio mere contingens et tamen adaequatum significatum ipsius est necessarium.

7 realiter *om. E*   9 magister] doctor *M* (*cf. supra, p. 94 lin. 33–4*)   13 deducendo] dicendo *E*

correspond to a categorical proposition. The inference is clear and will be explained below. Therefore, it must be said that these two propositions

The sun heats the house

and

The house is heated by the sun

are interchangeable. Nevertheless, their adequate significata are not really the same, since the house and the sun are not really the same.

Again, it follows from the preceding remarks that *that a man is white*, is not a man and whiteness, as one master of my order says it is, but precisely a man or what is white. For the proposition comes out true with respect to each of these, and not for whiteness. Thus, etc.

⟨*Arguments Deducing Absurd Conclusions from Thesis 4*⟩

I[a] argue against this thesis in many ways, by deducing from it many absurd conclusions commonly drawn by those who deny the way under discussion.

First ⟨Absurd⟩ Conclusion: A falsehood is known.

Proof: That a falsehood is, is known. But each falsehood existing[b] is a falsehood. Therefore, a falsehood is known. The inference is clear, since it is an argument in the third or fourth ⟨mood⟩ of the third figure.

Second ⟨Absurd⟩ Conclusion: The possible is impossible.

Proof: That this is (where 'this' indicates an impossible proposition) is impossible. That this is, is possible. Therefore, the possible is impossible. The inference is clear, since it is a demonstrative syllogism in the third figure. Proof of the second premiss: That this is, is true. Therefore, that this is, is possible. Proof of the first premiss: For this is impossible (where 'this' indicates the proposition

You are a donkey).

This is that this is. Therefore, that this is, is impossible. The inference is clear, as before, as is the premiss of the conclusion. Therefore, etc.

Third ⟨Absurd⟩ Conclusion: You know and you doubt the same proposition.

Proof: I suppose that you doubt the proposition

The king is sitting.

And you know the same proposition. Proof: You know that the proposition is. That the proposition is, is the proposition.[c] Therefore, you know the proposition.

Fourth ⟨Absurd⟩ Conclusion: Some proposition is merely contingent and nevertheless its adequate significatum is necessary.

Probatur: Et capio istam

Deus creat Sortem.

Haec est contingens, ut patet. Et tamen Deum creare Sortem est necessarium, quia hoc est necessarium, demonstrando Deum ⟨esse⟩. Et hoc est
5 Deum creare Sortem. Igitur etc.

  5ª conclusio: Sortes est Plato, dato quod ambo sint.

Nam Sortem differre a Platone est Sortes. Igitur Sortem esse et Platonem
esse et Sortem non esse Platonem est Sortes. Patet consequentia, ab
exposita ad suas exponentes. Sed ex consequente sequitur quod Platonem
10 esse est Sortes, (210ᵛᵃ M) tamquam a copulato extremo sine impedimento
praecedente ad alteram partem. Sed Platonem esse est Plato. Igitur Plato
est Sortes, et e contra.

  6ª conclusio: Ego possum facere me.

Probatur: Nam possum facere me currere. Sed ego sum me currere vel
15 possum esse me currere. Igitur ego possum facere me. Et ita probatur
quod ego possum facere omnes homines, quia possum facere omnes
homines sedere. Sed omnes homines sedere sunt vel possunt esse omnes
homines. Igitur etc.

  7ª conclusio: Solem calefacere domum est non sol.

20 Probatur: cum solem esse stat esse solem non calefacientem domum. Et
tamen cum solem calefacere domum non stat solem esse non calefacientem domum. Igitur solem esse non est solem calefacere domum.

  8ª conclusio: Antichristum fore est Antichristus, et tamen nullus
  Antichristus est.

25 Probatur: Deus scit Antichristum fore. Igitur Antichristum fore est Antichristus. Patet consequentia a simili: Deus (166ᵛᵃ E) scit Sortem esse.
Igitur Sortem esse est Sortes.

  9ª conclusio: Contingens est necessarium.

Probatur: Nam te esse est contingens. Et te esse est necessarium. Igitur
30 etc. Consequentia tenet cum maiori. Et minorem probo: Nam te esse vel
te non esse est necessarium. Sed quidquid et qualitercumque est te esse
vel te non esse, est te esse, quia te non esse non est aliquid nec aliqualiter.
Igitur te esse est necessarium.

  10ª conclusio: Tu es ita sapiens sicut Deus.

35 Probatur: Tu scis omnia. Sed Deus non scit plura quam omnia. Igitur etc.
Consequentia tenet cum minori. Et maiorem probo: Nam tu scis omnia

3 haec] hoc *E*   9 exposita] exposito *E*   ex] in *E*   20–2 et . . . domum¹
om. (hom.) *E*   21 cum] non *M, correxi*   22 calefacere] esse calefacientem *E*
31 et] vel *E*

Proof: I take the proposition

God creates Socrates.

This is contingent, as is clear. Nevertheless, that God creates Socrates, is necessary. For this is necessary (where 'this' indicates that God is), and this is that God creates Socrates. Therefore, etc.[d]

Fifth ⟨Absurd⟩ Conclusion: Granted that both Socrates and Plato are, Socrates is Plato.

Proof: *That Socrates is different from Plato*, is Socrates. Therefore, *that Socrates is, and Plato is, and Socrates is not Plato*, is Socrates. The inference is clear from the expounded proposition to the propositions expounding it. But from the conclusion it follows that *that Plato is* is Socrates. ⟨The inference goes over⟩ by replacement of a conjunctive extreme with one or another conjunct, when there is no preceding ⟨logical operator⟩ to stop this. But that Plato is, is Plato. Therefore, Plato is Socrates, and vice versa.[e]

Sixth ⟨Absurd⟩ Conclusion: I can make myself.

Proof: I can make myself to run. I am or can be myself running. Therefore, I can make myself. In this way, it is proved that I can make all men: I can make all men to sit. All men sitting, are or can be all men. Therefore, etc.[f]

Seventh ⟨Absurd⟩ Conclusion: That the sun heats the house, is not the sun.

Proof: It is consistent that the sun is, and that the sun is not heating the house. Nevertheless, it is not consistent that the sun heats the house and that the sun is not heating the house. Therefore, for the sun to be, is not for the sun to heat the house.[g]

Eighth ⟨Absurd⟩ Conclusion: That the Antichrist will be, is the Antichrist, and nevertheless there is no Antichrist.

Proof: God knows that the Antichrist will be. Therefore, that the Antichrist will be, is the Antichrist. The inference is clear, by analogy: God knows that Socrates is. Therefore, that Socrates is, is Socrates.[h]

Ninth ⟨Absurd⟩ Conclusion: A contingency is necessary.

Proof: That you are, is contingent. That you are, is necessary. Therefore, etc. The inference holds, as does the major. Proof of the minor: That you are or that you are not, is necessary. But whatever, and whatever way, that you are or that you are not, is: that, or in that way, is that you are. For that you are not, is not anything or anyhow. Therefore, that you are, is necessary.[i]

Tenth ⟨Absurd⟩ Conclusion: You are as wise as God.

Proof: You know all things. But God does not know more than all things. Therefore, etc. The inference holds, as does the minor. Proof of the major: You know that all things are. But that all things are, is all things.

esse. Sed omnia esse sunt omnia. Igitur tu scis omnia. Patet consequentia cum minori ex opinione. Et maiorem probo: Nam tu scis istam propositionem

Omnia sunt,

5 quam scis primo et adaequate significare omnia esse. Igitur etc.

11ᵃ conclusio: Aliqua propositio convertitur cum suo subiecto.

Probatur: Nam capiatur ista

Deus est.

Tunc sic: Quidquid significat ista propositio, significat eius subiectum, 10 et e converso. Igitur ista propositio convertitur cum eius subiecto. Patet consequentia. Nec valet si dicatur quod non convertitur, ex eo quod diversimode significant. Nam isti duo termini 'risibile' et 'homo' convertuntur, et tamen diversimode significant. Quare etc.

12ᵃ conclusio: Propositio mere contingens est propositio necessaria.

15 Probatur: Nam haec propositio est contingens

Deus est causa tui,

et eadem est necessaria. Igitur etc. Consequentia tenet cum maiori. Et minorem probo: Nam Deum esse causam tui est necessarium. Sed Deum esse causam tui est significatum adaequatum illius. Igitur illa est necessaria. 20 Consequentia tenet cum minori. Et maiorem probo: Nam Deum esse est necessarium. Sed Deum esse est Deum esse causam tui. Igitur, Deum esse causam tui est necessarium.

⟨*Responsio auctoris ad conclusiones absurdas*⟩

Ad haec respondetur negando omnes conclusiones adductas, non 25 obstante quod plures ipsarum concesserint huic conclusioni faventes qui me praecesserunt. Dimissis ergo talibus responsionibus plus ad fugam quam ad veritatem nitentibus, dico ergo ad primam conclusionem, negando ipsam. Et ad probationem nego consequentiam. Nec est syllogismus in tertia figura: primo quia maior non est alicuius quantitatis; secundo quia 30 in antecedente ly .scitur. sumitur officiabiliter, in consequente vero descriptibiliter;⁵ tertio quia in antecedente determinat complexum, in consequente vero incomplexum. Ideo deberet sic argui: Falsum esse

---

2 cum minori *om. E*   6 suo] eius *M*   10 subiecto] significato *E*   13 quare]
igitur (*etiam infra*) *E*   14 mere contingens] materiae contingentis *E*   26 talibus]
conclusionibus *add. M*   27 ergo *om. E*

Therefore, you know all things. The inference is clear, as is the minor, according to this opinion. Proof of the major: You know the proposition

All things are,

and you know that it primarily and adequately signifies that all things are. Therefore, etc.

> *Eleventh ⟨Absurd⟩ Conclusion*: Some proposition is interchangeable with its subject.

Proof: Take the proposition

God is.

Then I argue this way: Whatever the proposition signifies, its subject signifies, and vice versa. Therefore, the proposition is interchangeable with its subject. The inference is clear. Nor does it hold good if someone says that they are not interchangeable because they signify in different ways. For these two terms 'risible' and 'man' are interchangeable. Nevertheless, they signify in different ways. Therefore, etc.

> *Twelfth ⟨Absurd⟩ Conclusion*: A merely contingent proposition is a necessary proposition.

Proof: The proposition

God is the cause of you,

is contingent. The same proposition is necessary. Therefore, etc. The inference holds as does the major. Proof of the minor: That God is the cause of you, is necessary. That God is the cause of you, is the adequate significatum of that proposition. Therefore, that proposition is necessary. The inference holds, as does the minor. Proof of the major: That God is, is necessary. For God to be, is for God to be the cause of you.[j] Therefore, that God is the cause of you is necessary.

⟨*The Author's Reply to these Absurd Conclusions*⟩

I reply to these arguments by denying all the adduced conclusions, notwithstanding the fact that many of my predecessors who favoured Thesis 4 have granted many of these conclusions. I dismiss such replies as seeking evasion rather than the truth. Therefore, I reply *to the first ⟨absurd⟩ conclusion*, by denying it. In reply to the proof, I deny the inference. Nor is it a syllogism in the third figure: First, because the major is not of any quantity. Second, because 'is known' in the premiss is taken functionalizably, but in the conclusion describably.[k] Third, because in the premiss, it governs a complex, but in the conclusion a non-complex. Therefore, one ought to argue this way: That a falsehood is, is known. Whatever and

scitur. Sed quidquid et qualitercumque est falsum esse, est falsum. Igitur
aliqualiter esse scitur qualiter esse est falsum.

   Ad secundam conclusionem dico similiter negando ipsam. Et tunc ad
argumentum:

5   Hoc esse est impossibile.
       Et hoc esse est possibile.
       Igitur possibile est impossibile,
dicitur quod maior est falsa, cum ista propositio non sit impossibilis

       Hoc est, demonstrato uno impossibili.

10 Et ad probationem negatur consequentia, quia in antecedente sumitur
ly .impossibile. resolubiliter et in consequente officiabiliter. Ideo ex illo
antecedente solum sequitur quod aliquid vel aliqualiter quod vel qualiter
est hoc esse, est impossibile—et hoc est verum—⟨et non⟩ quod hoc esse
sit propositio ⟨im⟩possibilis—quod est falsum. Tertio, iterum, maior est
15 falsa, quia asserit hoc esse non posse esse—quod est impossibile.

   Ad tertiam conclusionem, respondeo iterum negando illam. Et concedo
quod illam propositionem dubito, et nego quod illam scio. Et cum dicitur:

       Illam esse scio,

concedo.

20   Et illam esse est ista.
       Igitur istam scio,

non valet consequentia propter rationes dictas in prima solutione. Sed
debet concludi:

       Igitur aliqualiter esse scio qualiter esse est haec propositio.

25 Ad quartam conclusionem, cum dicitur:

       Aliqua propositio est contingens, et tamen eius adaequatum signi-
       ficatum (210vb M) est necessarium,

dico quod ly .contingens. et ly .necessarium. possunt dupliciter sumi:
vel adiective pure dependenter a substantivo praecedente, vel in neutro
30 genere substantivata. Secundo modo concedo consequentiam. Sed primo
modo nego ipsam, quomodo communiter locutus sum in dictis meis. Et
tunc ad argumentum:

       Deum creare Sortem est necessarium.
       Et Deum creare Sortem est adaequatum significatum illius.

35   Igitur significatum illius est necessarium,

---

14 impossibilis] possibilis *ME, correxi*   tertio *om. M*   22 consequentia] argumentum *E*   30 substantivata] substantivo *ME, correxi (cf. supra, p. 70 lin. 8)*

whatever way that a falsehood is, is: that, or in that way, is a falsehood. Therefore, it is known that things are in some way such that their being in that way is a falsehood.

Similarly, I reply *to the second ⟨absurd⟩ conclusion*, by denying it. Then in reply to the argument:

That this is, is impossible.

That this is, is possible.

Therefore, the possible is impossible,

I say that the major is false, since the proposition

This is

(where 'this' indicates an impossible proposition) is not impossible. In reply to the proof, I deny the inference, since 'impossible' is taken as a resoluble term in the premiss, and as a functionalizable term in the conclusion. Therefore, from the premiss it follows only that something or some way, which or in which way *that this is* is, is impossible—and this is true—and not

That this is, is an impossible proposition,

which is false. Third, again, the major is false, since it asserts that *that this is* cannot be—which is impossible.

Again I reply *to the third ⟨absurd⟩ conclusion* by denying it. I grant that I doubt the proposition and deny that I know it. When it is said

I know that the proposition is,

I grant it. And

That the proposition is, is the proposition.

Therefore, I know the proposition

the inference does not hold good for the reasons stated in the first solution.[l] But one ought to conclude:

Therefore, I know that things are in some way such that their being in that way is this proposition.

In reply *to the fourth ⟨absurd⟩ conclusion*, when it is said

Some proposition is contingent and nevertheless its adequate significatum is necessary,

I say that 'contingent' and 'necessary' can be taken in two ways: either as pure adjectives depending on a preceding substantive or ⟨as adjectives⟩ in the neuter gender equivalent to a substantive.[m] Taken in the second way, I grant the inference. But in the first way, I deny it, in the way in which I have commonly stated in my claims. Then, in reply to the argument

That God creates Socrates, is necessary.

That God creates Socrates, is the adequate significatum of this proposition.

Therefore, the significatum of this proposition is necessary,

nego antecedens pro prima parte. Et ad argumentum:

> Deum esse est necessarium.
>
> Sed Deum esse est Deum creare Sortem.
>
> Igitur Deum creare Sortem est necessarium,

5 patet quod consequentia non valet. Sed deberet concludi:

> Igitur aliqualiter esse est necessarium qualiter esse est Deum creare Sortem.

Unde in simili non sequitur:

> Istam propositionem esse est scitum a te.
>
> 10 Sed istam esse est istam esse veram.
>
> Igitur istam esse veram est scitum a te.

Sed bene sequitur:

> Igitur aliqualiter esse est scitum a te qualiter esse est istam propositionem esse (166vb E) veram.

15 Ad quintam, dico quod Sortem differre a Platone est Sortes. Et ad argumentum nego consequentiam, quia illa propositio non habet exponi, sed ista

> Sortes differt a Platone.

Ad sextam, nego quod possum facere me ipsum. Et ad probationem:

> 20 Ego possum facere me currere.
>
> Sed ego sum me currere.
>
> Igitur possum facere me,

non valet argumentum. Et causa dicta est. Nam ly .facere. in antecedente determinat complexum et in consequente incomplexum. Ideo deberet 25 concludi:

> Igitur ego possum aliqualiter facere esse qualiter esse sum ego.

Haec enim propositio

> Ego possum facere me currere,

non plus asserit nisi quod ego possum facere actum vel operationem aliquam 30 quo vel qua ego possum currere. Sed ista

> Ego possum facere me ipsum,

asserit quod possum me ipsum producere aut de non esse ad esse derivare—quod est falsum.

Ad septimam conclusionem dico quod si sol calefacit domum, solem 35 calefacere domum est sol. Et ad rationem contra, non valet argumentum,

I deny the first part of the premiss. In reply to the argument

That God is, is necessary.
That God is, is God creating Socrates.
Therefore, that God creates Socrates, is necessary,

it is clear that the inference does not hold good. But one ought to conclude:

Therefore, it is necessary for things to be in some way such that their being in that way is for God to create Socrates.

Thus, by analogy, this does not follow:

That this proposition is, is known by you.
For this proposition to be, is for this proposition to be true.[n]
Therefore, that this proposition is true, is known by you.

But this does follow:

Therefore, that things are in some way such that for them to be in that way is for this proposition to be true, is known by you.

In reply *to the fifth ⟨absurd⟩ conclusion*, I say that *that Socrates is different from Plato* is Socrates. In reply to the argument, I deny the inference, since that proposition[o] does not have to be expounded, but the proposition

Socrates is different from Plato

does.

In reply *to the sixth ⟨absurd⟩ conclusion*, I deny that I can make myself. In reply to the proof:

I can make myself to run.
I am myself running.
Therefore, I can make myself,

the argument does not hold good and the reason has been stated. For 'make' in the premiss governs a complex and in the conclusion, a non-complex. Therefore, one ought to conclude:

Therefore, I can make things to be in some way such that I am their being in that way.

For the proposition

I can make myself to run

asserts no more than that I can produce an act or some operation by which I can run. But the proposition

I can make myself

asserts that I can produce myself or bring myself from non-existence to existence—which is false.

In reply *to the seventh ⟨absurd⟩ conclusion*, I say that if the sun heats the house, h tat the sun heats the house, is the sun. In reply to the argument,

non obstante quod minor sit falsa in sensu diviso. Sicut non sequitur:

> Stat te esse et te non esse currentem.

> Sed non stat te currere et non esse currentem.

> Igitur te esse non est te currere.

5   Ad octavam conclusionem similiter nego eam. Et tunc ad probationem:

> Deus scit Antichristum fore.

> Igitur Antichristum fore est ⟨Antichristus⟩,

nego consequentiam. Et ad probationem nego similitudinem, quia in una scientia Dei fertur super futurum quod non est, in alia vero super praesens.

10   Ad nonam nego quod te esse sit necessarium. Et ad probationem nego consequentiam. Sed bene sequitur:

> Igitur aliqualiter esse est necessarium qualiter esse est te esse, etc.

Ad decimam conclusionem nego quod ego sum ita sapiens sicut Deus, et nego quod sciam omnia. Et ad argumentum:

15   Tu scis omnia esse.

> Sed omnia esse sunt omnia.

> Igitur tu scis omnia,

patet per ea quae dicta sunt consequentiam non valere. Sed bene sequitur:

> Igitur tu scis aliqualiter esse qualiter esse est omnia.

20   Ad undecimam conclusionem similiter nego ipsam. Et ad probationem nego primo antecedens. Nam illa propositio

> Deus est

significat asinum ratione copulae sic significantis, et tamen ly .Deus. non significat asinum. Secundo nego consequentiam; quia dato quod quid-

25 quid significat illa propositio significat suum subiectum, quia tamen pro-positio significat quiescenter et non subiectum, quia significat adaequate complexe significabile et non subiectum, igitur non convertuntur. Quare etc.

Ultima conclusio etiam negatur. Et ratio negationis atque responsio ad obiectionem patet ex saepissime recitatis. Unde sicut non sequitur:

30   Contingenter iste homo est.

> Et iste homo est homo.

> Igitur contingenter homo est,

---

on the contrary, the argument does not hold good, notwithstanding that the minor is false in the sense of division. In the same way, this does not follow:

It is consistent that you are, and that you are not running.
It is not consistent that you are running and you are not running.
Therefore, for you to be, is not for you to run.

In reply *to the eighth* ⟨*absurd*⟩ *conclusion*, similarly, I deny it. Then, to the proof:

God knows that the Antichrist will be.
Therefore, that the Antichrist will be, is ⟨the Antichrist⟩,

I deny the inference. In reply to the proof, I deny the analogy, since in one proposition, the knowledge of God extends over the future which is not; but in the other, over the present.

In reply *to the ninth* ⟨*absurd*⟩ *conclusion*, I deny that *that you are* is necessary. In reply to the proof, I deny the inference. But this does follow:

Therefore, it is necessary that things are in some way such that for them to be in that way is for you to be, etc.

In reply *to the tenth* ⟨*absurd*⟩ *conclusion*, I deny that I am as wise as God. I deny that I know all things. In reply to the argument:

You know that all things are.
That all things are, is all things.
Therefore, you know all things,

it is clear from what has been said that the inference does not hold good. But this does follow:

Therefore, you know that things are in some way such that their being in that way is all things.

In reply *to the eleventh* ⟨*absurd*⟩ *conclusion*, similarly, I deny it. In reply to the proof, first I deny the premiss. For the proposition

God is

signifies a donkey by reason of the copula thus signifying. Nevertheless, 'God' does not signify a donkey. Second, I deny the inference. For granted that whatever the proposition signifies, its subject signifies, since nevertheless the proposition signifies quiescently and the subject does not, and since it signifies adequately what is signifiable by a complex and the subject does not, therefore they are not interchangeable. Therefore, etc.

In reply *to the last* ⟨*absurd*⟩ *conclusion*, I deny it, too. My reason for denying it, as well as my reply to the objection, is clear from what has been very often recited. Thus, just as this does not follow:

Contingently, this man is.
This man is a man.
Therefore, contingently a man is,

ita non sequitur:

> Istum hominem esse est contingens.
> Et istum hominem esse est hominem esse.
> Igitur hominem esse est contingens.

5 Similiter sicut non sequitur:

> Necessario homo est.
> Et omnis homo est albus.
> Igitur necessario homo albus est,

ita non sequitur:

10   Hominem esse est necessarium.
> Sed hominem esse est hominem esse album.
> Igitur hominem esse album est necessarium.

Sed bene sequitur:

> Igitur aliqualiter esse est necessarium, qualiter esse est hominem esse
15   album.

Et ita in proposito non sequitur:

> Deum esse est necessarium.
> Sed Deum esse est Deum esse causam tui.
> Igitur Deum esse causam tui est necessarium.

20 Sed debet inferri:

> Igitur aliqualiter esse est necessarium, qualiter esse est Deum esse
> causam tui.

⟨*Argumenta ultra contra quartam conclusionem*⟩

Adhuc arguitur contra conclusionem, (211ra M) ut responsali magis
25 detur materia respondendi.

⟨1⟩ Ex conclusione sequitur quod hoc posse esse est hoc, te demonstrato.
Consequentiam probo, quia bene sequitur:

> Hoc est, et hoc potest esse; igitur hoc est hoc posse esse,

quia generaliter sequitur:

30   Hoc est, et hoc fuit; igitur hoc est hoc fuisse.
> Hoc est, et hoc erit; igitur hoc est hoc fore.
> Hoc est, et hoc est album; igitur hoc est hoc esse album.

Sed consequens est falsum, quod probo sic:

> Hoc posse esse est primum simpliciter.

35   Igitur non est hoc,

te demonstrato. Consequentia bona, et antecedens probatur:

> Hoc posse esse necessitat voluntatem primi ad volendum hoc posse
> esse.

---

16 ita *om. E*   21 est²] necessarium *add. M*   22 tui] etc. *add. M*   24 magis]
maior *E*   39 esse] hoc *add. M*

so this does not follow:

> That this man is, is contingent.
> For this man to be, is for a man to be.
> Therefore, that a man is, is contingent.

Similarly, just as this does not follow:

> Necessarily a man is.
> Every man is white.
> Therefore, necessarily a white man is,

so this does not follow:

> That a man is, is necessary.
> For a man to be, is for a man to be white.
> Therefore, that a man is white, is necessary.

But this does follow:

> Therefore, it is necessary that things are in some way such that for them to be in that way is for a man to be white.

And so in the proposed case, this does not follow:

> That God is, is necessary.
> For God to be, is for God to be the cause of you.
> Therefore, that God is the cause of you, is necessary.

But ⟨one⟩ ought to infer:

> Therefore, it is necessary that things are in some way such that for them to be in that way is for God to be the cause of you.

⟨*More Arguments against Thesis 4*⟩

Further arguments against this thesis are set out, so that a respondent may have more material for articulating his reply.

⟨1⟩ It follows from Thesis 4 that *that this can be* is this (where 'this' indicates you). Proof of the inference: This does follow:

> This is, and this can be; therefore, this is that this can be.

For in general, it follows:

> This is, and this was; therefore, this is that this was.
> This is, and this will be; therefore, this is that this will be.
> This is, and this is white; therefore, this is that this is white.

But I[p] prove that the conclusion is false this way:

> That this can be, is the absolutely First Being.
> Therefore, it is not this (where 'this' indicates you).

The inference is good. Proof of the premiss:

> That this can be, necessitates the will of the First Being to will that this can be.

Igitur hoc posse esse est primum.

Patet consequentia, ex hoc quod voluntas primi non necessitatur ad volendum aliquid extra se. Antecedens patet, quia primum simpliciter necessarie vult hoc posse esse, quia vult hoc posse esse et non potest non velle
5 hoc posse esse. Igitur etc.

2° Arguitur sic:[6] Si significatum adaequatum propositionis est aliquid vel aliqua, sequitur quod res extra est (167ra E) adaequatum obiectum propositionis vel scientiae. Consequens est falsum, quia tunc multae scientiae essent de contingentibus aliter se habere tamquam de obiectis—quod
10 est falsum, accipiendo scientiam proprie. Nam ut ait Philosophus, sexto *Ethicorum*,[7] 'Omnes suspicamur, quod scimus non contingere aliter se habere.' Et ex hoc concludit quod scibile est aeternum ⟨et⟩ ex necessitate. Et eandem sententiam ponit primo *Posteriorum*.[8] Consequentia patet. Nam omnis res corruptibilis potest aliter se habere, secundum Philoso-
15 phum. Et secundum veritatem omnis res praeter Deum est contingens et non necessaria. Si autem res extra sunt obiecta scientiarum, mechanicae scientiae et physicae et geometricae et aliae plures essent de rebus aliis a Deo et contingentibus. Quare etc.

⟨2.1⟩ Confirmatur: Nam si res esset obiectum adaequatum scientiae,
20 eadem ratione res extra esset obiectum opinionis et fidei et erroris. Et per consequens contingeret quod idem homo idem sciret et opinaretur et crederet et etiam ignoraret—quae omnia sunt absurda. Patet consequentia. Nam contingit eundem scire quod Deus est, et opinari quod solus et immediate moveat caelum, credere quod sit trinus in personis, errare
25 putans quod sit vigore finitus.

⟨2.2⟩ Confirmatur secundo sic: Si res esset obiectum adaequatum scientiae, esset etiam obiectum assensus scientialis. Nam eidem assentimus quod scimus. Et simili ratione esset obiectum fidei. Ex hoc ulterius sequitur quod aliquis fidelis licite ita firmiter crederet diabolo sicut Deo. Nam
30 fidelis licite aeque firmiter credit quod diabolus non est omnipotens sicut quod Deus est omnipotens. Sequeretur etiam quod eidem simul assentiret et dissentiret—quae omnia sunt falsa.

⟨*Responsio ad haec argumenta*⟩

Ad istas rationes:

35 ⟨R1⟩ Ad primam, concedo quod hoc posse esse est hoc, te demonstrato.

---

2 necessitatur] necessitat *E*   3 aliquid *om. E*   6 propositionis *om. E*   7 adaequatum *om. E*   8 consequens] ergo *M*   9 essent] erunt *M*   11 contingere] contingit *E*   13 sententiam] scientiam *M*   17 scientiae et physicae *om. E*   19 confirmatur] consimiliter *M*   21 opinaretur] opinaret *ME*   22 ignoraret] imaginaret *M*   26 res] extra *add. E*   31 sequeretur] sequitur *E*   eidem] idem *E*

Therefore, that this can be, is the First Being.

The inference is clear, because the will of the First Being is not necessitated to will anything outside Itself. The premiss is clear, since the absolutely First Being necessarily wills that this can be, since It wills that this can be and cannot not will that this can be. Therefore, etc.

⟨2⟩ This argument is made: If the adequate significatum of a proposition is something or some things, it follows that a thing outside the mind is the adequate object of the proposition or of knowledge. The conclusion is false, since then many sciences would have as their objects contingent things that can be otherwise than they are—which is false, taking 'science' properly. For, as the Philosopher says in *Ethics*, Book VI ⟨1139^{b}19–21⟩, 'We all suppose that what we know cannot be otherwise than it is.' From this he concludes that the knowable is eternal and necessary. He advances the same opinion in *Posterior Analytics*, Book I ⟨c.1, 71^{b}14–15⟩. The inference is clear. For, according to the Philosopher, every corruptible thing can be otherwise than it is. And, according to truth, everything other than God is contingent and not necessary. But if things outside the mind are objects of the sciences, the sciences of mechanics and of physics and of geometry and many others would be about things other than God and thus about contingent things. Thus, etc.

⟨2.1⟩ Confirming argument: If a thing outside the mind were the adequate object of knowledge, by the same reasoning a thing outside the mind would be the object of opinion, and of faith, and of error. Consequently, it would happen that the same man would know and opine and believe and even be ignorant of the same thing—all of which are absurd. The inference is clear. For it happens that the same man knows that God is, and opines that He alone and immediately moves the sky, and believes that He is a Trinity of persons, and errs in thinking that He is finite in power.[q]

⟨2.2⟩ The second confirming argument is this: If a thing were the adequate object of knowledge, it would also be the object of knowledgeable assent. For we assent to the same thing that we know. By similar reasoning, it would be the object of faith. Further, it follows from this that a believer should rightfully believe the devil as firmly as God. For a believer rightfully believes, with equal firmness, that the devil is not omnipotent and that God is omnipotent. It would follow, too, that he would simultaneously assent to and dissent from the same thing. All of these are false.

⟨*Reply to these Arguments*⟩

In reply to the latter arguments:

⟨R1⟩ In reply to the first, I grant that *that this can be* is this (where 'this'

Et nego quod sit primum simpliciter aut quod necessitet voluntatem divinam. Et ad rationem:

Primum simpliciter necessario vult hoc posse esse.

Igitur hoc posse esse necessitat voluntatem divinam,

5 nego consequentiam. Nam si illa consequentia valeret, probarem quod tu necessitas intellectum divinum. Nam Deus necessario intelligit te. Igitur tu necessitas intellectum divinum. Antecedens patet, quia Deus intelligit te et non potest non intelligere te. Si ergo quaeritur, ex quo intellectus divinus necessario intelligit te, quid necessitat ipsum ad intelligendum te, 10 dico quod nulla creatura. Sed ipsamet divina essentia ut est species intelligibilis in qua relucet necessario non solum immensitas suae naturae, verum et quaelibet creatura possibilis aut imaginabilis, praesens, praeterita, aut futura. Ita in proposito dico quod hoc posse esse non necessitat voluntatem divinam, sed essentia divina ut est conceptus repraesentans vel 15 determinans hoc posse esse.

⟨R2⟩ Ad secundam rationem nego istam consequentiam:

Significatum adaequatum propositionis est aliquid.

Igitur aliquid est obiectum adaequatum scientiae vel propositionis.

Sed bene sequitur:

20 Igitur obiectum adaequatum propositionis vel scientiae est aliquid.

Pro quo est advertendum quod si A sit illa propositio

Homo est,

et B illa

Risibile est,

25 non debet concedi quod significatum adaequatum A est significatum adaequatum B, quia per istam assertive denotatur quod aliqualiter esse qualiter esse significatur adaequate per A significatur adaequate per B— quod est falsum. Et si arguitur sic:

Hominem esse est risibile esse.

30 Et hominem esse est significatum adaequatum A.

Et risibile esse est significatum adaequatum B.

Igitur significatum (211rb M) adaequatum A est significatum adae- quatum B,

non valet consequentia, quia in maiori est solum suppositio identica, in 35 consequente vero solum suppositio formalis. Sicut in simili, pono quod A sit bonitas in Deo et B sapientia in ipso. Et si proponitur:

Ratio formalis A est ratio formalis B,

6 necessitas] necessitares E   9 quid necessitat] quod necessitas E   21 sit]
est E   32-3 significatum[1] . . . B om. E   34 solum] sola E   35 solum] est
praecise E   36 proponitur] propono (etiam p. 188 lin. 21) E

indicates you). I deny that it is the absolutely First Being or that it necessitates the Divine Will. In reply to the argument:

The absolutely First Being necessarily wills that this can be.

Therefore, that this can be, necessitates the Divine Will,

I deny the inference. For if that inference holds good, I would prove that you necessitate the Divine Intellect. For God necessarily thinks of you. Therefore, you necessitate the Divine Intellect. The premiss is clear, since God thinks of you and cannot not think of you. If therefore someone asks, 'Given that the Divine Intellect necessarily thinks of you, what necessitates Him to think of you?' I say that no creature does, but the Divine Essence Itself, as It is an intelligible species in which there necessarily shines forth not only the immensity of Its own nature, but also each and every creature, whether possible or imaginable, present, past, or future. Thus, in the proposed case, I say that that this can be, does not necessitate the Divine Will, but the Divine Essence does, in so far as it is a concept representing or determining that this can be.

⟨R2⟩ In reply to the second argument, I deny the inference:

The adequate significatum of a proposition is something.

Therefore, something is the adequate object of knowledge or of a proposition.

But this does follow:

Therefore, the adequate object of a proposition or of knowledge is something.

For proof of this, one ought to notice that if A is the proposition

A man is,

and B the proposition

A risible is,

one ought not to grant that the adequate significatum of A is the adequate significatum of B. For what that proposition denotes affirmatively is that B adequately signifies that things are in some way such that their being in that way is adequately signified by A—which is false. If someone argues this way:

For a man to be, is for a risible to be.

That a man is, is the adequate significatum of A.

That a risible is, is the adequate significatum of B.

Therefore, the adequate significatum of A is the adequate significatum of B,

the inference does not hold good. For there is only identical *suppositio* in the major, but there is only formal *suppositio* in the conclusion. As, analogously, I posit that F is goodness in God and G is wisdom in Him. And if someone proposes:

The formal principle of F is the formal principle of G,

vel sic:

Formalitas *A* est formalitas *B*,

negatur. Et si arguitur:

A est *B*.

5   Et *A* est formalitas *A*.

Et *B* est formalitas *B*.

Igitur formalitas *A* est formalitas *B*, vel e converso,

non valet argumentum, propter mutationem suppositionis. Sed ad concludendum illud consequens oportet sumere pro maiori:

10   *A* est formaliter *B*,

—quod est falsum. Similiter ex illis praemissis debet concludi:

Igitur formalitas *A* est aliquid quod est formalitas *B*.

Ita in proposito debuit sumi pro maiori:

Hominem esse est formaliter risibile esse,

15 vel sic:

Hominem esse est adaequate risibile esse,

quorum quodlibet est falsum. Sed ex prioribus praemissis solum sequebatur quod aliqualiter esse qualiter esse est significatum (167rb E) adaequatum *A* est aliqualiter esse qualiter esse est significatum adaequatum *B*—

20 quod conceditur.

Item si proponitur:

Hominem esse est significatum adaequatum *B*,

nego, quia asserit quod hominem esse adaequate significatur per *B*—quod est falsum, sicut in priori exemplo:

25   *A* est ratio *B*, sive formalitas *B*,

quia utrobique est praedicatio formalis. Si vero proponitur:

Significatum adaequatum *B* est hominem esse,

concedo, quia est praedicatio identica et significat assertive, et convertitur, quod

30   Aliqualiter esse qualiter esse adaequate significatur per *B* est hominem esse.

Et si arguitur:

Significatum adaequatum *B* est hominem esse.

Igitur hominem esse est adaequatum significatum *B*,

5–6 formalitas$^{1-2}$] formaliter *E*   9 sumere] supponere *E*   12 formalitas^{2}]
formaliter *M*   18 qualiter esse *om. M*   19 esse^{2} *om. E*
28 et^{2} *om. M*

or thus:

The formality of *F* is the formality of *G*,

I deny it. And if one argues:

F is *G*.
F is the formality of *F*.
G is the formality of *G*.
Therefore, the formality of *F* is the formality of *G*, or vice versa,

the argument does not hold good, because of a change in *suppositio.*[r] But for drawing that conclusion, it is necessary to take the major to be

F is formally *G*,

which is false. Similarly, from these premisses, one ought to conclude:

Therefore, the formality of *F* is something which is the formality of *G*.

Thus in the proposed case, one ought to have taken the major to be

For a man to be, is formally for a risible to be,

or this:

For a man to be, is adequately for a risible to be,

each of which is false. From the previous premisses, it followed only that

For things to be in some way such that their being in that way is the adequate significatum of *A*, is for things to be in some way such that their being in that way is the adequate significatum of *B*,

which I grant.

Again, if someone proposes

That a man is, is the adequate significatum of *B*,

I deny it. For it asserts that *that a man is* is adequately signified by *B*—which is false; just as, in the previous example,

F is the formal principle of *G*, or formality of *G*,

since in both the predication is formal. But if someone proposes

The adequate significatum of *B* is that a man is,

I grant it, because there is identical predication and it signifies affirmatively and is interchangeable with

For things to be in some way such that their being in that way is adequately signified by *B*, is for a man to be.

If someone argues:

The adequate significatum of *B* is that a man is.
Therefore, that a man is, is the adequate significatum of *B*,[s]

non valet argumentum propter mutationem suppositionis. Sicut non sequitur:

> Ratio formalis *B* est *A*.
>
> Igitur *A* est ratio formalis *B*,

5 propter eandem causam. Sed bene sequitur:

> Igitur *A* est aliquid quod est ratio formalis *B*,

quia *A* est sapientia quae est ratio formalis *B*. Et si dicitur quod est conversio simplex, nego propter mutationem suppositionis.

Unde haec propositio

10 > Adaequatum significatum *B* est hominem esse

convertitur simpliciter in istam

> Hominem esse est aliqualiter esse qualiter esse adaequate signi-
> ficatur per *B*.

Ex his clarissime patet quod numquam adaequatum significatum subiecti
15 est adaequatum significatum totius propositionis, nec e contra. Immo nulla res est adaequatum significatum propositionis, licet significatum propositionis est aliqua res.

⟨R2.2⟩ Et sic patet solutio ad secundum argumentum cum suis con- firmationibus, cum nulla res sit obiectum adaequatum scientiae, sed
20 praecise aliqualiter esse. Et ita scientia est de impossibilibus aliter se habere ad modum Philosophi, quia hominem esse est necessarium, licet nullus homo necessario sit.

⟨R2.1⟩ Et patet etiam quod licet eadem res sit obiectum fidei, credulita- tis, ignorantiae et scientiae, non tamen obiectum adaequatum. Immo
25 obiectum adaequatum scientiae non est obiectum adaequatum ignorantiae nec credulitatis, nec e contra, licet taliter esse unius sit taliter esse alterius. Et sicut nulla res est obiectum adaequatum scientiae, sic nec assensus scien- tialis. Et ita non sequitur quod idem simul et semel assentiat et dissentiat eidem, supple adaequate. Quare etc.

30 ⟨*De Adaequatione Significati Ad Suum Signum*⟩
⟨*Capitulum Nonum*⟩

Ex praedictis posset colligi secundum declarationem in principio promissam de adaequatione significati ad suum signum et e converso.

18–19 confirmationibus] consimilibus *M*   19 cum] quomodo *M*   sit] est *M*
24 ignorantiae] imaginativae *M*   27 sicut] sic *M*   32 posset] potest *M*
33 promissam] promissum *M*

the argument does not hold good because of a change of *suppositio*. In the same way, this does not follow:

The formal principle of *G* is *F*.

Therefore, *F* is the formal principle of *G*,

for the same reason. But this does follow:

Therefore, *F* is something which is the formal principle of *G*.

For *F* is wisdom which is the formal principle of *G*. And if someone says that the argument is a simple conversion, I deny it, because of a change of *suppositio*.

Thus, the proposition

The adequate significatum of *B* is that a man is,

is absolutely interchangeable with the proposition

For a man to be, is for things to be in some way such that their being in that way is adequately signified by *B*.

It is most clearly obvious from these remarks, that the adequate significatum of a subject is never the adequate significatum of the whole proposition, nor vice versa. In fact, no thing is the adequate significatum of the proposition, although the significatum of the proposition is some thing.[t]

⟨R2.2⟩ Thus, the solution of the second argument, together with its confirming arguments, is clear. For *no thing* is the adequate object of knowledge, but precisely *that things are in some way*. Thus, knowledge is of what cannot possibly be otherwise than it is, according to the way of the Philosopher. For that a man is, is necessary, although no man necessarily is.

⟨R2.1⟩ It is clear, too, that although the same thing is the object of faith, of belief, of ignorance, and of knowledge, nevertheless, the same thing is not the adequate object. In fact, the adequate object of knowledge is not the adequate object of ignorance or belief, nor vice versa, although things being in such a way as we know may be ⟨really identical with⟩ their being in such a way as we are ignorant of. Just as no thing is the adequate object of knowledge, so no thing is the adequate object of knowledgeable assent. Thus, it does not follow that the same thing is simultaneously and at once assented to and dissented from (understand 'adequately'). Thus, etc.

⟨The Adequation of the Significatum to its Sign⟩
⟨Chapter Nine⟩

From the preceding remarks, one could gather, according to the explanation promised in the beginning, ⟨what is to be said⟩ about the adequation of a significatum to its sign, and vice versa. Nevertheless, having left aside

Verumtamen pro maiori evidentia et certitudine, dimissis opinionibus pluri-
mis quae longitudinem causarent scripturae ac temporis, pono aliquas
conclusiones.

⟨1⟩ *Prima* est ista: Significatum ⟨adaequatum⟩ termini quod ab
5   intellectu apprehenditur non dicitur esse tale quod toto signo
concipitur.

Patet. Nam si non esset alius terminus vel conceptus in mundo quam
conceptus proprius hominis, per illum apprehenderetur animal, substantia, et huiusmodi. Et non per alium conceptum. Igitur apprehenderetur
10 quodlibet illorum significatorum toto signo hominis. Et tamen patet quod
nullum illorum esset significatum adaequatum conceptus hominis.

2ᵃ conclusio: Significatum adaequatum termini quod ipse mentaliter
significat non dicitur illud (211ᵛᵃ M) quod prius tempore vel
natura virtuti repraesentatur.

15 Nam sicut ordine naturae prius est ens quam substantia, et prius substantia quam animal, et prius animal quam homo; ita ordine naturae conceptus hominis significat prius ens quam substantiam, et prius substantiam
quam animal, et prius animal quam hominem. Sicut etiam visio causata
a Sorte, sive species derivata ab obiecto sensibili per prius repraesentat
20 tale obiectum sub ratione magis communi quam minus communi, secundum quod declarat Aristoteles in prooemio *Physicorum*,[1] et tamen patet
quod ly .homo. non significat adaequate ens, substantiam, sive animal.

3ᵃ conclusio: Significatum adaequatum termini quod nunc declaratur
non dicitur esse illud quod totale nominatur.

25 Patet. Nam ille terminus 'homo' significat hominem, ens, substantiam,
animal, Sortem, Platonem, et omnes homines praesentes, praeteritos, et
futuros, aut imaginabiles; ex quibus fit totale significatum illius quod
tamen non est significatum adaequatum eiusdem, quia tunc haec esset
falsa:

30   Homo est,

quia iam non est totale significatum illius.

Ex quibus sequitur correlarie:

⟨1⟩ *Primo* quod significatum adaequatum propositionis non est illud
(167ᵛᵃ E) quod apprehenditur toto signo.

35 2° Sequitur quod significatum adaequatum propositionis non est illud
quod concipitur primo, sumendo ly .primo. exponibiliter.

---

5 apprehenditur] comprehenditur *M*   14 repraesentatur] repraesentat *M*

many opinions, which it would take a lot of writing and time ⟨to examine⟩, I assume certain theses to make ⟨my own explanation⟩ more evident and certain.

> *Thesis 1*: The adequate significatum of a term which is apprehended by the intellect is not so called because it is conceived of by means of the sign as a whole.

This is clear. For ⟨suppose⟩ there were no term or concept in the world other than the proper concept of man. Animal, substance, and the like would be apprehended through it and not through any other concept. Then, any of these significata would be apprehended by the sign as a whole, of man. Nevertheless, it is clear that none of them would be the adequate significatum of the concept of man.

> *Thesis 2*: The adequate significatum of a term, which the term itself signifies mentally, is not said to be that significatum which is represented to the ⟨intellectual⟩ power temporally or naturally prior ⟨to other significata⟩.

For, just as in the order of nature, being is prior to substance, and substance is prior to animal, and animal is prior to man; so in the order of nature, the concept of man signifies being prior to substance, and substance prior to animal, and animal prior to man. In the same way, also, the vision caused by Socrates, or the species derived from the sensible object, represents such an object under a more common notion prior to representing it under a less common notion, according to Aristotle's account at the beginning of the *Physics* ⟨Book I, c. 1, 184ᵃ23-4⟩. Nevertheless, it is clear that the term 'man' does not adequately signify being, substance, or animal.

> *Thesis 3*: The adequate significatum of a term as now being explained is not said to be the significatum which is called the whole significatum.

This is clear. For the term 'man' signifies man, being, substance, animal, Socrates, Plato, and all present, past, and future or imaginable men, from which its whole significatum is composed. Nevertheless, the whole significatum is not the adequate significatum of that term. For then the proposition

A man is

would be false, since its whole significatum is not now.

Corollaries follow from these theses.

> ⟨*Corollary*⟩ *1*: The adequate significatum of a proposition is not that which is apprehended by the sign as a whole.

It follows that

> ⟨*Corollary*⟩ *2*: The adequate significatum of a proposition is not that which is conceived of first, taking the term 'first' as exponible.ᵃ

3° Sequitur quod significatum adaequatum propositionis non est totale significatum ipsius.

Haec correlaria ex tribus istis conclusionibus manifeste sequuntur, ut patet discursive intuenti.

5   *4ᵃ conclusio* est ista: Significatum adaequatum termini est distincte apprehensum sub propria ratione quo nihil posterius concipitur sub formali denominatione.

Volo dicere quod si terminus aliquis significat distincte aliquid, aliqua vel aliqualiter sub propria ratione, et nihil posterius illo distincte significat sub
10 sua similiter formali denominatione, tale est significatum adaequatum illius termini.

Ista conclusio patet. Nam ex quo idem terminus significat quodlibet suum superius et quodlibet suum inferius et numquam adaequate, ut patet, nec potest assignari adaequatum significatum aliquo alio modo ex con-
15 clusionibus praemissis, igitur est deveniendum ad istum modum.

Ex quibus patet quod ly .homo. non significat primo et adaequate ens, substantiam, aut animal, quia licet quodlibet tale significet sub propria ratione et distincte, tamen in nullo illorum sistit sua significatio distincta, sed descendit in hominem posteriorem naturaliter ente, substantia, et
20 animali. Quia vero nihil posterius homine distincte significat sub propria ratione, ut Sortem vel Platonem et sic de aliis, sed solum in confuso, ideo significat hominem adaequate et non aliud significatum inferius aut superius ad hominem.

Ex quibus sequitur quod nullus terminus compositus significat adae-
25 quate alicuius partis adaequatum significatum, sicut sunt termini copulati aut disiuncti. Quilibet enim terminus copulatus vel disiunctus significat distincte cuiuslibet partis significatum, et prius naturaliter quam significa-tum totius. Nullum tamen talium significatorum est adaequatum, quia non sistit ibi, sed in suum posterius descendit, in quo quiescit distincta signi-
30 ficatione. Similiter tales termini complexi 'homo albus', 'homo niger', significant adaequate hominem album vel hominem nigrum, et non homi-nem nec album nec nigrum.

Item sequitur quod ly .omnis homo. significat adaequate omnem hominem et non hominem; quia licet significet distincte hominem, non
35 tamen ultimo, quia posterius est omnis homo, quam homo in quo sistit, quia ulterius nullum suum posterius, ut istum hominem et illum, distincte significat. Et ita consequenter dicatur quod ly .aliquis homo. significat

It follows that

> ⟨*Corollary*⟩ *3*: The adequate significatum of a proposition is not its whole significatum.

These corollaries manifestly follow from these three theses, as is clear to one who considers each corollary in turn.

> *Thesis 4*: The adequate significatum of a term is distinctly apprehended under a proper concept, to which significatum nothing posterior is ⟨distinctly⟩ conceived of under its formal denomination.

What I mean is that if some term distinctly signifies something, some things, or somehow, under its proper concept; and distinctly signifies nothing posterior to that ⟨significatum⟩ under its similarly formal denomination; such a ⟨significatum⟩ is the adequate significatum of the term.

This thesis is clear. For the same term signifies each of its superiors and each of its inferiors, and never signifies them adequately, as is clear. Nor can the adequate significatum be assigned in any other way, on the basis of the preceding theses. Therefore, one must arrive at this way of assigning it.

From these remarks, it is clear that 'man' does not primarily and adequately signify being, substance, or animal. For although it would signify any such things under its proper concept and distinctly, its distinct signification does not stop at any of them, but descends to man, which is naturally posterior to being, substance, and animal. But it signifies nothing posterior to man—such as Socrates or Plato, etc.—distinctly under a proper concept, but only confusedly. Therefore, ⟨the term 'man'⟩ adequately signifies man and no other significatum that is inferior or superior to man.

From these remarks, it follows that no composite term—such as a conjunctive or disjunctive term—adequately signifies the adequate significatum of any part. For any conjunctive or disjunctive term distinctly signifies the significatum of any of its parts and it signifies them naturally prior to signifying the significatum of the term as a whole. Nevertheless, no such significatum is adequate. For ⟨in signifying, the term⟩ does not stop there but descends to a significatum posterior ⟨to them⟩, and in this posterior significatum it rests with its signification distinct. Similarly, such complex terms as 'white man' and 'black man' adequately signify white man or black man, and neither man nor white nor black.

Again, it follows that 'every man' adequately signifies every man and not man. For although it distinctly signifies man, nevertheless it does not do so ultimately, since every man, in which ⟨significatum⟩ it rests, is posterior to a man. For beyond every man, there is no posterior significatum—such as this or that man—which it distinctly signifies. And so, consequently, we must say that 'some man' primarily signifies some man,

primo aliquem hominem, et non significat primo hominem. Et ly .nullus homo. significat primo nullum hominem.

Nec sequitur de se:

    Ly .omnis., .nullus. aut .aliquis. nihil significat.

5   Igitur ly .omnis homo. non significat primo omnem hominem,

quia licet de se non significet, tamen cum alio significat.

> 5^a *conclusio* est ista: Significatum adaequatum propositionis est aliqualiter esse qualiter esse implicite vel explicite (211vb M) egreditur a significatis adaequatis partium.

10 Patet, quia propositio significat adaequate implicite vel explicite ex compositione suarum partium. Igitur etc.

Verumtamen posset sophisma logicaliter assignare adaequatum significatum termini vel propositionis, dicendo quod significatum termini adaequatum dicitur esse illud quod denominationem consimilem vocaliter
15 gerit. Unde vocaliter iste terminus 'homo' habet denominationem consimilem cum homine suo significato. Significatum vero adaequatum propositionis dicitur esse illud quod esset oratio infinitiva, vel dictum huius, aut talis, dummodo esset dictum vel oratio infinitiva alicuius propositionis; ita quod Deum esse est adaequatum significatum huius propositionis

20   Deus est,

quia si per imaginationem esset oratio infinitiva, esset huius vel consimilis oratio infinitiva et nullius alterius. Sicut nec iam ly .Deum esse. Et ita universaliter de quibuslibet aliis dicatur. Quare etc.

Ex praedictis sequitur quod sicut non est possibile alicuius incomplexi
25 simpliciter aliqualiter complexe esse significatum adaequatum, sic non est possibile alicuius categoricae hypothetice significabile pro adaequato significato eidem communicari. Prima pars patet, quia aliter terminus simpliciter simplex significaret adaequate quiescenter verum vel falsum, et sic esset propositio. Immo tunc quaelibet propositio posset cum quolibet
30 (167vb E) suorum extremorum converti—quorum quodlibet est falsum. Secunda pars etiam patet, quia si tale significatum esset oratio infinitiva, non esset oratio infinitiva talis categoricae, immo unius hypotheticae.

2 significat primo *om. M*   4 nihil *om. M*   6 significet] significat *E*   12
assignare] assignari *E*   17 infinitiva] infinita (*etiam lin.* 18) *M*   huius] hoc *E*
18 propositionis *om. M*   22 iam] de *add. E*   31–*p.* 198 *lin.* 1 esset . . . significatum
om. (*hom.*) *M*

and does not primarily signify man. And the term 'no man' primarily signifies no man.

Nor does this follow of itself:

'Every', 'no', or 'some' signify nothing.

Therefore, 'every man' does not primarily signify every man.

For although 'every' does not signify of itself, it does signify together with another.

> *Thesis* 5: The adequate significatum of a proposition is things being in some way such that their being in that way comes out, implicitly or explicitly, from the adequate significata of its parts.

This is clear, since the proposition adequately signifies, implicitly or explicitly, by the composition of its parts. Therefore, etc.

Nevertheless, a sophisma could, logically, assign the adequate significatum of a term or of a proposition, by saying that the adequate significatum of a term is said to be that which bears an equiform denomination in its spoken form. Thus, the term 'man' in spoken form, has a denomination equiform with its own significatum, man. But the adequate significatum of a proposition is said to be that which its sentence-nominalization, or its dictum, or any such expression,[b] is, when there is a dictum or sentence-nominalization of a proposition. Thus, that God is, is the adequate significatum of the proposition

> God is.

For if it were a sentence-nominalization—imagine that it is—it would be the sentence-nominalization of this proposition or of one equiform with it, and not of any other. For example, now the sentence-nominalization 'that God is' ⟨would not be the adequate significatum of a proposition other than

> God is,

or one equiform with it⟩. The same thing may be said universally about any other propositions. Thus, etc.

From the preceding remarks, it follows that just as it is not possible for the adequate significatum of some ⟨expression⟩ that is absolutely non-complex to be somehow complex, so it is not possible for what is signifiable by a molecular proposition to be ascribed to a categorical proposition as the adequate significatum of that proposition. The first part is clear. Otherwise, an absolutely simple term would adequately signify quiescently a truth or a falsehood, and so would be a proposition. In fact, then, any proposition would be interchangeable with any of its extremes. Each of these is false. The second part is also clear. For if such a significatum were a sentence-nominalization, it would not be the sentence-nominalization of such a categorical but of a molecular proposition.

Similiter tale significatum hypotheticum non potest immediate egredi a significatis adaequatis partium talis categoricae. Igitur non potest esse adaequatum significatum illius.

Item sequitur quod non est possibile significatum adaequatum copula-
5 tivae esse significatum adaequatum disiunctivae vel condicionalis, nec e contra. Patet, quia alias propositio vera vel necessaria esset impossibilis vel falsa—quod non debet concedi. Unde licet harum propositionum

Tu es homo, et tu es animal,
Tu es homo vel tu es animal

10 eadem sint adaequata significata categoricarum, non tamen totalia signi-ficata hypotheticarum, quia significatum copulativae adaequatum con-surgit ex adaequatis significatis categoricarum et consignificatione vel modo significandi notae copulationis. Significatum autem illius disiun-ctivae adaequatum oritur ex adaequatis significatis earundem partium et
15 alia consignificatione vel modo significandi distincto specie a priori. Et ita de condicionalibus et aliis quibuscumque. Quare etc.

9 tu¹ . . . animal *om.* (*hom.*) *E*   12 categoricarum] earundem partium *M*   et] alia *add. M*   14 adaequatum] adaequate *M*

Similarly, such a molecular significatum cannot proceed immediately, from the adequate significata of the parts of such a categorical. Therefore ⟨a molecular significatum⟩ cannot be the adequate significatum of that ⟨categorical proposition⟩.

Again, it follows that it is not possible for the adequate significatum of a conjunctive proposition to be the adequate significatum of a disjunctive or conditional proposition, or vice versa. This is clear, since otherwise a true or a necessary proposition would be impossible or false—which should not be granted. Thus, although the adequate significata of the categoricals in the following propositions

You are a man and you are an animal,

⟨and⟩

You are a man or you are an animal,

are the same, nevertheless, the whole significata of the molecular propositions are not the same. For the adequate significatum of a conjunctive proposition arises from the adequate significata of the categoricals and the consignification or mode of signifying of the sign of conjunction. The adequate significatum of that disjunctive proposition, however, arises from the adequate significata of the same parts and a different consignification or mode of signifying, distinct in kind from the previous one. And so on, for conditionals and any other ⟨kinds of propositions⟩. Thus, etc.

FONTES

TRACTATUS DE VERITATE ET FALSITATE PROPOSITIONIS

Capitulum I

p. 4 n. 1 Auctor huius viae videtur Albertus de Saxonia (Albertucius). Cf. *Perutilis Logica*, tract. 1, c. 6 'De verbo' (ed. Venetiis 1522, f. 4ra–b) et tract. 6, c. 1 'De insolubilibus' (f. 43ra–vb). Cf. etiam Guillelmus de Ockham, *Summa Logicae*, Pars II, cc. 2–3 (*Opera Philosophica* I, ed. Ph. Boehner, G. Gál, S. Brown, St. Bonaventure, N.Y., 1974, pp. 249–58).

p. 4 n. 2 Pro prima et secunda conclusione, cf. Albertus, loc. cit.: 'Ex his sequitur quod omnis propositio affirmativa significat subiectum et praedicatum supponere pro eodem; et omnis propositio negativa significat quod subiectum et praedicatum non supponunt pro eodem. Secundo dico quod quando in propositione affirmativa non falsificante se pro eodem supponunt subiectum et praedicatum propositio est vera, et quando non supponunt pro eodem propositio est falsa' (f. 4ra lin. 27–38); 'Secunda suppositio quod omnem propositionem affirmativam veram esse est idem esse pro quo supponit eius subiectum et praedicatum et e converso, et ipsam esse falsam est non esse idem pro quo supponit eius subiectum et praedicatum et e contra. Tertia suppositio: omnem propositionem negativam veram esse est non esse idem pro quo supponit eius subiectum et praedicatum et e converso, et ipsam esse falsam est esse idem pro quo supponit subiectum et praedicatum. Quarta suppositio: omnis propositio affirmativa significat idem esse pro quo supponit subiectum et praedicatum, et hoc manifeste ostendit copula in ea affirmata' (f. 43ra lin. 36–43). Cf. etiam tract. 3, c. 1 'De propositionibus': 'propositio affirmativa dicitur illa in qua formale ipsius propositionis manet affirmativum . . . et per formale propositionis categoricae intelligo copulam verbalem' (f. 17va lin. 57–60).

p. 4 n. 3 Tertia conclusio non invenitur locis citatis supra, nota 1.

p. 4 n. 4 Cf. Albertus, op. cit., tract. 2, c. 6 'De regulis suppositionum terminorum': 'Nona regula est: syncategoremata per quae fit comparatio aequalitatis, ut sunt ista "quemadmodum", "sicut" et sic de aliis, confundunt terminos sequentes confuse distributive, semper intelligendo nisi aliud syncategorema impediat' (f. 13rb lin. 43–5).

p. 6 n. 5 Pro quarta conclusione, cf. Albertus, op. cit., tract. 1, c. 6: 'Sed diceres . . . taliter est qualiter per eam significatur. Et si sic tunc ipsa est vera; . . . Respondetur . . . quando dicitur ulterius "igitur est vera" negatur consequentia, quia si consequentia deberet valere oporteret quod praedicta propositio significaret taliter qualiter est et nullo modo aliter quam est' (f. 4rb lin. 19–25); tract. 6, c. 1: 'Et cum dicebatur . . . taliter est qualiter ipsa significat . . .; igitur ipsa est vera, nego consequentiam. Unde quamvis sit taliter qualiter ipsa significat, non tamen qualitercumque ipsa significat ita est, quod tamen oporteret ad hoc quod esset vera, sicut patet per descriptionem propositionis verae. Unde ad hoc quod propositio sit vera non sufficit quod taliter sit qualiter ipsa significat, sed requiritur quod qualitercumque significat ita est. Unde ista propositio "Homo est asinus" est falsa, et tamen taliter est qualiter ipsa significat, quia significat hominem esse et taliter est, sed quia cum hoc significat aliter quam est, ipsa est falsa' (f. 43vb lin. 17–27);

etiam tract. 3, c. 3 'De propositionibus habentibus plures causas veritatis': 'Prae-
mitto primo quod propositio vera est illa quae qualitercumque significat ita est.
Propositio autem falsa est illa quae non qualitercumque significat ita est' (f. 18ra
lin. 53–6).

p. 6 n. 6 Pro primo corollario, cf. Albertus, op. cit., tract. 1, c. 6: 'Sexto dico
quod omnis propositio significat se esse veram. Patet quia omnis propositio vel
est affirmativa vel est negativa. Si est affirmativa tunc per praedicta significat idem
esse pro quo supponit subiectum et praedicatum, et hoc est propositionem affirmativam esse veram. Si est negativa significat non esse idem pro quo supponit subiectum et praedicatum, et hoc est propositionem negativam esse veram' (f. 4rb lin.
1–5); tract. 6, c. 1: 'Quantum ad tertium sit prima conclusio: omnis propositio
affirmativa significat se esse veram. Probatur, quia omnis propositio affirmativa
significat idem esse pro quo supponit subiectum eius et praedicatum, per quartam
suppositionem, et omnem propositionem affirmativam esse veram est esse idem pro
quo supponit subiectum eius et praedicatum et e converso, per secundam suppositionem; ergo omnis propositio affirmativa significat se esse veram' (f. 43ra lin.
50–5).

p. 6 n. 7 Pro secundo corollario, vide supra, notam 2.

p. 6 n. 8 Pro tertio corollario, cf. Albertus, op. cit., tract. 1, c. 6: 'Quarto dico
quod quando subiectum et praedicatum alicuius propositionis affirmativae non
supponunt pro aliquo, talis propositio semper est falsa. Verbi gratia, dicendo
"Chimaera est chimaera", "Chimaera est opinabilis", "Chimaera est intelligibilis."
Patet quia ex quo est affirmativa non falsificans se, et cum ad veritatem talis propositionis affirmativae requiratur subiectum et praedicatum supponere pro eodem,
sequitur dictam propositionem affirmativam in qua subiectum non supponit pro
aliquo fore falsam. In ista enim subiectum et praedicatum non supponunt pro
eodem, ex quo non supponunt pro aliquo, quod tamen requiritur ad hoc quod
propositio affirmativa non falsificans se sit vera' (f. 4ra lin. 38–46).

p. 6 n. 9 Vide supra, notas 1 et 3.

p. 8 n. 10 Nos autem locum non invenimus.

p. 8 n. 11 Capitulum 'De gradu positivo' in *Logica Magna* non invenitur, sed
cf. ibidem, Pars I, tract. 9 'De dictione sicut' (ed. Venetiis 1499, f. 42ra lin. 40–
42rb lin. 35).

p. 8 n. 12 Cf. *Logica Magna*, Pars I, tract. 1 'De terminis' (f. 4vb lin. 40–52).

p. 12 n. 13 Cf. ibidem (f. 5ra lin. 28–39).

p. 12 n. 14 Cf. Albertus, op. cit., tract. 2, c. 6: 'Secunda regula: in propositione
indefinita subiectum non supponit determinate, sicut hic "Homo est animal" vel
"Homo non est animal" . . . regulae illae sunt tenendae tam pro terminis supponentibus materialiter quam pro terminis supponentibus personaliter. Tertia regula:
cuiuslibet propositionis particularis subiectum supponit determinate sicut etiam
subiectum propositionis indefinitae, sicut dicendo "Quidam homo est animal",
"Quidam homo non est animal" ' (f. 12vb lin. 19–26). Cf. etiam ibidem, f. 12va
lin. 37–44.

p. 14 n. 15 Cf. Albertus, op. cit., tract. 1, c. 6: 'Quinto dico propositionem
negativam cuius subiectum pro nullo supponit esse veram. Ex quo sequitur istam
esse veram "Chimaera non est chimaera"; et similiter istam "Vacuum non est
vacuum"; et similiter istam "Chimaera non est intelligibilis" ' (f. 4ra lin. 46–59).

p. 14 n. 16 Cf. Albertus, op. cit., tract. 2, c. 8 'De suppositione relativorum':
'Relativorum identitatis quaedam sunt reciproca, sicut "suus-sui", quaedam non

reciproca, ut "ille", "iste" . . . Tertia regula: relativum identitatis non reciprocum non supponit pro alio quam pro illo pro quo supponit suum antecedens, nam aliter non esset identitas in relatione, verbi gratia dicendo "Socrates currit et ipse movetur" ' (f. 14ra lin. 56–8, 14va lin. 25–8).

p. 14 n. 17 Cf. Albertus, op. cit., tract. 2, c. 10 'De ampliatione', *6a regula* (f. 15va lin. 63–5) verbo tenus.

p. 14 n. 18 Cf. Albertus, op. cit., tract. 2, c. 11 'De appellatione terminorum': 'Appellatio est proprietas praedicati. Solemus enim dicere praedicatum appellare suam formam in ordine ad verbum quod est copula illius propositionis. Unde praedicatum appellare suam formam est ipsum sub eadem forma, vel sub eadem voce, si sit terminus vocalis, sub qua praedicatur in propositione in qua appellat suam formam esse verificabile in propositione de praesenti de pronomine demonstrante illud pro quo supponit subiectum propositionis cuius est pars' (f. 16rb lin. 48–56). Cf. etiam Guillelmus de Ockham, *Summa Logicae*, Pars I, c. 72 (ed. cit., p. 216) et Walterus Burley (sive Burleigh), *De Puritate Artis Logicae Tractatus Longior*, tract. 1, Pars II (ed. Ph. Boehner, St. Bonaventure, N.Y., 1955, p. 49).

p. 14 n. 19 Cf. Albertus, op. cit., tract. 2, c. 11, *3a regula* (f. 16va lin. 38–42) verbo tenus.

p. 14 n. 20 Cf. *Logica Magna*, Pars I, tract. 2 'De suppositionibus' (f. 26ra lin. 16–21, f. 16ra lin. 30–40).

Capitulum II

p. 14 n. 1 Secundae viae auctor adhuc est ignotus. Quam tamen referunt Ricardus Feribrigge et Johannes Venator: cf. R. Feribrigge, *Logica* seu *Tractatus de Veritate Propositionum*, Pars I, c. 1 'De modis arguendi ad veritatem propositionis', *1a consequentia* MS. Patavii, Bibl. Univ. 1123, f. 79vb: vide Appendicem I, p. 215, lin. 11 et Johannes Venator, *Logica*, tract. III, c. 2 'De veritate et falsitate propositionis', *1a conclusio* (MS. Vat. lat. 2130, f. 105vb: vide Appendicem II, p. 243, lin. 20–8; quae ad verbum Paulus Venetus describit). Cf. etiam illa positio, quam tamquam 'scholae communis' recitat Willelmus Heytesbury, *De Veritate*: 'In ista materia tenet schola communis quod ad hoc quod aliqua propositio sit vera sufficit et requiritur quod ipsa significet praecise sicut est' (ed. Venetiis 1494, f. 184va lin. 24–6). Contra eam ponit Heytesbury argumenta (alia tamen ab iis quae Paulus Venetus ex Feribrigge et Venatore congregat: cf. infra notae 2 et 4) et improbat formas arguendi 'de probatione illius propositionis' scil. de vario modo exponendi dictionem exclusivam 'praecise', quae diversis auctoribus, non tamen ad nomen citatis, tribuit (ibidem, f. 184va lin. 26–184vb lin. 42; pro 'Tractatibus probationum' apud logicos saec. xiv, cf. A. Maierù, *Terminologia della tarda scolastica*, Romae 1972, pp. 393–498). Ad quaesitum principale sophismatis, suam exprimens sententiam sic respondet Heytesbury: 'Ad aliud quaesitum in alio articulo dico quod admisso cum modo loquendi quod aliqua propositio significet sicut est, quem modum volo sustinere gratia argumenti in materia concernente duos articulos sequentes, quia sermones sunt exponendi seu exemplificandi secundum materiam subiectam, ad haec dicitur quod ad hoc quod aliqua propositio sit vera sufficit quod ipsa praecise significet sicut est, sed non requiritur. Et causa est quia nulla negativa primarie praecise significat sicut est, nec aliqua propositio affirmativa de praeterito vel de futuro, nec aliqua propositio affirmativa de praesenti ubi principale verbum est hoc verbum "potest". Cuiusmodi est haec propositio "Antichristus potest esse". Nam Sortem non esse non est, nec Platonem fuisse est, nec Antichristum fore est, nec Antichristum posse esse est, ut patet per argumenta facta. Ad hoc quod aliqua propositio sit vera sufficit quod ita est totaliter sicut illa significat, quia quacumque propositione capta quae significat sicut est,

ita est totaliter sicut illa significat, sicut per argumenta facta ad istam partem patet. Nam formaliter sequitur "Quaecumque propositio detur, ita est sicut illa significat; ergo ita est totaliter sicut illa significat". Et ita conceditur quod ita est totaliter sicut haec propositio significat "Homo est asinus". Et consimiliter dictum est de quacumque propositione affirmativa sive vera sive falsa etc. Et si dicatur: quid requiritur ad hoc quod aliqua propositio sit vera? Dicitur quod si fiat quaestio de propositione affirmativa de praesenti quae non est ampliativa, ubi scilicet est verbum principale hoc verbum "est", cuiusmodi est haec "Deus est", est quod ad hoc quod haec sit vera sufficit et requiritur quod ipsa praecise significet sicut est affirmative directe. Si fiat quaestio de aliqua alia propositione, dicitur quod nihil est in re sufficiens et requisitum ad hoc quod sit vera. Nulla enim est nec potest esse causa in re quare negativa est vera, nec propositio de praeterito, nec de futuro, nec de ampliativo verbo. Nec potest esse aliqua causa in re de hoc quod aliqua talis est vera. Et ratio, quia ad hoc quod aliqua propositio de praesenti non ampliativa sit vera, non requiritur quod ipsa praecise significet sicut est. Verbi gratia, aliqua est talis propositio vera quae significat sicut non est. Nam haec propositio "Homo est" est vera et tamen significat quod homo est asinus' (ibidem, f. 185rb lin. 23–185va lin. 1). Cf. A. Maierù, 'Il problema della verità nelle opere di Guglielmo Heytesbury', *Studi Medievali*, 3a serie, VII. I (1966), 52–6.

p. 16 n. 2 Pro prima conclusione in contrarium, cf. Feribrigge, ibidem, *contra 1am consequentiam* (Appendix I, p. 215 lin. 24–7).

p. 16 n. 3 Cf. *Logica Magna*, Pars I, tract. 4 'De exclusivis' (ff. 34ra lin. 56–60, 35ra lin. 21–44).

p. 18 n. 4 Pro secunda conclusione in contrarium, cum argumentis ipsam probantibus, cf. Feribrigge, ibidem, *contra conversam 1ae consequentiae* (Appendix I, pp. 216 lin. 38–218 lin. 23) et Venator, tract. III, c. 2, *2a conclusio* (Appendix II, p. 245 lin. 32–47); tract. I, c. 7 'De significato propositionis', *3a et 4a conclusiones* (Appendix II, pp. 239 lin. 19–240 lin. 12). Quibus ambobus auctoribus, aut ad verbum aut similiter arguens, adhaeret Paulus Venetus.

p. 18 n. 5 Auctorem talis opinionis non invenimus.

p. 20 n. 6 Cf. *Logica Magna*, Pars II, tract. 2 'De propositione categorica' (f. 104ra lin. 20–104rb lin. 44).

p. 22 n. 7 Locus non inventus (forte ex *De Generatione et Corruptione* I, c. 10, 327^{b}22).

p. 24 n. 8 Cf. tract. 'De significato propositionis', c. 3, pp. 94–104.

Capitulum III

p. 24 n. 1 Tertiae viae auctor adhuc est ignotus. Refert eam cum probatione Feribrigge, ibidem, *2a consequentia* (Appendix I, p. 219 lin. 26–40) quem, vel ad verbum vel abbreviando, hic sequitur Paulus Venetus. Eandem viam forte innuit Venator, tract. III, c. 2, *3a conclusio* (Appendix II, p. 245 lin. 42–7). Pro sententia Heytesbury de hac via vide supra cap. II, notam 1.

p. 24 n. 2 Magister iste forte est Johannes Venator, ibidem, *contra 3am conclusionem* (Appendix II, pp. 246 lin. 1–247 lin. 25). Sed etiam cf. Feribrigge, ibidem, *contra 2am consequentiam* (Appendix I, pp. 220 lin. 6–221 lin. 21). Quos locos ambo forte prae oculis habuit Paulus Venetus, pro maiori parte tamen ex Venatore quasi verbum de verbo describens.

p. 30 n. 3 Cf. *Logica Magna*, Pars I, tract. 1 'De terminis' (ff. 2rb lin. 59–3vb lin. 23).

p. 36 n. 4 Etiam pro 'priori capitulo', quod dicit paulo supra, cf. cap. 2, supra, pp. 18–24.

Capitulum IV

p. 36 n. 1 Quartae viae auctor est adhuc ignotus. Quam referunt Feribrigge, ibidem, *3a consequentia* (Appendix I, p. 222 lin. 2–8) et Venator, tract. III, c. 2, *7a conclusio* (Appendix II, p. 247 lin. 26–8). Eandemque recitaverat Heytesbury: 'Alii dicunt quod ad hoc quod aliqua propositio sit vera sufficit et requiritur quod ita est totaliter sicut illa significat' (ed. cit., f. 185ra lin. 9–11); de qua via vide eiusdem Heytesbury sententiam, supra, cap. 2, notam 1.

p. 36 n. 2 Pro prima conclusione, cf. Feribrigge, ibidem, *contra 3am consequentiam* (Appendix I, pp. 222 lin. 9–223 lin. 3) et Venator, ibidem, *7a conclusio* (Appendix II, pp. 247 lin. 26–248 lin. 7); ex quorum utroque, paucis mutatis abbreviatis vel additis, videtur conflata hic a Paulo Veneto series argumentorum. Aliter haud tamen toto caelo, arguit contra quartam viam Heytesbury, ibidem (f. 185ra lin. 11–43).

p. 40 n. 3 Pro secunda conclusione, cf. Venator, ibidem, *8a conclusio* (Appendix II, p. 248 lin. 12–18).

p. 42 n. 4 Cf. supra, secunda conclusio contra secundam viam (cap. 2, p. 18) et secunda conclusio contra tertiam viam (cap. 3, p. 36).

Capitulum V

p. 42 n. 1 Quintae viae auctor videtur forte Ricardus Feribrigge. Cf. *Logica* seu *Tractatus de Veritate Propositionum*, Pars I, c. 3 'De veritate etc. sententia auctoris' (Appendix I, pp. 229–34); idemque apud Venator, tract. III, c. 2, *9a conclusio* (Appendix II, pp. 249–50).

p. 42 n. 2 Pro tribus conclusionibus huius viae, cf. Feribrigge, ibidem, 'Methodus etc.' (Appendix I, p. 229 lin. 8–32); idemque apud Venator, qui aliqua quae hic citantur omittit vel resumit (Appendix II, pp. 249 lin. 13–19).

p. 42 n. 3 Pro primo exemplo primae conclusionis, cf. Feribrigge, ibidem (Appendix I, p. 229 lin. 24–7). Cf. etiam Venator, ibidem (Appendix II, p. 249 lin. 20–3).

p. 42 n. 4 Pro ceteris exemplis cf. Feribrigge, ibidem (Appendix I, p. 229 lin. 28 sqq.).

p. 44 n. 5 Pro istis regulis, cf. Feribrigge, ibidem, 'Regulae etc.' (Appendix I, p. 231 lin. 33–43); idemque apud Venator, ibidem (Appendix II, p. 249 lin. 25–33).

p. 44 n. 6 Regulam in *Logica Magna* non invenimus. Sed cf. Venator, ibidem, 'contra opinionem' (Appendix II, p. 250 lin. 28–33).

p. 46 n. 7 Cf. *Logica Magna*, Pars I, tract. 5 'De regulis exclusivarum' (f. 35ra lin. 3–18).

Capitulum VI

p. 46 n. 1 Auctor huius viae est Petrus de Aliaco. Cf. *Insolubilia*, c. 2 de 'Quare sit propositio vera vel falsa', *3a conclusio* (ed. Parisiis 1498, sign. b$_{ii}$ra lin. 5–16) praecise ad verbum citata. Nota bene etiam omnia quae idem praemittit de propositione, de propositione mentali nec non de propositione mentali proprie dicta, in principio tractatus, c. 1 de 'Quid sit propositio': 'Primo ergo notandum est quod iste terminus "propositio" est analogus ad propositionem mentalem, vocalem, et scriptam et per

prius significat mentalem quam vocalem vel scriptam . . .' usque ad 'Et ista nota-
bilia diligenter prosequentibus sunt advertenda' (ibidem, sign. a_vivb lin. 40–a_viirb
lin. 41).

p. 46 n. 2 Sed contra, cf. Petrus de Aliaco, op. cit., c. 2 de 'Quare etc.': 'Quinta
conclusio erit ista quod quaelibet propositio mentalis proprie dicta simpliciter
categorica et de inesse, affirmativa, si sit vera ideo est vera quia qualitercumque
per eam secundum significationem eius totalem significatur esse, fuisse vel fore,
taliter est, fuit vel erit. Et quaelibet talis si sit falsa, propter causam oppositam est
falsa, scilicet quia aliqualiter secundum significationem eius totalem significatur
esse, fuisse aut fore, qualiter non est, non fuit nec erit. Sed quaelibet negativa talis
si est vera ideo est vera quia qualitercumque per eam secundum significationem
eius totalem significatur non fuisse, non esse nec fore, taliter non est, non fuit, nec
erit. Et quaelibet talis si est falsa propter causam oppositam est falsa, scilicet quia
aliqualiter per eam secundum significationem eius totalem significatur non esse,
non fuisse, non fore, qualiter est, fuit vel erit' (ibidem, sign. a_vivb lin. 40–a_viirb
lin. 41).

p. 48 n. 3 Scil. antecedens consequentiae ad probandum conclusionem, supra
p. 46 lin. 20–1.

p. 50 n. 4 Cf. *Logica Magna*, Pars I, tract. 1 'De terminis' (f. 5vb lin. 42–53).

Capitulum VII

p. 50 n. 1 Auctor huius viae forte est Johannes Venator, qui inter alias, has conclusiones affirmative ponit. Cf. *Logica*, tract. III, c. 2, *conclusiones 10a, 12a, 13a,
14a* (Appendix II, pp. 250–1).

p. 52 n. 2 Locus non inventus.

p. 52 n. 3 Cf. *Logica Magna*, Pars I, tract. 1 'De terminis' (f. 13rb lin. 3–9).

p. 54 n. 4 Cf. *Logica Magna*, Pars I, tract. 19 'De propositione exponibili' (f. 70va
lin. 21–70vb lin. 61).

p. 56 n. 5 Cf. *Logica Magna*, Pars II, tract. 15 'De insolubilibus', *7a conclusio*
(f. 195va lin. 47–195vb lin. 32).

Capitulum VIII

p. 56 n. 1 Octavae viae auctor est Petrus Mantuanus (Petrus Alboini). Cf. *Logica*,
tract. 'De veritate propositionis' (ed. Venetiis 1492, sign. D_3vb lin. 31–6 et D_3vb
lin. 54–D_iiiira lin. 6); locus hic verbatim recitatus a Paulo Veneto. Cf. etiam A.
Maierù, 'Il problema del significato nella logica di Pietro da Mantova', in *Miscellanea Mediaevalia*, Bd. 9, Berlin–New York, 1974.

p. 56 n. 2 Cf. *Logica Magna*, Pars II, tract. 1 'De propositione' (f. 101rb lin. 2–21).

p. 58 n. 3 Cf. supra c. 2, pp. 18 lin. 14–24 lin. 7.

p. 58 n. 4 Aristoteles, *Metaphysica* II, c. 1 993^{b}30–1.

p. 58 n. 5 Locum praecise ad verbum correspondentem non invenimus. Pro doctrina
autem cf. Petrus Mantuanus, *Logica*, tract. 'De veritate propositionis': 'Item
praesupponatur quod nihil potest intelligere intellectus humanus quod non possit
intelligere esse ens. Patet, quia ens est primum obiectum intellectus. Ideo tantum
ens seu aliquid potest intellectus humanus apprehendere aut intelligere' (ed. cit.
sign. D_iira lin. 27–31). Cf. etiam ibidem, tract. 'De probatione propositionis
exclusivae': 'Propositio exclusiva affirmativa in singulari numero de subiecto
simplici exponitur per copulativam compositam ex sua praeiacente et universali

negativa cuius subiectum est terminus infinitus oppositus contradictorie subiecto exclusivae, ut "Homo currit et nihil non homo currit; igitur tantum homo currit." Similiter "Tantum B instans et nihil non B instans erit instans; igitur tantum B instans erit instans." Et nondum debet sumi minor sic—"Nihil aliud quam B instans erit instans"—quia utraque exponens esset vera et exposita falsa, quia sua universalis de terminis transpositis esset falsa' (sign. B$_v$ra lin. 13–27); 'Item *quinto* data ista expositione sequitur quod tantum ens potest intelligi capiendo ly .ens. tran-scendenter, et per consequens praecise ens potest significari. Et consequenter sequitur ultra quod praecise verum potest significari, capiendo "verum" pro re vera. Et consequenter sequitur quod quacumque propositione data, quae aliquid significat, ipsa praecise verum significat, et per consequens nulla propositio falsum significat, capiendo "falsum" pro termino primae intentionis; et sequitur ultra quod falsum non potest intelligi, sicut non ens non potest intelligi' (sign. B$_v$rb lin. 9–17); 'Ad quintum cum infertur quod tantum ens potest intelligi et tantum ens potest signi-ficari dicitur negando consequentiam. Sed bene conceditur quod tantum ens intelligitur et quod tantum ens potest intellectus intelligere et quod praecise verum potest aliqua propositio significare, capiendo "verum" prout convertitur cum ly .aliquid. et ly .ens. Sed negatur illa quod tantum ens potest intelligi, quia illa significat quod tantum illud quod potest esse ens potest intelligi, eo quod ly .ens. supponit solum respectu huius verbi "potest" a quo accipit suppositionem, et non respectu illius verbi infinitivi "intelligi", quia si supponeret respectu illius verbi infinitivi et non respectu verbi principalis foret illa falsa "Antichristus potest esse", quia ly .Antichristus. supponeret respectu illius verbi infinitivi "esse" et per con-sequens staret pro eo quod est. Et ideo sunt tales falsae "Chimaera potest intelligi" et "Aliquod instans quod fuit potest fuisse" ' (sign. B$_v$va lin. 55–B$_v$vb lin. 7).

p. 60 n. 6 Cf. Petrus Mantuanus, op. cit., tract. 'De veritate propositionis': 'Item, haec propositio "Tu non es" significat te non esse. Et haec "Tu differs a te" signi-ficat te differre a te. Et haec "Non intelligibile est" significat non intelligibile esse. Et tamen non potest intelligi non intelligibile esse ens, nec te differre a te esse ens, nec te non esse ⟨esse⟩ ens' (ed. cit., sign. D$_{ii}$rb lin. 34–9); 'Ad ultimam formam dicitur quod hanc propositionem "Tu non es" significare te non esse intelligitur dupliciter. Uno modo quod haec "Tu non es" significet te non esse, id est quod haec te esse privative significet seu negative significet. Et isto modo qui satis est improprius, conceditur quod haec "Tu non es" significat te non esse, quia ista "Tu non es" te esse privative significat, aut te esse privative dat intelligere, et ita conceditur. Alio modo potest intelligi quod haec "Tu non es" significet te non esse, id est rem quae intelligitur esse te non esse haec propositio "Tu non es" significat, et ille modus est impossibilis. Frequenter tamen concedimus quod haec "Tu non es" significat te non esse, ubi argumenta praesentem difficultatem non exigant, vel ad primum sensum pro improprio derelictum. Et ita negatur quod haec "Non intelligibile est" significet non intelligibile esse, et haec "Tu differs a te" significet te differre a te etc' (sign. D$_{ii}$va lin. 7–21).

p. 62 n. 7 Cf. Petrus Mantuanus, op. cit., tract. 'De veritate propositionis': 'Praeterea sequitur quod omne significatum unius contradictoriorum est signi-ficatum alterius, et quidquid significatur per unum significatur per aliud. Patet illud ex ultima et penultima suppositione, quia si aliquid esset significatum unius quod non esset significatum alterius, hoc esset propter syncategorema quod est in una positum et non in alia. Sed syncategorema non variat significatum, quia nihil significat, sed solum variat modum significandi propositionis. Igitur etc. Et ante-cedens patet captis istis duobus contradictoriis—"Tu es", "Tu non es"—quorum primi significatum est te esse. Et idem etiam est significatum secundi, quia ly .non. quod ponitur in secunda nihil addit super significato terminorum primi contra-dictorii. Diversimode tamen te esse significatur per primum contradictorium et per

secundum. Ex quo sequitur quod si verum per unum contradictorium significatur, illudmet verum per aliud significatur. Et ideo non valet consequentia ista "Praecise verum ista propositio significat; igitur ista propositio est vera." Illa enim propositio "Tu non es" praecise verum significat quae tamen falsa est. False tamen verum significat, quia negative' (ed. cit. sign. D₃rb lin. 19–41).

Capitulum IX

p. 64 n. 1 Cf. *Logica Magna*, Pars II, tract. 15 'De insolubilibus', *opinio 15a* (f. 195vb lin. 56–66).

p. 64 n. 2 Pro primo argumento contra 2am conclusionem (in particulari p. 64 lin. 15–31), cf. Feribrigge, op. cit., Pars I, c. 3 'De veritate etc. sententia auctoris', *1um argumentum contra* (Appendix I, p. 232 lin. 26–34), simili ratione factum.

p. 64 n. 3 Pro secundo argumento (in particulari pp. 64 lin. 32–66 lin. 16), cf. Feribrigge, op. cit., c. 1 'De modis arguendi ad veritatem propositionis', *conclusio incidentalis* (Appendix I, p. 221 lin. 28–9) verbatim.

p. 66 n. 4 Pro tertio argumento (in particulari pp. 66 lin. 29–68 lin. 14), cf. Petrus Mantuanus, *Logica*, tract. 'De veritate propositionis': 'Sed incidit dubium utrum sit aliqua propositio quae non aliqualiter esse seu nullum significatum significet. Et arguitur quod sic: ⟨1⟩ Quia ista propositio "Si Antichristus est albus, Antichristus est coloratus" est propositio cuius nullum potest assignari significatum. Nullus enim posset intelligere quid foret quod si Antichristus est albus, Antichristus est coloratus, si foret. ⟨2⟩ Item, ista est propositio "Homo est non homo". Et tamen non aliqualiter esse illa significat. Quia si aliqualiter esse illa significaret, maxime hominem esse non hominem. Sed hoc est falsum, quia hominem esse non hominem non potest intelligi. Sed quod non potest intelligi significari non potest. Igitur illa hominem esse non hominem non significat. Patet consequentia. Et minor arguitur, quia hominem esse non hominem non potest intelligi esse verum et ens. Igitur etc. Quidquid enim potest intelligi, potest intelligi esse verum. Sed quidquid potest significari potest intelligi esse ens et verum. Igitur quidquid potest significari, potest intelligi esse ens et verum. Sed hominem esse non hominem potest significari. Igitur potest intelligi. Per primam responsionem. Consequens est falsum. Igitur etc. ⟨3⟩ Item tertio sic: Haec copulativa "Tu es et tu non es" est propositio quae non aliqualiter esse significat. Igitur etc. Arguitur antecedens: Quia te esse et te non esse non potest intellectus concipere simul, nec aliud significatum illa significat. Igitur non aliqualiter esse illa significat. Patet consequentia. Et probatur antecedens: Quia si te esse et te non esse intellectus posset simul comprehendere, potest per idem cuiuslibet consequentiae contradictorium consequentis intelligere cum antecedente—quod falsum est. Igitur etc.

'Oppositum tamen arguitur: Quia propositio est oratio verum vel falsum significans vel vere vel false significans. Igitur omnis propositio aliqualiter esse vere vel false significat.

'Ad quod dubium dicitur concedendo quod non quaelibet propositio aliqualiter esse significat, quia ista et illa et multae aliae—"Homo est asinus", "Differens ab homine est homo"—est propositio quae non aliqualiter esse significat, sicut etiam nullum est significatum illius "Homo est asinus", quia nec hominem esse asinum est significatum illorum trium terminorum qui sunt ista propositio "Homo est asinus", neque hominem esse est significatum istius "Homo est asinus", quia si hominem esse esset significatum illorum trium terminorum "Homo est asinus", per idem etiam esset significatum quorumlibet trium terminorum quorum unus esset ly .homo., et sic isti termini ly .homo., ly .est. et ly .chimaera. hominem esse haberent pro significato. Consequens falsum quia solum duorum illud est signi-

ficatum, scilicet istius termini "homo" et istius termini "est" ' (ed. cit. signi D₃ va lin. 3–46).

p. 68 n. 5 Cf. supra, c. 8 nota 5.

p. 68 n. 6 Pro quarto argumento, cf. Petrus Mantuanus, op. cit., tract. 'De veritate propositionis': 'Ex istis iam acceptis inferamus quod quacumque propositione data affirmativa, sive vera sive falsa, quae aliqualiter esse significet, praecise sicut est illa significat—quod sic arguitur: Quia haec propositio "Antichristus est" praecise sicut est significat, quia sicut est illa significat et non aliter quam sicut est illa significat. Igitur etc. Patet consequentia. Et maior antecedentis arguitur: Quia Antichristum esse illa significat. Et Antichristum esse est sicut est vel erit vel saltem intelligitur esse sicut est. Igitur sicut est illa significat. Patet consequentia expositorie. Sic enim debet sumi minor, quia hoc verbum "significat" extendit se ex parte post usque ad ea quae intelliguntur. Quae minor sic probatur: Quia Antichristum esse erit possibiliter esse et vere esse sicut est, vel intelligitur esse vere esse vel possibiliter esse sicut est. Igitur etc. Sed minor principalis argumenti arguitur, scilicet quod non aliter quam sicut est illa significat: Quia non aliter quam taliter qualiter est illa significat, quia praecise possibiliter esse per illam intelligitur aut significatur. Et praecise possibiliter esse est. Igitur non aliter quam sicut est illa significat. Sequitur igitur quod praecise sicut est illa "Antichristus est" significat. Et sicut arguitur de illa, ita etiam arguitur de ista "Adam fuit" et de quacumque alia affirmativa, quae aliqualiter esse significat' (ed. cit., sign. D₁₁va lin. 21–40).

p. 70 n. 7 Pro responsione ad 2um argumentum contra, cf. Feribrigge, op. cit., c. 1, conclusio incidentalis (Appendix I, p. 221 lin. 40–5).

p. 72 n. 8 Cf. tract. 'De significato propositionis', c. 4, p. 106 lin. 18–26.

p. 72 n. 9 Cf. ibidem, c. 3, p. 94.

p. 74 n. 10 Cf. Petrus Mantuanus, op. cit., tract. 'De veritate propositionis': 'Ad aliam formam dicitur negando antecedens, scilicet quod omnis propositio significat quidquid ad eam sequitur. Non enim est illud verum, nec de virtute sermonis nec de virtute intentionis, quia nihil sequitur ad propositionem nisi propositio. Nec est verum quod quaelibet propositio significat cuiuslibet propositionis significatum ad ipsam sequentis, quia ad illam "Tu curris" sequitur ista "Deus est", quae tamen non significat Deum esse; ad istam etiam "Tu differs a te" formaliter sequitur te currere, et tamen ista non significat te currere; aliter enim non staret solum prima impositio terminorum huius propositionis, cuius oppositum ponitur' (ed. cit., sign. D₃vb lin. 17–27).

TRACTATUS DE SIGNIFICATO PROPOSITIONIS

Capitulum I (et prooemium)

p. 80 n. 1 De significato propositionis multae apud logicos saec. XIV versabantur opiniones; quorum sententias in libris manuscriptis aut in incunabulis editionibus investigantes et studentes nuper publici iuris facere coeperunt viri docti, rerum tam philosophicarum quam historicarum periti. De quibus recentiorem bibliographiam collige ex J. Pinborg, *Logik und Semantik im Mittelalter: Ein Überblick*, Problemata, Stuttgart, 1972, pp. 189–95. Cf. etiam H. Schepers, "Holkot contra dicta Crathorn', *Philosophisches Jahrbuch*, 77 (1972), pp. 106–7.*

p. 80 n. 2 Cf. cap. 9, pp. 190–8.

p. 80 n. 3 Primae opinionis auctor adhuc incertus. Quam referunt Feribrigge, op. cit., Pars I, c. 2 'De significato propositionis' (Appendix I, p. 223 lin. 9–10)

* Vide Addenda et corrigenda, p. xvi.

et Venator, op. cit., tract. I, c. 7 'De significato propositionis' (Appendix II, p. 237 lin. 8–10). Etiam Heytesbury, ut secundam ex 'tribus opinionibus famosis', eam memorat. Cf. *De Veritate*: 'Penes materiam primi argumenti est iste articulus pertractandus: numquid Deum esse sit aliquid vel aliqualiter a Deo distinctus ... In ista materia sunt tres opiniones famosae, quarum *prima* dicit quod Deum esse est Deus, et quod Sortem esse est Sortes. *Secunda* opinio dicit quod Deum esse nihil est, sed est esse aliqualiter, id est modus Dei. *Tertia* opinio dicit quod Deum esse est oratio infinitiva, et eodem modo Sortem esse, et sic de aliis' (ed. cit., f. 183va lin. 54–183vb lin. 2).

p. 80 n. 4 Argumenta probantia hanc opinionem inveniuntur paene ad verbum etiam apud Feribrigge, ibidem, *1a opinio* (Appendix I, pp. 223 lin. 30–224 lin. 2). Textus Feribrigge iuxta codicem C (= Romae Bibl. Casanatensis MS. 85, D. IV. 3, f. 77va) hic respicitur.

p. 82 n. 5 Pro argumentis contra opinionem, cf. Feribrigge, ibidem, *argumenta contra 1am opinionem* (Appendix I, pp. 224 lin. 3–225 lin. 6); etiam Venator, ibidem, *2a conclusio* (Appendix II, p. 238 lin. 18–24, 35–42; p. 239 lin. 7–8). Ex quibus ambobus auctoribus, vel ad verbum vel saltem quoad rationem, haurit argumenta, sextum vero solum, forte, ad sui ipsius mentem inserens, Paulus Venetus.

p. 82 n. 6 Cf. c. 8, pp. 166 sqq.

p. 84 n. 7 Talem distinctionem modi intrinseci alibi in *Logica Magna* non invenimus.

p. 84 n. 8 Pro responsione ad rationes, cf. Feribrigge, ibidem, *3a opinio*, 'Responsio ad argumenta contra' (Appendix I, p. 228 lin. 6–33).

p. 84 n. 9 Cf. c. 6, pp. 136 sqq.

Capitulum II

p. 84 n. 1 Secundae opinionis auctor adhuc incertus. Quam referunt et Feribrigge, op. cit., Pars I, c. 2 'De significato propositionis' (Appendix I, p. 223 lin. 10–11) et Venator, op. cit., tract. I, c. 7 'De significato propositionis' (Appendix II, p. 237 lin. 13–14). Pro tribus argumentis ad probandum eandem, cf. Feribrigge, ibidem, *2a opinio* (Appendix I, p. 225 lin. 8–30) paene ad verbum; pro 1° et 2° argumento, cf. etiam Venator, ibidem, *contra 6am conclusionem* (Appendix II, p. 242 lin. 6–16).

p. 86 n. 2 *Peri Hermeneias*, c. 3, 16ᵇ24–5 (*De Interpretatione sive Periermenias*, transl. Boethii, Aristoteles latinus II. 1–2, ed. L. Minio-Paluello, Bruges–Paris, 1965, p. 7 lin. 18–19).

p. 86 n. 3 Ibidem, c. 13, 22ᵃ14–ᵇ28 (transl. Boethii, ibidem, pp. 29 lin. 8–32 lin. 3).

p. 86 n. 4 Pro argumentis contra secundam opinionem, cf. Feribrigge, ibidem, *argumenta contra 2am opinionem* (Appendix I, pp. 225 lin. 31–226 lin. 29) et Venator, ibidem, *6a conclusio* (Appendix II, pp. 240 lin. 28–241 lin. 7).

p. 88 n. 5 Petrus de Aliaco, *Insolubilia*, versus finem capituli de 'Quare sit propositio vera vel falsa', *3a conclusio*: 'Tertia conclusio quam pono probabiliter et assertive est pro intellectu praecedentis, scilicet quod Deus seu divina notitia est ipsi intellectui divino propositio vera' (ed. Parisiis 1498, sign. bᵥiva lin. 5–8).

p. 88 n. 6 Pro responsione ad rationes, cf. Feribrigge, ibidem, *responsio ad argumenta . . . contra 3am opinionem* (Appendix I, p. 228 lin. 24–47), qui ex aliquo simili fundamento arguit, quamvis Paulus Venetus videatur ad suam mentem reficere argumenta.

p. 90 n. 7 Cf. *Logica Magna*, Pars II, tract. 1 'De propositione categorica' (f. 102va lin. 71–vb lin. 2).

p. 90 n. 8 Cf. c. 6, pp. 142 lin. 27–144 lin. 33.

p. 90 n. 9 Huius opinionis auctor adhuc incertus. Quam refert Heytesbury, op. cit., *3a opinio* (cf. supra, 'De significato' c. 1 nota 3) et ponit contra eam argumenta (ed. cit., f. 184va lin. 1–21), alia tamen ab iis quae Paulus Venetus hic.

p. 92 n. 10 Pro prima opinione de suppositione materiali, cf. *Logica Magna*, Pars I, tract. 2 'De suppositionibus' (ed. Venetiis, 1499 f. 16rb lin. 1–11). Cf. etiam Paul of Venice, *Logica Magna* (*Tractatus de Suppositionibus*), edited and translated by A. R. Perreiah, Franciscan Institute Publications, Text Series 15, St. Bonaventure, N.Y., 1971, pp. 5–6; ubi haec opinio Vincentio Ferrer O.P. assignatur.

p. 92 n. 11 Cf. *Logica Magna*, ibidem (ed. Venetiis 1499, f. 16va lin. 42–53; etiam supra f. 16rb lin. 49–61. Ed. Perreiah, pp. 12–14 et p. 8).

p. 92 n. 12 Auctor huius opinionis adhuc ignotus.

Capitulum III

p. 94 n. 1 Cf. Gregorius Ariminensis O.E.S.A., *Super Primum et Secundum Sententiarum*, Prologus, q. 1, a. 1 (ed. Venetiis 1522, photostatice impressa, Franciscan Institute Publications, Text Series 7, St. Bonaventure, N.Y., 1955, ff. 1ra–2rb D–H). Cf. etiam M. Dal Pra, 'La teoria del significato totale della proposizione nel pensiero di Gregorio da Rimini', *Rivista critica di storia della filosofia*, 11 (1956), pp. 287–311. Etiam G. Pagallo 'Nota sulla logica di Paolo Veneto: la critica alla dottrina del complexe significabile di Gregorio da Rimini', *Atti del XII Congresso Internazionale di filosofia*, Firenze, 1960, pp. 183–93.

p. 96 n. 2 Pro dictis tertiae opinionis, cf. Gregorius Ariminensis, ibidem (ff. 1vb–2ra Q–P), ad verbum, paucis omissis. Cf. etiam Petrus de Aliaco, op. cit., in medio capituli de 'Quare sit propositio vera et falsa', *opinio recitata* post 'Dubitationes difficiles' (ed. cit., sign. b$_{iiii}$va lin. 18–vb lin. 26) verbo tenus, quamvis autem aliqua omittat quae hic recitat Paulus Venetus (scil. 'Et hoc modo . . . nihil esse', p. 96 lin. 14–16, et 'Nec hominem . . . ridere' p. 96 lin. 20–1).

p. 96 n. 3 *Categoriae*, c. 12, 14^{b}21–2 (editio composita, Aristoteles latinus I. 1–5, ed. L. Minio-Paluello, Bruges–Paris, 1961, p. 76 lin. 18–19).

p. 96 n. 4 Aristoteles, *Metaphysica* V, c. 7, 1017^{a}31–2.

p. 96 n. 5 Augustinus, *Contra Epistulam Manichaei quam vocant Fundamenti*, c. 40, §6, Migne, *Patrologia latina*, vol. 42, col. 205.

p. 98 n. 6 *Categoriae*, c. 4, 1^{b}25–7 (transl. Boethii, p. 6 lin. 26–30).

p. 98 n. 7 Ibidem, c. 5, 2^{a}34–^{b}6 (transl. Boethii, p. 8 lin. 3–15).

p. 100 n. 8 Pro quarto argumento contra tertiam opinionem de conclusione haeretica, cf. Petrus de Aliaco, op. cit., c. 2, *conclusio 1a* contra opinionem recitatam (vide supra notam 2): 'Secundo, illa opinio habet concedere quod illa complexe significabilia essent aeterna, saltem aliqua—quod est falsum, quia solus Deus est aeternus simpliciter loquendo. Consequentia patet, quia secundum eos mundum fore et Deum esse fuerunt ab aeterno, quae non erant Deus—quod est falsum et contra articulum Parisius condemnatum, in quo dicitur sic: "Dicere quod fuerunt multae veritates ab aeterno quae non fuerunt ipse Deus est error" ' (ed. cit., sign. b$_{v}$ra lin. 24–32). Cf. etiam Johannes Buridanus, *Sophismata*, c. 1, sophisma 5 'Complexe significabilia sunt chimaerae': 'Et arguitur etiam quod non erant sic complexe significabilia antequam esset aliquid praeter Deum . . . Item, oportet ea

esse aeterna, et nos tenemus ex fide nihil esse aeternum simpliciter praeter ipsum Deum' (ed. Parisiis 1493, sign. a₃ vb lin. 31–9).

p. 100 n. 9 Cf. H. Denifle et A. Chatelain, *Chartularium Universitatis Parisiensis*, vol. I, Paris, 1889, p. 546, '1277, Martii 7, Parisiis', articulo 52: 'Quod id, quod de se determinatur ut Deus, vel semper agit, vel nunquam; et multa sunt aeterna.'

p. 102 n. 10 Pro decimo et ultimo argumento contra tertiam opinionem, cf. Petrus de Aliaco, ibidem: 'Probatur primo, quia illa opinio habet concedere quod tale complexe significabile esset et tamen nihil esset, et quod nec esset substantia nec accidens, nec Deus nec creatura—quod videtur esse absurdum' (ed. cit., sign. bᵥra lin. 18–23). Cf. etiam Johannes Buridanus, ibidem: 'Item omne quod est, Deus est vel creatura dependens a Deo. Et tamen illa complexe significabilia non erant creaturae, quia erant antequam Deus aliquid crearet. Nec erant Deus, ut illi dicunt' (ed. cit., sign. a₃vb lin. 39–aᵢᵢᵢᵢra lin. 4).

Capitulum IV

p. 104 n. 1 Quartae opinionis auctor est absque dubio Petrus de Aliaco. Omnes enim conclusiones et dicta quae huic quartae opinioni attribuit hic, in quarto capitulo, Paulus Venetus, excerpta sunt verbatim aut paene ex Petrus de Aliaco, *Insolubilia*, c. 2 de 'Quare sit propositio vera vel falsa' (de medio usque fere ad finem, scil. ex 'tertia conclusio' usque ad 'et sic patet solutio secundae dubitationis'; ed. cit., sign. bᵥrb lin. 18–bᵥᵢvb lin. 33). Quare et nos ea non iterum recitabimus, sed si vis locum ad locum comparare, cf. Petrus de Aliaco, ibidem, *3a conclusio contra opinionem recitatam* (sign. bᵥrb lin. 18–27) pro: Paulus Venetus hic, p. 104 lin. 21–35; *6a et ultima conclusio contra eandem opinionem* (sign. bᵥva lin. 18–bᵥvb lin. 13) pro: p. 106 lin. 1–26; *responsio ad ₁am dubitationem et 1a conclusio ad declarationem eiusdem* (sign. bᵥvb lin. 22–bᵥᵢra lin. 6) pro: pp. 106 lin. 27–108 lin. 16; *4a propositio ad idem* (sign. bᵥᵢrb lin. 17–32) pro: p. 108 lin. 17–23; *responsio ad 2am dubitationem, 1a positio et 2a et 3a conclusio* (sign. bᵥᵢrb lin. 34–bᵥᵢva lin. 8) pro: p. 116 lin. 23–31; *responsio ad 2um et 3um argumentum 2ae dubitationis* (sign. bᵥᵢva lin. 31–bᵥᵢvb lin. 14) pro: p. 116 lin. 34–118 lin. 14; *responsio ad obiectionem* (sign. bᵥᵢvb lin. 29–31) pro: p. 118 lin. 15–16. Editionem huius tractatus Petri de Aliaco, cum aliis eiusdem auctoris opusculis, parant F. Del Punta et Joh. Pinborg.

p. 110 n. 2 Haec probatio praecise, supra non invenitur; sed cf. conclusio 4a ultimae opinionis, c. 8, pp. 166 sqq.

p. 120 n. 3 *Analytica Posteriora* I, c. 2, 71ᵇ15–16 (transl. Iacobi, Aristoteles latinus IV. 1–4, ed. L. Minio-Paluello, Bruges–Paris 1968, p. 7 lin. 10–11). Cf. etiam ibidem, c. 8, 75ᵇ24–5 (p. 20 lin. 22–3).

Capitulum V

p. 122 n. 1 Cf. supra, *Tractatus de Veritate Propositionis*, c. 2, pp. 20 lin. 1–22 lin. 19.

p. 122 n. 2 Magister ponens hanc conclusionem, sine dubio, est Johannes Venator. Cf. *Logica*, tract. I, c. 7, *8a conclusio* (Appendix II, p. 241 lin. 16–37), locus praecise ad verbum citatus.

p. 124 n. 3 Pro argumentis contra 8am conclusionem, cf. Venator, ibidem, *contra 8am conclusionem* (Appendix II, p. 242 lin. 17–31) ubi simili ratione qua Paulus Venetus arguitur. Cf. etiam idem, ibidem, 'Responsio ad argumenta facta contra conclusiones', *ad argumenta contra 8am conclusionem* (Appendix II, pp. 242 lin. 33–243 lin. 15).

p. 126 n. 4 Cf. *Logica Magna*, Pars II, tract. 9 'De hypotheticis propositionibus' (ed. cit., f. 131rb lin. 64–131va lin. 27).

p. 128 n. 5 Cf. conclusio 4a ultimae opinionis, c. 8, pp. 168 lin. 17–170 lin. 6.

Capitulum VI

p. 138 n. 1 Pro argumentis contra conclusiones, cf. Feribrigge, op. cit., Pars I, c. 3 'De veritate etc. sententia auctoris', *argumenta contra* (Appendix I, pp. 232 lin. 27–233 lin. 6) ubi simili ratione arguitur de propositione negativa 'Nullum hominem esse asinum est verum' (nota quae dicit Paulus Venetus, hic infra p. 140 lin. 9–10).

p. 140 n. 2 Responsionem videtur Paulus Venetus colligere ex duobus locis in Feribrigge. Cf. op. cit., Pars I, c. 3, 'Responsio ad argumenta in contrarium' (Appendix I, p. 233 lin. 23–37) et Pars II, c. 2 'De possibilitate, impossibilitate etc. opinio auctoris', 'argumenta contra opinionem' (Appendix I, p. 235 lin. 13–45).

p. 142 n. 3 Cf. *Logica Magna*, Pars I, tract. 20 'De propositione officiabili' (f. 73r–v; in particulari f. 73va lin. 62–70).

p. 144 n. 4 Cf. supra p. 140 lin. 20–4.

p. 152 n. 5 *Peri Hermeneias*, c. 13, 22^a32–8 (transl. Boethii, Aristoteles latinus II. 1–2, p. 30 lin. 1–7). Cf. Feribrigge, op. cit., Pars I, c. 3, 'Responsio ad argumenta in contrarium' (Appendix I, p. 233 lin. 39–42).

p. 154 n. 6 *Peri Hermeneias*, c. 13, 23^a7–11 (transl. Boethii, p. 33 lin. 1–6).

p. 154 n. 7 Ibidem, c. 9, 19^a12–16 (p. 16 lin. 15–18).

p. 154 n. 8 Ibidem, c. 9, 19^a27–32 (p. 17 lin. 7–13).

p. 156 n. 9 Ibidem, c. 9, 18^b9–11 (p. 14 lin. 14–16).

p. 156 n. 10 *Analytica Priora* I, c. 3, 25^a27–$^b26$, et c. 13, 32^a18–$^b3$ (transl. Boethii, Aristoteles latinus III. 1–4, ed. L. Minio-Paluello, Bruges–Paris, 1962, pp. 7 lin. 24–9 lin. 6 et pp. 26 lin. 12–27 lin. 12).

Capitulum VII

(sine notis)

Capitulum VIII

p. 168 n. 1 Cf. Feribrigge, op. cit., Pars I, c. 2 'De significato propositionis' (Appendix I, p. 223 lin. 11–21).

p. 170 n. 2 Cf. hic infra, p. 196 lin. 24 sqq.

p. 170 n. 3 Cf. Gregorius Ariminensis, *Super Primum et Secundum Sententiarum*, Prologus, q. 1, a. 1, '. . . nec quia homo est aut quia albedo est, aut etiam quia homo et albedo sunt, ideo haec est vera "Homo est albus", sed quia homo est albus . . .' (ed. cit., f. 1vb Q).

p. 170 n. 4 Pro conclusionibus istis ad absurdum, nota quod mutatis interdum verbis, sed communi ratione, aliquae inveniuntur apud Feribrigge, aliquae etiam apud Heytesbury. Pro 1a, 3a, 10a, et 11a conclusione cf. Feribrigge, ibidem, *3a opinio*, argumenta contra (Appendix I, p. 227 lin. 5–7, 14–17, 33–48). Pro 6a, 12a, 10a, 1a et 3a, hoc ordine relatis, cf. Heytesbury, *De Veritate, contra Iam opinionem* (ed. cit., f. 183vb lin. 24–38, 46–56; f. 184ra lin. 15–36, 39–43).

p. 174 n. 5 Cf. *Logica Magna*, Pars I, tract. 19 'De propositione officiabili' (ed. cit., f. 70va lin. 39–52).

p. 184 n. 6 Pro secundo argumento ultra contra 4am conclusionem ultimae opinionis, cf. Gregorius Ariminensis, op. cit., Prologus, q. 1, a. 1 (ed. cit. f. 1va–b M–O) fere ad verbum.

p. 184 n. 7 *Ethica Nicomachea* VI, c. 3, 1139^{b}20 (transl. R. Grosseteste Lincolniensis, Aristoteles lat. XXVI. 1–3, ed. R. A. Gauthier, Leiden–Bruxelles, 1972, p. 255 lin. 19–21).

p. 184 n. 8 *Analytica Posteriora* I, c. 2, 71^{b}15–16 (transl. Jacobi, Aristoteles lat. IV, 1–4, p. 7 lin. 10–11).

Capitulum IX

p. 192 n. 1 Aristoteles, *Physica* I, c. 1, 184^{a}23–4.

APPENDIX I

RICARDUS FERIBRIGGE

LOGICA SEU *TRACTATUS DE VERITATE PROPOSITIONUM*

MS. Patavii, Bibl. Univ. 1123, ff. 79va–87rb   5

⟨PARS PRIMA, CAPITULUM PRIMUM: DE MODIS ARGUENDI AD VERITATEM PROPOSITIONIS⟩

* * *

Assignantes namque causam veritatis propositionis ex hoc quod (f. 79vb) ita est totaliter sicut significatur per eam, ad probanda sophismata et quaslibet alias propositiones probandas, arguere triplici forma solent, quarum prima est haec: 10

⟨1⟩ Hoc sophisma significat praecise sicut est; ergo sophisma est verum.

Alii inter ⟨hunc⟩ modum arguendi et alium iam nominandum differentiam ponentes arguunt sic:

⟨2⟩ Praecise sicut est significat hoc sophisma, sive haec propositio; ergo haec propositio est vera.   15

Et dicunt quod e contra sequitur tamquam a per se causato ad per se causam, eo quod antecedens illius consequentiae est causa sufficiens consequentis. Tertia forma qua quidam arguunt ad partem affirmativam sophismatum probandorum est haec:

⟨3⟩ Ita est totaliter sicut haec propositio significat; ergo haec propositio est 20
vera.

⟨PRIMA CONSEQUENTIA⟩

⟨*Argumenta contra primam consequentiam*⟩

⟨1.1⟩ Contra primam formam arguitur sic: Ponatur quod A significet quod Deus est et quod homo est asinus. Isto posito patet quod A propositio non est 25 vera, et tamen significat praecise sicut est. Et ita est antecedens primae consequentiae verum et consequens falsum.

⟨1.1.1⟩ Quod A significat praecise sicut est probatur: A propositio significat sicut est et non aliter quam est. Ergo A propositio significat praecise sicut est. Consequentia probatur dupliciter: ⟨1.1.1a⟩ Primo sic: 'Sicut est et non aliter 30 quam est' et 'praecise sicut est' omnino convertuntur, quia qualitercumque est praecise sicut est, est sicut est et non aliter quam est, et e contra. Ergo si in aliqua propositione ex aliqua parte orationis ponitur alterum eorum, nullam diversitatem in significatione propositionis causabit quin causabit reliquum eorum positum ex eadem parte orationis. Consequentia patet per hoc, quia in quacumque pro- 35 positione ponuntur, ex eadem parte propositionis in quodcumque se extendit vis negationis importata per unum eorum, in idem praecise se extendit vis negationis importata per reliquum eorum.

⟨1.1.1b⟩ Secundo probatur prima consequentia sic: In hac propositione 'A significat praecise sicut est', denotatur exclusio solum respectu illius termini 'sicut est', et ita excluduntur solum opposita illius termini 'sicut est' positi a parte praedicati. Et per consequens non denotatur negatio sive exclusio respectu 5 totius compositionis, quia dictio importans negationem omnino postponitur actui copulandi. Ergo ex hoc quod A significat praecise sicut est, solum denotatur A significare sicut est et non aliter quam sicut est. Et per consequens non denotatur A non significare aliter quam est, ita quod negatio praecedat verbum.

Pro quo sciendum est quod propositionum in quibus diversimode ponuntur 10 termini exclusivi diversae sunt exponentes. Unde istae tres propositiones 'Haec propositio praecise significat sicut est' et 'Praecise sicut est significat haec propositio' et 'Haec propositio significat praecise sicut est', et omnia his similia diversimode habent exponi. Prima exponitur sic: haec propositio significat sicut est et haec propositio non est alia quam significans sicut est. Secunda exponitur 15 sic: sicut est significat haec propositio, et non sicut non est significat haec propositio. Vel non aliter quam sicut est significat haec propositio. Tertia exponitur sic: Haec propositio significat sicut est et non aliter quam est. Vel haec significat non aliter quam est. Ita quod in cuiuslibet talis propositionis exponibilis negativa exponente respectu eiusdem dictionis praeponitur negatio, respectu cuius 20 praeponitur nota exclusionis in propositione exponibili.

⟨1.1.1c⟩ Antecedens primae consequentiae propositae ⟨i.e. 1.1.1⟩ probatur sic: A significat quod Deus est. Et quod Deus est, est sicut est et non aliter quam est. Ergo A significat sicut est et non aliter quam est.

⟨1.1.1d⟩ Confirmatur argumentum sic: Sicut-est et praecise-sicut-est et sicut- 25 est-et-non-aliter-quam-est realiter sunt idem. Quia qualitercumque est sicut est, est praecise sicut est et etiam est sicut est et non aliter quam est. Ergo quidquid sive quaecumque dictio quae significat unum istorum significat quodlibet eorundem. Et per consequens quidquid significat sicut est, significat praecise sicut est et etiam sicut est et non aliter quam est.

30 ⟨1.1.1e⟩ Item probatur consequentia ista per a simili. Nam sequitur 'Video asinum, et asinus est non homo; ergo video non hominem.' Ergo, per a simili, 'Si A significat sicut est, et qualitercumque est sicut est, est sicut est et non aliter quam est; ergo A significat sicut est et non aliter quam est'—quod fuit primum antecedens probandum.

35 Patet ergo quod ista consequentia non valet (f. 80 ra): 'A significat praecise sicut est; ergo A est propositio vera'—quod est contra opinionem huiusmodi consequentias concedentium, etc.

⟨*Argumenta contra conversam primae consequentiae*⟩

Et iuxta eorum opinionis fundamentum probatur quod non valet consequentia 40 e contra:

⟨1'⟩ Haec propositio est vera; igitur haec propositio significat praecise sicut est.

Quia aliqua negativa de praesenti est vera, et aliqua affirmativa de futuro, et aliqua de praeterito, quarum nulla significat praecise sicut est, ad modum 45 loquendi huiusmodi consequentias concedentium. Ergo patet quod consequentia e contra non valet.

Et assumptum probatur pro qualibet parte. ⟨1'.1⟩ Et primo pro prima: Quia si aliqua negativa de praesenti vera significat praecise sicut est, sit ista 'Nulla

chimaera est.' Sed contra, si ista significat praecise sicut est, et ista praecise quod nulla chimaera est significat; ergo sic est quod nulla chimaera est.

Consequens falsum, quia quod nulla chimaera est nec est aliquid, nec aliqualiter. ⟨1′.1.1⟩ Quia si sit aliqualiter et non est principium simpliciter, ergo habet causam. Sed nulla est causa quare sic est quod nulla chimaera est. Ergo non sic est quod nulla chimaera est. Et quod nulla est causa quare sic est probatur, quia quod nulla chimaera est non est causa quare sic est quia nulla chimaera est. Quia non sequitur 'Nulla chimaera est; ergo sic est quod nulla chimaera est', eo quod ex pure negativa non sequitur affirmativa. Ergo antecedens non est sufficiens causa consequentis. Similiter dato quod nihil esset nec aliqualiter, adhuc nulla chimaera esset. Et tunc non sic esset quod nulla chimaera est. Ergo oppositum consequentis illius consequentiae est imaginabile cum antecedente—quod non est verum de consequentia simpliciter bona.

⟨1′.1.2⟩ Item nulla est causa positiva in re quare sic est quod nulla chimaera est. Probatur, quia non est aliqualiter in re, quin taliter non existente esset omnino sic quod nulla chimaera est, qualiter nunc est quod nulla chimaera est. Ergo nihil nec aliqualiter est causa positiva in re quare sic est quod nulla chimaera est, quin quodlibet vel qualitercumque esset causa sic esse. Ergo qua ratione aliquid esset causa sic esse, quodlibet esset causa sic esse. Consequens inconveniens. Non est enim conveniens dicere quod homo vel hominem esse est causa sic esse quod nulla chimaera est, cum causa et causatum ad invicem proportionentur.

⟨1′.1.3⟩ Item si aliqualiter vel aliquid sit nullam chimaeram esse, non est aliud quam nulla chimaera. Quia, ut probabitur inferius, si chimaeram esse sit aliqualiter, est chimaera. Ergo per idem, si nullam chimaeram esse sit aliqualiter, est nulla chimaera. Aut ergo nihil, aut quodlibet est nulla chimaera. Si sit aliquid, eadem ratione quodlibet et qualitercumque esse est nulla chimaera. Ergo quodlibet et qualitercumque esse est nullam chimaeram esse. Et cum aliqualiter esse sit contingens, ergo aliqualiter contingens est nullam chimaeram esse. Ergo contingens est nullam chimaeram esse—quod negant omnes viam suppositam sustinentes.

⟨1′.1.4⟩ Item esse quod nulla chimaera est, vel est per se esse vel esse alteri inhaerens. Non secundo modo, quia in nullo est subiective existens, eo quod omni subiecto corrupto vel non existente, esset omnino nullam chimaeram esse, sicut est nunc, si est. Similiter si esset in aliquo subiecto, eadem ratione esset in quolibet. Et cum aliquod sit corruptibile, ergo esset in aliquo subiecto corruptibili. Consequens falsum, cum necessarium est quod nulla chimaera est, et ita erit in aeternum. Igitur etc. Si nullam chimaeram esse sit esse per se, ergo quocumque alio non existente sic esse esset. Et ita si Deus non esset, sic esse quod nulla chimaera est esset. Et per consequens esset principium simpliciter, cum nullam causam haberet—quod est absurdum dicere.

Sed forte dicitur quod nullam chimaeram esse, nec est esse per se, nec esse in alio, sed esse quo est aliud; sicut quidam ponunt de modis affirmativis quod esse-per-quod sive -quo, non est esse-in, nec etiam esse-ad est esse-in. Unde dicunt, 'Nullus modus est in subiecto, sed est quo est subiectum; nulla relatio est in subiecto, sed ad subiectum.'

Et contra illud arguitur per Aristotelem in *Praedicamentis* ⟨c. 5, 2ᵃ34–ᵇ6⟩, 'Omnia aut sunt in primis substantiis, (f. 8orb) aut de primis dicuntur.' Si ergo nullam chimaeram esse est, aut est in aliqua substantia aut de substantia dicitur. Sed non dicitur de substantia. Ergo est in substantia.

Contra illud quod dicitur de relationibus arguitur dupliciter sic: ⟨a⟩ Omnis
relatio realis est accidens secundum Aristotelem. Et accidentis esse est alteri
inesse secundum eundem. Ergo relationis esse est esse in subiecto. ⟨b⟩ Item si
propter hoc quod modus est quo est subiectum, ideo non est in subiecto; per
5 idem forma non est in materia, quia est quo est materia ens actu, et albedo non
est in albo, quia est quo album est album.

Et quia inferius contra hanc opinionem arguetur, ideo probandum est quod non
sic est sicut aliqua propositio vera et affirmativa de praeterito et de futuro significat. ⟨1′.2.1⟩ Quoniam ex Caesarem fuisse non sequitur sic esse quod Caesar fuit,
10 nec aliqualiter esse positive. Quia si nihil esset nec aliqualiter, nec umquam erit
aliquid nec aliqualiter, non minus Caesar fuit, eo quod iuxta principium Agatho-
nis commendatum ab Aristotele, sexto *Ethicorum*, capitulo secundo ⟨1139ᵇ10–11⟩,
'Hoc solo privatur Deus, genita facere ingenita.' Patet ergo quod ex hoc quod
Caesar fuit non sequitur aliqualiter esse, nec ita esse quod Caesar fuit.

15 ⟨1′.2.2⟩ Et quod nulla est causa quare sic est quod Caesar fuit, arguendum est
omnino sicut argutum est de negativa vera de praesenti.

⟨1′.2.3⟩ Item si Caesarem fuisse sit aliquid vel aliqualiter, est realiter idem cum
Caesare praeterito, sicut inferius ostendetur. Sed nihil nec aliqualiter est Caesar
praeteritus. Ergo nihil nec aliqualiter est Caesarem fuisse. Consequentia patet
20 de se.

⟨1′.3⟩ Consimiliter arguendum est de propositione affirmativa vera de futuro,
cuius subiecto non correspondet aliqua res significata de praesenti. Cuiusmodi
est haec propositio 'Antichristus erit', supposita eius veritate. Et consimilibus
formis arguendum est ad illam sicut ad priora.

25 Forte respondetur pro omnibus argumentis ad hoc factis quod quando existit
actualiter propositio significans Antichristum fore, tunc est ita quod Antichristus erit, vel sicut significatur per istam propositionem sic significantem non
est nisi esse in signo.

⟨1′.3.1⟩ Sed tale esse non est esse simpliciter sed secundum quid, cum secun-
30 dum Philosophum secundo *Posteriorum* ⟨c. 7, 92ᵇ6–8⟩ multa significantur quae
non sunt, et ita habent esse in suis signis. Ergo ex hoc quod sic esse est in propositione tamquam in suo signo, non sequitur sic esse simpliciter. Quia non est
aliud dicere quod Antichristus erit est in propositione sic significante tamquam
in suo signo, quam dicere quod propositio sic significans significat quod Anti-
35 christus erit. Sed non sequitur 'Quod Antichristus erit, significatur per propositionem; ergo quod Antichristus erit, est.' Ergo nec sequitur 'Quod Antichristus
erit, est in propositione sicut in signo; ergo quod Antichristus erit, est.' Immo
est fallacia secundum quid et simpliciter.

⟨1′.3.2⟩ Similiter iuxta istam responsionem probatur quod Antichristus est.
40 Quia sicut sequitur 'Antichristum fore significatur per propositionem; ergo
Antichristum fore est', ergo ita sequitur 'Antichristus significatur per subiectum
istius propositionis "Antichristus est"; ergo Antichristus est.' Ergo aequaliter
sequitur 'Antichristus est in suo signo; ergo Antichristus est', sicut sequitur
'Antichristum fore est in suo signo; ergo Antichristum fore est.'

45 ⟨1′.3.3⟩ Item ex hac responsione probatur quod quaelibet propositio significat
praecise sicut est, et ita sicut sequitur 'Haec propositio est vera; ergo significat
praecise sicut est', ita sequitur 'Haec propositio est falsa; ergo significat praecise
sicut est.' Assumptum probatur: Cuiuslibet propositionis significatum non minus
habet esse in suo signo quam alicuius propositionis significatum, cum quaelibet

propositio aequaliter significat suum significatum, sicut alia. Ergo si sic est quod nulla chimaera est, quia sic est in suo signo; ergo sic est quod homo est asinus, quia sic est in suo signo.

Pro isto forte dicitur quod differentia est de significato propositionis verae et de significato propositionis falsae. Quia in ista propositione 'Nulla chimaera est', 5 et in qualibet tali propositione vera, sic esse in signo, vel in propositione sic significante, non solum est causa quare sic est quod nulla chimaera est, sed quia nulla chimaera est et haec propositio 'Nulla chimaera est' sic significat. Sed non sic est de ista propositione 'Homo est asinus.'

Haec responsio (f. 8ova) commendabilis, eo quod accedit ad actionem unius 10 maximi dubii in hac materia, sicut inferius patebit. Contra hanc responsionem arguitur: Si causa sic esse quod nulla chimaera est, est quia nulla chimaera est et quia haec propositio sic significat—cum haec coniunctio 'quia' sit nota causae —ergo assumitur nullam chimaeram esse, esse causam ad probandum sic esse quod nulla chimaera est. Sed quod assumitur esse causam, assumitur esse. Ergo 15 assumitur esse quod nulla chimaera est, ad probandum sic esse quod nulla chimaera est. Et per consequens idem assumitur ad probationem sui ipsius. Ergo petitio principii.

Patet ergo quod nec negativa vera de praesenti, nec affirmativa vera de praeterito vel de futuro, cuius veritas non dependet super aliqua re existente, signi- 20 ficat sicut est, ad modum loquendi ponentium significata propositionum esse modos rerum. Patet ergo quod non valet haec consequentia 'Haec propositio est vera; ergo significat praecise sicut est.' Et ita patet quod per se causa veritatis propositionis non est ex hoc quod propositio significat praecise sicut est—quod est contra istam opinionem tenentes.   25

⟨SECUNDA CONSEQUENTIA⟩

Improbata prima consequentia causam veritatis propositionum assignantium, iam restat improbare secundam, quae fuit haec:

⟨2⟩ Praecise sicut est significat *A* propositio; ergo *A* propositio est vera.

Et primo probatur ista consequentia per argumentum illam consequentiam con- 30 cedentium. Secundo ex eorum proprio fundamento probatur consequentiam non valere. Tertio quacumque propositione signata, sive vera, sive falsa, quod praecise sicut est illa significat iuxta opinionem hic sustinendam ostendetur.

⟨*Argumenta pro secunda consequentia*⟩

Quod consequentia est bona probatur: Si praecise sicut est significat *A* 35 propositio, ergo sicut est significat *A* propositio et non aliter quam est significat *A* propositio. Consequentia patet ab exclusiva ad exponentem. Et si non aliter quam est significat *A* propositio, ergo *A* propositio non est falsa.

Consequentia patet quia ex opposito sequitur oppositum. Sequitur enim '*A* propositio est falsa; ergo aliter quam est *A* significat.' Probatur ista consequentia, 40 quia si non sequitur, ponatur oppositum consequentis cum antecedente. Et ponatur quod *A* significat quod tu es asinus vel tu curris, supposito quod non curras. Tunc sic: *A* propositio est falsa, et non aliter quam est *A* significat, et aliqualiter significat. Ergo praecise sicut est significat. Et solum significat quod tu es asinus vel tu curris. Ergo sic est. Sed non sic est quod tu curris. Ergo sic 45

est quod homo est asinus. Consequens impossibile. Ergo patet illa consequentia.
Et ex consequente sequitur 'A propositio non est falsa, et A propositio est; ergo
est vera.' Ergo, a primo ad ultimum, si praecise sicut est significat A propositio,
ergo A propositio est vera. Quae fuit secunda consequentia principaliter pro-
5 banda.

⟨*Argumenta contra secundam consequentiam*⟩

    Ad cuius improbationem arguitur multis modis: ⟨2.1⟩ Primo sic: Praecise
sicut est significat propositio falsa. Ergo consequentia non valet. ⟨2.1.1⟩ Assumptum probatur: Praecise sicut est significans est propositio falsa. Ergo praecise
10 sicut est significat propositio falsa. Probatur ista consequentia: Praecise
sicut est significans est propositio falsa. Ergo sicut est significans est propositio
falsa, et non sicut non est significans est propositio falsa. Et ultra, ergo non sicut
non est significat propositio falsa. Ex quibus omnibus sequitur quod praecise
sicut est significat propositio falsa. Et penultima consequentia probatur, quia ex
15 opposito sequitur oppositum. Sequitur enim 'Sicut non est significat propositio
falsa; ergo sicut non est significans est propositio falsa.'
    ⟨2.1.1.1⟩ Assumptum primae consequentiae ⟨i.e. 2.1.1⟩ probatur: Propositio
falsa est praecise sicut est significans. Ergo praecise sicut est significans est
propositio falsa. Antecedens huius consequentiae probatur per prius. Et con-
20 sequentia probatur dupliciter: ⟨a⟩ Primo per conversionem simplicem. ⟨b⟩
Secundo sic: In quacumque indefinita affirmativa denotatur praedicatum
particulariter dici de subiecto, ita quod subiecti et praedicati est omnino suppositio convertibilis. Ergo sive ponatur unus terminus pro subiecto sive alius, non
erit diversitas ex parte veritatis vel falsitatis. Quia non est differentia quoad
25 veritatem sive dicam 'Homo est animal' sive 'Animal est homo.' Ergo eadem
ratione non est differentia sive dicam 'Praecise sicut est significans est propositio
falsa' sive 'Propositio falsa est praecise sicut est significans.' Ergo patet consequentia probanda.
    ⟨2.1.1.2⟩ Item sic: Aliquid praecise sicut est significans est propositio falsa.
30 Ergo praecise sicut est significans est propositio falsa. Consequentia patet a particulari affirmativa ad suam indefinitam in eisdem terminis.
    ⟨2.1.1.3⟩ Item supponitur quod omnis propositio falsa significat (f. 80vb) sicut
est. Tunc tantum sicut est significans est propositio falsa. Ergo praecise sicut est
significans est propositio falsa. Consequentia patet per hoc quod 'praecise',
35 'tantum', et 'solummodo' et omnes tales termini exclusivi convertuntur. Ergo
omnes propositiones in quibus ponuntur, omnibus ceteris manentibus eisdem,
convertuntur.
    Forte negatur antecedens illius argumenti, et dicitur quod 'praecise' denotat
exclusionem respectu modi et 'tantum' solum respectu rei.
40   Sed quod illud nihil est probatur: Sed quia ex hoc quod 'praecise' denotat
exclusionem respectu modi, hoc solum est ratione termini cui apponitur, et
haec dictio 'tantum' excludit respectu rei, est etiam ratione termini cui apponitur.
Quia nulla dictio exclusiva in se ipsa aliquam rem significat, sed solummodo
modum excludit. Unde cum iste terminus 'praecise' apponitur termino signi-
45 ficanti rem, excludit respectu rei, et illa dictio 'tantum' similiter. Sicut patet in
istis 'Praecise Deus est' et 'Tantum Deus est', quia per utramque denotatur quod
Deus est et nihil aliud quam Deus est. Sed cum dicitur 'Praecise sicut est significat A propositio' sive 'Tantum sicut est significat A propositio', denotatur

quod sicut est significat *A* propositio, et non sicut non est vel non aliter quam est significat *A* propositio. Et sic de aliis dictionibus exclusivis. Patet ergo quod non magis est aliqua earum nata excludere respectu modi quam rei. Ergo patet prima consequentia.

Assumptum probatur: Omnis propositio falsa est sicut est significans. Ergo 5 tantum sicut est significans est propositio falsa. Consequentia patet ab universali ad exclusivam de terminis transpositis. Et antecedens patet ex casu.

Item probatur idem per exponentes. Quia sicut est significans est propositio falsa, et nihil aliud quam sicut est significans est propositio falsa. Ergo tantum sicut est significans est propositio falsa—quod fuit probandum. 10

⟨2.2⟩ Item arguitur principaliter ad improbationem secundae consequentiae principaliter improbandae: Praecise sicut est significat haec propositio 'Antichristus est.' Et illa non est vera, ut supponitur. Igitur etc. Antecedens arguitur: Praecise quod Antichristus est haec significat, et sic est. Ergo etc.

Minor arguitur sic: Tali modo est. Ergo sic est. Consequentia patet per hoc 15 quod iste terminus 'sic' et hoc nomen 'tale' similitudinem duorum similium significant. Antecedens probatur: Aliquo tali modo est. Ergo tali modo est.

Consequentia patet. Antecedens probatur: Quod tu es homo, est. Et quod tu es homo est aliquis talis modus qualis est quod Antichristus est. Ergo aliquo tali modo est. Antecedens probatur: Uterque illorum est modus possibilis. Ergo 20 talis est unus qualis est alius.

*   *   *

⟨*Conclusio incidentalis*⟩

Ex isto et paucis additis probatur quod nulla est causa quam solebant sophistae assignare falsitatis propositionis. Quia non ex eo quod aliqua propositio significat aliter quam est, quia nulla est talis, ut probatum est. Nec ex hoc quod aliqua 25 propositio significat sicut non est, quia quaelibet negativa vera et quaelibet affirmativa vera de praeterito et de futuro, quorum veritas non dependet super aliquo de praesenti, significant sicut non est, ut prius probatum est.

Item probatur de omni propositione quod nulla significat sicut non est. Quia si aliqua propositio significat aliqualiter qualiter non est, ergo aliqua propositio 30 significat aliqualiter et aliqualiter non est. Consequentia patet per hoc quod arguitur a propositione in qua ponitur terminus relativus ad copulativam de eisdem terminis, sine negatione et sine distributione praeposita termino relativo, sola mutatione facta termini relativi in suum antecedens. Ut patet hic 'Video hominem quem tu vides; ergo video hominem et hominem vides.' Similiter 35 sequitur si negatio postponitur termino relativo, ut 'Aliqualiter currit Sortes qualiter non currit Plato; ergo aliqualiter currit Sortes et aliqualiter non currit Plato.' Et consequens primae consequentiae falsum, quia 'Qualitercumque est, est; ergo non aliqualiter non est.'

*   *   *

Nec valet hoc argumentum, per quod illud probant 'Haec propositio significat 40 aliqualiter qualiter non est. Ergo haec significat aliqualiter et aliqualiter non est.' Sed sequitur quod haec propositio significat aliqualiter et aliqualiter qualiter haec significat non est. Et isto modo mutandum est relativum in suum antecedens. Et universaliter cum terminis ampliativis oportet sic reduplicare. Cuiusmodi sunt isti termini 'posse', 'velle', 'intelligere', 'significare' et huiusmodi. 45

*   *   *

(f. 82rb) Tertiam consequentiam principaliter improbandam qua quidam ad probationem sophismatum arguunt, ex hoc ultimo argumento satis liquet non valere, quae in forma est haec:

5　　⟨3⟩ Ita est totaliter sicut hoc sophisma significat; ergo hoc sophisma est verum.

Et per ly .ita. demonstratur modus quo hoc sophisma significat, sive relative teneatur quod significet modum quo significat sophisma.

⟨Argumenta contra tertiam consequentiam⟩

10　　⟨3.1⟩ Aliter tamen ex proprio fundamento in hac (f. 82va) materia loquentium, improbatur eadem consequentia, posito quod haec propositio 'Chimaera est' significaret chimaeram esse et Deum esse. Tunc ita est totaliter sicut haec propositio significat, et tamen illa non est vera. Ergo etc.

Antecedens probatur: Ita est totaliter—demonstrando per ly .ita. Deum esse—
15　et ita haec propositio significat. Ergo ita est totaliter sicut haec propositio significat. Consequentia probatur, quia haec dictio 'sicut' est dictio relativa et convertitur cum suo antecedente, quando non sequitur illam terminus confusus per eandem dictionem. Quia ubi sequitur terminus confusus non valet consequentia. Unde non sequitur 'Sortes est ita fortis, et ita fortis est aliquis homo
20　mundi; ergo Sortes est ita fortis sicut aliquis homo mundi.' Sed ubi nullus terminus confundibilis sequitur est consequentia bona. Unde sequitur 'Sortes est ita fortis, et ita fortis est Plato; ergo Sortes est ita fortis sicut est Plato', quamvis appareat alicui illam consequentiam non valere, ut posito quod Sortes sit minus fortis Platone—quod tamen non est verum.

25　　⟨3.2⟩ Item arguitur fortius ad idem, posito quod haec propositio 'Chimaera est' significet praecise primarie. Tunc chimaeram esse est totaliter sicut haec propositio significat. Ergo ita—demonstrando chimaeram esse—est totaliter sicut haec propositio significat.

　　⟨3.2.1⟩ Consequentia patet intuenti, et antecedens probatur: Chimaeram esse
30　est totale significatum huius propositionis. Et totale significatum huius propositionis est totaliter sicut haec propositio significat. Ergo etc. ⟨3.2.1a⟩ Patet consequentia, et antecedens probatur, primo pro prima parte: Quia chimaeram esse est significatum ab hac propositione. Et non aliud, nec aliquis alius modus est significatum ab hac propositione, iuxta hic loquentes. Ergo chimaeram esse
35　est totale significatum ab hac propositione.

　　⟨3.2.1b⟩ Secunda pars antecedentis probatur: Nam istae propositiones convertuntur—'Haec propositio significat totale significatum huius propositionis' et 'Haec propositio significat totaliter sicut haec propositio significat'—cum ex utraque sequitur alia. Ergo praedicata et subiecta convertuntur. Ergo praedicata
40　convertuntur. Et si sic, ergo totaliter sicut haec propositio significat, est totale significatum huius propositionis. Ergo per conversionem sequitur 'Totale significatum huius propositionis est totaliter sicut haec propositio significat'—quae fuit secunda pars antecedentis probanda.

Et confirmatur sic: Nam si totale significatum illius non sit totaliter sicut haec
45　propositio significat, tunc staret aliquid vel aliquam propositionem significare totale significatum illius propositionis et non significare totaliter sicut illa significat, vel e contra. Ergo cum non stat aliquid significare unum quod non significat

reliquum, nec e contra; ergo si aliquid vel aliqualiter sit totale significatum huius, idem vel taliter est totaliter sicut haec propositio significat—ex quo deducendum est ulterius sicut prius, etc.

⟨CAPITULUM SECUNDUM: DE SIGNIFICATO PROPOSITIONIS⟩

Improbatis communibus modis arguendi quibus solebant arguere ad probanda sophismata veritatem propositionum assignantes, iam restat inquirere consequenter quid sit quod per propositionem veram significatur, de quo tres sunt opiniones: ⟨1⟩ Una universaliter affirmat significatum propositionis verae esse modum rei. ⟨2⟩ Secunda ponit significatum propositionis esse compositionem mentis vel intellectus componentis vel dividentis. ⟨3⟩ Tertia, quam reputo ceteris veriorem ponit ⟨i⟩ quod cuiuslibet propositionis verae affirmativae de praesenti, cuius verbum principale non est verbum ampliativum nec praedicatum, est res eadem quae significatur per aliquam partium eiusdem propositionis, sicut inferius declarabitur. In casu pluribus existentibus eiusdem partibus diversas res significantibus, sicut res diversae per partes illas diversas significantur, ita significata illius propositionis sunt res plures. Verbi gratia, significatum huius propositionis 'Deus est' est Deum esse, et Deum esse non est aliud quam Deus. Similiter haec propositio 'Sol calefacit domum' significat solem calefacere domum, quod non est aliud quam sol; et significat domum calefieri a sole, quod non est aliud quam domus. Ulterius dicit haec opinio ⟨ii⟩ quod nullius negativae verae significatum est aliquid vel aliqualiter vel (f. 82vb) aliqua; ⟨iii⟩ nec etiam alicuius affirmativae verae de futuro, cuius subiecto non correspondet aliqua res de praesenti; ⟨iv⟩ nec alicuius propositionis affirmativae de praeterito per cuius subiectum res principaliter significata non existit; ⟨v⟩ nec alicuius propositionis verae de praesenti cuius praedicatum est terminus distrahens, ut 'Homo est mortuus' vel terminus ampliativus, et res significata per subiectum non sit, ut 'Chimaera est opinabilis.'

⟨PRIMA OPINIO⟩

⟨*Argumenta pro prima opinione*⟩

⟨1.1⟩ Una ratio super quam prima opinio fundatur est haec: Cuiuslibet propositionis verae significatum est ubique. Sed nihil praeter substantiam immaterialem est ubique, nec potest esse ubique. Ergo cuiuslibet propositionis verae significatum est modus rei et non res.

Antecedens probant de hac propositione 'Tu es': Ubique est verum quod tu es. Ergo ubique est quod tu es. Et quod tu es haec propositio significat. Ergo ubique est significatum huius propositionis, et sic arguunt de qualibet propositione vera. Et antecedens probant sic: Ubicumque scitur quod tu es, ibi est verum quod tu es. Sed nullum est ubi in mundo quin staret, absque mutatione tui a loco in quo es, quod ibi sciatur quod tu es. Ergo in omni loco stat quod ibi sit verum quod tu es. Sed ubicumque esset verum quod tu es, si ibi sciretur quod tu es, nunc aliqualiter est verum ibi quod tu es, sicut tunc. Ergo nunc ubique est verum quod tu es.

⟨1.2⟩ Alia ratione fundatur haec opinio sic: Haec propositio 'Nulla chimaera est' est propositio vera. Ergo suum significatum est verum. Et ultra, ergo suum significatum est. Sed suum significatum non est res, quia quod nulla chimaera

est non est res alicuius praedicamenti, ut patet inductive. Ergo est modus rei. Et sic de aliis.

⟨*Argumenta contra primam opinionem*⟩

⟨C1⟩ Contra hanc opinionem arguitur sic: ubicumque est significatum alicuius
5 propositionis, ibi est significatum subiecti vel praedicati. Ergo si ubique est significatum propositionis verae, ubique est significatum subiecti vel praedicati eiusdem. Sit ergo haec vera 'Sortes est', tunc sic: Ubique est significatum illius propositionis. Ergo ubique est significatum subiecti. Sed Sortes est significatum per subiectum. Ergo ubique est. Consequens falsum. Ergo illud ex quo sequitur.
10 Sed forte negatur haec consequentia 'Ubique est significatum huius "Sortes est"; ergo ubique est significatum subiecti.' Contra, ubicumque est significatum adaequatum per duo ex quibus resultat unum significatum, ibi est utriusque illorum significatum. Sed significatum propositionis aggregat in se significata partium ex quibus componitur. Ergo ubicumque est significatum propositionis,
15 ibi est significatum utriusque partis. Assumptum patet, nam sicut haec propositio significat Sortem esse, ita altera pars significat Sortem et altera esse, ex quibus hoc totum componitur, Sortem esse. Ex isto sequitur immediate quod Sortes est pars illius modi.

⟨C2⟩ Item cum significatum illius 'Sortes est' praecise sit significatum suarum
20 partium, seu ex illis compositum, cum una pars significat Sortem et altera esse quod non distinguitur realiter a Sorte cuius est esse, ergo significatum per totam propositionem non distinguitur realiter a Sorte. Quod esse Sortis non distinguitur a Sorte, vide in parte ubi tractabitur problema de universalibus.

⟨C3⟩ Item si significatum propositionis verae sit modus ubique existens, ergo
25 Sortem currere est modus· ubique existens, dato quod haec sit vera 'Sortes currit.' Et si sic, ergo si Sortes incipiat currere, tunc efficiens cursum Sortis ubique efficit istum modum qui est Sortem currere. Consequentia probatur: Ubique est Sortem currere postquam nullibi fuit Sortem currere. Ergo ubique efficitur Sortem currere. Et a nullo alio quam ab efficiente Sortem currere.
30 Ergo ab efficiente cursum Sortis fiet ubique Sortem currere. Et hoc apparet mirabile, quod non posset alicubi fieri mutatio nisi ubique fuerit mutatio. Istud accedit ad opinionem antiquorum qui dixerunt quod uno motu moventur omnia, et Heracliti qui dixit omnia esse in continuo motu.

⟨C4⟩ Item ex isto sequitur 'Hoc quod scio—te esse—non est aliud quam iste
35 modus qui est te esse.' Item per positionem sequitur quod omnis scientia est scientia (f. 83ra) modorum. Et tunc sequitur quod scientia esset sine propositionibus sicut est scientia divinorum. Et homo tunc nihil sciret nisi modos rerum. Item sequitur quod intelligentiae solum modos rerum sciunt.

⟨C5⟩ Item si significatum propositionis verae sit modus, ita quod non res,
40 aut ergo huiusmodi modus est simplex aut compositum. Si simplex, ergo uno simplici nomine potest significari. Consequentia patet per hoc quod conceptus de simplici potest esse simplex, et illi conceptui simplici potest simplex pars orationis correspondere, cum iuxta variationem conceptuum variantur partes orationis. Et tunc sequitur quod non quodlibet incomplexorum significat
45 substantiam vel qualitatem, et sic de ceteris, cum illa simplex vox non significat rem, sed solum modum rei. Si talis modus sit compositum, cum simplex praecedit compositionem, ergo staret simplex esse non existente huiusmodi modo. Consequens falsum, quia si Deus est, est quod Deus est; et ita non stat

Deum esse, qui est res simplex, nisi quod Deus est sit, qui est modus quem significat propositio vera.

⟨C6⟩ Item sequitur quod non potest intelligi Deum esse pluribus non existentibus. Consequens falsum. Et quod hoc sequitur probatur ex hoc quod non est intelligibile quod Deus est non existente quod Deus est. Et si est quod Deus est, 5 cum quod Deus est sit complexum, plura sunt. Patet ergo consequentia.

⟨SECUNDA OPINIO⟩

⟨*Argumenta pro secunda opinione*⟩

Secunda opinio fundatur super duo dicta Aristotelis et super assumptum in ultima ratione ad opinionem primam.   10

⟨2.1⟩ In primo *Peri Hermeneias* ⟨c. 3, 16ᵇ24–5⟩ dicit Aristoteles quod hoc verbum 'est' significat quandam compositionem quam sine compositis non est intelligere. Ergo significatum per totam huiusmodi propositionem 'Sortes est', 'Homo est animal' et huiusmodi non est res extra mentem, sed aliqua compositio mentis. Tenet consequentia per hoc quod huic verbo 'est' non correspondet aliquid 15 extra mentem iuxta auctoritatem allegatam.

⟨2.2⟩ Item fundatur super dictum Aristotelis secundo *Peri Hermeneias* ⟨c. 13, 22ᵃ14–ᵇ28⟩ ubi dicit quod 'Necesse est esse' et 'Impossibile est non esse' convertuntur. Unde per eum istae propositiones convertuntur 'Necesse est nullam chimaeram esse' et 'Impossibile est chimaeram esse.' Sed nihil nec aliqualiter 20 extra intellectum est nullam chimaeram esse. Ergo est solum compositio intellectualis quae est necessaria ad modum loquendi Aristotelis. Quia aliter non diceret in secundo *Peri Hermeneias* ⟨c. 13, 22ᵃ14–ᵇ28⟩ illa converti 'Non possibile est non esse' et 'Necessario est esse', cum una sit negativa et alia affirmativa. Si enim intelligeret 'non esse extra intellectum', ut dicit haec opinio illae propositiones 25 essent impertinentes.

⟨2.3⟩ Item nisi significatum propositionis verae sit in mente solum, nullius propositionis verae negativae, nec affirmativae verae de praeterito vel de futuro, per cuius subiectum non significatur res existens, esset significatum verum, ut dicit haec opinio.   30

⟨*Argumenta contra secundam opinionem*⟩

⟨C1⟩ Contra hanc opinionem arguitur sic: Quia iuxta illam non valet hoc argumentum 'Deus est; ergo Deum esse est verum', quia antecedens necessarium et consequens contingens. Quia si nulla compositio intellectus esset, non esset verum Deum esse. Sed quod nulla talis compositio sit, est possibile. Ergo quod 35 non sit verum Deum esse est possibile—ex quo sequitur quod Deum esse esse verum est contingens.

⟨C2⟩ Item sequitur non existente compositione intellectus 'Deum esse non est possibile.' Quia haec propositio 'Deum esse est possibile' significat quod talis compositio mentis 'Deum esse' est possibile—quod est falsum nulla compositione 40 mentis existente. Ergo tunc, Deum esse, non est possibile. Ergo non est possibile Deum esse. Et ultra, ergo impossibile est Deum esse. Consequentia tenet per Aristotelem secundo *Peri Hermeneias* ⟨c. 13, 22ᵃ14–ᵇ28⟩ ubi se fundat haec opinio.

⟨C3⟩ Item sequitur non existente intellectu componente 'Non est ita quod Deus est, nec est verum quod Deus est.'   45

⟨C4⟩ Sequitur etiam haec conclusio 'Iam necesse est Deum esse, et iam desinit esse Deum esse', posito quod aliquis iam intelligat Deum esse et quod immediate post hoc instans nullus intellectus (f. 83rb) intelligat componendo.

⟨C5⟩ Item posito quod nullus intellectus intelligat componendo, tunc non scitur
5 Deum esse, eo quod Deum esse non est, et quod non est, non scitur.

⟨C6⟩ Item principaliter contra hanc opinionem arguitur sic: Ista compositio in mente significat Deum esse, et non significat seipsam. Ergo Deum esse significat aliquid vel aliqualiter quod vel qualiter non est compositio mentis. Assumptum probatur: Per hanc intelligitur Deum esse, et quod intelligitur per istam
10 significatur. Ergo Deum esse significatur per istam. Sed quidquid significat propositio in voce, significat propositio sibi correspondens in intellectu et e contra, quia voces significant res mediante conceptu. Ergo si compositio mentalis significat Deum esse quod non est in intellectu sed ad extra, ergo illa in voce significat Deum esse quod non solum est compositio mentis sed aliquid ad
15 extra.

⟨C7⟩ Item si haec propositio 'Deus est' significat solum compositionem mentis, ergo partes istius compositionis mentalis significant. Cum ergo propositio affirmativa de praesenti significat rem significatam per subiectum esse rem significatam per praedicatum, ergo haec propositio 'Deus est' solum significat
20 unam intentionem in anima correspondentem huic termino vocali 'Deum esse'. Et ita non magis est haec vera 'Deus est' quam haec 'Chimaera est.'

⟨C8⟩ Item ex hoc sequitur quod haec propositio est falsa 'Homo est animal', quia haec intentio 'homo' non est haec intentio 'animal'.

⟨C9⟩ Item sequitur quod propositio in mente solum significat seipsam, vel
25 oportet ponere simul in mente unam aliam compositionem sibi correspondentem et sic esset processus in infinitum.

⟨C10⟩ Item ex ista opinione sequitur quod tu potes facere Deum esse, quia potes esse causa effectiva huius compositionis mentalis Deum esse. Et Deum esse nihil aliud est quam talis compositio mentalis. Ergo potes facere Deum esse.

30   ⟨TERTIA OPINIO⟩

⟨*Argumenta pro tertia opinione*⟩

Tertia opinio et ultima, inter omnes verissima cuilibet veritatem rei curanti magis quam verba, super hanc rationem fundatur:

⟨3.1⟩ In ista propositione 'Deus est' iste terminus 'Deus' significat Deum, et
35 iste terminus 'est' significat esse—quod significatum realiter non differt ab ente, cum nullius rei esse aliqualiter ab eo cuius est differt. Ergo totum significatum per istam propositionem non est aliud ab eo quod significant isti duo—'Deus', 'ens'—licet modus significandi sit diversus. Confirmatio huius rationis habetur in obiectionibus contra secundam opinionem recitatis.

40 ⟨3.2⟩ Aliter fundatur haec opinio: Si nihil nec aliqualiter esset nisi A, quae esset res simplicissima quae imaginari posset, adhuc ita esset quod A est. Et tunc nullus modus esset. Ergo quod A est tunc esset realiter ipsum A. Et nunc quod A est, est idem quod tunc esset. Ergo nunc si A est, quod A est est ipsum A.

Hae duae rationes cum aliis contra secundam opinionem factis sunt pro hac
45 opinione ad praesens.

⟨*Argumenta contra tertiam opinionem*⟩

Contra hanc opinionem sunt argumenta super quae se fundaverunt opiniones improbatae. Aliter contra istam arguitur sic:

⟨C1⟩ Si Deum esse est Deus, et Sortem esse est Sortes, et falsum esse est falsum. Tunc sic: Falsum esse est falsum. Et falsum esse est verum. Ergo falsum 5 est verum. Consequens impossibile. Et etiam ex hoc sequitur quod falsum scitur, eo quod falsum esse scitur.

⟨C2⟩ Item sic: Si Sortem esse est Sortes, et Sortem esse album est Sortes albus, ergo Sortem esse album est Sortes. Consequens falsum, quia aliquid sequitur ex Sortem esse album quod non sequitur ex Sorte. Ergo Sortem esse 10 album non est Sortes. Antecedens probatur sic: Ex Sortem esse album, sequitur quod albedo est. Et ex Sorte non sequitur quod albedo est. Ergo etc. Antecedens patet de se.

⟨C3⟩ Item ex hoc sequitur quod homo est scitus et quod homo est dubitatus —quae non communiter intelliguntur. Et quod illa sequuntur probatur: Homi- 15 nem esse est scitum a te. Et hominem esse est homo, ut prius. Ergo homo est scitus a te. Et sic de aliis.

⟨C4⟩ Item ex hoc sequitur quod Sortes facit se ipsum, quia sequitur 'Sortes facit Sortem currere, (f. 83va) et Sortem currere est Sortes; ergo Sortes facit Sortem.' Consequens falsum. 20

⟨C5⟩ Item si Sortes est Sortem esse album, et Sortes erit, ergo quandocumque Sortes erit, Sortem esse album erit. Consequens falsum, quia aliquando Sortes erit niger et in illo instanti Sortem esse album non erit, quia tunc non erit albus. Et tunc Sortes erit. Ergo non quandocumque Sortes erit, Sortem esse album erit.

⟨C6⟩ Item fortius sic: Si quando Sortes erit niger, Sortem esse album erit, 25 ergo tunc quod Sortes est albus erit, cum idem sit realiter quod Sortes est albus et Sortem esse album. Et ultra, ergo tunc erit quod Sortes est albus—ex quo sequitur quod Sortes tunc erit albus.

⟨C7⟩ Item si sic, ergo quando Sortes erit niger, erit haec vera 'Sortes est albus' —quod probatur: Quia quod Sortes est albus tunc erit. Et illa propositio 'Sortes 30 est albus' praecise sic significabit tunc. Ergo haec propositio tunc erit vera—ex quo sequitur quod tunc Sortes erit albus, sicut prius.

⟨C8⟩ Item sequitur quod quilibet sciens seu credens hanc propositionem 'Quodlibet est' esset ita sapiens sicut Deus. Quia talis sciret omnia esse. Et omnia esse sunt omnia. Ergo talis sciret omnia. Et magis sciens non est Deus. 35 Ergo etc.

⟨C9⟩ Item ex hoc sequitur quod idem significat subiectum propositionis et tota illa propositio. Quia cum Deum esse sit Deus, idem praecise significat iste terminus 'Deus' sicut haec propositio 'Deus est.' Et ex hoc sequitur quod subiectum propositionis et ipsa propositio convertuntur. Sequitur enim 'Quid- 40 quid significat *A* significat *B* et e contra; ergo *A* et *B* convertuntur.'

Huic forte dicitur quod non sequitur, quia licet idem significant, non tamen eodem modo. Contra istud arguitur sic: Istae propositiones convertuntur— 'Homo est', 'Risibile est.' Et tamen idem significando diversis modis significant. Ergo etc. 45

Ex isto sequitur quod intelligendo istum terminum 'Deus' vel istum terminum 'homo' intelligit homo verum vel falsum, sicut hanc 'Deus est' vel hanc 'Homo est', cum altera Deum esse significat et altera hominem esse quarum utraque est vera. Frustra ergo ponitur hoc verbum 'est' dicendo 'Deus est', 'Homo est.'

⟨C10⟩ Item haec est vera affirmativa de praesenti 'Chimaera est opinabilis.' Et significatum illius non est aliqua res positiva. Ergo etc. Minor probatur: Si chimaeram esse opinabilem aliquid esset, illud esset chimaera. Sed nulla chimaera est res. Ergo etc.

5   Haec argumenta contra hanc opinionem ad praesens sufficiunt.

⟨*Responsio ad argumenta contra tertiam opinionem, quae sunt rationes pro prima et secunda opinione*⟩

Ad argumenta contra hanc opinionem adducta consequenter respondetur.

⟨R1.1⟩ Primo ad primum, quando dicebatur primam opinionem fundari super
10   hoc quod cuiuslibet propositionis verae affirmativae de praesenti significatum est ubique, et non quaelibet res significata per aliquam partem eius est ubique; ergo etc.—negatur antecedens. Et quando arguitur quod sic, de significato istius propositionis 'Tu es' quod illud est ubique, negatur. Nec est verum quod asserebatur, scilicet quod ubique est quod tu es. Et quando arguitur sic: ubicumque
15   est verum vel scitur quod tu es, ibi est quod tu es, sed ubique est verum vel scitur quod tu es; ergo etc.—conceditur consequentia. Et negatur maior, quoniam sicut non ubicumque est verum quod tu es ens, ibi est quod tu es ens, ita nec ubicumque est verum quod tu es, ibi est quod tu es. Quia non sequitur 'Hic est verum quod tu es; ergo hic est quod tu es', ut patet in aliis. Non enim sequitur
20   'Hic video te; ergo tu es hic', 'Hic intelligo te; ergo tu es hic', et sic item.

⟨R1.2⟩ Ad aliud quando dicitur 'Haec est vera "Nulla chimaera est"'; ergo significatum huius est verum'—conceditur consequentia et consequens. Et non sequitur ultra 'Ergo significatum huius est', sicut postea patebit.

⟨R2.1⟩ Ad primum argumentum super quod se fundat secunda opinio, respon-
25   detur distinguendo assumptum, eo quod potest intelligi quod hoc verbum 'est' sic significat compositionem, ita quod per actum animae illi verbo convenienter correspondentem repraesentetur compositio. Et ille sensus est falsus, sicut loquendo de significatione idem debet significari per vocem et per conceptum illi correspondentem. Vel aliter quod hoc verbum 'est' significat compositionem,
30   scilicet quod huic verbo 'est' in propositione vocali posito correspondet compositio mentis cuius loco hoc verbo utimur ad exprimendum quid concipimus in intellectu. (f. 83vb) Et sic intelligit Aristoteles. Et ad istum sensum negatur consequentia.

⟨R2.2⟩ Ad aliud super quod se fundat eadem opinio, quando arguitur per
35   Aristotelem secundo *Peri Hermeneias* ⟨c. 13, 22ª14–b28⟩ illas propositiones converti 'Necesse est nullam chimaeram esse' et 'Impossibile est aliquam chimaeram esse' etc.—respondetur quod omnis talis terminus modalis—'necesse', 'possibile', 'impossibile', 'contingens', 'verum', 'falsum'—apud Aristotelem est terminus distrahens vel ampliativus, cuiusmodi sunt 'intelligibile', 'opinabile', 'volubile'*,
40   'significabile' et huiusmodi. Et non debent intelligi a parte praedicati, cum de vocibus significantibus aliqua quae non sunt aliquis istorum praedicetur per hoc verbum 'est'. Ideo Aristoteles intelligit quod hae propositiones convertuntur— 'Nullam chimaeram esse est necessarium' et 'Aliquam chimaeram esse est impossibile'—quarum prima significat quod nullam chimaeram esse est intelligi-
45   bile per hanc propositionem, dato quod sit, 'Nulla chimaera est'—quod sic intellectum non potest esse falsum**. Unde tales termini dicuntur modales eo quod modificant nobis quales huiusmodi propositiones essent, si essent.

*   *   *

* *scil.* 'volibile'   ** Vide Addenda et corrigenda, p. xvi.

⟨CAPITULUM TERTIUM: DE VERITATE ET CAUSA VERITATIS PROPOSITIONIS SENTENTIA AUCTORIS⟩

⟨*Methodus ad causam veritatis propositionis categoricae inquiredam*⟩

(f. 84rb) Cum ex praemissis pateat quod non ex eo quod ita est ex parte rei sicut propositio significat est propositio vera, nec ex eo quod ita non est sicut propositio 5 significat, est propositio falsa; causam veritatis et falsitatis propositionis categoricae ostendens, consequenter est methodus inquirendus.

Pro quo notandum est quod

⟨1⟩ Eo quod propositio aliqua praecise rem quae est significat esse, vel rem quae non est significat non esse, est propositio affirmativa vel negativa de 10 praesenti vera.

Et

⟨2⟩ Ex eo quod propositio aliqua praecise rem quae erit significet fore, vel rem quae non erit significet non fore, est propositio affirmativa vel negativa de futuro vera.   15

Etiam

⟨3⟩ Eo quod aliqua propositio praecise rem quae fuit significat fuisse vel rem quae non fuit significat non fuisse, est propositio affirmativa vel negativa de praeterito vera.

Et intelligo hic 'rem' generalius quam 'aliquid'. Accipitur enim hic pro omni tali 20 quod potest rationari, vel de quo potest esse ratio, cum hoc nomen 'res' dicitur de reor–reris.

Et hae propositiones hic positae non stricte sed ad sententias ad quas hic ponuntur sunt intelligendae. Exemplum primae propositionis: Sit *A* ista 'Deus est' et *B* ista 'Nullus homo est asinus.' Tunc ex eo quod *A* praecise quod Deus est signi- 25 ficat, et Deus est, est *A* propositio vera. Et eo quod *B* praecise quod nullus homo est asinus significat, et nullus homo est asinus, est *B* propositio vera.

Sed haec negativa 'Nullus homo est asinus' quae assumitur in antecedente, ex quo cum aliquo assumpto sequitur quod *B* propositio est vera, non ponitur pro causa, sed ut fiat mentio per illam quod illa affirmativa assumpta—scilicet 30 '*B* praecise quod nullus homo est asinus significat'—est causa veritatis *B* ubi non impeditur per illud quod affirmative significatur per contradictorium *B*, quae est haec 'Homo est asinus.' Unde sola significatio qua *B* significat quod nullus homo est asinus est causa a parte rei quare *B* est vera. Sed ex propositione assumpta ab illa causa per se non formaliter sequitur *B* esse verum, cum causa 35 ista per illud quod significat contradictorium *B* potest impediri. Et saltem si non sit ita hic, tamen ita est de multis negativis contingentibus, sicut non sequitur '*B* praecise quod tu non curris significat; ergo tu non curris.' Sed de negativa praeassumpta bene sequitur, cum eius causalitas per eius contradictorium non potest impediri. Exemplum huius apparet in naturalibus, dato quod aliquid esset 40 quod haberet albedinem per totum, non habens contrarium admixtum. Tunc albedo esset causa formalis a parte rei per quam illud est album. Et tamen non sequitur 'Hoc habet albedinem per totum; ergo hoc est album.' Sed oportet addere sibi unam propositionem per quam denotatur non impediri hoc esse album per contrarium illius albedinis, sic arguendo 'Hoc habet albedinem per 45 totum et sine contrario admixto; ergo hoc est album.' Et sic est in proposito etc.

Sed ad veritatem propositionis verae affirmativae de praesenti, tam requiritur

significatio quam significat talis affirmativa de praesenti, cuius praedicatum non
est terminus distrahens nec ampliativus, quam etiam esse rei significatae. Unde
ad hoc quod haec propositio sit vera 'Deus est', requiritur quod Deus sit et
praecise quod Deus est haec significet. Et si aliud significet affirmative requiritur
5 quod illud sit.

Causa quare negativa (f. 84va) assumpta cum affirmativa ad probandum
negativam esse veram non assumitur pro aliqua causa a parte rei est haec: Nam
notum est quod talis negativa secundum suum esse non est causa essendi huius
propositionis conclusae ex illa et ex alia, quacumque data, sicut nec est aliqua alia
10 propositio, nec esse potest. Et si significatum per talem negativam esset causa
significati per consequens conclusum ex illa negativa et affirmativa cum qua
assumitur, cum universaliter quod est causa alicuius realiter est, ergo oportet
concedi quod significatum per propositionem negativam a parte rei est—quod
tamen improbatum et negatum est.
15   Ex quibus inferendum est quod intellectus istius propositionis in libro *Praedi-*
camentorum ⟨c. 5, 4ᵇ8–10⟩, qui a logicis communiter poni solet, huius scilicet non
est verus 'In eo quod res est vel non est, est oratio vera vel falsa.' Solet enim dici
quod iste terminus 'in eo' dicit causam sive circumstantiam esse. Et sic sumendo
istum terminum dici solet quod in eo quod res est quam significat affirmativa de
20 praesenti, est affirmativa illa vera; et in eo quod res non est, quam rem non esse
significat negativa de praesenti, est talis negativa vera; et in eo quod res est quam
negativa significat non esse, est negativa falsa; et in eo quod res non est quam
affirmativa significat esse, est affirmativa falsa. Ex quo sequitur ad intellectum
istum quod rem non esse est causa veritatis negativae, et rem non esse est causa
25 falsitatis affirmativae, ut plane patet ex iam dictis.

Unde non sic sed aliter habet illa auctoritas intelligi loco quo eam ponit
Aristoteles. Dicit enim capitulo 'De substantia' prope finem ⟨c. 5, 4ᵇ8–10⟩ quod
'in eo quod res est vel non est, est oratio vera vel falsa, non ex eo quod ipsa
oratio sit susceptibilis contrariorum.' Per quam auctoritatem ibi, ut patet per
30 textum Augustini, intelligit istum intellectum: In eo quod res est postquam non
fuit, sive per mutationem ad esse rei, est oratio significans rem esse vera postquam non fuit vera. Et in eo quod res non est, id est per mutationem ab esse rei
ad non esse, est oratio significans rem esse falsa postquam non fuit falsa. Nam
sic patet ex processu textus. Loquitur enim ibi quomodo est oratio vera postquam
35 non fuit vera, vel falsa postquam non fuit falsa; et numquid hoc sit per mutationem factam in re vel per mutationem factam in oratione. Aliter enim ad
nullum intellectum sanum adderet illi propositioni hanc negativam 'non in eo
quod ipsa oratio sit susceptibilis contrariorum.'

Et si allegatur contra istum sensum propositio in eodem libro capitulo quo
40 'Prius' ⟨c. 12, 14ᵇ21–2⟩ ad illud potest dici quod non dicit ibi quod 'in eo quod
res est' etc., immo dicit quod 'dum res est vel non est, est oratio vera vel falsa.'*
Et illud non est contra praedicta. Et licet in addendo primum modum prioritatis
dicat rem esse priusquam oratio sit vera significans rem sic esse et quod res sit
causa veritatis, et quod oratio numquam sit causa rei, quia ut ex praedictis patet
45 idem est esse quod verum; non tamen dicit alicubi in processu isto quod rem
non esse vel privatio rei sit aliquo modo causa quare oratio sit vera, ut patet
cuilibet qui textus sententiam Aristotelis noverit.

Consimiliter dico quod causa veritatis huiusmodi propositionum affirma-

* Vide Addenda et corrigenda, p. xvi.

tivarum, quarum verba principalia sunt ampliativa vel praedicata termini
ampliativi est significatio qua significat aliqua huiusmodi suum significatum.
Et etiam alia causa potest dici quaelibet res nata intellectum huius rei significabilis intellectui facere intentione vel causare. Exemplum huius: Causa
veritatis huius propositionis 'Chimaera est significabilis' est significatio sive actus 5
componendi quo componitur haec propositio vel sibi correspondens in anima.
Vel cum hoc quodlibet natum facere intellectui simplicem intentionem significare
de chimaera, quoniam quodlibet tale potest esse causa propter quam significaret
chimaeram. Sed brevius et satis vere dicitur quod a parte rei, causa veritatis
huius propositionis 'Chimaera est significabilis' est sua significatio qua significat 10
chimaeram esse significabilem. Et licet ex propositione affirmativa quae est
causa suae veritatis sequitur quod haec propositio est vera, tamen de aliis non
(f. 84vb) sequitur, sicut superius de albedine et subiecto albo patet.

   Ideo ad hoc quod propositio assumpta inferatur ab effectu ex propositione
affirmativa assumpta ex causa eiusdem effectus, oportet accipere aliquam 15
propositionem quae a nulla causa assumitur. Sed sufficit quod illa propositio
quae probatur esse vera, sit vera, quae probabiliter potest dici causa esse suae
veritatis, causa scilicet materialis dato quod veritas distinguatur a propositione
vera—quod dici potest. Vel si non dicitur, et similiter dicendum est quod
huiusmodi propositio a nulla causa assumitur a parte rei, quae solummodo potest 20
esse causa inferens vel inferendi.

   Similiter est ponendum de futuro et de praeterito quod sola significatio qua
propositio affirmativa significat rem fore quae erit, vel rem fore rem quae erit,
est causa veritatis propositionis affirmativae de futuro, et sola significatio qua
significat affirmativa de praeterito rem fuisse quae fuit, vel rem fuisse rem quae 25
fuit, est causa veritatis propositionis affirmativae de praeterito. Similiter propositio negativa de praeterito vel de futuro est vera per significationem qua significat rem non fuisse quae non fuit, vel rem non fore quae non erit. Et in eo quod
propositio de praeterito vel de futuro significat rem fore quae non erit, vel rem
non fore quae erit, cum aliis additis significantibus mensuram temporis vel alia- 30
rum circumstantiarum, vel rem fuisse quae non fuit, vel rem non fuisse quae
fuit, est propositio falsa.

⟨*Regulae causam veritatis propositionis ostendentes sive definitio propositionis
   verae vel falsae*⟩

   Sed quia forsan diceret aliquis quod his omnibus positis non habetur regula 35
causam veritatis propositionis universaliter ostendens, ideo duae breves regulae
sunt ponendae quarum prima est haec:

   ⟨1⟩ Omnis propositio finite vel determinate praecise verum significans est
      propositio vera.

Alia   40

   ⟨2⟩ Omnis propositio finite vel determinate praecise falsum significans est
      falsa.

Et intelligendum est hic 'verum' vel 'falsum' pro significato vero vel falso. Et
istum modum loquendi habet Boethius in *Topicis*, ubi dicit propositionis
descriptionem esse hanc 'Propositio est oratio verum vel falsum significans.' 45

   Ideo notandum est quid sit ratio veri et quid falsi. Pro quo dicendum est quod
isti duo termini 'verum' et 'falsum' sunt praedicabiles de terminis significantibus

significata propositionum, et sunt termini ampliativi, sicut sunt huiusmodi
nomina 'intellectum', 'intelligibile', 'opinatum', 'opinabile', 'significatum',
'significabile'. Unde omne intellectum non esse quod non est, non esse est verum;
et omne intellectum esse quod est, esse est verum; et omne intellectum fuisse
5 quod fuit, et intellectum non fuisse quod non fuit, et intellectum fore quod erit,
et intellectum non fore quod non erit. Et semper apponendum est cum aliis
circumstantiis temporis vel loci, sicut alias dictum est. Et isto modo concedendum
est quod nullum hominem esse asinum est verum, Antichristum fore est verum,
Caesarem fuisse est verum. Et non sequitur ultra, 'ergo nullum hominem esse
10 asinum est' et sic de ceteris, sicut non sequitur 'Antichristum fore est intellectum; ergo Antichristum fore est.' Et ita dicendum est de falso quod intellectum
non esse quod est, non esse est falsum; et intellectum esse quod non est, et sic de
ceteris.

Unde verum, sumptum pro significato vero, est ens intellectum per cuius in-
15 tellectionem intellectus intelligentis illud verificatur. Falsum est ens intellectum
per cuius intellectionem intellectus intelligentis illud obliquatur sive falsatur.
Unde iuxta haec dicta, solummodo quando intelligitur nullum hominem esse
asinum, tunc nullum hominem esse asinum est verum, et sic de ceteris. Sed ut
largius accipiatur verum pro vero in habitu, tunc accipitur pro intelligibili esse
20 quod est, vel pro intelligibili non esse quod non est, et sic de ceteris quae significantur per propositionem de praeterito vel de futuro. Et istum modum loquendi
habet Aristoteles secundo *Metaphysicae*, ubi separat ens verum a sua considera-
tione, et etiam a scientia ibi tradita, cum huiusmodi esse non habeat esse reale
extra animam, sed solummodo esse intellectum vel esse intelligibile. Et ideo
25 large dico ne videar dictis philosophorum repugnare de vero et falso.

⟨*Argumenta contra istam viam*⟩

⟨1⟩ Contra ista arguitur sic: Si nullum hominem esse asinum est verum, ergo
verum est nullum hominem esse (f. 85ra) asinum. Ergo aliquid vel aliqualiter est
nullum hominem esse asinum, ex quo immediate sequitur quod nullum hominem
30 esse asinum est aliquid vel aliqualiter—quod superius saepius est negatum.
Prima consequentia de se patet, et secunda probatur: Quia si nec aliquid nec
aliqualiter est nullum hominem esse asinum, nullum verum est nullum hominem
esse asinum, cum omne verum sit aliquid vel aliqualiter. Quia quod verum sit
et nec aliquid nec aliqualiter nec aliquale, intellectus capere non potest.
35 Ista ratio confirmatur: Si verum est nullum hominem esse asinum, et non
aliud verum quam nullum hominem esse asinum; ergo nullum hominem esse
asinum est nullum hominem esse asinum—ex quo sequitur quod nullum
hominem esse asinum est. Consequentia patet a tertio adiacente quod non est
terminus ampliativus nec distrahens, ad secundum adiacens, quem modum
40 arguendi probat Philosophus secundo *Peri Hermeneias* ⟨c. 11, 21ᵃ18–33⟩.*

⟨2⟩ Item ad principale arguitur sic: Si illud quod significatur per negativam
est verum, eadem ratione scitur. Et ultra sequitur quod illud quod significatur per
negativam est. Consequentia patet per hoc quod non ens non scitur, eo quod scire
est rem per causam cognoscere. Sed quod non est non habet causam. Ergo etc.
45 Sed oppositum probatur tam de scientia proprie dicta quam de scientia communiter dicta. ⟨a⟩ Nam significatum propositionis negativae creditur absque
haesitatione existente veritate propositionis significantis illud significatum. Ergo

---

* Cf. etiam W. Burley, *Super artem veterem,* ad locum (ed. Venetiis 1519, f. 86va-b).

significatum propositionis negativae scitur. Confirmatur per exemplum: Nullum hominem esse asinum creditur sine haesitatione. Et nullum hominem esse asinum est verum. Ergo nullum hominem esse asinum scitur. Consequentia per hoc patet quod nulla alia causa requiritur ad scientiam communiter dictam. Et maior similiter, quia esset nimis fatuus qui non crederet se ipsum non esse asinum et 5 quemlibet alium hominem, si de illo consideraret.

⟨b⟩ Item quod significatum propositionis negativae scitur scientia proprie dicta, probatur: Aliqua est demonstratio negativa, ut patet primo *Posteriorum* ⟨c. 25⟩. Ergo, cum demonstratio est syllogismus faciens scire, ergo per aliquam demonstrationem acquiritur scientia de significato propositionis negativae. Pro- 10 batur consequentia per hoc quod per demonstrationem acquiritur scientia significati per conclusionem. Ergo etc.

Huic forte dicitur quod per demonstrationem acquiritur scientia conclusionis et non rei significatae per conclusionem, ut videtur Philosophus innuere in eodem loco. Et ita non sequitur. 15

Contra illud arguitur sic: Scire conclusionem est scire conclusionem esse et e contra, ut superius probatum est, eo quod conclusionem esse est ipsa conclusio. Sed aequaliter contingit scire propositionem falsam esse sicut propositionem veram. Ergo aequaliter contingit scire per demonstrationem conclusionem quae est propositio falsa sicut vera—quod non est verum. Quia si conclusio est falsa, 20 altera praemissarum est falsa; et sic non omnis demonstratio esset ex veris— cuius oppositum patet in primo *Posteriorum* ⟨c. 2, 71ᵇ20–2⟩. Igitur etc.

⟨*Responsio ad argumenta in contrarium*⟩

⟨R1⟩ Ad primum istorum respondetur negando consequentiam primam, cum arguitur 'Nullum hominem esse asinum est verum; ergo verum est nullum 25 hominem esse asinum.' Sicut non sequitur 'Nullum hominem esse asinum est intellectum vel intelligibile, per cuius intellectionem intellectus certificatur vel habitualiter est certificabilis—et vocatur habitualiter certificabilis quando absque mutatione istius intelligibilis, ab ipso intelligibili certificaretur intellectus si ipsum intelligibile intelligeret. Ergo intellectum vel intelligibile per cuius intelle- 30 ctionem certificatur intellectus vel habitualiter est certificabilis, est nullum hominem esse asinum.' Non magis valet haec consequentia quam haec 'Chimaera est intellectum; ergo intellectum est chimaera.'

Unde pono istas conclusiones: 'Nullum hominem esse asinum est verum, et non est verum nullum hominem esse asinum', 'Te esse Romae est possibile, et 35 non est possibile te esse Romae', cum nec aliquid nec aliquale est te esse Romae, 'Te esse asinum est impossibile, et non est impossibile te esse asinum.' Et si arguitur (f. 85rb) contra unam istarum conclusionum sic: non est possibile te esse Romae; ergo impossibile est te esse Romae—negatur consequentia. Et si allegatur Aristoteles secundo *Peri Hermeneias* ⟨c. 13, 22ᵃ14–ᵇ28⟩ ubi dicit ista con- 40 verti 'Non possibile est esse' et 'Impossibile est esse', dicitur quod omnes illi termini debent intelligi a parte praedicati, scilicet 'possibile', 'impossibile'. Unde istas intelligit converti—'Te esse Romae non est possibile' et 'Te esse Romae est impossibile', supposito quod te esse Romae sit intellectum vel intelligibile. 45

⟨R2⟩ Ad aliud, quando arguitur 'Significatum propositionis negativae scitur; ergo significatum propositionis negativae est'—negatur consequentia. Et quando dicitur 'Scire est rem per causam cognoscere, sed quod non est non habet

causam; igitur etc.'—dicendum est quod Aristoteles utitur in suo modo loquendi
scientia conclusionis pro scientia rei significatae per conclusionem quae est ex
scientia praemissarum, sumpta pro scientia significatorum per praemissas. Vult
ergo intelligere per auctoritatem allegatam quod scientia conclusionis vel scire
5 aliquam conclusionem perfecte, hoc est significatum conclusionis mediante conclusione, tamquam per medium repraesentativum illius sciti, est scire per causam
illius conclusionis, videlicet per praemissas quae sunt quodammodo causae conclusionis, cum sint prius scibiles. Et etiam significata per ipsas prius sunt scibilia quam
significatum conclusionis. Nec perfecte potest aliquis scire significatum per con-
10 clusionem ex illis illatam, nisi prius sciantur significata per praemissas. Et ita intelligit Philosophus per causam istius sciti praemissas ex quibus infertur conclusio.

Vel aliter dici potest quod scire est rem per causam cognoscere, id est scire
demonstrative quod significatur per conclusionem demonstrationis est scire per
causam, id est per scientiam praemissarum, sive per habitum praemissarum,
15 quae scientia vel qui habitus est causa scientiae conclusionis. Et iste est intellectus
generalis ad quodlibet scibile demonstrative, sive fuerit significatum conclusionis
negativae sive affirmativae de praesenti vel de praeterito vel de futuro.

Sed communi modo loquendi de scire, scire quod significatur per conclusionem
affirmativam de praesenti est per causam positivam a parte rei, et scire illud per
20 quod scitur est scire causam illius sciti. Sed ista cognitio generalis acquisita est
per cuiuslibet propositionis significati demonstrabilis demonstrationem.

Sed dubitaret aliquis qualiter aliquod significatum esset scitum quod non est,
cum quodlibet significatum est cognitum et quodlibet cognitum est. Probatur: Nam
tertio* *Metaphysicae* unumquodque sicut se habet ad esse, ita ad cognosci et e
25 contra. Ergo aequaliter est res cognoscibilis et ens et e contra. Ergo non stat
significatum propositionis negativae esse cognitum vel cognoscibile et non esse.
Et per consequens nec est scitum, cum non sit ens.

Ad istud respondeo concedendo sicut prius, quod significatum propositionis
negativae nec est aliquid nec aliqualiter nec aliqua, et tamen est cognitum et
30 scitum. Consimiliter concedo de significato propositionis de praeterito et de
futuro, quod declaro sic: Sicut omnis sensatio est cognitio obiecti sensibilis, ita
omnis intellectio rei intelligibilis est cognitio obiecti intelligibilis. Sed ut patet
contingit intelligere plura quae non sunt, ita et cognoscere multa quae non sunt.
Et tunc dico ad auctoritatem quod non plus intelligit nisi quod quaelibet res
35 quantum est causata, de se est cognita vel nata facere cognitionem quantum
a parte sui. Nec ex illo sequitur e converso quod in quantum est aliquid cognoscibile in tantum est. Aliquid enim est cognoscibile quod cognitionem facere non
potest, sicut sunt non entia, ut quod nulla chimaera est, et quod Caesar fuit, et
huiusmodi, quae solummodo cognoscuntur per cognitionem factam ex aliis. Et
40 per hoc patet responsio ad argumentum.

* * *

⟨PARS SECUNDA, CAPITULUM SECUNDUM: DE POSSIBILITATE, IMPOSSIBILITATE ETC. OPINIO AUCTORIS⟩

⟨*Opinio quae tamquam insufficiens ab auctore reprobatur*⟩

45 (f. 86vb) His taliter improbatis dicitur forte consequenter ex dictis de veritate et
falsitate propositionum quod universaliter

---

* *pro*: secundo. Cf. *Metaphysica* II, c. 1 993^{b}30–1.

⟨1⟩ Ex hoc quod possibile est rem esse vel rem esse rem, quam rem esse rem significatur per aliquam propositionem, est propositio affirmativa (f. 87ra) possibilis de praesenti,

et hoc intelligendo modo quo prius dictum est in capitulo praecedente. Similiter,

⟨2⟩ Eo quod possibile est rem non esse vel rem non esse rem etc., est pro- 5
positio negativa possibilis de praesenti.

Et similiter dicendum est de propositione de futuro et de praeterito. Et omnino consimiliter est dicendum de necessaria contingenti et ⟨im⟩possibili.

⟨*Argumenta contra istam opinionem*⟩

Contra ista multipliciter arguitur: ⟨1⟩ Primo, ista 'Nullus homo est asinus' est 10
possibilis. Et non est possibile nullum hominem esse asinum. Ergo non ex hoc quod possibile est rem non esse rem, est negativa sic praecise significans possibilis. Assumptum probatur: Quia si possibile est nullum hominem esse asinum, et possibile est quo posito in esse non accidit impossibile, ergo si poneretur in esse quod nullus homo est asinus, non accidit impossibile. Et si sic, sequitur quod 15
possibile est esse quod nullus homo est asinus—quod saepius est improbatum. Et consequentia satis patet, et minor est Aristotelis primo *Priorum* ⟨c. 13, 32ª18– 20⟩ et primo *De generatione* et Boethii et auctoris *Sex Principiorum.*

Item si possibile est nullum hominem esse asinum, ergo aliqua potentia est possibile nullum hominem esse asinum. Sed cum omnis potentia est deter- 20
minata per actum vel ad actum ordinata, ergo potentia qua possibile est nullum hominem esse asinum est ordinata ad actum vel per actum determinata. Sed ad nullum alium actum ordinatur vel per alium actum terminatur, quam per nullum hominem esse asinum. Ergo nullum hominem esse asinum est actus. Et si sic, ergo nullum hominem esse asinum est. 25

Item si possibile est nullum hominem esse asinum, cum solum illud quod potest esse sit possibile, ergo potest esse quod nullus homo est asinus. Sed nullum hominem esse asinum non potest esse. Hoc probatur quia nullus homo potest aliter esse asinus quam nunc nullus homo est asinus. Ergo si potest esse quod nullus homo est asinus, nunc est quod nullus homo est asinus—quod 30
tamen est contra prius posita.

Item non necesse est nullum hominem esse asinum. Et tamen propositio sic praecise significans est necessaria. Ergo non ex hoc. Et tunc antecedens pro- batur: Quia si necesse est nullum hominem esse asinum, cum necesse sit in- ferius ad verum, sequitur quod verum est nullum hominem esse asinum; ex 35
quo sequitur, ut praeargutum est, quod nullum hominem esse asinum est.

Item arguitur ad idem sic: Si verum est nullum hominem esse asinum, ergo aliqua veritate est verum nullum hominem esse asinum. Quod si detur aliqua, ergo verum est nullum hominem esse asinum veritate rei vel veritate composi- tionis sive intellectus. Non primo modo, ut patet capitulo praecedente. Quod 40
non secundo modo probatur: Nam veritas intellectus sive compositionis est adaequatio intellectus ad rem. Sed si adaequatio intellectus ad rem fuerit veritas illa qua verum est quod nullus homo est asinus, illa esset adaequatio intellectus ad rem illam quae est nullum hominem esse asinum. Ergo nullum hominem esse asinum est res. Consequens impossibile. 45

* * *

(f. 87rb) Item specialiter sic: Non est contingens rem esse nec rem non esse.

Ergo non ex hoc etc. Assumptum probatur: Contingentia est potentia indifferens ad utramque partem contradictionis. Sed in re non est potentia indifferens ad utramque partem contradictionis. Ergo etc. Antecedens probatur de quacumque re existente: Quia ad esse illius non est potentia, saltem distincta contra actum.
5 Ergo si in re existente sit aliqua contingentia sive potentia indifferens ad esse et ad non esse, illa est potentia determinata actu. Sed nulla talis est indifferens ad esse et ad non esse, cum esse magis se habet ad esse.

Item actus terminat potentiam. Sed illud quod nihil est non potest terminare. Ergo ad non esse, cum nihil sit, non potest esse potentia. Et ita apparet quod non
10 sit contingentia ad utrumlibet contradictoriorum, cum nihil sit, nec potest esse contingentia. Ergo sicut non est aliqua contingentia in re sic nec in propositione.

APPENDIX II

JOHANNES VENATOR

LOGICA

MS. Vat. lat. 2130, ff. 73rb–76vb; 105vb–108rb

⟨TRACTATUS PRIMUS, CAP. VII: DE SIGNIFICATO   5
PROPOSITIONIS⟩

(f. 73rb) Septimo contingit dubitare circa materiam significati propositionis seu significabilis complexe, in qua materia diversae sunt positiones: ⟨1⟩ Una est ponens significatum propositionis verae esse modum rei, sic quod nullo modo est res. Verbi gratia dicit quod Deum esse non est res, et quod Sortem esse sit   10
modus rei ubique existens. Et similiter quod chimaeram non esse (f. 73va) est modus rei.

⟨2⟩ Secunda positio ponit quod Deum esse nec est modus nec Deus, sed est compositio mentalis.

⟨3⟩ Tertia ponit quod Deum esse est Deus, et similiter quod Sortem esse est   15
Sortes, supposito quod Sortes sit; solem calefacere domum est sol calefaciens domum; et quod solem fuisse est sol praeteritus; et solem fore est sol futurus. Sed Antichristum fore nihil est, supposito quod Antichristus non sit. Ulterius dicitur quod nullius negativae propositionis verae significatum adaequatum est. Sic patet quod nullam chimaeram esse non est, et similiter Deum non esse solem   20
non est.

⟨*Aliquae conclusiones pro declaratione materiae huius*⟩

Pro declaratione materiae huius sit

1a conclusio: Deum esse non est modus distinctus a Deo.

⟨1.1⟩ Probatur: Nam dato opposito conclusionis, sequitur ista conclusio impossi-   25
bilis 'Duo sunt dei.' Probatur: Deus est Deus. Et Deum esse est Deus. Et Deum esse non est Deus, per positionem. Ergo duo sunt dei. Patet consequentia. Et sumptum probatur: Quam repugnat Deum esse sine Deo, tam repugnat Deo ipsum esse sine Deum esse, et e converso. Ergo qua ratione Deus est Deus, pari ratione Deum esse est Deus.   30

⟨1.2⟩ Item secundo, Deum esse est Deus. Ergo Deum esse non est modus distinctus a Deo. Patet consequentia. Et antecedens probatum est.

⟨1.3⟩ Item tertio, dato opposito conclusionis sequitur ista 'Si Deus est, infinita sunt.' Probatur: Si Deus est, Deum esse est, et Deum esse ⟨esse⟩ est, et sic in infinitum. Ergo etc.   35

⟨1.4⟩ Item quarto, sequitur ista conclusio 'Tantum Deus est, et infinita sunt', posito isto casu quod Deus est et nihil aliud quam Deus est. Tunc patet prima pars conclusionis. Et secunda probatur: Infiniti modi sunt. Ergo infinita sunt.

Patet consequentia. Et antecedens probatur: Deum esse est, et Deum esse esse
est, et sic sine statu. Et Deum esse non est Deum esse ⟨esse⟩. Ergo etc.

⟨1.5⟩ Item quinto, dato opposito conclusionis sequitur ista conclusio 'Hoc
non est Deus'—demonstrando causam primam. Probatur: Omnis Deus est hoc
5 posse esse. Sed hoc non esse Deum est posse esse. Ergo hoc non est Deus. Patet
discursus et similiter minor iuxta adversarium. Et maior probatur: Stat sine
contradictione Deum posse esse sine hoc, eo quod ista stant simul—'Deus potest
esse' et 'Hoc non est.' Sed non stat Deum posse esse sine Deo, sic quod stat
quod Deum posse esse est et quod Deus non est, nec e converso. Ergo maior.

10 ⟨1.6⟩ Item sexto, sequitur ista conclusio 'Mere contingens est necesse.'
Probatur: Te esse vel te non esse est necesse. Et qualitercumque est te esse vel
te non esse, est contingens. Ergo contingens est necesse. Patet consequentia et
similiter maior iuxta positionem. Et minor probatur: Qualitercumque est te
esse, est contingens. Et te non esse non (f. 73vb) est, ut suppono. Ergo qualiter-
15 cumque est te esse vel te non esse est contingens. Patet consequentia. Nam
sequitur generaliter 'Omnis homo est, et nulla chimaera est; ergo omnis homo
est vel chimaera est.'

2a conclusio principalis: Te esse non distinguitur a te.

20 ⟨2.1⟩ Probatur: Nam dato opposito conclusionis sequitur ista conclusio 'Tu es
ubique', te solum Bacharati existente. Probatur: Ubicumque est aliquid inte-
grum ex pluribus partibus est quaelibet eius pars. Sed significatum huius propositionis 'Tu es tu' est quoddam significatum ex te et significato praedicati. Et
significatum istius propositionis est ubique, ut dicit positio. Ergo tu es ubique.
25 Et tu es solum Bacharati. Ergo etc.

⟨2.2⟩ Item sequitur alia conclusio: Dato opposito conclusionis sequitur ista
conclusio—valet quod aliquid est idem tibi, quod non est idem tibi. Probatur:
Et suppono quod tu sis. Tunc ista propositio 'Tu es tu' significans praecise
quod tu es tu, est vera. Arguo tunc sic: Significatum istius propositionis est
30 modus distinctus a te, sicut totum integrale distinguitur a parte sua. Ergo illud
significatum non est idem tibi. Et quod sit idem tibi probatur: Cui quaelibet
pars integralis est eadem, idem totum est idem eidem. Sed significatum subiecti
est idem tibi. Et tunc tuum ⟨esse⟩ est idem tibi, supposito adhuc quod 'es' esse
significat, et significatum praedicati est idem tibi, quae integrant significatum
35 huius propositionis. Ergo illud significatum istius propositionis est idem tibi.

⟨2.3⟩ Item tertio sequitur ista conclusio 'Ubique tu curris.' Et suppono quod
aliquis efficiat cursum suum. Tunc sic: Ubicumque est cursus tuus, tu curris.
Sed ubique est cursus tuus. Ergo ubique tu curris. Patet consequentia. Et
similiter maior eo quod cursus est in determinato subiecto. Et minor probatur:
40 Ubique efficitur cursus tuus. Ergo ubique est cursus tuus. Tenet consequentia,
et antecedens probatur: Ubicumque efficitur te currere, ibi efficitur cursus tuus.
Sed ubique efficitur te currere. Ergo ubique efficitur cursus tuus. Patet consequentia ex eo quod ubique est te currere postquam non fuit.

⟨2.4⟩ Item quarto, positis te et tuis partibus et subductis quibuscumque aliis
45 positivis absolutis et respectivis, ponitur te esse. Sed si te esse distingueretur
a te, te esse non esset, subductis quibuscumque positivis absolutis et respectivis
praeter te et tuas partes. Ergo tu es te esse.

⟨2.5⟩ Item quinto, si te esse est modus, vel igitur est modus in te vel extra te.
Non extra te, quia tunc ad corruptionem tui non desineret te esse, eo quod

nullum absolutum desineret esse ad mutationem factam in alio. Nec te esse est
modus in te, quia tu es naturaliter prior omni existente (f. 74ra) in te. Et universaliter stat prius esse sine posteriori. Ergo stat te esse, quamvis te esse non sit.

⟨2.6⟩ Item sexto, omne tale cuius esse est in alio est accidens. Sed te esse est
tale cuius esse est in alio. Ergo te esse est accidens. Maior sic probatur: Ens prima 5
sui divisione dividitur in esse per se et in esse in alio, in cuius divisionis secunda
parte includitur solum accidens. Sed generaliter omne divisum praedicatur de
suis dividentibus. Et minor patet ex eo quod te esse non est ens per se.

⟨2.7⟩ Item septimo, dato quod te esse est modus, sequitur quod unus modus
est duo modi. Probo: Nam tenentes quod te esse est modus, tenent quod te 10
differre a Sorte est unus modus. Tunc sic: Te differre a Sorte est duo modi vel
tres. Et te differre a Sorte est unus modus. Ergo unus modus est duo modi vel
tres. Patet consequentia, et minor similiter. Et maior probatur sic: Te esse, et
Sortem esse, et te non esse Sortem, sunt tres modi vel duo. Ergo te differre
a Sorte est vel sunt tres modi vel duo. Patet consequentia ab exponentibus ad 15
expositam. Similiter illae propositiones convertuntur 'Tu differs a Sorte, et tu
es' et 'Sortes est, et tu non es Sortes.' Et dicta istarum sunt. Ergo dicta istarum
convertuntur. Consequentia nota prout postea videbitur.

3a conclusio principalis: Non est quod nulla chimaera est.

⟨3.1⟩ Probatur sic: Quod nulla chimaera est non est primum simpliciter. Et quod 20
nulla chimaera est non habet causam. Ergo non est quod nulla chimaera est.
Patet consequentia, et antecedens similiter pro prima parte. Et pro secunda
parte probatur: ⟨3.1.1⟩ Nullam chimaeram esse non est causa quare sic est quod
nulla chimaera est. Nec est aliqua alia causa positiva quare sic est quod nulla
chimaera est. Ergo non sic est quod nulla chimaera est. ⟨3.1.1a⟩ Assumptum pro 25
prima parte probatur sic: Ista consequentia deficit 'Nulla chimaera est; igitur
est quod nulla chimaera est', ut patet per regulam superius probatam—scilicet
quod ex nulla negativa sequitur affirmativa. ⟨3.1.1b⟩ Item secundo quod non
valet probatur: Oppositum consequentis illius consequentiae est compossibile
antecedenti eiusdem. Ergo consequentia nulla. Assumptum arguitur: Utrumque 30
istorum sequitur ex mere negativa. Nam sequitur 'Nihil est nec aliqualiter est;
ergo nulla chimaera est.' Similiter sequitur 'Non est quod nulla chimaeraest'.
Ergo etc.

⟨3.1.2⟩ Item tertio arguitur quod non sit aliqua causa positiva quod nulla
chimaera est. Probatur: Non est aliqualiter in re quin taliter non existente sic 35
omnino nulla chimaera esset qualiter nunc nulla chimaera est. Et etiam si aliqualiter sit nullam chimaeram esse. (f. 74rb) Ergo nihil in re est causa positiva
sic esse quod nulla chimaera est, quoniam quodlibet et qualitercumque esse erit
causa sic esse quod nulla chimaera est. Consequens est inconveniens. Non enim
conveniens est dicere quod homo est causa sic esse quod nulla chimaera est, cum 40
causa et causatum aliqualiter ad invicem proportionentur. Et notum est quod
hominem esse, et esse quod nulla chimaera est, nullatenus ad invicem propor-
tionantur vel conveniunt. Immo si utrumque istorum foret, maxime ad invicem
disproportionarentur.

⟨3.2⟩ Item quarto, si nihil esset nec aliqualiter, tunc non esset quod nulla 45
chimaera est. Sed iam aeque bene nulla chimaera est, sicut tunc nulla chimaera
esset. Ergo iam non est quod nulla chimaera est.

⟨3.3⟩ Item quinto, si est quod nulla chimaera est, vel ergo est per se existens

vel alteri inhaerens. Non secundo modo, quia non esset ratio quare inesset uni individuo, quin pari ratione omni. Et sic unum accidens esset subiectum alterius accidentis—quod est impossibile eo quod permanentius esset in ⟨im⟩permanentiori.

5   *4a conclusio*: Adam fuisse non est, supposito quod nullus Adam est.

⟨4.1⟩ Probatur: Non stat Deum esse sine Deo, vel non stat te esse sine te. Ergo per idem non stat Adam fuisse sine Adam. Sed Adam non est. Ergo Adam fuisse non est.

⟨4.2⟩ Item secundo, subductis omnibus absolutis a Deo, et hac propositione 10 'Adam fuit' cum suis partibus sic significantibus, adhuc haec propositio esset vera, significando primo Adam fuisse. Sed tunc Adam fuisse non esset. Ergo per idem nec nunc ex quo Adam non est.

⟨4.3⟩ Item tertio, Adam fuisse est. Ergo Adam fuisse est substantia vel accidens. Patet consequentia per sufficientem divisionem. Sed consequens est falsum, quia 15 Adam fuisse non est substantia ut patet. Nec est accidens ut satis patet per praearguta, quia non posset assignari subiectum eius. Ergo etc.

⟨4.4⟩ Item quarto, tota ratio quare ponitur ita esse quod Adam fuit, est ista 'Adam fuit; ergo ita est quod Adam fuit.' Sed ista consequentia non valet. Probatur: Quia si nihil nec aliqualiter esset, non esset Adam fuisse. Ergo nec 20 nunc est Adam fuisse.

5a conclusio: Antichristum fore non est, supposito quod Antichristus non est.

Probatur: Antichristum fore non est Antichristus futurus. Ergo Antichristum fore non est. Patet consequentia iuxta hoc, quia si Deum esse est, Deum esse est Deus, et si Sortem esse est, Sortem esse est Sortes. Patet ergo per idem 'Si 25 Antichristum fore est, Antichristum fore est Antichristus futurus.' (f. 74va) Sed Antichristum fore non est Antichristus futurus eo quod nihil nec aliqualiter est Antichristus futurus. Ergo etc.

6a conclusio: Deum esse non est compositio mentalis, et similiter Sortem esse non est compositio mentalis.

30 ⟨6.1⟩ Probatur: Dato opposito conclusionis sequitur ista conclusio 'Ex necessario sequitur contingens ad utrumlibet'—quae conclusio est impossibilis. Antecedens probatur: Ista consequentia est bona 'Deus est; ergo Deum esse est verum.' Et antecedens istius consequentiae est necessarium apud ponentes oppositum conclusionis. Et consequens est mere contingens—quod sic probatur: Deducta 35 compositione mentali, nec verum nec necessarium est Deum esse eo quod nulla esset compositio mentalis intellectus. Et consequentia patet eo quod arguitur a propositione ad eius dictum ad bonum intellectum.

⟨6.2⟩ Item sequitur ista conclusio 'Quod desinet esse non desinet esse.' Probatur: Ista consequentia est bona 'Deus est; ergo verum est Deum esse' ut 40 patet statim. Ergo etc. Consequentia deducitur. Et ponatur quod omnis compositio mentalis desinat esse. Tunc sic: Deum esse desinet esse. Et Deum esse non desinet esse eo quod Deum esse est necessarium.

⟨6.3⟩ Item sequitur ista conclusio 'Aliquid significat quod non significat', sumendo [quod] ly .quod. relative. Probatur sic: Sit *A* ista compositio mentalis, 45 scilicet 'Deus est.' Et patet quod *A* significat quod Deus est. Et idem *A* non significat, ut probabitur. Ergo etc. ⟨a⟩ Prima pars probatur: *A* significat, et *A* non solum significat seipsum. Ergo *A* significat aliud a se. Et nihil potest poni

nisi Deum esse, quod sit res extra. Ergo etc. ⟨b⟩ Et quod *A* non significat sic res
ad extra probatur: Quidquid significat compositio mentalis significat vox ei
correspondens mediante ista compositione, cum vox significet istam mediante
conceptu, ut vult Philosophus primo *Peri Hermeneias*, capitulo primo, ubi sic
inquit: 'voces sunt earum quae sunt in anima passionum notae' ⟨c. 1, 16ª3–4⟩. Sed 5
conceptus iste significat rem extra, ut probatum est. Ergo vox significat rem
extra. Et sic non solum significatum propositionis est compositio mentalis.

⟨6.4⟩ Item sequitur quod ego possum facere Deum esse eo quod possum
facere talem compositionem mentalem 'Deus est.'

> *7a conclusio* principalis est ista: Deum esse est Deus, et solem esse est sol, 10
> et solem fuisse est sol praeteritus, et solem fore est sol futurus, et Sortem
> currere est Sortes currens, supposito quod Sortes currat.

Patet conclusio: Nam ex eo quod Deum esse est, et Deum esse non est modus
nec accidens ut probatum est, nec Deum esse est substantia distincta a Deo, nec
Deum esse est compositio mentalis; ergo relinquitur quod Deum esse est Deus. 15

8a conclusio: Deum non esse solem (f. 74vb) est Deus.

⟨8.1.1⟩ Probatur: Deus est. Et Deus non est sol. Ergo Deus est Deum non esse
solem. Patet consequentia. Nam sequitur generaliter 'Ego sum, ego sum albus;
ergo ego sum me esse album.' Similiter, 'Ego sum, et ego ero; ergo ego sum me
fore.' Ergo per idem in proposito. 20

⟨8.1.2⟩ Item tota causa movens aliquos ad oppositum est ista 'Si nihil esset nec
aliqualiter, Deum non esse solem non esset; sed iam aeque bene Deus non est
sol, sicut tunc non esset sol; ergo per idem iam Deum non esse solem non est.'
Sed quod illa ratio non debet movere probatur: Nam data ista responsione
sequitur ista conclusio. Probatur: Deum esse non est. Ergo Deus non est. Patet 25
consequentia, et antecedens probatur: Deum esse vel Deum non esse, non est.
Sed qualitercumque est Deum esse vel Deum non esse, est Deum esse. Ergo
Deum esse non est. Tenet consequentia, et antecedens probatur: Si nihil esset
nec aliqualiter, Deum esse vel Deum non esse, non esset. Sed aeque bene Deus
est vel Deus non est, sicut tunc Deus esset vel Deus non esset. Ergo iam Deum 30
esse vel Deum non esse, non est.

⟨8.2⟩ Item posset sic argui: Deum esse non solem est Deus. Ergo Deum esse
et Deum non esse solem est Deus. Patet consequentia, quia arguitur a convertibili ad convertibile. Et ultra, ergo Deum non esse solem est Deus. Et quod sic
arguitur patet, quia illae propositiones convertuntur, scilicet ista copulativa 35
'Deus non est sol et Deus est' et illa, scilicet 'Deus est non sol.' Et dicta illarum
propositionum sunt. Ergo dicta illarum convertuntur.

⟨*Argumenta contra praedictas conclusiones*⟩

*   *   *

(f. 75ra) *Contra tertiam conclusionem* arguitur sic: Tu scis nullam chimaeram
esse. Ergo a te scitur nullam chimaeram esse. Tenet consequentia, ex eo quod 40
arguitur ab activa ad suam passivam. Et sequitur ultra 'Ergo scitum est a te
nullam chimaeram esse.' Tenet consequentia. Et ultra, ergo nullam chimaeram
esse est scitum a te. Ex quo sequitur quod nullam chimaeram esse est. Et antecedens principale arguitur: Tu scis illam propositionem 'Nulla chimaera est.'
Et tu scis istam significare primo quod nulla chimaera est. Ergo tu scis quod nulla 45
chimaera est.

Item, haec est vera 'Nulla chimaera est.' Ergo est sicut ipsa significat. Patet consequentia, ut videtur per descriptionem propositionis verae ex quo veritas est adaequatio rei ad intellectum. Et sequitur ultra 'Est sicut haec propositio significat, et haec significat primo nullam chimaeram esse; ergo est quod nulla
5 chimaera est.'

*   *   *

(f. 75rb) *Contra sextam conclusionem* arguitur per Aristotelem primo *Peri Hermeneias*, capitulo 'De verbo' in fine, ubi dicit quod 'hoc verbum "est" significat quandam compositionem quam sine extremis non est intelligere' ⟨c. 3, 16^b 24–5⟩. Et per consequens significatum istius propositionis 'Deus est', scilicet Deum
10 esse, non est aliquid extra mentem.

Item Aristoteles secundo *Peri Hermeneias*, capitulo 'De modalibus' ⟨c. 13, 22^{a}14–^{b}28⟩ dicit converti illas 'Necesse est non esse', 'Impossibile est esse', ita quod idem est dicere 'Necesse est nullam chimaeram esse' et 'Impossibile est chimaeram esse.' Modo clarum est quod nihil est nec aliqualiter nullam chimaeram
15 esse extra mentem. Ergo ad veritatem huius propositionis 'Nulla chimaera est' ⟨requiritur⟩ quod nullam chimaeram esse sumatur pro compositione intellectus.

*   *   *

(f. 75vb) *Contra octavam conclusionem* arguitur sic: Deus est Deum non esse solem. Ergo Deus est solem non esse Deum. Patet consequentia a convertibili ad convertibile tamquam a totali extremo. Et consequens est falsum. Ergo et
20 antecedens. Et quod sic convertantur probatur sic: Istae propositiones 'Deus non est sol', 'Sol non est Deus' mutuo se inferunt, et quidquid significat una significat reliqua. Ergo convertuntur. Et sunt de simplici subiecto et praedicato. Tunc sic: Istae convertuntur et sunt de simplici subiecto et praedicato. Et dicta istarum sunt. Ergo dicta istarum convertuntur.
25 Modo probatur quod consequens, scilicet istud 'Deus est solem non esse Deum' est falsum. Nam sequitur 'Deus est solem non esse Deum; ergo Deus est sol non Deus.' Patet consequentia. Nam sequitur: 'Tu es te esse album; ergo tu es tu albus', 'Sortes est Sortem currere; ergo Sortes est Sortes currens', 'Antichristus est Antichristum fore; ergo Antichristus est Antichristus futurus.'
30 Ergo per idem in proposito. Videntur etiam contra istam conclusionem argumenta facta contra primam et secundam conclusionem.

⟨*Responsio ad argumenta facta contra conclusiones*⟩

*   *   *

(f. 76vb) Ad argumenta facta *contra conclusionem octavam*, dicitur concedendo quod Deus est Deum non esse solem, et negatur ista 'Deus est solem non esse
35 Deum.' Et ulterius negatur quod ista dicta convertuntur. Et ad eius probationem dicitur quod aliquas propositiones converti potest intelligi dupliciter, scilicet proprie et improprie. Proprie quando convertibilitas consurgit ex convertibilitate subiectorum ceteris paribus vel praedicatorum tentis ceteris paribus vel utrorumque. Et isto modo istae propositiones convertuntur 'Homo currit', 'Risibile
40 currit.' Alio modo quando mutuo se inferunt, et cum hoc quidquid significat una, significat reliqua. Primo modo dictum est verum, et non secundo modo.

Sed quia argumenta facta *contra tertiam conclusionem** videntur esse contra octavam, ideo respondetur ad ea. Concedo quod non est quod chimaera non est. Similiter quod non est quod Deus non est. Et similiter quod non est quod
45 Sortes non est. Sed supposito quod Sortes sit, dico quod Sortes est Sortem

---

* *An potius*: pro tertia conclusione? (Cf. supra, p. 239 lin. 20–47.)

non esse Platonem. Et ulterius conceditur quod Sortem non esse Platonem, habet causam. Nam quidquid est causa Sortis est causa Sortem non esse Platonem. Et tunc ad argumentum quando arguitur 'Si nihil esset nec aliqualiter, tunc non esset quod Sortes non est Plato; sed nunc aeque bene Sortes non est Plato sicut tunc: ergo nunc non est quod Sortes non est Plato', negatur 5 consequentia. Nam per idem probaretur quod ego non sum me esse vel me non esse—quod est manifeste falsum.

Ad aliud quando arguitur 'Non est aliqualiter in re quin taliter non existente omnino Deus non esset sol, sicut et nunc Deus non est sol . . .', conceditur. Et ulterius negatur ista consequentia 'Si nihil esset nec aliqualiter, Deum non esse 10 solem non esset; ergo et nunc Deum non esse solem non est.' Unde dico quod Deum non [non] esse solem est ex eo quod Deus est. Sed tunc non esset eo quod tunc Deus non esset. Et per hoc patet responsio ad omnia alia. Et similiter concedi potest ista conclusio 'Quod nullus homo est asinus, est homo, si homo est et nullus homo est asinus.' 15

⟨TRACTATUS TERTIUS, CAP. II: DE VERITATE ET FALSITATE PROPOSITIONIS⟩

⟨*Prima conclusio*⟩

(f. 105vb) Circa veritatem et falsitatem propositionis sit

> *1a conclusio ista*: Si haec propositio vel illa—quacumque demonstrata— 20 significat praecise sicut est, haec propositio est vera.

Probatur: Si haec propositio significat praecise sicut est, haec propositio significat sicut est, et haec propositio non significat sicut non est. Patet consequentia ab exposita ad eius exponentes. Et ultra, si haec propositio significat sicut est, et haec propositio (f. 106ra) non significat sicut non est, haec propositio est et 25 haec propositio non est falsa. Et sequitur ultra, ergo haec propositio est vera. Ergo—a primo ad ultimum—si haec propositio significat praecise sicut est, haec propositio est vera.

⟨*Argumenta contra primam conclusionem*⟩

⟨1⟩ Contra istam conclusionem arguitur: Aliqua propositio falsa significat 30 praecise sicut est. Igitur non si haec propositio vel illa significat praecise sicut est, est haec propositio vera. Patet consequentia iuxta conclusionem. ⟨1.1⟩ Et antecedens probatur sic: Et sit *A* ista propositio 'Deus est asinus' quae etiam significat Deum esse ens. Tunc sic: *A* significat praecise sicut est. Et idem *A* est propositio falsa. Ergo propositio falsa significat praecise sicut est. Patet conse- 35 quentia, et similiter minor. ⟨1.1.1⟩ Et maior probatur sic: *A* significat sicut est et non aliter quam sicut est. Ergo *A* significat praecise sicut est. ⟨1.1.1a⟩ Tenet consequentia, quia ly .sicut est et non aliter quam est. et ly .praecise sicut est. convertuntur. Ergo si in aliqua propositione ex aliqua parte ponitur alterum illorum, nullam diversitatem in significatione propositionis faciet vel causabit 40 quam non causabit reliquum eorum simili modo positum. ⟨1.1.1ai⟩ Consequentia patet per hoc quod in quacumque propositione ponuntur huiusmodi consimilia vel convertibilia, consimiliter ex eadem parte propositionis in quodcumque transit vis negationis importata per unum et per reliquum se extendit. ⟨1.1.1aii⟩ Et quod isti duo termini convertuntur—scilicet ly .praecise sicut est. et .sicut 45

est et non aliter quam sicut est.—probatur: Quia qualitercumque est praecise sicut est, est sicut est et non aliter quam sicut est, et e contra. Ergo convertuntur.

⟨1.1.1b⟩ Secundo probatur principalis conclusio probanda: Sicut in hac propositione '*A* significat praecise sicut est' denotatur exclusio solummodo
5 respectu illius termini 'sicut est' et sic excluduntur solummodo opposita illius termini 'sicut est' positi a parte praedicati. Sed ex hoc quod sit exclusio oppositorum istius termini 'sicut est' non denotatur negatio totius compositionis, cum dictio importans negationem, si qua sit, postponitur actui copulandi. Ergo ex hoc quod *A* significat praecise sicut est, non sequitur *A* non significare aliter
10 quam est, cum nulla negatio nec aliquid habens vim negationis aliqualiter praecedit copulam propositionis.

⟨1.1.1c⟩ Modo probatur antecedens illud, scilicet '*A* significat sicut est et non aliter quam sicut est.' *A* significat quod Deus est. Et quod Deus est, est sicut est et non aliter quam sicut est. Ergo *A* significat sicut est et non aliter quam sicut est.
15 ⟨1.1.1d⟩ Confirmatur: Sicut-est, praecise-sicut-est, et sicut-est-et-non-aliter-quam-sicut-est, realiter idem sunt. Ergo quaelibet oratio vel dictio quae significat unum eorum, significat quodlibet eorum. Et per consequens quidquid significat sicut est, significat praecise sicut est et significat sicut est et non aliter quam sicut est. Assumptum huius probatur: Qualitercumque est sicut est, est praecise sicut
20 est, et sicut est et non aliter quam sicut est. Ergo sicut-est est idem realiter cum praecise-sicut-est et sicut-est-et-non-aliter-quam-sicut-est.

⟨1.1.1e⟩ Item confirmatur modus arguendi. Nam sequitur 'Video asinum, et asinus est non homo; ergo video non hominem.' Ergo per idem sequitur '*A* significat sicut est; et sicut est, est sicut est et non aliter quam sicut est; ergo *A*
25 significat sicut est et non aliter quam sicut est.'

Pro istis argumentis aliqui concedunt istam conclusionem 'Aliqua propositio (f. 106rb) falsa significat praecise sicut est' et negant istam conclusionem 'Haec propositio significat praecise sicut est; ergo praecise sicut est haec propositio significat.' Similiter, negant istam 'Haec propositio significat praecise sicut est;
30 ergo haec propositio est vera', dicentes istas propositiones—scilicet 'Praecise sicut est significat haec propositio' et 'Haec propositio significat praecise sicut est'—diversimode esse exponendas. Ita scilicet quod respectu cuiuscumque dictionis praecedat nota exclusionis in aliqua istarum propositionum, respectu eiusdem debet praecedere negatio importata per notam illam exclusionis in neg-
35 ativa exponente. Unde primam et secundam istarum exponunt sic: Haec propositio significat sicut est, et haec propositio non significat aliter quam sicut est. Sed tertiam—scilicet hanc 'Haec propositio significat praecise sicut est'—exponunt sic: Haec propositio significat sicut est et haec propositio significat non aliter quam sicut est. Planum autem dicunt isti esse quod in qualibet istarum propositi-
40 onum exponibilium negativa exponente, respectu eiusdem dictionis praeponitur negatio, respectu cuius praeponitur nota exclusionis in propositione exponibili*.

⟨*Ad argumenta facta contra primam conclusionem*⟩

Non obstantibus istis argumentis conceditur prima conclusio, et ulterius admitto suppositionem. ⟨R1.1⟩ Et ulterius, quando sic arguitur '*A* significat
45 praecise sicut est, et *A* est propositio falsa; ergo etc.', negatur prima pars antecedentis. ⟨R1.1.1⟩ Et ad probationem quando dicitur '*A* significat sicut est et non aliter quam sicut est; igitur *A* significat praecise sicut est', dicitur negando

---

* Cf. Feribrigge, *Logica*, Pars I, c. 1, *1ᵃ consequentia* (Appendix I, p. 216 lin. 9–20).

consequentiam. ⟨R1.1.1a⟩ Et ad probationem consequentiae, quando dicitur 'Isti termini "praecise sicut est" et ly .sicut est et non aliter quam sicut est. omnino convertuntur; ergo si in aliqua propositione etc.', negatur antecedens et similiter consequentia. Unde non sequitur apud multos 'Scio hoc esse triangulum; ergo scio hoc esse figuram habentem tres angulos aequales duobus 5 rectis.' Immo multis modis fallit, ut patet ex superius dictis.

⟨R1.1.1aii⟩ Et ad probationem antecedentis, quando dicitur 'Qualitercumque est praecise sicut est, est sicut est et non aliter quam sicut est et e contra; ergo isti termini convertuntur', negatur consequentia. Unde dato isto modo arguendi sequitur ista conclusio 'Omne ens est Deus.' Probatur: Tantum Deus est ens. 10 Ergo omne ens est Deus. Patet consequentia, et antecedens probatur: Deus est ens. Ergo tantum Deus est ens. Probatur consequentia: Isti termini 'Deus', 'tantum Deus' convertuntur ceteris paribus. Ergo consequentia bona. Assumptum probatur: Quidquid est Deus est tantum Deus. Et quidquid est tantum Deus est Deus. Ergo isti termini convertuntur.   15

⟨R1.1.1b⟩ Ad confirmationem quae magis est colorata, quando sic arguitur— 'In hac propositione "*A* significat praecise sicut est" denotatur exclusio solum respectu istius termini "sicut est", et ita excluduntur solum opposita istius termini "sicut est". Sed ex hoc quod fit exclusio oppositorum istius termini non denotatur respectu totius compositionis, cum dictio importans negationem, si 20 qua sit omnino, postponitur actui copulandi, etc.'—negatur secunda pars antecedentis. Unde licet dictio importans negationem postponatur actui copulandi, adhuc denotatur negatio respectu totius compositionis, ut patet in talibus— 'Sortes est melior Platone', 'Tu es differens ab asino.'

⟨R1.1.1d⟩ Ad aliud argumentum, quando arguitur 'Quidquid est praecise sicut 25 est, est sicut est, et e contra, etc.; ergo si aliqua propositio significat sicut est, illa significat (f. 106va) praecise sicut est, et e contra', ⟨negatur consequentia.⟩ Unde non sequitur 'Quidquid est homo, est tantum homo, et e contra; ergo si hominem video, tantum hominem video' vel 'Si homo currit, tantum homo currit.'   30

⟨Secunda conclusio⟩

2a conclusio: Non si haec propositio est vera, haec propositio significat praecise sicut est.

Probatur: Et sit *A* ista propositio negativa 'Antichristus non est', supposito quod Antichristus non sit. Tunc: Haec propositio est vera—demonstrando *A*. 35 Et haec propositio non significat praecise sicut est. Igitur non si haec propositio est vera, haec propositio significat praecise sicut est. Patet consequentia. Et antecedens pro prima parte patet, et probatur pro secunda parte: Haec significat Antichristum non esse. Et Antichristum non esse non est nec hoc est esse, ut probatum est superius, capitulo 'De significabili complexe'. Ergo haec propositio 40 non significat praecise sicut est.

⟨Tertia conclusio⟩

Si praecise sicut est significat haec propositio, sicut est significat haec propositio ⟨. . .⟩ Et si praecise sicut est significat haec propositio, haec propositio est vera. Similiter, si praecise sicut est significat haec propositio, haec propositio 45 significat praecise sicut est; et ultra, igitur haec propositio est vera. Ergo a primo etc.

⟨Argumenta contra tertiam conclusionem⟩

Contra istam conclusionem arguitur multipliciter.

⟨3.1⟩ Primo sic: Praecise sicut est significat *A* propositio falsa. Ergo non si praecise sicut est significat haec propositio, haec propositio est vera. Patet con-
5 sequentia, et antecedens probatur: Sit *A* ista propositio 'Deus est asinus.' Tunc sic: Praecise sicut est significans est *A* propositio falsa. Ergo praecise sicut est significat *A* propositio falsa. Probatur consequentia: Praecise sicut est significans est *A* propositio falsa. Ergo sicut est significans est *A* propositio falsa et non sicut non est significans est *A* propositio falsa. Patet consequentia ab exposita ad
10 eius exponentes. Et sequitur ultra, ergo sicut est significat *A* propositio falsa et non sicut non est significat *A* propositio falsa—quod sic probatur, quia ex opposito consequentis sequitur oppositum antecedentis. Nam sequitur 'Sicut non est significat *A* propositio falsa; ergo sicut non est significans est *A* propositio falsa.' De alia parte patet patenter consequentia.
15 ⟨3.1.1⟩ Et probatur antecedens: *A* propositio falsa est praecise sicut est signi-ficans. Ergo praecise sicut est significans est *A* propositio falsa. Patet consequentia per conversionem simplicem. Item in quacumque indefinita affirmativa denotatur praedicatum praecise dici de subiecto, sic quod subiecti et praedicati sit eadem suppositio et aequalis seu convertibilis praecise. Ergo si imponitur unus terminus
20 pro subiecto sive alter non est differentia quoad veritatem vel falsitatem enun-tiandam.

⟨3.1.2⟩ Item aliquid praecise sicut est significans est *A* propositio falsa. Igitur praecise sicut est significans est propositio falsa. Patet consequentia ex eo quod affirmative a particulari ad eius indefinitam in eisdem terminis omnino tenet
25 consequentia. Illud sic patet: Nam propositio singularis vel particularis, sola demptione signi, fit indefinita. Et talis est in proposito.

⟨3.1.3⟩ Item supposito quod omnis propositio falsa significat sicut est, tunc sic: Tantum sicut est significans est propositio falsa. Ergo praecise sicut est significans est propositio falsa. Consequentia patet ex hoc quod 'praecise',
30 'tantum', 'tantummodo', 'solum' et omnes huiusmodi termini exclusivi con-vertuntur. Ergo propositiones in quibus simpliciter ponuntur, omnibus ceteris paribus manentibus eisdem, simpliciter (f. 106vb) convertuntur.

Hic forte negatur assumptum huius rationis propter hoc quod 'praecise' denotat exclusionem respectu modi solum, et 'tantum', 'tantummodo' respectu
35 rei.

Contra: Nam quod 'praecise' denotat exclusionem respectu modi, hoc est ratione termini est (*sic: dele* est) cui apponitur. Et etiam quod ille terminus 'solummodo' denotat exclusionem rei, hoc est ratione termini cui apponitur, quoniam in seipsis nullam rem significatam important, immo dumtaxat modum
40 excludendi rei. Unde cum ly .praecise. apponitur termino significanti rem, solum exclusionem oppositorum rei significatae per terminum cui apponitur denotat, ut cum dicitur 'praecise Deus est', denotat quod Deus est et quod nihil aliud quam Deus est, et cum dicitur 'praecise sicut est significat *A* propositio', denotatur quod sicut est significat *A* propositio, et non sicut non est vel non
45 aliter quam est significat *A* propositio. Consimiliter est de aliis dictionibus exclusivis, ut cum dicitur 'Tantum vel solummodo sicut est significat *A* proposi-tio', denotatur quod sicut est significat *A* propositio, et non sicut non est significat *A* propositio. Et cum dicitur 'Tantum vel tantummodo Deus est', denotatur quod Deus est et quod nihil aliud quam Deus est. Patet ergo quod cuiuslibet

istarum dictionum exclusivarum non magis est facere exclusionem rei quam
modi—quod si sic, sequitur quod quacumque illarum amota ab aliqua propositione, alia earum apposita loco eiusdem, praecise idem significat haec vel
alia propositio.

Ex quo patet modus iste arguendi 'Tantum sicut est significans est propositio 5
falsa; ergo praecise sicut est significans est propositio falsa.' Cuius antecedens
sic arguitur: Omnis propositio falsa est sicut est significans. Igitur tantum sicut
est significans est propositio falsa. Tenet consequentia per regulam generalem,
scilicet ab universali affirmativa ad eius exclusivam etc.

⟨3.1.4⟩ Item sicut est significans est propositio falsa. Et nihil aliud quam sicut 10
est significans est propositio falsa. Igitur tantum sicut est significans est propositio falsa. Tenet consequentia ab exponentibus ad expositam. Et antecedens
suppositum est. Ergo etc.

⟨3.2⟩ Item praecise sicut est significat haec propositio falsa 'Antichristus est.'
Ergo non si praecise sicut est significat haec propositio, haec propositio est vera. 15
Tenet consequentia, et antecedens probatur: Praecise quod Antichristus est,
haec propositio significat, et sic est. Ergo praecise sicut est haec propositio
significat.

⟨3.2.1⟩ Minor sic arguitur: Tali modo est; ergo sic est. Consequentia probatur
per hoc quod ly .sic. denotat similitudinem duorum similium, sicut hoc nomen 20
'talis'. Et antecedens probatur: Aliquo tali modo est. Ergo tali modo est. Patet
consequentia. Et antecedens probatur: Quod tu es homo, est. Et quod tu es homo,
est aliquis talis modus qualis est quod Antichristus est. Ergo aliquo tali modo est.
Consequentia probatur: Uterque istorum modorum est possibilis. Ergo talis
est unus eorum qualis est alter. 25

* * *

⟨*Septima conclusio*⟩

(f. 107rb) *7a conclusio*: Non si ita est totaliter sicut haec propositio significat,
haec propositio est vera quacumque demonstrata.

⟨7.1⟩ Probatur: Et capio istam propositionem 'Tu es asinus', et sis tu. Tum ita
est totaliter sicut haec significat, quae est propositio falsa. Ergo non si ita est 30
totaliter sicut haec propositio significat, haec propositio est vera. Patet consequentia. ⟨7.1.1⟩ Et antecedens arguitur: Te esse est totaliter sicut haec significat, et te esse est ita. Ergo ita est totaliter sicut haec significat. Patet syllogismus,
et sequitur ultra intentum. ⟨7.1.1.1⟩ Et antecedens probatur: Te esse est aliqualiter totaliter sicut haec significat. Ergo te esse est totaliter sicut haec significat. 35
Patet consequentia, ex eo quod ex opposito consequentis sequitur oppositum
antecedentis. Similiter sequitur in aliis 'Tu es quidam totus homo; ergo tu es
totus homo.'

⟨7.1.1.2⟩ Item te esse est totaliter. Et te esse haec significat. Ergo te esse est
totaliter sicut haec significat. Patet consequentia per hoc quod ly .sicut. est 40
terminus relativus. Ergo convertitur cum suo antecedente et nota copulationis,
ubi non sequitur terminus confundibilis per eandem—quod additur quia non
sequitur 'Sortes est sic fortis, et ita fortis est aliquis homo mundi; ergo Sortes
est ita fortis sicut aliquis homo mundi.'

Contra, ibi non est aliquis terminus confundibilis, quia bene sequitur. Unde 45
sequitur 'Sortes est sic fortis, et sic fortis est Plato; ergo Sortes est ita fortis sicut

Plato.' Sed tamen aliqualiter consequentia disparet, supposito quod Plato est
fortior Sorte.

⟨7.1.1.3⟩ Item te esse est totale significatum illius 'Tu es asinus.' Ergo te esse
est totaliter sicut haec significat. Consequentia est nota. Et similiter antecedens.

5   ⟨7.1.1.4⟩ Item te esse est aliqualiter sicut haec significat. Ergo te esse est
totaliter sicut haec significat. Patet consequentia, quia qualitercumque est
totaliter est aliqualiter, et e converso. Ergo etc.

⟨7.1.2⟩ Item aliqualiter totaliter sicut haec significat, est. Ergo totaliter (f.
107va) sicut haec significat, est. Tenet consequentia a particulari ad eius indefini-
10   tam 'Sicut haec significat etc.', eo quod dempto signo particulari, remanet propositio indefinita sibi correspondens.

⟨*Octava conclusio*⟩

     8a conclusio: Non si aliqua propositio est vera, ita est totaliter sicut ipsa
     significat.

15   Ista satis patet per superius dicta. Similiter dico quod ⟨si⟩ haec propositio 'Deus
est' cras praecise significat solem esse omnino, patet istam consequentiam non
valere 'Haec "Deus est" est vera; ergo ita est totaliter sicut ipsa significat'—
demonstrando per ly .ita. Deum esse.

⟨*Nona conclusio*⟩

                              *   *   *

20 ⟨*Definitiones cuiusdam auctoris*⟩

     Circa istam materiam aliqui ponunt aliquas definitiones propositionis quarum
prima patet ex ista:

     ⟨1⟩ Propositio affirmativa vera de praeterito est propositio quae praecise
     significat primo et affirmative sicut fuit.

25   *2a definitio*: Propositio affirmativa vera de futuro est propositio quae
     praecise significat primo et affirmative sicut erit.

     3a definitio: Propositio negativa de praesenti de inesse [est] quae significat
     primo et negative sicut non est, est propositio vera.

⟨*Contra definitiones*⟩

30   Contra primam et secundam definitiones arguitur: Nam datis istis sequitur
ista conclusio 'Propositio vera est propositio falsa.' Quod sic arguitur: Et signo
istam propositionem 'Hoc fuit'—demonstrando *B* quod fuit. Tunc haec est
vera, ut patet. Et quod haec est falsa arguitur: Haec est affirmativa de praeterito
quae praecise significat primo et affirmative sicut non fuit. Ergo haec est falsa.
35   Patet consequentia (f. 107vb) iuxta descriptionem datam. Assumptum probatur:
Haec praecise significat primo et affirmative hoc fuisse. Et hoc fuisse non fuit eo
quod numquam fuit hoc fuisse, quia nec in *B* instanti nec ante *B* instans, nec
post, ut patet deducenti.

     Contra tertiam definitionem arguitur: Nam data ipsa, sequitur ista conclusio
40   quod ista 'Deus non est' est vera. Probatur: Omnis propositio negativa de
praesenti et de inesse, quae praecise et primo negative significat sicut non est,
est propositio vera. Sed ista 'Deus non est' est huiusmodi. Igitur est vera. Discursus patet in Darii. Et minor probatur pro hac particula quod haec significat

praecise primo sicut non est. Nam haec significat praecise primo negative Deum non esse. Et Deum non esse non est. Igitur etc.

Item aliqua propositio negativa de praesenti vera praecise significat primo negative sicut est. Ergo definitio nulla. Antecedens probatur: Et capiatur ista 'Deus non est sol.' Tunc haec praecise significat primo negative sicut est. Et 5 haec est propositio negativa de praesenti vera. Ergo propositio negativa de praesenti vera praecise significat primo negative sicut est. Antecedens pro secunda parte patet. Et pro prima parte arguitur: Haec praecise significat primo negative Deum non esse solem. Et Deum non esse solem est. Ergo haec praecise significat primo negative sicut est. Patet consequens iuxta istos. Et antecedens 10 est superius probatum.

⟨*Opinio alterius auctoris*⟩

Circa istam materiam alii* dicunt quod aliqua propositio

⟨1⟩ Eo quod praecise quod est significat esse, vel quod non est significat non esse, est propositio affirmativa vel negativa vera de praesenti. 15

Et

⟨2⟩ Ex eo quod propositio significat quod erit fore, vel quod non erit non fore, est propositio affirmativa vel negativa vera de futuro.

Et consimiliter est de propositione de praeterito, variando differentias temporis. Ita quod sic opinantes concedunt istas consequentias 'Deus est, et haec propositio 20 praecise Deum esse significat; igitur haec est vera' et 'Nulla chimaera est, et haec "Nulla chimaera est" praecise nullam chimaeram esse significat; igitur haec est vera.' Et ulterius dicunt et concedunt quod nullam chimaeram esse est necessario, et tamen non est necessarium nullam chimaeram esse; et quod hominem esse asinum est impossibile, et non impossibile est hominem esse asinum. Ulterius 25 ponunt isti descriptiones propositionis verae vel falsae:

⟨*1a descriptio*⟩: Omnis propositio vera praecise verum significat determinate vel definite, et omnis propositio definite sive finite praecise verum significans est propositio vera.

Ita quod sequitur 'Praecise verum significat haec propositio; ergo haec propositio 30 est vera' et e contra.

⟨*Alia descriptio*⟩: Omnis propositio falsum significans est propositio falsa, et e contra.

Et ulterius ponunt isti intellectum istius propositionis 'In eo quod res est vel non est, est propositio vera vel falsa . . .', supponendo quod ly .eo. dicit circumstantiam 35 causae: in eo quod res est postquam non fuit, sive per mutationem ad esse rei, est propositio significans rem esse vera postquam fuit falsa; et in eo quod res non est, id est in eo quod mutatio est ab non esse rei ad esse, est propositio falsa postquam non fuit falsa.

⟨*Contra istam opinionem*⟩ 40

Contra istam rationem (f. 108ra) quoad istas particulas: Quod nullam chi-maeram esse est necessarium, et quod hominem esse asinum est impossibile, et similes sufficienter argutum est superius in primo tractatu. Verumtamen arguitur adhuc contra eas: Nam sicut iam non est nec potest esse, nullam chimaeram esse

* Cf. Feribrigge, *Logica*, Pars I, c. 3 (Appendix I, pp. 229–31).

non est nec potest esse. Ergo qua ratione chimaeram esse non necessarium, per idem nullam chimaeram esse non est necessarium.

Si dicitur quod non est simile, pro tanto quia nulla propositio necessaria significat nullam chimaeram esse—contra, ex hoc sequitur quod contingens est
5 necessarium. Probatur: Te esse vel te non esse est necessarium. Et qualitercumque est te esse vel te non esse, est contingens. Ergo contingens est necessarium. Discursus patet. Et minor probatur: Qualitercumque est te esse est contingens. Et te non esse non est, nec potest esse. Ergo qualitercumque est te esse vel te non esse, est contingens.
10 Item concessa 'Hominem esse asinum est impossibile', sequitur quod ex negativa sequitur affirmativa. Probatur: Nam ista nulla ratione conceditur nisi quia sequitur 'Hominem esse asinum non est possibile; igitur hominem esse asinum est impossibile.' Sed constat quod antecedens est mere negativum et consequens affirmativum. Et per consequens consequentia non valet.
15 Item contra definitionem propositionis verae arguitur: Aliqua propositio vera non praecise verum significat. Ergo definitio nulla. Assumptum probatur: Aliqua propositio vera hominem esse asinum significat. Ergo aliqua propositio vera non praecise verum significat. Patet consequentia. Et antecedens patet de ista 'Homo est animal' et similiter de ista disiunctiva 'Homo est asinus vel nullus
20 homo est asinus.' Contra secundam definitionem arguitur sic: Aliqua propositio falsum significans est vera. Ergo descriptio nulla. Patet consequentia. Et antecedens patet de praedictis duabus propositionibus. Et patet totum per superius dicta.

Item contra hoc quod dicit istum modum arguendi convertibiliter tenere
25 'Deus est, et haec propositio "Deus est" praecise Deum esse significat; igitur haec est vera.' Nam non sequitur 'Homo est animal, et praecise hominem esse animal haec "Antichristus est animal" significat; igitur haec "Antichristus est animal" est vera.' Et quod non sequitur, probatur: Nam antecedens istius consequentiae est verum. Et consequens eiusdem est falsum. Ergo etc. Et quod
30 antecedens est verum pro prima parte patet apud istos. Et secunda pars probatur: Praecise Antichristum esse animal haec significat. Ergo praecise hominem esse animal haec significat. Patet consequentia apud omnes ex quo arguitur ab inferiori ad suum superius affirmative a parte subiecti in quantum totale extremum dictione exclusiva immediate praecedente. Nam sequitur generaliter
35 'Tantum Antichristus currit; igitur tantum homo currit', 'Tantum homo currit; igitur tantum animal currit', et sic discurrendo per omnia. Et antecedens istius consequentiae est verum apud sic ponentes. Ergo etc.

⟨*Decima conclusio*⟩

    10a conclusio: Si Deus est, et haec propositio—quacumque demonstrata—
40   est propositio una significans primo quod Deus est, haec propositio est vera.

Et dicitur bene 'una' propter propositiones multiplices.

⟨*Undecima conclusio*⟩

    11a conclusio: Non si Deus est, et haec propositio 'Deus est' significat primo
45   Deum esse, haec propositio est vera.

Probatur: Nam dato quod esset una virtus infinitae potentiae activae, producens propositionem simplicem per quam intelligitur primo tam Deum esse, quam chimaeram esse, haec propositio esset falsa, ut patet. Et de tali non sequeretur 'Deus est, et haec propositio significat primo Deum esse; ergo haec propositio est vera.' (f. 108rb)   5

⟨*Duodecima conclusio*⟩

    12a conclusio: Si Sortes fuit, et haec propositio est una significans primo quod Sortes fuit, haec propositio est vera.

⟨*Tertiadecima conclusio*⟩

    13a conclusio: Si Sortes erit, et haec propositio est una significans primo 10 quod Sortes erit, haec propositio est vera.

⟨*Quartadecima conclusio*⟩

    14a conclusio: Si nulla chimaera est, et haec propositio est una significans primo quod nulla chimaera est, haec propositio est vera.

*   *   *

NOTES TO *ON THE TRUTH AND FALSITY OF PROPOSITIONS*

Chapter *1*

p. 5 n. a Unless one follows the edition, so that Thesis 2 states that 'it is a *necessary* and sufficient condition', nothing in the theses will entail the second part of Corollary 2—'and false when they do supposit for the same thing'—which, Paul claims, follows from the theses of this opinion. This reading is further justified by the fact that the author of this opinion, Albert of Saxony, does think that it is a necessary, as well as a sufficient, condition of the truth of a negative proposition that its subject and predicate do not supposit for the same thing. The edition states no proof for Thesis 2. But since proofs are given for the other three theses, we have followed the manuscript in stating one. The proof is only a proof that it is a 'sufficient condition', however, since, according to the manuscript, Thesis 2 states only that it is a 'sufficient condition'. The corresponding proof that it is a 'necessary condition' would be as follows: It is a sufficient condition of the truth of an affirmative proposition that they supposit for the same thing. Therefore, it is a necessary condition of the truth of a negative proposition opposite to it, that they do not supposit for the same thing. The latter argument could be based on Thesis 1, however, only if Thesis 1 stated that it is a sufficient, as well as a necessary, condition of the truth of an affirmative proposition that its subject and predicate supposit for the same thing—a claim to which Albert of Saxony certainly subscribes. Thus, it may be that the texts of both the manuscript and the edition are defective here.

p. 5 n. b Paul defines '*suppositio*' by saying that '*suppositio* is the signification of a term . . . for something or some things in a proposition . . .' (*Logica Magna*, Part I, 'On the *Suppositio* of Terms', fol. 16ra, lin. 30–3 (ed.)). Confused and distributive *suppositio* is a division of personal *suppositio*, which Paul describes as follows: 'Confused distributive *suppositio* is divided into mobile and immobile *suppositio*. Confused, distributive mobile *suppositio* is the signification of a common term under which one can descend, given the proper means of inference, to the conjunction of all of its singulars, and conversely, given the same means of inference. For this follows: This animal runs and that animal runs and so on for the other singulars, and these are all of the animals; therefore every animal runs. Conversely, this follows, given the same minor premiss: Every animal runs, and these are all of the animals; therefore this animal runs and that animal runs and so on for the other singulars.' Terms following 'as' have confused, distributive mobile *suppositio* (see *Logica Magna*, Part I, 'On the Expression "As" ', fol. 42ra–b (ed.)).

p. 7 n. c 'Discretely' here may be an allusion to the fact that the author of this opinion gives two types of criteria for the truth or falsity of propositions: Theses 1 and 2 specify criteria of truth in terms of the relative *suppositiones* of the subject and predicate terms in propositions, whereas Theses 3 and 4 specify criteria in terms of a characteristic of the signification of a proposition.

p. 7 n. d Counter-Thesis 1 is a denial of Thesis 1 of this opinion.

p. 9 n. e That is, from the false propositions 'People are not people' and 'Socrates and Plato are not men.' The extremes of these propositions do not supposit for the same thing (singular) because they supposit for the same things (plural).

p. 9 n. f Against the proof of Thesis 1.

p. 9 n. g Against the proof of Thesis 3.

p. 9 n. h Against Thesis 4.

p. 9 n. i In *Logica Magna*, Part I, 'On Terms', c. 2 'Naturally Significant and Arbitrarily Significant Terms', Paul notes that 'The third opinion, which is acceptable as compared with the others, maintains that each term signifies its superior and anything inferior to it, *per se* as well as *per accidens*' (fol. 6va, lin. 38–40 (ed.); Kretzmann transl.). He goes on to say that '. . . When it is said that each term signifies anything superior to it and anything inferior to it, this must not be understood to mean that each term signifies each significatum of its superior or of its inferior term. The term "man" does not signify donkey or cow, each of which is the significatum of the term "animal", nor does it signify stone or wood, each of which is a significatum of the term "body". Similarly, the term "white man" is inferior to the term "man", but "man" does not signify whiteness, which "white man" does signify. The opinion is therefore to be understood to mean that each term secondarily signifies whatever its superior or inferior term primarily signifies. Thus, the term "man" secondarily signifies animal and, consequently, the term "animal" primarily signifies it as well. Likewise the term "white man" primarily signifies white man, and "man" secondarily signifies the same thing' (ibid., fol. 6vb, lin. 38–51 (ed.); Kretzmann transl.). Since Paul thinks that a proposition 'signifies by the composition of its parts' (see p. 11), it is easy to see why he thinks 'A man is an animal' signifies that a man is a donkey. 'Animal' secondarily signifies what 'donkey' primarily signifies: viz. a donkey. Therefore, '. . . the proposition "A man is an animal" signifies that a man is a donkey not primarily but secondarily' (*Logica Magna*, Part I, 'On Terms', c. 3, fol. 10vb, lin. 29–30 (ed.); Kretzmann transl.). Again, Paul says, 'Similarly, take the proposition "A man is an animal". It is true and yet it signifies infinitely many falsities. For it signifies that a man is a donkey, a goat, a lion, and so on, each of which is false' (ibid., fol. 4vb, lin. 49–52 (ed.); Kretzmann transl.).

p. 9 n. j I use fused participles ('a man being a donkey' and 'God existing') rather than that-clauses ('that a man is a donkey' and 'that God is') to translate the accusative plus the infinitive, because it better preserves the ambiguities of Paul's argument.

p. 11 n. k According to Paul's usage, a sentence-nominalization corresponding to a spoken or written proposition is the name of the adequate significatum of the proposition ('On the Truth and Falsity of Propositions', ch. 7, pp. 55, 57). Thus, 'God existing or a man being a donkey' names the adequate significatum of 'God is or a man is a donkey.' And Paul's claim that 'God is or a man is a donkey' signifies *God existing or a man being a donkey* is thus correct. What is at issue, however, is not whether the proposition signifies *God existing or a man being a donkey*, but whether it signifies *God existing*, or signifies *a man being a donkey*. Paul derives an affirmative answer to the latter from an affirmative answer to the former, by means of the principle that a whole signifies by the composition of its parts. ('On the Truth and Falsity of Propositions', ch. 1, proof of Counter-Thesis 4, p. 11; ch. 2, pp. 17, 19; 'On the Significatum of a Proposition', ch. 9, Thesis 5, pp. 197–9.)

p. 11 n. l Counter-Thesis 4 is a denial of Corollary 1 of the First Way.

p. 11 n. m In *Sophismata*, ch. 8, 'Insolubles', John Buridan says that he used to hold that every categorical proposition signifies itself to be true. But he argues against it using an argument similar to Paul's. (See *Sophisms on Meaning and Truth*, translated by T. K. Scott, New York, 1964, pp. 194–5.)

p. 11 n. n This is against the proof of Thesis 1.

p. 11 n. o This is a denial of Corollary 2 of Thesis 4.

p. 11 n. p This is a supposition which Paul rejects. See his discussion of Counter-Thesis 7 below.

p. 13 n. q Counter-Thesis 6 is a denial of Corollary 3.

p. 13 n. r Paul similarly spells out what it is for 'chimera' to signify, in terms of a counterfactual: 'I say that the mental term *chimera* does signify a chimera because of a certain association and resemblance. As for the argument—There is no resemblance between the intention and a chimera; therefore, etc.—I reject the inference. Although the mental term *chimera* does not signify a chimera because of an association and resemblance which is, it is enough that it signifies a chimera because of an association and resemblance which there would be if a chimera existed . . .' (*Logica Magna*, Part I, 'On Terms', ch. 2, fol. 5rb, lin. 32–7 (ed.); Kretzmann transl.).

p. 15 n. s This proof depends on the fact that it is contrary to revelation to deny that the Antichrist will be. Hence, Albert will not want to admit that the second part of the conjunctive proposition is true. And, by his own rules, he can avoid this only by allowing that 'Antichrist' supposits for something in the first part of the conjunctive proposition.

p. 15 n. t Ampliation is the expansion of the natural or normal *suppositio* of a common term by means of certain verbs or verbs taken together with certain modifiers. If the natural *suppositio* of 'man' is taken to be every extant individual man, then the term 'will be' or 'is future' produces an ampliation—an enlargement—in the *suppositio*, so that 'man' supposits for every individual man that does or will exist; 'was' or 'is past', so that 'man' supposits for every individual man that either does exist or did exist; 'can', or 'is possibly', so that 'man' supposits for every individual man that either does or can exist (see *Logica Magna*, Part I, 'On the *Suppositio* of Terms', fol. 25va, lin. 21–45, 25vb, lin. 38–72 (ed.)).

p. 15 n. u The saying that in past- and future-tense propositions and in modal propositions of possibility, 'the predicate appellates its own form' was already referred to as an 'ancient' saying by Walter Burleigh (*Tractatus De Proprietatibus Terminorum, Secunda Pars, De appellatione*, ed. Philotheus Boehner, St. Bonaventure, N.Y., 1955, p. 49) and was accordingly given 'reverent' and therefore different interpretations by disagreeing logicians. Paul quotes Albert's explanation of the saying here. According to it, to say that the predicate 'an animal' appellates its own form in the future-tense proposition 'Socrates will be an animal', is to say that the present-tense proposition 'This is an animal' (where 'this' indicates Socrates) will be true at some time.

None of this shows that the author of this opinion should, to be consistent, agree that 'chimera' supposits for something in 'A chimera is believed in' or 'A chimera is thought of.' For, although Albert of Saxony allows that verbs such as 'think of', 'know', 'cognize', and 'signify' ampliate the *suppositio* over past, present, and future time, as well as over possibles, he does not say that the *suppositio* is ampliated over impossibles. And a chimera is impossible.

Chapter 2

p. 17 n. a In discussing exclusives of the fourth order, Paul says that 'no proposition in the world signifies precisely as things are. Nor does any proposition signify precisely otherwise than things are. For every false proposition signifies an infinite number of truths; and every true proposition, an infinite number of falsehoods' (*Logica Magna*, Part I, 'On Exclusives', fol. 35ra, lin. 21–4 (ed.)). The latter is

a consequence of Paul's views about primary and secondary signification, outlined above, p. 9 n. i.

Of course, if no proposition signifies precisely as things are, the proposition 'if *A* signifies precisely as things are, *A* is true' will be true for every *A* because of the falsity of the antecedent. But it will also follow that a proposition's signifying precisely as things are cannot serve as a criterion of truth, as adherents of the Second Way claim it will.

p. 17 n. b For their exposition, see the first proof of their Thesis above.

p. 17 n. c Paul elaborates this point in *Logica Magna*, Part I, 'On Terms', where he distinguishes between spoken or written terms' being significant (which they are provided that the appropriate conventions exist) and their actually signifying: '. . . a term is significant even while it is not actually signifying. On this basis it is granted that there are many truths in a closed book—not because they are actually signifying, but because they will be significant of what is true when they have been apprehended, and without any new imposition. Otherwise it follows that you make the Gospel and the whole of Sacred Scripture true whenever you wish, and anew, simply by opening such a closed book and considering the things written down in it. By closing that book you would consequently destroy the whole of Sacred Scripture and the Gospel truth, which sounds less good. Thus in accordance with ordinary usage one thing is called actually true, another potentially true. A thing actually true is what I call a proposition actually signifying primarily *per se* what is true—e.g. "A man is an animal"—provided that this is signifying in that way to someone. But a thing potentially true is what I call not simply what can be true, but rather something written, spoken, or mental not actually being apprehended, which although it is not now signifying either will signify hereafter without any new imposition or is naturally suited to signify' (ibid., fol. 5vb, lin. 43–60 (ed.); Kretzmann transl.).

p. 21 n. d The first premiss is 'There being no chimera, is not the cause by which it is that no chimera is.'

p. 21 n. e According to Paul, in *Logica Magna*, Part II, 'On Categorical Propositions', fol. 104ra, lin. 20–fol. 104rb, lin. 45 (ed.), negative categorical propositions can be divided into pregnant negative categorical propositions and non-pregnant negative categorical propositions. The former include 'any exponible negative proposition from which any of the propositions expounding it, follows by a formal inference'. Propositions of this sort include exclusives, reduplicatives in which the exclusive term or note of reduplication is not denied, proper negative exceptive propositions, and other negative mobile exponible propositions in which the term having mobile *suppositio* is not denied. Non-pregnant negative categorical propositions include any negative categorical proposition that is not exponible or that is not a proposition of the above-mentioned sorts. He later goes on to explain that it is only from non-pregnant negative categorical propositions that affirmative categoricals without any modal term, do not follow. For from a pregnant negative categorical, any of the propositions that expound it follow by a formal inference. Sometimes the expounding propositions include affirmative propositions of the second or third adjacent. For example, the propositions 'Socrates exists' and 'Socrates is running' follow by a formal inference from, and are among the propositions that expound 'No man but Socrates is running.'

p. 25 n. f I shall occasionally italicize sentence-nominalizations in order to make it clear where they begin and end. The italicization does not indicate that the sentence-nominalizations are being mentioned rather than used. This is always indicated by quotation marks or by setting the expression off on a line by itself.

p. 25 n. ǧ Paul's remarks here are based on his own view of what (if anything) the significatum of a proposition is. See 'On the Significatum of a Proposition', Fifth Opinion, chs. 5–8, pp. 123–91.

Chapter 3

p. 25 n. a This thesis is not, as Paul suggests, the converse of the thesis of the Second Way. For in Latin the antecedents of the theses of the Second and Third Ways have the same subject and predicate terms, and their consequents are the same. They differ in word order. As a result of this difference, the antecedent of the thesis of the Second Way is an exclusive of the fourth order; but the antecedent of the thesis of the Third Way is an exclusive of the first order, since the exclusive term 'precisely' governs both the subject and the predicate term (*Logica Magna*, Part I, 'On Exclusives', fol. 34ra, lin. 49–59 (ed.); see p. 45 n. e below). Master Richard Feribrigge makes something of this difference in word order and the resultant difference in expositions in his discussions of these opinions (see 'On the Truth of Categorical Propositions', First Part of the First Chapter, fol. 79vb).

In the First and Second Ways, I have translated '*sicut est*' as 'as things are', since this makes the meaning clearer. In translating the Third Way, however, I have translated '*sicut est*' as 'the way it is' instead, in an effort to imitate the ambiguities of the Latin on which many of the arguments offered by a certain Master against the Third Way turn. Since in the end Paul thinks this view can be refuted by the same arguments that refuted the Second Way (see pp. 17–25), his main objective in discussing the Third Way seems to be to reject the other Master's critique of it.

p. 27 n. b This Master's arguments against the Third Way depend on a certain ambiguity in the Latin sentence '*Praecise sicut est significans est A propositio falsa.*' If it is punctuated after the first '*est*' ('*Praecise sicut est, significans est A propositio falsa*'), then it is equivalent to (i) 'The false proposition A signifies precisely as things are.' On the other hand, if it is punctuated after '*significans*' ('*Praecise sicut est significans, est A propositio falsa*'), it is equivalent to (ii) 'It is precisely in so far as A is a sign that A is a false proposition.' Understanding a comma after 'sign'—(iii) 'Precisely the way it is a sign, is A a false proposition'— it can be understood as equivalent to (ii). Understanding a comma after the first 'is' and an 'of' after 'precisely'—(iv) 'Precisely of the way it is, a sign is A, a false proposition'—it can be taken as equivalent to (i). I shall not supply either the commas or the 'of', however, in order to preserve the ambiguity of the sentence.

As Paul notes on pp. 29, 31 this argument turns on a fallacy of ambiguity. The inference is valid only if the premiss is understood as (iv). But the subsequent proof of the premiss establishes only (iii). Further, the premiss is true, only when it is understood as (iii).

p. 27 n. c Paul locates the flaw of this proof in the second inference (see pp. 29, 31 below). The first conclusion—'The way it is a sign is A a false proposition'— follows and is true if it means that it is in so far as proposition A is a sign, and not in so far as it is anything else, that A is false. But interpreted in this way, 'a sign' is taken together with 'the way it is' (as in (iii) in p. 27 n. b above) and not together with the principal copula. The second inference to 'The way it is, is signified by A, a false proposition, and it is not so that the way it is not is signified by A, a false proposition' presupposes that 'a sign' is taken together with the main verb (as in (iv) in p. 27 n. b).

p. 27 n. d That is, the inference from 'Not: the way it is, is signified by A, a false proposition' to 'Not: the way it is a sign is A a false proposition.'

p. 27 n. e Once again, Paul points out in his critique (on pp. 29–31) that the inference is a simple conversion only if 'a sign' in the conclusion is taken together, not with the principal copula, but with 'precisely the way it is' (as it is in (iii) in p. 27 n. b above).

p. 27 n. f The pretended inference here is from 'Some C is D' or 'Something that is C is D' to 'C is D'. Paul criticizes this Master's application of the rule on pp. 31, 33.

p. 29 n. g The assumption is plausible if one thinks, as Paul does, that propositions signify by the composition of their parts and that a term (secondarily) signifies whatever its inferior or superior term primarily signifies (see p. 9 n. i above). Accordingly, Paul grants this assumption (see p. 33).

p. 29 n. h The pretended inference here is from 'Every C is D' to 'Precisely D is C.' Paul argues that the inference here is not actually an instance of this rule (see p. 33).

p. 29 n. i That is, from 'Precisely the way it is a sign is A a false proposition' to 'Therefore, the way it is a sign is A a false proposition, and not the way it is not a sign is A a false proposition' (p. 27 above).

p. 31 n. j The inference would hold if 'sign' were taken with the principal copula as 'part of the predicate'—'⟨Of⟩ the way it is not, a sign is A, a false proposition.' But on the present assumption that 'sign' is 'part of the subject' so that the conclusion is 'The way it is a sign, is A a false proposition', the inference fails.

p. 31 n. k Paul says that the proposition 'Precisely the way it is a sign is A a false proposition' has no quantity, because it is an exclusive of the first order (see p. 25 n. a above) and he has argued that 'no exclusive of the first order has any quantity' (*Logica Magna*, Part II, 'On the Quantity of Propositions', fols. 107vb–113rb). He notes that if exclusives of the first order were of any quantity, they would have to be either universal, particular, indefinite, or singular. He then proceeds to argue that, given his definitions of what it is for a proposition to be universal, particular, indefinite, or singular, respectively, exclusives of the first order fit none of them and hence have no quantity.

p. 31 n. l Paul grants 'Something precisely the way it is a sign, is A a false proposition' because it asserts that something is the false proposition A, precisely in so far as that thing is a sign. He does not grant 'Something ⟨that is⟩ precisely ⟨of⟩ the way it is, a sign is A, a false proposition', because that proposition asserts that A signifies precisely the way it is.

p. 33 n. m Paul's point is that the Master whose arguments he is attacking must, in order to defend his inferences, suppose that the inference from 'Some C is D' or 'Something that is C is D' to 'C is D' and from 'Some C is' to 'C is' are valid, not only where 'C' and 'D' are non-complex terms such as 'man' and 'animal', but also where 'C' and 'D' are compounds of a syncategorematic together with a categorematic term. On that assumption, 'Something that is only God is' will entail 'Only God is', where 'C' is 'only God'—which is absurd.

p. 33 n. n The rule appealed to in this Master's argument was that 'Every C is D; therefore precisely D is C' is a good inference. The rule is sound, if 'C' and 'D' are interpreted correctly. But what it warrants is an inference from 'Every false proposition signifies (i.e. is a sign of) the way it is' to 'Precisely a sign of the way it is, is a false proposition', and not to 'Precisely the way it is, a false proposition signifies'—the conclusion this Master draws.

p. 33 n. o This claim is puzzling, since for all Paul has said, it would seem that

A signifies that you are Socrates and *B* signifies that you are Plato. Since every proposition signifies by the composition of its parts, the conjunction of *A* and *B* would signify that you are Socrates and that you are Plato.

Paul has evidently neglected to lay down the case that the conjunction of *A* and *B* actually signifies only some truth to someone and that it does not actually signify its adequate significatum. When such a case has been laid down, Paul's argument here parallels those he gave in defence of Counter-Thesis 1, against the Second Way.

Chapter 4

p. 37 n. a Paul's main criticism of the Fourth Way rests on his understanding of the distinction between the categorematic and syncategorematic uses of '*totaliter*' or 'wholly'. This distinction parallels that between the categorematic and syn-categorematic uses of '*totus*' or 'whole' which Paul explains in *Logica Magna*, Part I. Briefly, '*totus*' is taken syncategorematically when it governs the principal copula of the proposition, and categorematically when it does not govern the principal copula of the proposition. It cannot govern the principal copula either (i) if it is placed after it in the proposition, as it is in 'A runner is Socrates as a whole'; or (ii) if it occurs before the principal copula but after another syncate-gorematic word, as it does in 'Some Socrates as a whole is a man.' In its categore-matic sense, Paul says, it is equivalent to 'something' or 'being', so that 'Some Socrates as a whole is a man' is equivalent to 'Some human being is Socrates' or 'Someone who is some Socrates, is a man' (ibid., fol. 57rb, lin. 6–12 (ed.)). It occurs in its syncategorematic sense if it occurs before the principal copula and is not preceded by some syncategorematic word. So understood, it is equivalent to 'whatever quantitative or integral part of'. Thus, it occurs syncategorematically in 'The whole of this wood is combustible', which is equivalent to 'Every integral part of this wood is combustible' (ibid., fol. 56ra, lin. 27–38 (ed.)). Paul thus ties the distinction between categorematic and syncategorematic occurrences of '*totus*' to word order.

When adherents of the Fourth Way advance the thesis that if things are so wholly as a proposition signifies, the proposition is true, they doubtless intended the 'wholly' to be taken syncategorematically. So understood, the thesis would assert that if things are so however the proposition signifies, the proposition is true. Or, more simply, it asserts that if all of the significata of a proposition are true, the proposition is true. On this interpretation, the Fourth Way would not differ sig-nificantly from the Second and Third Ways. And Paul would reject this claim on the ground that every proposition signifies infinitely many falsehoods. (See p. 17 n. a above.)

Paul takes their statement of the thesis at face value, however. Since 'wholly' occurs in it after the principal copula, Paul insists that it cannot be taken syncate-gorematically but only categorematically. So understood, the thesis asserts that if some significatum of the proposition is true, the proposition is true. Given Paul's doctrines of primary and secondary signification and his distinction between being significant and actually signifying, this claim is obviously false.

The soundness of Paul's criticism is questionable, however, since his tying the distinction between categorematic and syncategorematic uses of 'wholly' to word order seems arbitrary. Peter of Spain (*Summulae Logicales, Tractatus Distributionum*, ed. J. P. Mullaly, Notre Dame, 1945, pp. 90–4), William Ockham (*Summa Logicae*, Part II, ch. 6, ed. Philotheus Boehner, Gedeon Gál, and Stephen Brown, St. Bonaventure, 1974, pp. 267–9), and Walter Burleigh, (*De Puritate Artis Logicae, Tractatus Brevior*, Part I, Particula II, ed. Boehner, p. 256), all distinguish these uses of '*totus*', but none of them links the different senses with word order.

p. 37 n. b In this first set of criticisms labelled (1.1), Paul understands 'so' to be interchangeable with 'true'.

p. 39 n. c The second, third, and fourth arguments conclude only that *that such and such* 'is wholly as *A* signifies' and not *that such and such* 'is wholly *so* as *A* signifies'. Paul evidently does not think they are equivalent, since in the first argument he takes the trouble to infer the latter from the former by means of an additional premiss 'That you are, is so.' Probably, he thinks that having argued this once, he does not have to re-establish it each time.

p. 39 n. d The mistake here is that there is a shift from a categorematic to a syncategorematic use of 'as a whole' in the inference from the premiss to the conclusion. The premiss is equivalent to 'A runner is some Socrates.' The conclusion, however, implies that each part of Socrates is a runner. See p. 37 n. a.

p. 41 n. e Similarly, these inferences fail because of a fallacy of equivocation: in the premiss, although the 'wholly' and 'as a whole' precede the copula, they are preceded by another syncategorematic term and therefore must be taken categorematically. In the conclusion, however, they occur before the copula and are not preceded by another syncategorematic term. Hence they must be taken syncategorematically.

p. 41 n. f In the arguments labelled (1.2), Paul does not take 'so' to be interchangeable with 'true', but rather understands it to indicate the proposition's adequate significatum. Part of the point of this criticism is that adherents of the Fourth Way should explicitly specify how 'so' is to be understood, if they wish to buttress their position against such refutations.

Chapter 5

p. 43 n. a '*aliquid*', translated as 'something', is used by the author of this opinion for concreta: some really existing mode or substance. '*res*', translated 'thing', is used more broadly for whatever can be thought of.

p. 43 n. b The etymology is possibly correct for both English and Latin: cf. Lewis and Short's *Latin Dictionary*, s.v.: '[etym. dub.; perh. root ra- of reor, ratus; cf. Germ. Ding; Engl. thing, from denken, to think; prop., that which is thought of; cf. also *logos*, Lid. and Scott, 9]'.

p. 45 n. c Paul's criticism here seems fallacious. When the author of the Fifth Way says that if *A* precisely signifies that what is, is, *A* is true, he is not claiming that if *A*'s adequate significatum is correctly labelled by the that-clause 'that what is, is' or 'that this, which is, is', then *A* is true. Rather he means to say that if a proposition signifies *that this is* (where 'this' indicates something that is), it is true. The Fifth Way's claim is thus that 'You are running' is true because it signifies that this is (where 'this' indicates something that is—viz. you running).

Even if Paul had correctly construed the theses of the Fifth Way, however, he would have rejected them. For the adequate significatum of 'You are running' is named by its sentence-nominalization. And the sentence-nominalization of 'You are running' is neither 'that this is' nor 'that *that you are running*, is', but 'that you are running' or 'you running'.

p. 45 n. d Note that according to the Christian doctrines of the general resurrection and life after death, both Caesar and the Antichrist will exist in the future.

p. 45 n. e Exclusive propositions are said to be of different orders depending on how much of the proposition falls within the scope of the exclusive term. According to Paul, in *Logica Magna*, Part I, 'On Exclusives', '. . . an exclusive proposition of the first order is one in which the exclusive term governs, whether implicitly or

explicitly, both the subject and the predicate of the exclusive proposition. For example, "Only a man runs", "Only a man does not run."

'An exclusive proposition of the second order is one in which the exclusive term governs, whether implicitly or explicitly, the predicate as a whole together with the copula. For example, "This man only runs", "This only does not run."

'A proposition of the third order is said to be one in which the exclusive term governs only the predicate. For example "You are only a man".

'An exclusive proposition of the fourth order is one in which the exclusive term governs only part of the predicate or part of the subject. For example, "I see only Socrates", "Proposition A signifies precisely as things are."

'An exclusive proposition of the fifth order is one in which the exclusive term is placed at the end. For example, "You are thus only or precisely" . . .' (fol. 34ra, lin. 17-59 (ed.)).

p. 45 n. f The Second, Third, Fourth, and Fifth Ways all try to arrive at a criterion of truth by identifying some characteristic feature of the significata of true propositions that distinguishes them from false ones. The feature the first three of these focus on and try with varying success to formulate is that of signifying as things are and not signifying as things are not. Paul's reaction is that if by 'signifying' they mean 'is significant of' (see p. 17 n. c), the condition is too strong, in that it cannot be satisfied by any proposition. For, according to Paul, every proposition signifies infinitely many truths and infinitely many falsehoods (see p. 9 n. i). If by 'signifying' they mean 'actually signifying to someone', then the condition is both too strong and too weak. For a true proposition may actually signify only falsehoods to someone; and a false proposition may actually signify only truths to someone.

The sufficient condition suggested by the Fifth Way differs from those of the Second and Third Ways, in that it is an exclusive of the second, as opposed to the fourth or first order. This makes a substantial difference to its meaning. Focusing on this fact, Paul argues that the condition suggested by the Fifth Way is too weak. For 'A precisely signifies that what is, is' means merely that A is not a not-sign, but a sign that what is, is. All false propositions meet this condition. For they are all signs, and not not-signs, of infinitely many truths, although it is not the case that they signify precisely truths.

p. 45 n. g Notice that Paul's inference does hold good here, since 'A precisely signifies that that man runs' is an exclusive of the *second* order. For as such it means merely that A is not a not-sign, but a sign of that man running. Given Paul's doctrine of primary and secondary signification, it does indeed follow that A is not a not-sign, but a sign of a man running. The corresponding inference for exclusives of the *fourth* order—from 'A signifies precisely that that man runs' to 'A signifies precisely that a man runs'—does not hold good, however.

p. 47 n. h Again, as an exclusive of the second order, 'You precisely see Socrates' is expounded by 'You see Socrates' and 'You are not a non-beholder of Socrates', from which 'You see a man' and 'You are not a non-beholder of a man' follow respectively.

p. 47 n. i The consequent, 'It is precisely a sign of the truth' is an exclusive of the third order. According to Paul, 'An affirmative exclusive proposition of the third order is expounded as an affirmative exclusive of the second order is. Thus, the proposition "You are only a man" is expounded this way: "You are a man and you are not a not-man" . . .' (*Logica Magna*, Part I, 'On Exclusives', fol. 34vb, lin. 61-4 (ed.)). Accordingly, 'It is precisely a sign of the truth' is expounded by 'It is a sign of the truth' and 'It is not a not-sign of the truth'—which is, of course, compatible with 'It is precisely a sign of a falsehood', similarly expounded.

Chapter 6

p. 49 n. a It is difficult to understand how it is logically possible that a mental term or proposition should exist and fail to be significant. For Paul says, 'Some categorematic terms signify naturally and others arbitrarily. I call a term naturally significant which signifies something which it is impossible for it not to signify as long as it is significant.

'It is in this way that mental terms naturally signify themselves and their separate significata, for they cannot signify without primarily representing themselves and their separate significata to the understanding . . .' (*Logica Magna*, Part I, 'On Terms', c. 2, fol. 3vb, lin. 26–8 (ed.); Kretzmann transl.). If it is impossible that the mental term 'man' does not signify men so long as it is significant, and if 'a mental term signifies a thing because of association with and accidental resemblance to such a thing' (ibid., fol. 4ra, lin. 44–5 (ed.); Kretzmann transl.), it would seem that such a term could exist and fail to be significant only if it could exist and fail to be related to things by accidental resemblance. Yet Paul insists that for a term to be significant, this relation need not actually obtain; it suffices that it would obtain if certain relata existed. This suffices even if, as in the case of the term 'chimera', it is impossible that such relata (viz. chimeras) exist (see p. 13 n. r).

p. 51 n. b Paul has the following to say about arbitrarily significant signs: 'A term such as "man" or "animal" is said to signify arbitrarily, therefore, because it moves the understanding to conceive of something or other not as a result of association or resemblance (as does the mental term subordinate to it), but by institution, convention, or agreement . . .' (*Logica Magna*, Part I, 'On Terms', c. 2, fol. 4va, lin. 22–6 (ed.); Kretzmann transl.). Paul's assertion of Counter-Thesis 3 suggests that he would not agree with William Ockham (*Summa Logicae* I, c. 1, ed. Boehner, pp. 8–9, and *Commentary on Peri Hermeneias*, Prologue) in saying that they are conventions that written and spoken signs should signify what mental signs signify naturally.

p. 51 n. c This reason is unconvincing, since the fact that the adequate significatum might really exist and the spoken sounds or inscriptions really exist, and the latter not be propositions, does not show that the latter are not made propositions by being related to the adequate significatum. In fact, in his discussion of arbitrarily significant signs, Paul suggests that this is part of what the conventions accomplish (*Logica Magna*, Part I, 'On Terms', c. 2). Whether or not Paul can consistently claim that the mental entities that are mental propositions might exist and fail to be apt actually to signify their adequate significata has already been questioned in p. 49 n. a above.

Chapter 7

p. 51 n. a A multiplex proposition is one that has more than one meaning. Ambiguous propositions such as 'The house is near the bank' are multiplex.

p. 53 n. b This criticism does not seem fair. It is not true that every spoken or written proposition is unambiguous. Perhaps what Paul is getting at is that 'one' should be replaced by 'unambiguous'.

p. 53 n. c A proposition can signify that such-and-such prior to signifying that so-and-so, even if that so-and-so is the adequate significatum of that proposition, provided that the priority in question is a priority of nature or of duration (see Counter-Thesis 4, p. 55; see also 'On the Significatum of a Proposition', c. 9, Thesis 2, p. 193). The priority with which a proposition signifies its adequate significatum prior to its secondary significata is a priority of distinctness (see 'On the Significatum of a Proposition', c. 9, Thesis 4, pp. 195, 197).

p. 55 n. d Paul alludes here and elsewhere ('On the Significatum of a Proposition', ch. 4, p. 121) to a fairly common scholastic account of how God conceives of things. Although all agreed that God does not conceive of some things at a time before He conceives of others, but eternally and immutably thinks of whatever He thinks of, nevertheless a number of philosophers (e.g. Aquinas, Henry of Ghent, and Duns Scotus) thought they could distinguish a natural priority and posteriority among God's thoughts. According to them, God first perfectly conceives of the Divine Essence as it is in Itself. Aquinas (in his *Commentary on the Sentences* I, d. 36, a. 2, and *Summa Theologiae* I, q. 15, a. 2) and Henry of Ghent (*Quodlibeta* VIII, q. 8 & IX, q. 2) say that He next (in the order of natural priority) conceives of Himself as imitable in many determinate ways, and by means of thus conceiving of Himself He comes to conceive of all creatures (actual and possible) perfectly. By contrast, Scotus says that God conceives of creatures as they are in themselves perfectly and then, comparing them with the Divine Essence, thinks of them as imitations of It (*Lectura* I, d. 35, q. u). God's concepts of things other than Himself that are producible, were called 'divine ideas'. Aquinas (*Summa Theologiae* I, q. 15, a. 3, ad 1um), Scotus (ibid.), and Ockham (*Commentary on the Sentences* I, d. 35, q. 5 G) seem to have thought that there was a divine idea proper to each particular creature. Henry of Ghent maintained, however, that God perfectly conceives of everything producible merely by having ideas proper to each species together with an idea of matter (*Quodlibeta* III, q. 1 A–B; VII, q. 1–2). Since privations, negations, and impossibilities are not producible, they claimed that God did not have proper ideas of them, but rather conceived of them by conceiving of possible, positive things (Aquinas, *Summa Theologiae* I, q. 15, a. 3, ad 1um; Scotus, *Ordinatio* I, d. 43, q. u).

p. 55 n. e A term is taken as functionalizable if it is among the 'terms that limit a proposition to the compounded sense or the divided sense and to various compositions according to various arrangements in propositions. For example, terms signifying mental acts, such as "know", "understand", "wish", "imagine", "perceive", "believe", "doubt", and the like...' (*Logica Magna*, Part I, 'On Terms', c. 4, fol. 13rb, lin. 9–13 (ed.); Kretzmann transl.). Other functionalizable terms include modal terms such as 'possible', 'impossible', 'necessary', and 'contingent'. Presumably 'primarily' is taken as functionalizable if and only if the occurrence of 'primarily' makes the proposition apt to a distinction between senses of composition and division.

p. 55 n. f This alleged sufficient condition for the truth of a proposition comes very close to the one Paul sets out in Thesis 1 of the Ninth Way. The difference is that Paul adds in the antecedent 'and it is not inconsistent that *A* should be true' as it is in the case of an insoluble proposition with a true adequate significatum.

p. 55 n. g The indirect discourse form or sentence-nominalization in Latin is the *oratio infinitiva*—an expression in which the subject is put into the accusative and the verb into the infinitive form. I usually translate this construction with the that-clause construction, since the latter is the normal indirect discourse form in English. Sometimes I translate it with an infinitive construction ('for *C* to be *D*') or a fused participle ('*C* being *D*') to bring out the force of the argument. Accordingly, I have translated '*orationes infinitivae*' as 'sentence-nominalizations'.

Chapter 8

p. 57 n. a Paul explains that '... not only an indicative utterance is called a proposition, but also an imperative, supplicative, optative, and subjunctive. For the intellect gives assent or dissent to each of these. But the intellect assents to or dissents from only truths or falsehoods. Therefore, each of these utterances is true or false and consequently is a proposition. The premiss is clear from experience.

First, with respect to imperatives, I say that the intellect assents to or dissents from "Peter, read" and does not await a further determination. The same thing is clear with respect to supplicatives such as "God have mercy on me". Again, with respect to optatives, such as "Would that I might read". For the latter is interchangeable with the utterance "I hope that I may read", which is a proposition. Therefore, so is the other. Again I prove it with respect to subjunctives. For the conditional "If the Antichrist were white, the Antichrist would be coloured" is true and holds good. Therefore, it has an antecedent and consequent. But the only antecedent it has is "The Antichrist were white" and the only consequent is "The Antichrist would be coloured." Therefore the latter two are propositions, and they are contrary-to-fact utterances. Therefore, a contrary-to-fact utterance is a proposition.' Paul explains further that 'Nevertheless, it can be said with probability that utterances of the sorts mentioned above are indicative, if not explicitly, then implicitly, since they are subordinate to indicative mental expressions. For an utterance such as "Peter, read" is subordinate to the mental expression "I want, I order you to read, Peter." And an utterance such as "God have mercy on me" is subordinate to the mental expression "I pray, God, that you will have mercy on me." But it is clear that each of these mental expressions is indicative. The same thing can be said with respect to optatives, that they are implicitly indicative. For example, "Would that I might read." I say that it has, explicitly, neither a subject nor a predicate, but it does implicitly in the "Would". Thus the subject is "I", the copula is "am", and the predicate is the whole expression "wishing that I may read" ' (*Logica Magna*, Part II, 'On Propositions', fol. 101rb, lin. 2–21, ed.).

p. 59 n. b Paul is here focusing on Peter of Mantua's claim (in the second paragraph of Paul's summary on p. 57 that 'the intellect is rendered incorrect when nothing in reality corresponds to the composition of terms (or did correspond or will correspond, according to the tense of the proposition)'. In fact, the latter remark is inconsistent with Peter of Mantua's other assertion 'that a proposition renders the intellect correct because through it the intellect conceives . . . negatively, that a thing that is not is not . . .' (first paragraph of Paul's summary, p. 57). For it would seem that through the proposition 'No chimera is', the intellect conceives that a thing, which in fact is not, is not.

Chapter 9

p. 65 n. a That is, '*verum*' can be taken as a modal operator, operating on a proposition or its nominalization, or it can be taken as being in the neuter gender equivalent to a substantive ('*aliquid verum*'). Paul usually expresses this contrast by saying that '*verum*' can be taken either as a *modal* and functionalizable term or *nominally* as a resoluble term. But in his general explanation of what it is for terms to be resoluble or functionalizable, his wording suggests that a term is being taken nominally when it is functionalizable: 'Note, however, that when "possible", "contingent", and the like are taken nominally, they can be taken in one of two ways in a proposition, either as functionalizable or as resoluble. Taken in the first way, they are syncategorematic words, as has been said. But taken in the second way they are categorematic and signify possible or contingent beings . . .' (*Logica Magna*, Part I, 'On Terms', c. 1, fol. 2rb, lin. 71–2–fol. 2va, lin. 1–3 (ed.); Kretzmann transl.). And in c. 4 of the same treatise, he remarks, 'Of mediate terms some are resoluble, such as nouns, verbs, adverbs, and participles that have inferiors in predication. For example, "man", "moves", "somewhere", with respect to which these are inferior: "this", "runs", "there" ' (ibid., fol. 13ra, lin. 71–2–fol. 13rb lin. 1–3 (ed.); Kretzmann transl.).

p. 65 n. b In Latin, the adjective '*verum*' may stand alone as the subject of a proposition, but the corresponding English adjective 'true' cannot. Consequently,

where '*verum*' stands now in the subject-position, now in the predicate position, I have translated it by 'a truth'. The occurrence of the indefinite article must not be taken to beg the question of whether 'a truth' is a functionalizable term or a nominal, resoluble term. Rather 'a truth' must be understood to be ambiguous in the same way as Paul understands '*verum*' to be (see p. 65 n. a above). To remind the reader of this, I have put the indefinite article in brackets. I have followed the same policy in translating the Latin adjectives '*contingens*', '*possibile*', '*necessarium*', and '*necesse*' in 'On the Significatum of a Proposition', ch. 6.

p. 69 n. c In discussing functionalizable propositions (i.e. a proposition containing a functionalizable term, see p. 55 n. d), Paul gives the following criterion for when they are to be taken in the sense of composition, and when in the sense of division: '. . . whenever the mode absolutely precedes the categorical or hypothetical nominalization, there is a sense of composition. And when it comes between the verb of the nominalization and the first extreme, it is taken in the sense of division. But when it is placed at the end after the nominalization, the proposition can be taken in either way, in the sense of composition and in the sense of division. An example of the first is "It is possible that Socrates runs" or "I know that *A* is true." An example of the second is "For Socrates, it is impossible to run" or "*A* I doubt to be true." An example of the third is "That the creator is God is necessary" or "That *A* is true, is believed by you" . . .' (*Logica Magna*, Part I, 'On the Compounded and Divided Sense', fol. 76va, lin. 15–25 (ed.)). When the functionalizable verb 'signifies' is placed in front of the nominalization (as in the translation) or at the end (as in the Latin) it can occur in the sense of composition; at the middle or the end, in the sense of division. If '*Antichristum esse illa significat*' were taken in the sense of division, it would imply that some existing thing is the Antichrist, and that thing is signified to be by 'The Antichrist is'—which would imply that the Antichrist exists. What the framer of the argument points out is that, given the position of the functionalizable verb, the proposition can be taken in the sense of composition. So taken, the verb 'signifies' ampliates the *suppositio* of the terms beyond actually existing things, to those things which are understood.

p. 73 n. d That is, those who hold Gregory of Rimini's opinion about the quiddity of the adequate significatum of a proposition. (See 'On the Significatum of a Proposition', ch. 3.)

p. 73 n. e Perhaps Paul thinks that only something positive can be an object for the intellect (see Seventh Way, Counter-Thesis 4, p. 55). As he explains in 'On the Significatum of a Proposition', Fifth Way, Theses 3 and 4, pp. 157–90, the adequate significatum of a true proposition about the present that lacks an ampliative or distracting term, is formally distinct from but really the same as what is adequately signified by its subject or predicate term and is therefore something positive which can be an object for the intellect. But in the case of false propositions, as well as true propositions that contain ampliative or distracting terms, the adequate significatum is not some thing, some things, or somehow. Therefore, the adequate significatum of a false proposition would not be something positive in the nature of things that could serve as an object for the intellect.

p. 75 n. f That is, assuming (contrary to fact, in some cases) that the first proposition is merely contingent, rather than impossible.
We have followed the manuscript in reading 'sign' rather than '**significatum**' in '. . . because its sign—viz. "A man is"—follows materially or formally from the proposition . . .' and 'because its sign follows formally from that proposition' for two reasons. First 'A man is' is not the label for the significatum of any proposition. Paul explains in 'On the Significatum of a Proposition', c. 9, pp. 197–9, that the adequate significatum of a proposition is to be labelled by the sentence-

nominalization corresponding to the proposition that adequately signifies it. 'A man is' is, however, the sign that adequately signifies that a man is and is a token proposition that is entailed by 'A man is a not-man.' Second, if one reads 'significatum' with the edition, then the pronoun 'its' must refer to the proposition 'A man is a not-man.' The fact that the significatum of 'A man is a not-man'—viz. that a man is a not-man—follows from that proposition by a formal or material inference, is irrelevant to the point Paul wishes to make.

p. 75 n. g Presumably, just as God understands positive things prior to understanding negations and privations (Seventh Way, defence of Counter-Thesis 4, p. 55) because the former are naturally prior to the latter, so He would understand affirmative propositions prior to understanding their negations, because their significata are naturally prior.

p. 77 n. h There is a discourse of nature, since He understands some things naturally prior to understanding others.

NOTES TO *ON THE SIGNIFICATUM OF A PROPOSITION*

Chapter 1

p. 83 n. a The last argument is as much a repetition of the proof of the conclusion as a proof of the first premiss.

p. 83 n. b That is, 'It is true that God is and only God is' would be inconsistent. For that God is, would be a complex. If it is true that God is, then that complex exists and the simple being God exists. Thus many—i.e. the complex mode and the simple thing—would exist.

p. 85 n. c We have not found who divides intrinsic modes in just this way, nor have we located any further discussion of it by Paul. 'Thisness' was a term used by Scotists to refer to the individuating principle. 'Existence in reality' may contrast with mere existence in the intellect as an object of thought.

p. 85 n. d The order of dependence alluded to in the first part of the proposition is the order or dependence of one thing upon another for its existence. Among things that are only formally distinct, such a dependence does exist. But it does not obtain among really distinct things. See p. 159 n. d below.

p. 85 n. e See p. 65 n. a above.

Chapter 2

p. 87 n. a In this argument, Paul assumes that 'That God is, is necessarily *true*' entails 'That God is, is necessarily *existent*.' But not all medieval logicians understood necessary truth in this way. Apparently, William Ockham did not, since he writes: 'Nevertheless, with respect to necessary propositions it must be known that a proposition is not called necessary because it is always true, but because it is true if it exists and cannot be false. For example, the mental proposition "God exists" is necessary, not because it is always true—since if it does not exist, it is not true— but because if it is, it is true and cannot be false . . .' (*Summa Logicae* II, c. 9, ed. Boehner, Gál, and Brown, p. 275). Robert Holkot develops Ockham's position with more consistency, e.g. in *Quodlibetal Questions* I, q. 6, ed. E. A. Moody in 'A Quodlibetal Question of Robert Holkot, O.P. On the Problem of the Objects of Knowledge and Belief', *Speculum*, 39 (1964), 59–65.

p. 91 n. b In *Logica Magna*, Part II, 'On Categorical Propositions', Paul explains that '. . . some categorical propositions are of the second adjacent, some of the third adjacent, and some of neither the second nor the third adjacent. A categorical proposition of the second adjacent is one that has only a subject and a copula for its principal parts. For example, "You are." A categorical proposition of the third adjacent is one that has a subject, predicate, and copula as its principle parts. For example, "A man is an animal." A categorical proposition that is neither of the second nor of the third adjacents is one which lacks a subject and a predicate and a copula (such as "am", "are", or "is"). For example, the "and vice versa" in the proposition "Every man is an animal and vice versa." In addition, the proposition "Socrates runs" is neither of the second nor the third adjacent, since it lacks a substantive verb, notwithstanding the fact that it has a principal verb' (fol. 102va, lin.

61–vb, lin. 7 (ed.)). He then proceeds to explain how propositions of the second adjacent are not found among mental propositions, since all mental propositions involve a mental act of compounding and dividing. But the mind 'can never compound or divide unless it compounds a subject with a predicate or divides a subject from a predicate by means of an act of affirming or denying. For it says in *Peri Hermeneias*, Part I, that the verb "is" signifies a certain composition which cannot be understood without extremes. Nevertheless, the opposite of this is commonly found in spoken or written discourse' (fol. 102vb, lin. 9–23 (ed.)). Hence there can be no mental proposition without both a subject and a predicate and hence none that has a subject and copula but no predicate.

p. 91 n. c The force of the argument depends on the ambiguity between taking 'that God is' to be mentioned and taking it to be used. I have omitted the quotes to preserve the ambiguity. Paul points out this mistake on p. 93.

p. 93 n. d Paul is here alluding to two views about when a term can have material *suppositio*, which he discussed in *Logica Magna*, Part I, 'On the *Suppositio* of Terms'. A term 'man' has material *suppositio* when it stands in a proposition for the sound or mark tokens conventionally associated with that term rather than for those things (such as Socrates and Plato) that it was imposed to signify. According to one view, '. . . A term has material *suppositio* without the requirement that some sign of materiality precede it. But it suffices merely that the term of first intention is drawn by a term of second intention ⟨in the predicate⟩ to such simple and material *suppositio*, where it is assumed as a basic principle that subjects are of the sort of which their predicates can be asserted. Therefore, they grant the propositions "Man is a species", "Animal is a genus", "Every animal is a name", "Every man is not a species" and they deny the propositions "Every man is a name" and "Some man is a species", etc. . . .' (fol. 16rb, lin. 1–11 (ed.)). On this view, the same inscription type is used when a term is mentioned—i.e. used to talk about itself—as when it is used to talk about the things that it has been imposed to signify. But a term will have material *suppositio* only if it is the subject of a proposition whose predicate is a term that signifies signs, as in 'Man is a name.' Paul thinks 'the adequate significatum of a proposition' is not a term that is apt to signify signs. Hence, on this position about material *suppositio*, the subject of 'That God is, is the adequate significatum of a proposition' cannot have material *suppositio*. Of course, in claiming that 'the adequate significatum of a proposition' does not supposit for signs, Paul is begging the question.

According to another view, however, '. . . a term cannot have simple or material *suppositio* without the requirement of a term or sign of materiality. In fact, neither does such a term of second imposition suffice to draw the term of first imposition to such simple or material *suppositio*' (fol. 16rb, lin. 49–54). Signs of materiality in contemporary use are quotation marks. Thus, one ordinarily would say that 'Man is a name' is ungrammatical for ' "Man" is a name.' In fourteenth- and fifteenth-century Latin, however, the standard sign of materiality was 'li' or 'ly' prefixed to the term in question. On this view, the subject of 'That God is, is a sentence-nominalization' cannot have material *suppositio* because there is no sign of materiality preceding it or enclosing it. Hence the proposition is false.

Paul's own view about material *suppositio* is a compromise between these two. He thinks that syncategorematic terms, such as 'every', that signify things other than themselves and tokens of the same term type, only in conjunction with other terms, can supposit materially even if there is no sign of materiality in the proposition: e.g. 'Every is a noun.' But categorematic terms cannot supposit materially unless they are operated on by some sign of materiality. Thus 'Man is a noun' is false, while ' "Man" is a noun' is true (fols. 16vb–17rb (ed.)).

p. 95 n. e The question of the objects of knowledge, belief, doubt, etc. was much

debated. For an introduction to the early fourteenth-century discussion, see E. A. Moody, loc. cit. on p. 87 n. a. See also Heinrich Shepers, 'Holkot contra dicta Crathorn', *Philosophisches Jahrbuch* (1970), 320–54, and ibid. (1972), 106–36.

Chapter 3

p. 95 n. a The expression '*complexe significabile*' is so associated with Gregory of Rimini's discussion that Paul finds it necessary only to use that expression to bring Gregory's theory to the reader's mind (see 'On the Truth and Falsity of Propositions', ch. 9, p. 73; 'On the Significatum of a Proposition', ch. 4, p. 111). Gregory uses '*complexe significabile*' (an adjective modified by an adverb) as a noun expression labelling what can be signified only by a complex of terms or a proposition. In English, however, where it is necessary to expand it to render it 'signifiable by a complex' or 'what can be signified by a complex', it loses some of its impact as a concise technical term.

p. 97 n. b What can be signified by a single term as well as a complex of terms.

p. 99 n. c See 'On the Truth and Falsity of Propositions', above, p. 15 n. t.

p. 99 n. d Paul's point here is clear and correct: viz. that a relative clause introduced by 'that' or 'which' ('*qui*', '*quae*', or '*quod*') can be changed, *salva veritate*, to an independent clause by substituting a sign of conjunction together with a demonstrative pronoun for 'that' or 'which'. But Paul's terminology is unusual. For he uses '*relativum nominis*' (translated 'noun-relative' or, more literally, 'relative of a noun') to refer to the relative pronoun '*quod*' and '*relativum pronominis*' (translated 'pronoun-relative' or, more literally, 'relative of a pronoun') to refer to '*illud*', which would normally be called a demonstrative pronoun. Paul apparently takes himself to be following standard usage when he identifies, not only the relative pronouns '*qui*', '*quae*', and '*quod*', but also the demonstrative pronouns '*iste*', '*ille*', and '*hic*', as non-reciprocal relatives of identity (*Logica Magna*, Part I, 'On the *Suppositio* of Terms', fol. 28va, lin. 26–7 (ed.)). But why in the present passage does he distinguish '*quod*' as a *noun*-relative, and '*illud*' as a *pronoun*-relative? The answer is not that the antecedent of '*quod*' is a noun whereas the antecedent of '*illud*' is a pronoun: for the antecedent of each is the indefinite pronoun '*aliquid*'. Unfortunately, we have not been able to find a place in which Paul, or any of his contemporaries or predecessors, explicitly explains this terminology. Paul does say that demonstrative pronouns such as '*iste*', '*ille*', and '*hic*' are immediate terms that are not further resolvable into others (*Logica Magna*, Part I, 'On Terms', fol. 12vb lin. 1–16). Thus, one might hypothesize that a noun-relative is a resoluble pronoun, while a pronoun-relative is a non-resoluble pronoun. But, in another work attributed to Paul it is remarked that whereas some relatives are resoluble in the way that '*quod*' is here, some *noun-relatives* are not thus resoluble: 'The inference is clear, since a relative that does not have confused *suppositio* is resoluble either into a relative pronoun together with a sign of conjunction or into a relative pronoun together with a sign of disjunction . . .' But 'no noun-relative that is limited to confused *suppositio*', as 'whatever' or 'whoever' would be, 'is in general resoluble into a relative pronoun together with a sign of conjunction' (*Quadratura* II, Sophisma 22, fol. 34va-vb (Venice, 1493)).

p. 103 n. e Here Paul alludes to the common medieval doctrine that the duration of creatures that begin to be and cease to be is measured by time; that of creatures that begin to be and do not cease to be, by *aevum*; and that of God, who neither begins nor ceases to be, by eternity. This doctrine is discussed and challenged by William Ockham, *Commentary on the Sentences* II, q. 13.

Chapter 4

p. 105 n. a *Nothing* is, because many *things* are.

p. 107 n. b The author of this way apparently agrees with Paul that a term such as 'man' signifies whatever is superior or inferior to it in the praedicamental line, as well as for men. But whereas Paul would say that we can distinguish among these significata, primary significata which it distinctly signifies and for which it supposits (see ch. 9 below), the author of this opinion seems to think no criterion for making such a distinction can be found.

p. 109 n. c See Addenda et corrigenda, p. xvi.

p. 111 n. d Ailly has argued that because some propositions signify many things, there is *nothing* that the proposition as a whole signifies. Paul is here alluding to his own view (elaborated more fully in chapters 7 and 8 than anywhere earlier in this treatise) that although some propositions may signify many things, the adequate significatum of an affirmative categorical present-tense proposition is really identical with, but formally distinct from the supposita of the subject or predicate. In the example, the proposition 'Socrates is a beholder of a donkey' signifies both Socrates and a donkey, but its adequate significatum is really identical with only one thing—viz. Socrates, who is the adequate significatum of the subject.

p. 111 n. e That is, he rejects a view such as that endorsed by Gregory of Rimini (see ch. 3, pp. 95, 97 above).

p. 113 n. f On some accounts (though not on Paul's, see p. 93 n. d), 'Runs' could occur as a noun having material *suppositio* in ' Runs is in the indicative mood.'

p. 113 n. g In *Logica Magna*, Part I, 'On the *Suppositio* of Terms', Paul explains that 'Some complex terms are non-quiescently significant (e.g. "white man", "for God to be"); but some are quiescently significant (e.g. "A man is white", "God exists") . . .' (fol. 16vb, lin. 28–30 (ed.)). Complete propositions are said to signify 'quiescently' presumably because they express a complete thought upon the grasping of which the intellect *rests*, without expecting some further determination. (See 'On the Truth and Falsity of Propositions', p. 57 n. a.) By contrast, nouns modified by adjectives and infinitive expressions do not express such complete thoughts, and neither do non-complex terms. Note that Paul's usage does not seem to accord with that of Aristotle in *Peri Hermeneias*, ch. 3, 16b19 ff. For Aristotle says there that 'the speaker arrests his thought and the hearer pauses', when a verb is uttered by itself as a name.

p. 113 n. h One expression is equiform with another if it is a token of the same type.

p. 115 n. i The point here is that the accusative is grammatical and the nominative is not. Since there is no difference in English between the accusative and nominative of the term 'God', I have switched to the capitalized personal pronouns 'He' and 'Him'.

p. 121 n. j See p. 55 n. d above.

Chapter 5

p. 123 n. a That is, to assert Thesis 1.

p. 127 n. b Paul's point is that an indefinite proposition of the form '(An) *A* or *B* is *C*' is interchangeable with the disjunction '(An) *A* is *C* or (a) *B* is *C*.' But propositions of the form 'Every *A* or *B* is *C*' are not interchangeable with the corresponding disjunctive proposition 'Every *A* is *C* or every *B* is *C*', but rather with 'Every *A* is *C* and every *B* is *C*.' See *Logica Magna*, Part II, 'On Disjunctives', fol. 131rb, lin. 64–131va, lin. 27 (ed.), for Paul's explanation of this point.

p. 135 n. c Paul here imagines someone arguing that the significatum of some negative proposition—viz. 'No chimera is'—is something, because it is you. The argument turns on ambiguities in the Latin phrase *'nullam chimaeram esse'*. The latter is most naturally translated by 'that no chimera is', or less naturally by 'no chimera existing', which are sentence-nominalizations of 'No chimera is' or 'No chimera exists', respectively. But the phrase could also be translated by 'Not any chimera exists', which is ambiguous between 'not-any chimera-existing' (a sentence-nominalization of 'Not any chimera exists' and hence the label of its adequate significatum) and 'not any-chimera-existing' (which might be liberally construed as a negation sign followed by a sentence-nominalization of 'Some chimera exists' or 'A chimera exists'). Paul points out that the latter is also ambiguous between 'the negation of the adequate significatum of "A chimera exists" ' and 'something that is not the adequate significatum of "A chimera exists".' And he maintains that while it is true that you are something that is neither the adequate significatum of 'No chimera is' nor of 'Not any chimera exists' nor of 'A chimera exists', it is false that you are the negation of these adequate significata.

p. 135 n. d Viz. 'The negation of a chimera existing, is.'

p. 137 n. e That is, he grants that a chimera is and that a man is a donkey, are not anything, any things, or anyhow. But he does not grant that *that no chimera is* is something, some things, or somehow.

p. 137 n. f Because nothing is the negation of a chimera existing.

p. 137 n. g Which would, taken in that way, assert that the adequate significatum of 'No chimera exists' is something which is not a chimera existing. But Paul has argued that *that no chimera exists* is not anything, any things, or anyhow.

p. 137 n. h When the premiss is taken in the first way, it is false and impossible, since it signifies that you are a pure negation. The inference holds because anything follows from an impossible proposition. Taken in the second way, the premiss asserts that you are something other than you being a donkey. The conclusion is false, however, because according to Thesis I, you not being a donkey is the adequate significatum of the *negative* proposition 'You are not a donkey' and as such is nothing.

Chapter 6

p. 139 n. a In Latin, the construction *'Antichristus fore est Antichristus futurus'* is ambiguous. (i) *'futurus'* can be taken as an adjective modifying *'Antichristus'*, in which case the sentence is equivalent to 'That the Antichrist will be, is the Antichrist-to-be', or 'That the Antichrist will be, is the future Antichrist.' From either of these, one can legitimately infer 'That the Antichrist will be, is'; just as one can infer 'She is' from 'She is a bride-to-be' or 'She is a future bride.' (ii) But *'futurus'* is the future active participle of the verb 'to be'. And by a natural extension of classical usage, medievals allowed *'futurus'* to combine with the present-tense copula to form a periphrastic tense equivalent to the future tense copula. So taken, the above claim is equivalent to 'That the Antichrist will be, will be the Antichrist', from which one cannot infer 'That the Antichrist will be, is', but only 'That the Antichrist will be, will be.' This ambiguity seems to be imitated in English by 'That the Antichrist will be, is the Antichrist to be.'

Paul sees a parallel ambiguity in the Latin *'Adam fuisse est Adam praeteritus'*. *'Praeteritus'* is the perfect passive participle of the verb *'praetereo'* (to pass by). As such, it combines with the present-tense copula to form a verb of the perfect tense and passive voice (to have been passed), which does not function in the same way as the past-tense copula, since it cannot take a predicate adjective or predicate

noun. And I have not been able to find any English expression that indicates the past tense and that is ambiguous in the way that Paul's argument requires.

p. 139 n. b See p. 91 n. b above.

p. 139 n. c Paul writes in *Logica Magna*, Part I, 'On the *Suppositio* of Terms', that '. . . participles alone are distracting terms, since they must distract the present tense copula . . .' (fol. 25vb, lin. 45–6 (ed.)). The copula together with the distracting term, brings about an ampliation of the *suppositio*. See p. 15 n. t above.

p. 139 n. d Paul says literally 'as participles', since '*futurus*' and '*praeteritus*' are participles in Latin. And he is here appealing to the common-place rule of medieval logic that the copula plus a participle of a given verb is equivalent to a form of that verb in a non-periphrastic tense. For example, '*est currens*' is equivalent to '*currit*'. That applying this rule as Paul does involves a stretching of classical usage has been pointed out in p. 139 n. a above. Since I translate '*futurus*' here by 'to be', and since 'to be' is not a participle, I have translated '*participialiter*' by 'part of a periphrastic tense formation'.

p. 139 n. e See p. 65 n. b above.

p. 141 n. f For Paul's understanding of this rule, see p. 151.

p. 143 n. g Paul finds this absurd only when one is not dealing with insolubles. See *Logica Magna*, Part II, 'On Insolubles', Opinion Fifteen, Article 3, Thesis 2, fol. 195rb lin. 49–57 (ed.).

p. 143 n. h Paul does not think this is absurd where insolubles are concerned either. See ibid., Thesis 5, fol. 195va, lin. 15–28 (ed.).

p. 145 n. i See p. 65 n. a above.

p. 145 n. j I do not systematically distinguish between '*ita*' and '*sic*', but I do here for the sake of the argument.

p. 147 n. k Paul says the proposition does not have any quantity and is therefore not indefinite, because when '*verum*' ('a truth') is taken as a modal term, it is a syn-categorematic term and thus not the sort of term that can be operated on by a syncategorematic term. But when '*verum*' is taken as a nominal term, it is the sort of term that can be operated on by a syncategorematic.

p. 147 n. l See p. 65 nn. a and b above.

p. 149 n. m See p. 15 n. t and p. 139 n. c above.

p. 149 n. n See pp. 143, 145, where Paul turns Feribrigge's arguments against his own position.

p. 149 n. o That is, by some created truth.

p. 157 n. p Consider propositions of the form '*N* is *M*' and '*M* is *N*', where substitutions for '*M*' include terms such as '⟨a⟩ truth' (*verum*), '⟨a⟩ falsehood' (*falsum*), '⟨a⟩ necessity' (*necesse*), '⟨an⟩ impossibility' (*impossibile*), '⟨a⟩ contingency' (*contingens*), and '⟨a⟩ possibility' (*possibile*); and substitutions for '*N*' are sentence-nominalizations. The opinion under consideration has maintained (i) that propositions of the form '*N* is *M*' do not entail '*N* is something or somehow', but (ii) propositions of the form '*M* is *N*' do entail 'Something or somehow is *N*.'

Paul is here trying to reduce to an absurdity the suggestion that the Philosopher would accept (ii), by considering cases where the substitution for '*N*' is a negated nominalization—i.e. the nominalization of a negative proposition. Such nominalizations, according to Paul, signify the adequate significata of the corresponding negative propositions. But, by Paul's Thesis 1, the adequate significata of such propositions is not anything, any things, or anyhow. Hence, where such substitutions

for '*N*' are concerned, 'Something or somehow is *N*' is false. And if (ii) is true, then by *modus tollens*, propositions of the form '*M* is *N*' are also false for such substitutions. But the Philosopher repeatedly asserts propositions of this form.

For example, consider '⟨A⟩ truth is that no chimera is.' By (ii), this would entail 'Something or somehow is that no chimera is.' But that no chimera is, is the adequate significatum of the negative categorical proposition 'No chimera is.' By Thesis 1, it is false that something or somehow is that no chimera is. By *modus tollens*, the proposition '⟨A⟩ truth is that no chimera is' is likewise false. Similarly for other negated propositions.

Chapter 7

p. 157 n. a This stipulation is made because the adequate significata of some propositions are not anything, any things, or anyhow—e.g. true negative propositions such as 'No chimera is.' See Thesis 1 above.

p. 159 n. b I translate the accusative plus the infinitive with the fused participle construction here, because a fused participle such as 'God existing' gives a smoother English translation.

p. 159 n. c It is difficult to find an English word that captures the force of '*ratio*'. Often, '*ratio*' is equivalent to 'concept', where concepts are essentially mind-dependent—whether they are identified with really existent mental acts, or with the objects of such acts, in so far as those objects have the non-real mode of existence in the intellect. Sometimes '*ratio*' means 'definition', where a definition is a combination of words or concepts that expresses, by specifying a genus and differentia, the essence of a thing. The *rationes* of which Paul speaks, however, are neither essentially mind-dependent, nor are they linguistic entities. Rather they are in really existing things as really identical with but formally distinct from them and from each other (see next note). The genus and differentia that constitute a thing's essence are among such *rationes*. And it is a distinction of such *rationes* in things, prior to the intellect's activity in thinking them distinct, that justifies its conceiving of them by distinct concepts. Hence, *rationes* here cannot be concepts or definitions.

If not, it is tempting to suppose that they are what essential definitions express. The trouble with this suggestion is that most of the *rationes* Paul discusses—e.g. the *rationes* of being, life, *God existing, a man being an animal*—do not have definitions in terms of genus and differentia.

Perhaps Paul's use of '*ratio*' here is covered by the broadest contemporary use of 'property'. Unfortunately, 'property' is a correct translation of '*proprietas*', which is the abstract noun corresponding to '*proprium*'. In medieval philosophy, a *proprium* is, strictly speaking, a feature shared by all and only the members of a given species, or less technically for a feature peculiar to some individual. Hence '*proprietas*' picks out a special sub-class of properties (in the contemporary sense). '*Ratio*' does not have this connotation.

By a process of elimination, I have decided to translate '*ratio*' most often by 'notion' and occasionally by 'formal principle'. It is true that in ordinary English, 'notion' is most often used to refer to mind-dependent entities such as thoughts or ideas. But there is some precedent for using 'notion' to stand for some real thing other than a thought or idea in Aquinas's use of '*notio*' to refer to the real relations in God by which the Father is related to the Son and Holy Spirit and by which each of them is related to the Father. Such notions as Paternity and Filiation are not really distinct from the Divine Persons of Father and Son, respectively. But notions are signified by abstract concepts and are that *by which* God is three persons, whereas persons are signified by concrete concepts and are *who* God is. (*Summa Theologiae* I, q. 32, a. 2, c.) Aquinas does not use '*notiones*' to refer to other

divine attributes such as wisdom and justice, but he does draw analogies between such notions and the divine attributes. So in translating '*ratio*' by 'notion' I will be making a natural extension of Aquinas's usage. Again, it is true that 'principle' is a correct translation of '*principium*'. And medieval philosophers sometimes use the latter to refer to the indemonstrable, first premisses of a science. But it is clear that the *rationes* under discussion here are neither arguments, nor premisses of an argument. And these philosophers also speak of the principles (*principia*) of things when they wish to refer to those things from which other things take their origin. Paul uses '*ratio*' in this context to refer to something similar to '*principium*' in the latter sense. For *rationes* are metaphysical constituents of things that are really the same as but formally distinct from the thing and from each other. To make it clear that *rationes* are not the efficient causes from which things take their origin, however, I shall translate '*ratio*' by '*formal* principle'.

p. 159 n. d The notion of a formal distinction was brought to prominence in the philosophy of Duns Scotus. It served as a mean between a distinction of reason and a real distinction. According to some medieval usage, there is a distinction of reason between x and y, if and only if x and y are in fact conceived of by means of distinct concepts. But there can be no distinction of reason between x and y if there are no intellects or if no intellects ever think of x and y or think of them as distinct. If everyone mistakenly thought x and y were to be conceived of only under the same concepts, there would be no distinction of reason between them. On the other hand, there is a real distinction between x and y if and only if it is logically possible that x should exist apart from y and/or logically possible that y should exist apart from x. Scotus thought that sometimes, even though x and y are not really distinct, we want to say that our conceiving of x and y by means of different concepts is justified by what exists in the nature of things prior to and apart from any activity of the intellect. When, prior to and apart from any activity of the intellect, x and y are apt to be thought of by means of distinct concepts, x and y are formally distinct. Thus, Scotus says that the attributes of God are formally, though not really, distinct (*Ordinatio* I, d. 8, pars 1, q. 4, n. 186 (ed. P. C. Balic, Vatican City, 1956), vol. 4, p. 254. *Lectura* I, d. 8, pars 1, q. 4, nn. 156–9; vol. 17 (1966), pp. 56–7). Similarly, the Divine Persons are formally, but not really distinct from the Divine Essence (*Ordinatio* I, d. 2, q. 1–4, n. 388, vol. 2 (1950), pp. 349–50). Scotus gives the following criterion of formal identity: '. . . Moreover, I say that there is a formal identity, where that which is said to be formally the same as something else includes that with which it is identical in its formal quidditative principle, and does so *per se* in the first way . . .' (*Ordinatio* I, d. 2, pars 2, q. 1–4, n. 403; vol. 2 (1950), pp. 356–7. Cf. *Lectura* I, d. 2, pars 2, q. 1–4, n. 275; vol. 16 (1960), pp. 216–7). By the same token, x and y are formally distinct, if and only if (i) if x and y are definable, then x is not included in the definition of y and y is not included in the definition of x; and (ii) if x and y are not definable in terms of genus and differentia, then if they were so definable, x would not be included in the definition of y and y would not be included in the definition of x; and (iii) x and y are really the same (*Ordinatio* I, d. 8, pars 1, q. 4, n. 193; vol. 4 (1956), pp. 261–2).

p. 161 n. e I have rendered '*Deum esse*' by the fused participle 'God existing' rather than by 'that God exists' in order to give these fallacious arguments more superficial plausibility.

p. 161 n. f Not Paul.

p. 161 n. g 'God existing' is ambiguous between 'God, who exists' and a sentence-nominalization, and hence a label of the adequate significatum of 'God exists.' If God and the adequate significatum of 'God exists' were really distinct, there would be many (i.e. two) Gods existing. For the First Being, which exists,

would be one God existing. And the adequate significatum of 'God exists', which is by hypothesis really distinct from the First Being, is God existing. Hence, there would be two Gods existing.

p. 163 n. h In the premiss the supposita are really identical, but in the conclusion they are asserted to be formally identical as well. The inference does not hold because those things that are really the same can be formally distinct.

p. 163 n. i That is, in the premiss the *suppositio* is for the divine essence, but in the conclusion it is for persons. The claim is that the Father and the Son are one Essence, but distinct Persons.

p. 167 n. j Scotus would say that Father and the essence are really the same but formally distinct ('by real identity, although not formal', *Ord.* I, d. 2, pars 2, q. 1–4, n. 410; vol. 2 (1950), p. 360; nn. 416–17, p. 364).

Chapter 8

p. 171 n. a Not Paul.

p. 171 n. b I have used the fused participle construction here, because in English 'each falsehood existing' is grammatical, but 'each that a falsehood is' is not grammatical.

p. 171 n. c By an application of Paul's Thesis 4, the adequate significatum of 'The proposition is'—viz. that the proposition is—is really identical with the adequate significatum of its subject.

p. 173 n. d Paul's opponent is apparently applying Thesis 4 to conclude that each of *that God creates Socrates* and *that God is* is really identical with God. Inferring that *that God creates Socrates* is identical with *that God is*, he argues that if the latter is necessary, so is the former.

p. 173 n. e The rule invoked is that inferences of the form '*A* and *B* are *C*; therefore, *A* is *C*' hold good. This Master then pretends that inferences of the form 'that *p* and *q* is so-and-so; therefore that *q* is so-and-so' are instances of the first schema as well.

p. 173 n. f As noted many times, the accusative plus the infinitive in Latin can be translated by a that-clause, an infinitive phrase, or a fused participle in English. The force of these arguments can best be brought out by translating '*me currere*' and '*omnes homines sedere*', respectively, with an infinitive phrase in the first premiss and a fused participle in the second premiss.

p. 173 n. g As Paul's opponent suggests it would be, if Thesis 4 were true. For by Paul's application of Thesis 4, both *that the sun is* and *that the sun heats the house* would be really identical with the sun.

p. 173 n. h The arguments here are elliptical, and it is not clear what the analogy appealed to is. I suggest that their proponent may be using the following strategy: He begins with the assumption that 'God knows that *p*' entails 'It is so that *p*.' He then invokes Paul's rule to tell him what in particular *that p* is, and misreads the rule to say that it is always the adequate significatum of the subject or of the predicate of the corresponding proposition. Thus, the adequate significata of the subjects of 'Socrates is' and 'The Antichrist will be' are Socrates and the Antichrist, respectively.

Paul rejects the analogy. If 'so' is taken as a nominal, transcendental term, then it is only where God's knowledge of the present, and not His knowledge of the past and future is concerned, that 'God knows that *p*' entails 'It is so that *p*.' For only true, affirmative, categorical propositions *of the present tense*, whose predicates

contain no distracting terms, have adequate significata that are something or some-how. Thus, the above argument holds where the adequate significatum of 'Socrates is' is concerned, but not for that of 'The Antichrist will be.' My conjecture thus fits with Paul's terse reply (see p. 181 below).

p. 173 n. i The inference pretended here is of the following form: A or B is C and B is not C (since B isn't anything); therefore A is C. This is supposed to hold whatever, or whatever way, is substituted for 'C'.

p. 173 n. j This premiss would be defended as follows: By Paul's Thesis 4, the adequate signification of each of 'God is the cause of you' and 'God is' is really identical with God. But the adequate significatum of 'God is' is for God to be. And the adequate significatum of 'God is the cause of you' is for God to be the cause of you. Therefore, for God to be, is for God to be the cause of you. p. 171 n. c.

p. 175 n. k Paul explains in *Logica Magna*, Part I, 'On Functionalizable Terms', that 'a describable proposition is, therefore, one in which one of the previously mentioned verbs that is primarily provable of a proposition, determines a complex. Thus the proposition "I know proposition A" is described and proved as follows: "I know the primary significatum of proposition A and I know that it is primarily signified by A; therefore, I know proposition A." Notice I add the "primarily" because this does not follow: "I know the primary significatum of A and I know that it is signified by A; therefore I know A." For suppose that A is the proposition "God is", which I believe firmly and without any hesitation to be false. Suppose further that I firmly know that God is, and I also know that significatum is signified by A, but I believe that it is signified by A secondarily. Having assumed this case, it is clear that I know the primary significatum of A, since I know that God is, and I know, too, that that significatum is signified by A, according to the case. Nevertheless, I do not know the proposition A, since I firmly believed it to be false . . .' (fol. 70va, lin. 38–53 (ed.)).

p. 177 n. l That is, in Paul's reply to the argument for the First Absurd Conclusion (pp. 175, 177 above).

p. 177 n. m In Latin, adjectives have gender. When they occur as modifying a noun, they must agree with that noun in gender and number. On the other hand, they may stand alone and play the role of nouns. The adjective '*contingens*' here could be either feminine, so that it agrees with and modifies the feminine noun '*propositio*'. Or it could be neuter, in which case it would not modify anything but would be equivalent to '*res contingens*' (contingent thing). Similarly, '*necessarium*' is neuter and could be taken as modifying the neuter subject '*significatum*'. But it could also be understood as standing alone and equivalent to '*res necessaria*' (necessary thing).

p. 179 n. n Again, I have translated '*istam propositionem esse*' by an infinitive expression in the second premiss here because we would not say 'That this proposition is, is that this proposition is true' in English.

p. 179 n. o. That is, the proposition '*That Socrates is different from Plato* is Socrates.'

p. 183 n. p Not Paul.

p. 185 n. q Holkot replies to similar objections. See E. A. Moody, loc. cit. on p. 87 n. a.

p. 189 n. r In 'F is G', 'F' and 'G' supposit for God with whom F and G are both really identical. But in 'F is the formality of F', 'F' supposits for the formal principle F; similarly for 'G' in 'G is the formality of G.' Therefore, there is a change of *suppositio* in the argument.

p. 189 n. s Apparently the word order is supposed to dictate whether the *suppositio*

is 'formal' or 'real and identical', as Paul says. 'The adequate significatum of B' can have real or identical *suppositio* only when it occurs in the subject position and has formal *suppositio* when it occurs in the predicate position.

p. 191 n. t Again, the word order is supposed to dictate whether the *suppositio* is 'formal' or 'real'. The claim is that 'the adequate significatum of the proposition' can have 'real *suppositio*', only when it is in the subject position and not when it is in the predicate position.

Chapter 9

p. 193 n. a That is, the adequate significatum is not that which is conceived of prior to the other significata, where the priority is understood to be temporal, formal, natural, or priority according to goodness and honour (see *Logica Magna*, Part II, 'On Molecular Propositions', fol. 150ra, lin. 44–150vb, lin. 30 (ed.)).

p. 197 n. b As noted above, in English these include that-clauses, infinitive expressions, and fused participles. Paul usually uses the accusative plus the infinitive, but he does use a *quod*-clause construction in expressing the significatum of a proposition in Opinion V, p. 144. But Paul does not believe that the adequate significatum of a proposition is an infinitive expression or a that-clause. This is the opinion which he rejected on pp. 91, 93 above. Following what Paul says about non-complexes, he evidently means to say that in the spoken form, the adequate significatum of a proposition bears an equiform denomination with the infinitive expression or that-clause form of a proposition.

INDEXES

Bold type is used to indicate a reference to the Notes on pages 201–14 and 252–76

I. INDEX OF MANUSCRIPTS

II. INDEX OF AUTHORS AND THEIR WORKS

III. BOOKS AND ARTICLES CITED

Antonio Cittadini: *Logica Minor* Cod. Urb. lat. 1381, f. 2^r: p. xi, n. 1; p. xiv, n. 2.

Dal Pra, M.: 'La teoria del significato totale della proposizione nel pensiero di Gregorio da Rimini', *Rivista critica di storia della filosofia*, 11 (1956), pp. 287–311: **p. 94 n. 1,** p. 211

Denifle, H. and Chatelain, A.: *Chartularium Universitatis Parisiensis*, vol. I, Paris, 1889: **p. 100 n. 9**, p. 212

De Rijk, L. M.: ed. *Logica Modernorum* II (Assen, 1967)

Domenico Bianchelli (*Menghus Blanchellus Faventinus*): *Commentarius super Logicam Pauli Veneti* (Tarvisii, 1476): p. xiv, n. 2

Menghi Faventini Subtilissime Expositiones Questionesque super Summulis Magistri Pauli Veneti, una cum Argutissimis Additionibus Jacobi Ritii Aretini et Manfredi de Medicis (Venetiis, 1542): p. viii n. 2

Emden, A. B.: *A Biographical Register of the University of Oxford to A.D. 1500* (Oxford, 1959), vol. 2, 'John Huntman,' pp. 987–8: p. x, n. 1; vol. 3, 'Paolo Veneto', pp. 1944–5: p. vii, n. 1; p. viii, n. 1

Gauthier, R. A.: ed. *Ethica Nicomachea* (transl. R. Grosseteste Lincolniensis, Aristoteles lat. XXVI. 1–3, Leiden–Bruxelles, 1972): **p. 184 n. 7**, p. 214

James Ricci (*Jacobus Ritius Aretinus*): *Menghi Faventini Subtilissime Expositiones Questionesque super Summulis Magistri Pauli Veneti, una cum Argutissimis Additionibus Jacobi Ritii Aretini et Manfredi de Medicis* (Venetiis, 1542): p. viii n. 2

Kretzmann, Norman: 'Medieval Logicians on the Meaning of *Propositio*', *Journal of Philosophy*, vol. 65 (1970), pp. 767–87: p. xi, n. 2

translator of *Logica Magna*, 'On terms': p. xiv

Lohr, C. H.: 'A Note on the Manuscripts of Paulus Venetus Logica', *Manuscripta*, 1973: p. viii n. 5

Maier, A.: *Codices Vaticani Latini, Codices 2118–2192* (Romae, 1961): p. viii n. 5; p. xii n. 2

Maierù, A.: 'Il problema della verità nelle opere di Guglielmo Heytesbury', *Studi Medievali*, 3a serie, VII. I (1966), 52–6: **p. 14 n. 1**, p. 204

'Il problema del significato nella logica di Pietro da Mantova', *Miscellanea Mediaevalia*, Bd. 9, Berlin–N.Y., 1974: **p. 56 n. 1**, p. 206

Terminologia della tarda scolastica, Rome, 1972: **p. 14 n. 1**, p. 203

Manfred Medici (*Manfredus de Medicis*): *Menghi Faventini Subtilissime Expositiones Questionesque super Summulis Magistri Pauli Veneti, una cum Argutissimis Additionibus Jacobi Ritii Aretini et Manfredi de Medicis* (Venetiis, 1542): p. viii n. 2

Minio-Paluello, L.: ed. *Analytica Posteriora* (trans. Iacobi, Aristoteles latinus IV. 1–4, Bruges–Paris, 1968): **p. 120 n. 3**, p. 212

ed. *Analytica Priora* (transl. Boethii, Aristoteles latinus III. 1–4, Bruges–Paris, 1962): **p. 156 n. 10**, p. 213

ed. *Categoriae* (transl. Boethii, Aristoteles latinus I. 1–5, Bruges–Paris, 1961): **p. 96 n. 3**, p. 211; **p. 98 nn. 6, 7**, p. 211

ed. *De Interpretatione sive Periermenias* (transl. Boethii, Aristoteles latinus II. 1–2, Bruges–Paris, 1965): **p. 86 nn. 2, 3**, p. 210; **p. 154 nn. 5, 6, 7, 8, 9**, p. 213

Moody, E. A. 'A Quodlibetal Question of Robert Holkot, O.P. On the Problem of the Objects of Knowledge and Belief', *Speculum*, 39 (1964), 59–65: **p. 87 n. a.**, p. 266; **p. 95 n. e**, pp. 267–8; **p. 185 n. r**, p. 275

Nardi, Bruno: *Saggi sull' aristotelismo Padovano dal secolo XIV al XVI* (G. C. Sansoni Editore, Firenze, 1958): p. xi n. 1; p. xiv n. 2

Pagallo, G.: 'Nota sulla logica di Paolo Veneto: la critica alla dottrina del complexe significabile di Gregorio da Rimini', *Atti del XII Congresso Internazionale di filosophia*, Firenze, 1960, pp. 183–93: **p. 94 n. 1**, p. 211

Perreiah, Allan R.: ed. and transl. *Logica Magna, Tractatus de Suppositionibus*, St. Bonaventure, 1971: p. viii n. 3; **p. 92 nn. 10, 11**, p. 211

Pinborg, J.: *Logik und Semantik im Mittelalter: Ein Überblick*, Problemata, Stuttgart, 1972: **p. 80 n. 1**, p. 209

Prantl, C.: *Geschichte der Logik im Abendlande*, v. IV (Graz, 1955): p. xi n. 2

Risse, Wilhelm: *Bibliographia Logica Verzeichnis der Druckschriften zur Logik mit Angabe ihrer Fundorte*, Band I, Hildesheim, 1965: p. viii n. 4

Scott, T. K.: translator of *Sophisms on Meaning and Truth*, New York, 1964: **p. 11 n. m**, p. 253

Shepers, Heinrich: 'Holkot contra dicta Crathorn', *Philosophisches Jahrbuch* (1970), 320–54 and ibid. (1972), 106–36: **p. 80 n. 1**, p. 209; **p. 95 n. e**, pp. 267–8

IV. DOCTRINAL INDEX

Accident (*accidens*): cannot pass from subject to subject: *2nd Way*, p. 23; less permanent than a substance: *2nd Way*, p. 23.

Adequate significatum (*significatum adaequatum*):

what is it? is that of a true proposition a mode of a thing and not a thing? *1st Op.*, pp. 81–5; is that of a true proposition a composition of the mind? *2nd Op.*, pp. 85–9; is that of a proposition a sentence-nominalization? *DO*, pp. 91–3; is that of a proposition the proposition itself? *ADO*, pp. 93–5; is that of a proposition Gregory of Rimini's *complexe significabilium*? *3rd Op.*, pp. 95–105; of any proposition, whose a.s. has a place in reality, is somehow distinct from its statable subject or predicate: *5th Op.*, pp. 157–61; of any true, affirmative, present-tense proposition that has no ampliative or distracting term, is really identical with its principal significatum: *5th Op.*, pp. 167–71; cf. **p. 173 n. h,** pp. 274–5; of a negative proposition is not anything, any things, or anyhow: *5th Op.*, p. 123; of no affirmative categorical proposition whose subject or predicate has nothing over and above a sign corresponding to it is something or somehow, some kind or so much, creator or creature: *5th Op.*, p. 137; of a proposition is things being in some way (*aliqualiter esse*) such that their being in that way comes out implicitly or explicitly from the adequate significata of its parts: *5th Op.*, p. 197; of a proposition that signifies many whole distinct significata is those wholes only if the proposition comes out true when its substantival extremes supposit for them: *5th Op.*, p. 169; of 'This donkey is a man's' is a donkey and not a man: *5th Op.*, p. 169; of 'Socrates' beholder is Plato' is Plato and not Socrates: *5th Op.*, p. 169; of 'Socrates is different from Plato' is Socrates and not Socrates and Plato: *5th Op.*, p. 169; of 'Men are men' and 'There are people' is identical with many: *5th Op.*, p. 169; of 'The sun heats the house' is the sun and not the sun and the house: *5th Op.*, p. 169; of 'The house is heated by the sun' is the house: *5th Op.*, pp. 169–71; of 'A man is white' is not a man and whiteness but precisely a man: *5th Op.*, p. 171; no thing is the a.s. of a proposition although the significatum of a proposition is something: *5th Op.*, p. 191; cf. *4th Op.*, pp. 105, 109–11; that of the subject is never that of the whole proposition or vice versa: *5th Op.*, p. 191; of a conjunctive proposition exists, only if those of both conjuncts exist: *5th Op.*, p. 133; of a disjunctive proposition exists, if that of one of its parts exists: *5th Op.*, p. 133; of a true proposition may not be signified by that proposition: *4th Way*, p. 43

its adequation to its sign: changed by syncategorematics: *8th Way*, pp. 61–3; of a term apprehended by the intellect is not so called because it is conceived of by means of the sign as a whole: *5th Op.*, p. 193; not that which is represented to the intellectual power temporally or naturally prior to other significata: *5th Op.*, p. 193; not the significatum which is called the whole significatum: *5th Op.*, p. 193; is distinctly apprehended under a proper concept by which significatum nothing posterior is distinctly conceived under its formal denomination: *5th Op.*, p. 195; of a composite term is not that of any of its

parts: *5th Op.*, p. 195; could be said to have an equiform denomination with its spoken form: *5th Op.*, p. 197; of an absolutely non-complex expression cannot be in any way complex: *5th Op.*, p. 197; of a proposition is not that which is apprehended by the sign as a whole: *5th Op.*, p. 193; not that which is conceived of first, taking 'first' as an exponible: *5th Op.*, p. 193; not the whole significatum: *5th Op.*, p. 195; of a conjunctive cannot be that of a categorical: *5th Op.*, pp. 169–71; of a disjunctive proposition cannot be that of a conjunctive: *5th Op.*, p. 197; of a molecular proposition cannot be that of a categorical: *5th Op.*, pp. 197–9; cf. *7th Way*, p. 55

   its relation to truth and falsity: if the a.s. of a proposition is false, the proposition is false: *9th Way*, p. 63; if the a.s. of a proposition is true, and it is not inconsistent that the proposition, thus adequately signifying, should be true, the proposition is true: *9th Way*, p. 63; if a proposition is false and it is not inconsistent that its a.s. should be false, its a.s. is false: *9th Way*, p. 63; of some false proposition is true: *7th Way*, pp. 55–7; *9th Way*, p. 63

Adjacent (*adiacens*): propositions of the second and third a. distinguished: *2nd Op.*, p. 91; **p. 91 n. b**, p. 266; propositions of the second a. cannot be found in the mind: *2nd Op.*, p. 91; propositions of both the second and third a. may be included in propositions expounding pregnant negative propositions: **p. 21 n. e**, p. 255; inference from a proposition of the third a. to a proposition of the second a. where the propositions are affirmative and there are no distracting terms, holds: *5th Op.*, p. 139

Aevum: the measure of creatures that begin to be but do not cease to be: *3rd Op.*, p. 103; **p. 103 n. e**, p. 268

Aliqualiter: identified by Doctors of Paul's order with *nullum chimaeram esse*: *2nd Way*, p. 24; identified by Gregory of Rimini and his followers with the adequate significatum of 'If the Antichrist is white, the Antichrist is coloured': *9th Way*, p. 73; *aliqualiter esse*: the adequate significatum of a proposition, according to Paul of Venice: *5th Op.*, pp. 175–91; the adequate object of knowledge: *5th Op.*, p. 191

Ampliation (*ampliatio*): defined: **p. 15 n. 5**, p. 254; **p. 139 n. c**, p. 271; affects the adequate significatum of the proposition: *5th Op.*, p. 167; of the subject in a future-tense proposition or a proposition with a present-tense copula and future-tense predicate, to stand for things that will be: *1st Way*, p. 15; by the verb 'signifies of the term' following it to range over those that are thought of: *9th Way*, p. 69; **p. 69 n. c**, p. 264; by '⟨a⟩ truth', '⟨a⟩ falsity' and modal terms: *5th Op.*, c. 6, p. 149; according to Albert of Saxony: **p. 15 n. u**, p. 254

The Antichrist (*Antichristus*): does not exist in reality: *1st Way*, p. 13; will exist in the future, according to Christian doctrine: **p. 45 n. d**, p. 259; God knows that he will exist: *5th Op.*, p. 173; is supposited for by 'the Antichrist' in 'The Antichrist is the Antichrist and he will not be': *1st Way*, p. 13

Appellation (*appellatio*): discussed: **p. 15 n. u**, p. 254; in every future-tense proposition, the predicate following the verb appellates its own form: *1st Way*, p. 15; **p. 15 n. u**, p. 254

As (*sicut*): *2nd and 3rd Ways: passim*; sometimes taken relatively: *4th Way*, p. 39; renders the *suppositio* of terms following it confused, distributive, and mobile: **p. 5**; **p. 5 n. b**, p. 252

Being (*esse/ens*): inherent or *per se*: *2nd Way*, pp. 21–3

   positive (*ens positivum*): not identical with negations, privations, falsehoods, and impossibilities that are not signs: *5th Op.*, p. 151; naturally prior to negations and privations: **p. 77 n. g**, p. 265; understood prior to negations and privations: **p. 73 n. e**, p. 264; **p. 75 n. g**, p. 265; by God in its own proper idea: *7th Way*, p. 55; **p. 55 n. d**, p. 262

Chimera (*chimaera*): could not exist in reality: *1st Way*, p. 13; is supposited for by the term 'chimera' in 'A chimera is a chimera' or 'A chimera is thought of': *1st Way*, p. 13; the term 'chimera' supposits for something in an affirmative present-tense or future-tense proposition: *1st Way*, pp. 13–15; signifies something: *1st Way*, pp. 13–15; **p. 13 n. r**, p. 254. Cf. *Nullum chimaeram esse*

Complex: of terms is a proposition: **p. 95 n. a**, p. 268; what can be signified by one: cf. *Complexe significabile*

Complexe significabile: according to Gregory of Rimini: is the significatum of a proposition: *3rd Op.*, pp. 95–105; **p. 95 n. a**, p. 268; is something (*aliquid*) where 'something' is taken in the first or second ways but not in the third way: *3rd Op.*, p. 97; many were from eternity and none was God: *3rd Op.*, p. 101; rejected by the author of the *4th Op.*, p. 111; partisans thereof say that the significata—that if the Antichrist is white, the Antichrist is coloured, and that no chimera is—would not be something or some things but somehow: *9th Way*, p. 73; according to Paul of Venice, formally distinct from those signifiable by a non-complex: *5th Op.*, p. 159

Composition of the mind or intellect (*compositio mentis vel intellectus*): exists precisely contingently: *2nd Op.*, p. 87; some will exist only if a created intellect thinks of something: *2nd Op.*, p. 89; none existed before the production of the world: *2nd Op.*, p. 89; cannot be understood without extreme terms, according to the Philosopher: *2nd Op.*, p. 87; its truth is the adequation of the intellect to things: *5th Op.*, p. 141; whether it is the adequate significatum to a true proposition: *2nd Op.*, pp. 85–9

Contingent/⟨a⟩ contingency (*contingens*): taken either as a pure adjective or as an adjective in the neuter gender equivalent to a substantive: *5th Op.*, p. 177; sometimes taken as a functionalizable term: *5th Op.*, p. 145

Describably (*descriptibiliter*): defined: **p. 175 n. k**, p. 275; 'is known' so taken where it governs a non-complex: *5th Op.*, p. 175

Difference (*differentia*): obtains only among really distinct things: *5th Op.*, p. 167

Distinction (*distinctio*): real distinction, formal distinction, and distinction of reason contrasted: **p. 159 n. d**, p. 273

   formal: Scotus's criterion for: **p. 159 n. d**, p. 273; does not involve a difference: *5th Op.*, p. 167; where there is a f.d. but no real distinction, there is an order of dependence for existence: **p. 85 n. d**, p. 267

   real: implies a difference: *5th Op.*, p. 167

Divine Essence (*essentia divina*): alone is measured by eternity: *3rd Op.*, p. 103; is an intelligible species that represents Itself and everything else to the Divine Intellect: *2nd Way*, p. 19; cf. God and Divine Intellect; is always the first object of the Divine Intellect: *3rd Op.*, pp. 101–3; is a sort of proposition for the Divine Intellect: *2nd Op.*, p. 89; *4th Op.*, pp. 111, 117; as a true proposition before the creation of the world: *2nd Op.*, p. 89; intuitively sees that it is: *3rd Op.*, p. 101; an intuitive vision of it has neither an extrinsic term nor an extrinsic cause: *3rd Op.*, p. 101; the Father does not differ, but is distinct from it: *5th Op.*, p. 167; cf. Divine Persons.

Divine Intellect (*intellectus divinus*): no created thing represents itself or its significatum to it, but everything is signified or represented to it by the Divine Essence: *2nd Way*, p. 19; God or the Divine Cognition is a true proposition for it: *4th Op.*, pp. 117–19; always has the Divine Essence as its first object: *3rd Op.*, pp. 101–3; thinks each possible positive thing in its own idea, but impossibles, privations, and negations in the ideas of possible positive things: *7th Way*, p. 55; **p. 55 n. d**, p. 262; *4th Op.*, p. 121; necessarily thinks of you but is necessitated by no creature: *5th Op.*, p. 187; simultaneously has the thought that you are and that you are not: *9th Way*, p. 77

proposition of the third adjacent to a proposition of the second adjacent, where the proposition is affirmative and where there is no distracting verb or predicate, holds: *5th Op.*, p. 139; from the universal to the exclusive with the terms transposed, holds: *3rd Way*, p. 29; whether that from an affirmative proposition in which a relative term is posited to a conjunctive proposition formed using the same terms with only a change of the relative to its antecedent, holds: *9th Way*, pp. 67, 71–3

Infinite (*infinita, -um*): distinction between God and that God is: *5th Op.*, p. 161; number of formal principles (*rationes*) is consistent with divine simplicity: *5th Op.*, p. 165; predicate taken absolutely negatively or somehow positively: *5th Op.*, p. 135

Intellect (*intellectus*): has only positive beings as its object: *7th Way*, p. 55; **p. 73 n. e**, p. 264; only the truth can be its object: *9th Way*, p. 73; cannot simultaneously (by the simultaneity of nature) have the thought that you are and that you are not, but can by the simultaneity of duration: *9th Way*, p. 75; can at one and the same time think the premiss, the conclusion, and the opposite of the conclusion: *9th Way*, p. 77; thinks of man by the same act by which it thinks of the species man: *ADO*, p. 95. Cf. Divine Intellect and God

Knowledge (*scientia*): whether the adequate object of knowledge is anything outside of the mind: *5th Op.*, pp. 185–7, 191; cf. **p. 95 n. e**, pp. 267–8; is not only of modes: *1st Op.*, p. 83; its adequate object is no thing, but precisely that things are in some way (*aliqualiter esse*): *5th Op.*, p. 191; properly speaking is of incorruptibles and those that cannot be otherwise than they are: *4th Op.*, p. 121; *5th Op.*, p. 185; by which it is known that God is, is that by which the proposition is known: *ADO*, p. 95

'A man is an animal' (*Homo est animal*): may actually signify a falsehood no less primarily than a truth: *6th Way*, p. 53; signifies that a man is a donkey, a goat, a cow, etc.: *1st Way*, p. 9; **p. 9 n. i**, p. 253; *3rd Way*, p. 37; *5th Way*, p. 47; is precisely a sign of a falsehood when it does: *5th Way*, p. 47; signifies a man, a donkey, a lion, etc., but not adequately: *5th Op.*, p. 169

Modes (*modi*): posterior to quiddities: *1st Op.*, p. 83; kinds of: intrinsic or extrinsic: *1st Op.*, pp. 83–5; intrinsic modes four-fold: **p. 84 n. 7**, p. 210; **p. 85 n. e**, p. 266; simple or complex: *1st Op.*, p. 83; simple can be signified by a simple name: *1st. Op.*, p. 83; whether they are the significata of true propositions: *1st Op.*, pp. 81–5

Multiplex: defined: **p. 51 n. a**, p. 261; proposition: *7th Way*, p. 51

Necessary, it is (*necesse est*): whether interchangeable with 'It is not impossible' (*impossibile non est*): *2nd Op.*, pp. 87–91

No chimera existing: cf. *Nullam chimaeram esse*

Non-pregnant (*non-praegnans*): non-pregnant and pregnant negative propositions distinguished: **p. 21 n. e**, p. 55; negative proposition does not entail an affirmative proposition without any modal term: *2nd Way*, p. 21

Non-quiescently (*non quiescenter*): defined: **p. 113 n. f**, p. 269; an infinitive expression signifies thus: *4th Op.*, p. 113

Notion/formal principle (*ratio*): meaning explained: **p. 159 n. c**, pp. 272–3
   distinction of: how much they are distinct is proportional to how much they are: *5th Op.*, p. 161; infinite ones more distinct from one another than finite ones: *5th Op.*, p. 161; that of a complex and a non-complex formally

p. 159; adequate significatum is p. to other significata: in distinctness: *5th Op.*, p. 195; cf. **p. 53 n. c**, p. 261; not by temporal, formal, or natural priority or by priority according to goodness or honor: **p. 193 n. a**, p. 276

Privations (*privationes*): and negations can be thought of: *8th Way*, p. 59; understood posterior to positive beings: **p. 73 n. e**, p. 264; **p. 75 n. g**, p. 265; thought of by God in the ideas of possible positive things: p. 55; **p. 55 n. d**, p. 262; whether it can be thought that a man is a not-man: *9th Way*, pp. 67–9, 73

Pronoun-relative (*relativum pronominis*): p. 99; **p. 99 n. d**, p. 268

Proposition (*propositio*): either in the indicative, imperative, optative, or subjunctive moods: *8th Way*, p. 57; **p. 57 n. a**, pp. 262–3; cf. p. xiii; God is one for the Divine Intellect: *4th Op.*, pp. 117–19; possible that no created proposition should exist: *ADO*, p. 95

    so called from what? no conventional p. so-called from a relation to a mental p.: *6th Way*, p. 47; none so-called intrinsically, but all extrinsically: *6th Way*, p. 49; **p. 49 n. a**, p. 261; none so-called from a relation to a vital power actually being applied or exercised: *6th Way*, p. 51; none so-called from a relation to a power, quiescently perceptive of the true or the false: *6th Way*, p. 51; none so-called from a relation to its own primary or adequate significatum: *6th Way*, p. 51, **p. 51 n. c**, p. 261

    each is somehow significant: *9th Way*, p. 73

    how does it signify? only by the composition of its parts: *1st Way*, p. 11; **p. 11 n. k**, p. 253; *4th Op.*, p. 113; **p. 29 n. g**, p. 257; **p. 33 n. o**, pp. 257–8; signifies primarily its own significatum and secondarily those of each of its parts: *2nd Way*, pp. 17–19; none signifies precisely as things are: **p. 17 n. a**, p. 254; every false one signifies an infinite number of truths: **p. 17 n. a**, pp. 254–5; every true one signifies an infinite number of falsehoods: **p. 17 n. a**, p. 254; **p. 9 n. i**, p. 253; **p. 37 n. a**, p. 258; some false and impossible one signifies the truth prior to the false and impossible: *6th Way*, p. 53; some true and necessary proposition signifies the false prior to the truth: *6th Way*, p. 53

    what does it signify? whether it is its own adequate significatum? *ADO*, pp. 93–5; no thing is the adequate significatum of a p. but the adequate significatum of a p. is something: *5th Op.*, p. 191; cf. **p. 191 n. t**, p. 276

suppositio of: cannot have personal *suppositio*: *5th Op.*, p. 129

quantity of: cf. Quantity

truth of: cf. Truth

kinds of:

    affirmative (*propositio affirmativa*): whether true if and only if its subject and predicate supposit for the same thing? *1st Way*, pp. 5–7; whether every one signifies itself to be true? *1st Way*, pp. 7, 11; whether one in the present tense is false if its subject supposits for nothing? *1st Way*, pp. 7, 13; whether any indefinite one signifies that its subject and predicate have the same, equal, or precisely convertible *suppositio*: *3rd Way*, pp. 27, 31; one that is not so called implicitly or explicitly from an oblique term converts with a proposition formed by adding an exclusive to its predicate: *5th Way*, p. 47

    conditional (*propositio condicionalis*): not possible for its adequate significatum to be identical with that of a disjunctive proposition, or vice versa: *5th Op.*, p. 199

    conjunctive (*propositio copulativa*): true only if both parts are true: *5th Op.*, p. 133; its adequate significatum: arises from the adequate significata of the categoricals together with the consignification of the sign of conjunction: *5th Op.*, p. 199; cannot be identical with that of a disjunctive proposition:

5th Op., p. 199; exists only if the significatum of both parts exists: *5th Op.*, p. 133

disjunctive (*propositio disiunctiva*): rendered true because of a true part: *1st Way*, p. 11; *5th Op.*, p. 133; signifies the significatum of each of its parts: *1st way*, pp. 9–11; its adequate significatum arises from those of the categoricals and the consignification of the sign of disjunction: *5th Op.*, p. 199; its adequate significatum cannot be identical with that of a conjunctive or conditional proposition: *5th Op.*, p. 199; is one that cannot be grasped by the intellect unless the intellect grasps its first part: *1st Way*, p. 11

exclusive (*propositio exclusiva*): four different orders distinguished: **p. 45 n. e**, pp. 259–60; the first order: **p. 25 n. a**, p. 256; **p. 31 n. k**, p. 257; the second order: **p. 45 nn. g, h**, **p. 47 n. i**, p. 260; the third order: **p. 47 n. i**, p. 260; the fourth order: *2nd Way*, p. 17; **p. 17 n. a**, pp. 254–5; **p. 25 n. a**, p. 256; the inference from the universal to the e.p. with the terms transposed holds good: *3rd Way*, p. 29

future-tense (*propositio de futuro*): some do not signify primarily as things are: *2nd Way*, pp. 19, 23

indefinite (*propositio indefinita*): entailed by the corresponding particular proposition: *3rd Way*, p. 29; whether a singular proposition becomes one when its applicative is removed: *3rd Way*, pp. 27, 33; whether the subject and predicate of an affirmative one have the same, equal, or precisely convertible *suppositio*: *3rd Way*, pp. 27, 31

insoluble (*insolubilis*): commonly not said to be false because of a false significatum but because it asserts itself to be false or not true or because of some premiss in the case implies it is false: *9th Way*, p. 65; cf. **p. 55 n. f**, p. 262; *7th Way*, p. 57; what rules of inference hold: **p. 143 nn. g, h**, p. 271; 'The Antichrist is' is not one: *9th Way*, p. 69

molecular (*propositio hypothetica*): *5th Op.*, pp. 197–9; the significatum adequate to it is not adequate to a categorical proposition: *7th Way*, pp. 55–7

negative (*propositio negativa*): whether true if and only if its subject and predicate do not supposit for the same thing: *1st Way*, pp. 5–11; some— e.g. 'No chimera is'—do not signify primarily as things are: *2nd Way*, pp. 19–23; some have nothing in reality corresponding to them by which the intellect is rendered correct: *8th Way*, p. 59; pregnant vs. non-pregnant ones distinguished: **p. 21 n. e**, p. 255

past-tense (*propositio de praeterito*): some do not signify primarily as things are: *2nd Way*, pp. 19, 23–5

universal (*propositio universalis*): the inference from one to the exclusive with the terms transposed holds good: *3rd Way*, p. 29

Quiescently (*quiescenter*): defined: **p. 113 n. f**, p. 269; an absolutely simple term does not adequately signify a truth and a falsehood thus: *5th Op.*, p. 197; the Divine Intellect signifies thus: *4th Op.*, p. 117; a proposition signifies thus, but its subject does not: *5th Op.*, p. 181. Cf. Non-quiescently

Quantity (*quantitas*): of a proposition: **p. 31 n. k**, p. 257; '⟨A⟩ truth is that the Antichrist will be' is not of any quantity when 'a truth' is taken as a modal or functionalizable term: *5th Op.*, c. 6, p. 147; cf. **p. 147 n. k**, p. 271; 'Precisely the way it is a sign is *A* a false proposition' (*Praecise sicut est significans est A propositio falsa*) is not of any quantity: *3rd Way*, pp. 31–3; **p. 31 n. k**, p. 257; 'That a falsehood is, is known' is not of any quantity: *5th Op.*, p. 175

Ratio: cf. Notion/formal principle

Really identical (*idem realiter*): what is r.i. can be formally distinct: **p. 163 n. h**,

Suppositio:
  kinds of:
    different views about material and simple: *DO*, p. 93; **p. 93 n. d**, p. 267; an
      expression that can be a proposition on its own can have only material
      supposition as the subject of a proposition: *4th Op.*, p. 117
    personal *suppositio*: confused and distributive with 'as': *1st Way*, p. 5; **p. 5
      n. b**, p. 252; rendered merely confused by an exclusion sign: *5th Way*,
      p. 45; determinate: *1st Way*, p. 13; *3rd Op.*, pp. 99–101; had by the
      subject of an indefinite proposition: *3rd Op.*, p. 99; makes it possible to
      descend to all of the supposita: *3rd Op.*, p. 101; for divine persons: *5th Op.*,
      p. 163; **p. 163 n. i**, p. 274; *5th Op.*, p. 165; formal: *5th Op.*, pp. 163, 187;
      p. 163 n. h, p. 274; real and identical: *5th Op.*, pp. 163, 187; **p. 163 n. h**,
      p. 274; essential: *5th Op.*, p. 163; **p. 163 n. i**, p. 274; word order dictates
      whether it is real or formal: *5th Op.*, pp. 189–91; **p. 189 n. s**, pp. 275–6;
      p. 191 n. t, p. 276; can be had by an infinitive expression in the subject
      position: *4th Op.*, pp. 113–17
  'chimera' supposits for a chimera even though none does or could exist in
    reality: *1st Way*, pp. 13–15
  a relative pronoun has s. for something only if its antecedent does: *1st Way*,
    p. 15

Term/Terminus (*terminus*):
  of an act: *5th Op.*, p. 141; whether what neither is nor can be, cannot be or
    have a terminus: *5th Op.*, p. 141
  of a proposition:
    kinds of:
      conjunctive (*terminus compositus*): distinctly signifies the significatum of any
        of its parts and does so naturally prior to signifying its adequate significa-
        tum: *5th Op.*, p. 195
      disjunctive (*terminus disiunctus*): signifies the adequate significatum of any
        part distinctly and naturally prior to the significatum of the term as a
        whole: *5th Op.*, p. 195
      distracting (*terminus distrahens*): defined: **p. 15 n. t**, p. 254; **p. 139 n. c**,
        p. 271; '⟨a⟩ truth', '⟨a⟩ falsity', and modal terms distract the principal
        copula: *5th Op.*, p. 149; affects the adequate significatum of the proposi-
        tion in which it occurs: *5th Op.*, p. 167
      functionalizable (*terminus officiabilis*): has more force when it precedes the
        expression it governs than when it follows it: *5th Op.*, p. 143; when taken
        in the sense of composition and when taken in the sense of division:
        p. 69 n. c, p. 264; '⟨a⟩ truth', '⟨a⟩ possibility', '⟨an⟩ impossibility',
        '⟨a⟩ necessity', '⟨a⟩ contingency' so taken: *5th Op.*, pp. 145, 177; 'is
        known' so taken when it governs a complex: *5th Op.*, p. 175; 'primarily'
        so taken: *7th Way*, p. 55; 'so' (*ita*) and 'as' (*sic*) so taken: *5th Op.*, p. 145
      resoluble (*terminus resolubilis*): distinguished from modal and functionaliz-
        able: **p. 65 n. a**, p. 263; '⟨a⟩ truth', '⟨a⟩ possibility', '⟨an⟩ impossibility',
        '⟨a⟩ necessity', and '⟨a⟩ contingency' so taken: *5th Op.*, pp. 145–9, 177;
        'is distinct' so taken: *5th Op.*, p. 165
      syncategorematic (*syncategorema*): signify together with another but not of
        itself: *8th Way*, p. 63; false that one would not change the significatum
        but only the mode of signifying: *8th Way*, pp. 61–3
      transcendental (*transcendens*): 'something' (*aliquid*) so taken: *3rd Op.*,
        p. 101; '⟨a⟩ truth' so taken: *5th Op.*, p. 147
  That if the Antichrist is white, the Antichrist is coloured: false that no one can
    understand what it would be, because some say it is God, and some anything